Career
Adaptability

Mark L. Savickas

Career Adaptability

ISBN: 978-1-7341178-3-7 (paperback)
ISBN: 978-1-7341178-4-4 (casebound)

Printed in USA by 48HrBooks
www.48HrBooks.com

To the one who inspired this book,

my mother

May Savickas

Table of Contents

Chapters

INTRODUCTION

The Career Construction Model of Adaptation

The construct of career adaptability first drew attention when Donald Super encountered difficulties in extending his model of career maturity (1955) from adolescents to adults. The concept of maturation did not adequately comprehend adult work lives. Consequently, Super and Knasel (1981) suggested replacing the concept of career maturity with that of *career adaptability* when considering adult career development. I adopted the term in Career Construction Theory (CCT), explaining that maturity fit an organismic world view, while adaptability better fits the contextual world view of CCT (Savickas, 1997, 2005, 2019a). In the present book I explain the construct of career adaptability and position it as a core component in the career adaptation model proposed by CCT.

In the following Chapters, I formally review and synthesize empirical findings about career adaptability and integrate them into a body of scientific knowledge that can serve as a basis for further conceptualization and investigation. I organized the integration using a conceptual framework for programmatic research suggested by Edwards and Cronbach (1952) and Crites (1969).

The framework organizes programmatic research on career adaptability using a sequential strategy that progresses across five different stages with distinct research methods: survey, technique, critical, theoretical, and applied. The s*urvey research* concentrated on the existing literature related to career adaptability, followed by reflection on the findings that identified dimensions of the construct and variables to which it may relate. *Technique research* developed operational definitions with which to observe, quantify, and measure career adaptability. The third strategy of *critical research* used the measures to establish a coherent nomological network of empirical relationships between career adaptability and related constructs. The fourth stage involved *theoretical research* to test hypotheses concerning relations among adaptivity, adaptability, adapting, and adaptation. The final stage, which has

1

just recently begun, is *applied research* to determine how educational, counseling, and coaching interventions might develop the career adaptability of students and employees.

Survey Research

Chapter 1 traces the emergence of *adaptability* as an important construct in career theory and positions it as a core component in a process model of career adaptation. Then the Career Construction Theory (CCT) model of adaptation and its components are defined and described. Distinctions are made among adaptive readiness, adaptability resources, adapting responses, adaptation results, and their interplay. In addition, the differences between adapting beliefs and behaviors are addressed, particularly highlighting beliefs about work volition and career decision-making self-efficacy. Chapter 1 concludes with an admonition about semantic and pragmatic meanings of the terms in the adaptation model.

Technique Research

Chapter 2 addresses the operational definitions of the adaptation model constructs in terms of measurement inventories. The Chapter begins with an explanation of how the proactive personality trait and the Five Factor Model traits of openness and conscientiousness serve as preferred representations of adaptive readiness in the CCT model of adaptation. The next section describes how the *Career Adapt-Abilities Scale* (*CAAS*) was constructed and initially validated by a team of researchers from 13 countries. Chapter 2 concludes with a discussion of measures for adapting responses.

Chapter 3 addresses the construct validity of the *CAAS* by reporting, in turn, evidence from 37 confirmatory factor-analytic studies in 24 countries, six studies of factorial invariance, and a set of studies showing convergent and discriminant validity for the *CAAS*.

Chapter 4 deals with the test-retest reliability and rank-order stability of *CAAS* scores. The first section of the Chapter considers five studies that have examined the temporal stability of *CAAS* scores. The second section of the Chapter discusses score profiles for groups and individuals.

Chapter 5 describes alternative forms of the *CAAS*. The forms include a 12-item short form, a behavioral measure, and a Francophone version that adds seven additional items to the *CAAS*. The Chapter also includes a discussion of a measure for Cooperation as an interpersonal resource to support adapting behaviors. Chapter 5 concludes by explaining a set of descriptors that may be used as a coding scheme in qualitative research that analyzes interview transcripts.

Critical Research

Chapters 6 concentrates on familial antecedents of individuals' career adaptability. It presents evidence that families and significant others foster the development of career adaptability in adolescents through career-specific parental behaviors and social support.

Chapter 7 describes significant biographical experiences, activities, and achievements that seem to foster development of career adaptability in later life.

Chapter 8 describes how the adaptations required by seeking and maintaining a job activate the use of self-regulatory resources to deal with employability, unemployment, job insecurity, and refugee resettlement.

Theoretical Research

Chapter 9 discusses how researchers have investigated the relation of adaptive readiness to adaptability resources by representing adaptive readiness in terms of three different models of personality organization -- single trait models, hierarchical trait models, and motivation models. The career adaptation model distinguishes between traits as indicators of *readiness* to activate adaptability responses from motivation as indicators of *willingness*.

Chapter 10 addresses studies that examine the relation of adaptability resources to the actual adapting *responses* used to construct a career and manage job transitions. The first section of this Chapter addresses adapting responses that have been represented in terms of enacting behaviors and the second section addresses adapting beliefs.

Chapter 11 reviews the relation of adaptability resources to adaptation results, independent of adapting behaviors. The first section addresses outcomes that pertain to individuals; the second section addresses adaptation outcomes that pertain to a job; and the third section addresses adaptation outcomes that pertain to career success, satisfaction, and stability.

Chapter 12 discusses the CCT proposition that adaptability resources mediate the relation between adaptive readiness and adapting responses. The studies in this Chapter are organized according to how the researchers represented adapting responses in terms of exploring, decision-making difficulties, career self-management strategies, and career engagement.

Chapter 13 discusses studies that examine the CCT proposition that adaptability resources mediate between adaptive readiness and adaptation results. In these studies, researchers operationally defined adaptation results as academic satisfaction, job performance, career success and satisfaction, work identification, work engagement, and personal growth initiative.

Chapter 14 reviews nine studies that examined the CCT proposition about the function of adapting responses as mediators between adaptability resources and adaptation results. The adaptation outcomes were represented as promotability, career prospects, daily adapting behaviors.

Chapter 15 describes the results of nine studies in seven countries that tested the full four-component model of career adaptation.

Chapter 16 summarizes literature reviews of research on the *CAAS* and the CCT adaptation model. The different literature reviews used narrative, meta-analytic, and scientometric methods.

Applied Research

Chapter 17 describes career-related experiences that have been shown to develop career adaptability resources, namely academic advising, internships, and supervisor feedback.

Chapter 18 discusses four types of counseling and educational interventions that increase participants' career adaptability resources and adapting responses.

Afterword

Chapter 19 summarizes the book and ends with suggestions for future research.

CHAPTER 1

CAREER ADAPTABILITY:
A 21st CENTURY CONSTRUCT

In the 21st century, the global economy of post-industrial society begets employment instability. For most people, the new economy has replaced life-time employment in a 30-year career with a series of contingent positions that consist of projects and assignments. Job changes and transitions have become increasingly common among adults because of the reorganization of work-life and employment into careers characterized as boundaryless (Arthur, 1994) and protean (Hall, 2004). The move from *institutionalized* life-course patterns to *individualized* biographies has made workers responsible for managing their own de-standardized careers. In the context of greater complexity and diversity of career paths, it has become important for individuals to manage their own careers, make multiple transitions, and keep up with new demands on the job. Today, continuous adaptation to the work environment is crucial to achieve job success and maintain career satisfaction (Morrison, 1977).

This individualization of work-life as a biography of choice required innovation in career theory and interventions. The mid-twentieth century constructs of career development and maturity do not comprehend the individualized, de-institutionalized, and de-standardized career trajectories of post-modern societies that are rife with uncertainty and risk. Thus, Super and Knasel (1981) argued for a more forward-looking and proactive construct to replace "maturity," one that "allows greater emphasis to be given to the novel, non-maturational problems which presently confront many people" (p. 199). They proposed the construct of "career adaptability" and defined it as "readiness to cope with changing work and working conditions" (p. 195). Today, adaptability is key to managing the complexity of one's career in the midst of transformations wrought by a fourth industrial revolution that has reshaped social institutions and patterns of employment. To manage a 21st century work life, individuals must develop the adaptability required to deal with the challenges and changes presented by the new employment patterns.

An excellent description and analysis of the early development of the *adaptability* construct appeared in an article by Goodman (1994). She explained how Douglas Hall (1986) promoted the construct of adaptation in organizational psychology, arguing that career adaptability is central to achieving career effectiveness in a changing environment and important in enabling individuals to manage shifting social demands. Subsequently, Hall and Mirvis (1995) asserted that the ability to adapt to changing tasks, engage in life-long learning, and regulate one's career direction were critical for both (a) managing one's career rather than developing it and (b) meeting employers' demand for an increasingly adaptable workforce. Hall and Mirvis (1995) emphasized the need for contemporary workers to develop the "meta-skills" of career identity and personal adaptability. These two higher-order qualities or meta-competencies engender the capacity to master specific skills. In this sense, adaptability and identity are each a meta-skill, that is, a skill required for learning how to learn. Mastering a meta-competency enables one to learn many specific skills.

Career Construction Theory (CCT) characterizes career adaptability as a psychosocial strength or capacity for solving unfamiliar, complex, and ill-defined problems presented by developmental vocational tasks, occupational transitions, and work troubles. Building on Morrison and Hall's (2002) description of adaptability as the capacity to change in responding to a new situation, CCT conceptualizes adaptability as *self-regulation resources* that individuals activate to manage career changes or challenges. Self-regulation denotes attitudes, beliefs, and competencies that enable people to override impulses and select their own responses in enacting behaviors that move them toward a goal (Karoly, 1993). Activation of self-regulation resources in the career domain occurs in response to organizational, social, or task changes such as the school-to-work transition or job loss. In CCT, the self-regulation resources that constitute career adaptability are a component in a more extensive model of career adaptation.

The Career Adaptation Model

People construct careers through actions that implement their self-concepts and manifest their vocational interests in work roles. Viewing career construction as a series of attempts to fit a self into work roles concentrates attention on adaptation to repeated transitions from school-to-work, from job to job, and from occupation to occupation. This adaptation is motivated and guided by the goal of bringing inner needs and outer opportunities into harmony. Adaptation, or goodness of fit, is indicated by success, satisfaction, and stability.

The word *adapt* comes from the Latin meaning *to fit* or *to join*. Over time, subtle distinctions have been made using the root word *adapt* -- including adaptivity, adaptability, adapting, and adaptation. The CCT model of self-regulation (Savickas, 2019a, 2020) uses these words to denote a sequence of preparatory and performance components ranging across adaptive *readiness*, adaptability *resources*, adapting *responses*, and adaptation *results*. People are more or less prepared to change, vary in their resources to manage change, demonstrate more or less action when change is required, and experience different outcome levels. The following section explains how the CCT model of career adaptation distinguishes among the constructs of adaptivity, adaptability, adapting, and adaptation.

Adaptive Readiness

The CCT adaptation model begins with the personality trait of adaptivity, defined as a disposition of *personal readiness* and *motivational willingness* to make changes in response to vocational development tasks, occupational transitions, and work troubles. As a dispositional trait, career adaptivity acts as a filter through which individuals interpret the environment and, when needed, activate self-regulation processes to better adjust to imminent and intermediate transitions. As a motivational orientation, adaptivity guides and maintains movement across transitions.

Functioning as a disposition or an abstract, global trait (Funder, 1991), adaptivity involves a compound mixture of multiple specific personality traits. Thus, CCT considers adaptivity to have more explanatory power across a broad range of situations and behaviors than does a single trait. A narrow trait such as proactivity may increase the strength of correlations when predicting a particular behavior, yet it decreases the range of behaviors that may be predicted. Career adaptivity becomes increasingly stable and durable over time yet remains situation-specific in being relevant to some life situations yet not others.

Adaptivity as a personality trait may be conceptualized as a perspective or a subjective evaluation of relative significance that helps individuals interpret the environment and activate self-regulation resources (in this case career adapt-abilities) in order to better adjust to that environment. Adaptive readiness prompts activation of adaptability resources when they are needed. People do not routinely engage career adaptability resources. Rather, they activate them to effectively manage career challenges and changes. Career adaptivity influences the determination to begin engaging self-regulation resources when transitions are imminent or control opportunities are available. The requirement to change may be imposed by external social forces or by internal affective reactions. For example, external forces include graduating from school or losing a job. A need to change or desire for a new challenge also may arise internally. For example, floundering on the job or boredom may lead a worker to consider changing positions.

During transitions, highly adaptive individuals activate their adaptability resources and engage adapting responses to bridge the transition. Furthermore, individuals who display stronger self-regulation may (a) choose better strategies to respond to occupational transitions, (b) more fully acknowledge their emotions, (c) recover more rapidly from psychological distress, and

9

(d) show greater motivation to develop their adaptability resources (Savickas, 2005, 2020).

Individuals differ in their personal readiness and motivational willingness to cope with changes and challenges. People vary widely in how quickly they activate adaptability resources and engage adapting responses. For example, some students start to anticipate their occupations in junior high school, while other students begin after they graduate. Some employees activate adaptability resources at the first hint of potential job loss while other employees wait until they receive their final unemployment check. Individuals must reach some subjective threshold before they activate resources and enact responses. They must reach a point at which they can no longer continue routine activities by tolerating dissatisfaction and assimilating the changes. In both externally imposed tensions and internally experienced anxiety, a threshold of disequilibrium must be crossed before individuals activate the resources that guide goal-directed activity. At some point of their own or others making, individuals need to accommodate to the disequilibrium by changing self, context, or both. The required accommodations typically prompt feelings of distress that fuel the readiness and bolster the motivational willingness to adapt. It is easier for individuals to cope with this distress if they have developed the psychosocial resources that enable them to change their situations. The CCT adaptation model suggests that individuals who demonstrate adaptive readiness are more likely to develop career adaptability resources.

Adaptability Resources

The *American Psychological Association Dictionary of Psychology* (Vandenbos, 2015) defines adaptability as "the capacity to make appropriate responses to changed or changing situations; the ability to modify or adjust one's behavior in meeting different circumstances or different people" (p. 18). In general, adaptability as a self-regulation "capacity" or "ability" increases the degree to which human behavior is flexible and able to adapt (Baumeister & Vohs, 2007). Career adaptability denotes self-regulation

10

resources for coping with unfamiliar, complex, and ill-defined problems presented by current and anticipated vocational development tasks, occupational transitions, and work troubles that, to some degree large or small, alter an individual's social integration (Savickas, 1997). These self-regulation strengths are not at the core of the individual, they reside at the intersection of person-in-environment. Thus, adaptability refers to psychosocial competencies that develop through interactions between the inner and outer worlds of a person. In this sense, adaptability resources are a form of human capital, defined as accumulated transactional competencies and knowledge gained through education and experience (Arthur & Sheffrin, 2003). Consequently, career adaptability is more malleable than personality traits and more susceptible to the boundary conditions imposed by cultural and contextual influences. Societies vary in the degree to which they prompt the formation of adaptability because social groups provide different opportunities and imperatives to develop and express psychosocial resources and transactional competencies.

CCT conceptualizes career adaptability as a self-regulation system with multiple subsystems. It is not a single structure but an aggregate construct, that is, a composite of resources that serve development. CCT configures the psychosocial resources that constitute the meta-competence of career adaptability in a multi-dimensional and hierarchical model. The first level consists of specific attitudes, beliefs, and competencies -- the ABCs of career construction that shape the actual problem-solving strategies and adapting behaviors that individuals use to respond to changing demands. At the second level of the hierarchy, these ABCs are grouped into four dimensions of career adaptability resources called *adapt-abilities*. Together, these four adapt-abilities combine at the third level into a global indicator of career adaptability. The four particular adapt-ability dimensions of general career adaptability are Concern, Control, Curiosity, and Confidence.

11

Concern denotes a future orientation and inclination to anticipate and prepare for career moves. Awareness of imminent and intermediate transitions disposes an individual to prepare for what might come next.

Control denotes taking responsibility for building a career. Control inclines individuals to become deliberate and conscientious in shaping their work environments as well as to exert influence on what may come next. Healthy control originates in the self. The target of career Control in the environment not within the self.

Curiosity denotes an inquisitiveness about possible selves in various educational and vocational roles. Curiosity inclines individuals to engage in exploration of self as well as educational and vocational opportunities.

Confidence denotes assuredness to make realistic career decisions and move toward educational and vocational goals. Career Confidence supports an expectation of success and the persistent pursuit of aspirations in the face of obstacles.

Individuals use these four transactional and psychosocial resources to form strategies for navigating successfully through unfamiliar and complex environments. Thus when vocational tasks, occupational transitions, or work troubles occur, the adaptable individual is conceptualized as (a) focusing *concern* on the vocational future, (b) wanting to *control* what comes next, (c) being *curious* about possible selves and future scenarios, and (d) having the *confidence* to pursue desired outcomes. Increasing a client's career adapt-abilities is a central goal of career education and coaching. Strong adaptability is linked, through adapting behaviors, to a host of positive work-related outcomes. Table 1 presents definitions of and descriptive qualities for the four career adapt-abilities

Table 1. Adapt-Ability Resources Defined and Described

Adapt-Ability Resources	Descriptive Qualities
Concern - oriented toward the future and inclined to anticipate and prepare for career moves.	aware, oriented, anticipating, involved, planful
Control - disposed toward deliberateness and conscientious in building a career	conscientious, responsible, assertive, reliable, disciplined
Curiosity - given to inquisitiveness about possible selves, opportunities, and information.	open, inquisitive, exploratory, imaginative, innovative
Confidence - assuredness to make realistic career decisions and solve problems in moving toward occupational goals.	resilient, assured, flexible, efficient, persistent, steadfast

CCT does not propose the four adapt-abilities as a straightforward, sequential combination of constituent parts. Rather, individuals draw upon adaptability resources as an ensemble of coordinated psychological capacities with which to form adapting strategies and responses. The coordination of these complex resources requires the exercise of self-influence to form strategies and actions aimed at achieving adaptation goals. Thus, an ensemble of adaptability resources themselves shape the actual adapting behaviors and condition an individual's self-extension into the social environment. As already described, adaptability resources are in

13

varying states of activation relative to moving toward educational-vocational goals and bridging career transitions. In sum, career adaptability resources are self-regulatory, psychosocial resources that an individual activates to form strategies and shape adapting responses to deal with vocational development tasks, occupational transitions, and work troubles.

Adapting Responses

Adaptability refers to self-regulation resources. In comparison, adapting refers to actual responses -- both conative beliefs and strategic behaviors -- intended to bring about change to better meet personal aspirations and environmental demands. Thus, adapting responses include both beliefs about and performance of behaviors that address novel situations and changing conditions (Ployhart & Bliese, 2006). For CCT, adapting responses move an individual through a transition to a new equilibrium or adaptation. Recall that CCT defines adaptivity as a stable dispositional trait involving an action orientation. Adaptivity is expressed behaviorally in terms of adapting responses, with adaptability serving as a mediator variable. In other words, individuals who display stronger adapt-abilities are more likely to enact effective adapting responses. For example, individuals who possess more curiosity about changes or challenges are more likely to engage in exploratory responses such as information seeking, self-reflection, and occupational daydreaming. CCT makes a clear distinction between adapt-abilities as resources and adapting as responses. For example, the adapt-ability of Concern includes the resources of a future orientation and planfulness whereas a related adapting response is the behavior of actually planning how to move from a currently experienced situation to a currently desired situation.

Career adapt-abilities are presumed to be more stable over time than the actual adapting beliefs and behaviors, which are more proximal to day-to-day life circumstances, but not as stable as the personality trait of adaptivity. CCT conceptualizes dynamic and reciprocal relations between individuals' career adaptability and actual adapting responses. Across time, the continuing course of

14

career adapting responses and adaptation results may contribute to strengthening career adapt-abilities, but this latter process is likely to require an extended accumulation of behaviors yielding successful outcomes that eventually translate into expanding and deepening the repertoire of human strengths or adapt-abilities. For example, ongoing career exploration yielding useful insights and learning that advance a person to a gratifying career choice is likely to strengthen the adapt-ability resource of career Curiosity. This gradual process constitutes a reciprocal relationship between components of the adaptation model. Success at planning increases planful concern, solving problems increases confidence, and so on.

Career Adapting Behaviors

Career adapting behaviors center on mastering vocational development tasks, dealing with occupational transitions, and coping with work troubles and contingencies. CCT views adapting to these tasks, transitions, and troubles as fostered principally by five sets of generic behaviors, each named for their constructive actions relative to work-roles: orientation, exploration, establishment, management, and disengagement. As each call for adaptation approaches, individuals can adapt more effectively if they meet changing conditions with growing awareness and information-seeking followed by informed decision making, trial behaviors leading to a commitment projected forward for a certain time period, active role management, and eventually forward-looking disengagement. These constructive activities form a cycle of adapting performance as an individual moves through a work role across time, whether it be of short or long duration. Most individuals periodically repeat the cycle when they find themselves in changing conditions, whether the change be in work-role demands or transition to a new role.

The CCT model evaluates adapting responses as either integrative coping, adjustive defending, or maladaptive fragmenting (Shaffer, 1936; Haan, 1977). *Integrative coping*, which is oriented to reality, both solves a problem and reduces tension and anxiety, moving the individual to greater stability at a higher level of organization, possibly involving a transformative development. Sometimes individuals cannot fully respond to a baffling problem so instead they adjust by reducing negative emotions. *Adjustive defending*, which distorts reality, does not solve a problem yet does reduce tension and anxiety. Adjustive defending may produce small, incremental change. Very often adjustive responses persist because temporary reduction in anxiety reinforces them. Nevertheless, anxiety and tension eventually return because the problem itself has not been resolved. Adjustive responses are often shaped by concern and curiosity or by control and confidence but not by all four adapt-ability resources. The third category of responses is neither integrative nor adjustive. *Maladaptive fragmenting* neither solves a problem nor reduces negative emotions because the behavior is guided by idiosyncratic thoughts and feelings that do not correspond to reality nor change the existing state of affairs. Chronic use of maladaptive responses may result in repeated mistakes, personal difficulties, social withdrawal, or unregulated emotional reactions such as fearfulness and demoralization.

Career Adapting Beliefs

As already explained, adapting responses include both conative beliefs and strategic behaviors intended to bring about change to better meet environmental demands. Research on the CCT adaptation model has empirically identified three conative variables that mediate between adaptability resources and adapting behaviors. *Conation* refers to the connection of knowledge and affect to behavior and involves desire, volition, and striving. Its etymology traces to the Latin *conatio*, meaning "attempting to act." In the CCT adaptation model, conative refers to a striving, intention, or effort to enact adapting responses. Based on relevant beliefs, individuals choose adapting behaviors to address the situation, which in turn determine the adaptation results.

In CCT, *conative beliefs* about one's control of and effectiveness in performing specific behaviors mediate the relation between adaptability resources and adapting behaviors. A mediator influences the effect of an independent variable on a dependent one. The mediating variable is affected by the independent variable and in turn affects the dependent variable. The CCT model of career adaptation highlights three conative mediators between adaptability resources and adapting behaviors, namely *constructivist beliefs* about career decision making (Xu, 2020a), *work volition* from the psychology of working theory (Blustein, 2006) and *career decision-making self-efficacy* from the social-cognitive model of career self-management (Lent & Brown, 2013).

Constructivist beliefs. To supplement the role of career adaptability in CCT, Xu (2020a) developed and measured constructivist beliefs about the goal of making a decision and the reality of a good career choice. Xu explained that career adaptability and constructivist beliefs represent two distinct and complementary variables in the career construction process. While career adaptability pertains to self-regulatory capacities needed for construction, career decision-making constructivist beliefs denote whether one conceptualizes career decision making and development as construction processes. In his study, Xu (2020a) concentrated on two types of constructivist beliefs. The first type concentrates on alternative goals for decision making, whether a choice may be good-enough or optimal. Xu used the term "satisficing" to denote a decision-making strategy that aims for a choice that may satisfy and suffice. The second type of beliefs pertain to the idea that the goodness of a career choice is open to change and depends on choice implementation. Xu explained that an agentic construction of a good career path focuses on choice implementation and adjustment. By contrast, a decision maker may believe that a career choice leads to a prescribed implementation with a predetermined outcome. To measure each type of belief, Xu developed a scale with two six-item subscales. The sacrificing scale items range between the poles of a good enough choice versus the best choice. Sample items read, "One should look for a good enough career choice" and "There is no optimal career choice." The agentic construction scale items range between the poles of a fixed versus fluid choice. Sample items for agentic beliefs read, "How one implements a chosen career determines one's career success" and "Career success relies on good execution and adjustment of one's career choice."

After completing a study to develop the scale, Xu (2020a) conducted an initial validity study using a diverse sample comprised of 292 individuals who ranged in age from 18 to 25 years (M = 23.51, SD = 1.93). Of the sample, 63% were females and about half were students. In addition to the *Constructivist Belief in Career Decision Making Scale (CBCDS)*, participants responded to the (a) *CAAS*; (b) the *Career Decision Ambiguity Tolerance Scale–Revised* (Xu & Tracey, 2015), which measures the tendency to avoid and withdraw from ambiguity in career decision making; and (c) the *Career Indecision Profile–Short* (CIP-Short; Xu & Tracey, 2017), which measures career indecision resulting from negative affectivity, choice/commitment anxiety, lack of readiness, and interpersonal conflicts. Results indicated that the *CAAS* total score correlated -.18 to satisficing decision and .43 to agentic creation. Xu (2020a) suggested that the negative correlations could be regarded as a passive and dysfunctional strategy that individuals with stronger adaptability resources tend to avoid during career decision making. By contrast, agentic creation beliefs correlated as expected to career adaptability. With regard to causes for indecision, the *CAAS* total score correlated -.43 to negative affectivity, -.34 to choice/commitment anxiety, -.56 to lack of readiness, and -.26 to interpersonal conflicts. Of note, the strongest correlations of indecision causes to the *CAAS* total score were to lack of readiness, which involves difficulty in initiating a career decision-making process --- possibly because of limited career adaptability resources. With regard to decision-making ambiguity tolerance, the *CAAS* total score correlated .48 to preference for ambiguity, .31 to tolerance of ambiguity, .46 to confidence in coping with ambiguity, and -.25 to aversion and withdrawal from ambiguity. Regression analyses indicated that the *CBCDS* explained additional variance for career indecision and career decision ambiguity management beyond career adaptability, providing strong evidence for incremental validity of the *CBCDS* beyond career adaptability. The results indicated that the *CBCDS* scores improved the R^2 by 2% for negative affect, 5% for choice commitment, 10% for lack of readiness, 14% for interpersonal conflict, 19% for preference, 13% for tolerance, 10%, for confidence, and 20% for aversion. Xu (2020a) concluded that constructivist beliefs could play a salient role in the process and outcome of career decision making. Before applying a career construction intervention, Xu suggested that counselors assess clients' constructivist beliefs to determine whether a constructionist approach to career counseling fits a client's expectations.

Work volition. The word "volition" derives from the Latin verb "velle," meaning "to will" or "to wish." Accordingly, the *Merriam-Webster Dictionary* defines volition as the power, right, or opportunity to make one's own choices or decisions. In vocational psychology, the term *work volition* refers to the will to make career decisions on one's own despite external constraints. Duffy, Diemer, Perry, Laurenzia, and Torrey (2012) linguistically explained work volition as the "perceived capacity to make occupational choices despite constraints" (p. 402) and operationally defined it with the 13-item *Work Volition Scale*, which has subscales for volition, financial constraints, and structural constraints. The Volition Subscale consists of four items:

> I've been able to choose the jobs I have wanted.
> I can do the kind of work I want, despite external barriers.
> I feel total control over my job choices.
> I feel able to change jobs if I want to.

Concurrently, Duffy, Diemer, and Jadidian (2016) developed the *Work Volition Scale–Student Version* for university students. It measures the perceived capacity to make future occupational choices despite constraints using the two factors of volition (seven items) and constraint (ten items). Dealing with future choices, six of the seven Volition Subscale items use the word "will," primarily expressing capacity yet also implying futurity.

> I will be able to change jobs if I want to.
> Discrimination will not affect my ability to choose a job.

I will be able to choose jobs that I want.

I will learn how to find my own way in the world of work.

I feel total control over my future job choices.

I will be able to do the kind of work I want to, despite external barriers.

Once I enter the work world, I will easily find a new job if I want to.

In publishing the *Work Volition Scale*, Duffy and his colleagues (2012) suggested that researchers explore "the place of work volition in more elaborate models of work satisfaction and general well-being, with work volition being placed as both a predictor and as an outcome" (p. 410). Nevertheless, in studies of its position in the CCT model of adaptation, most researchers have focused on just volition, not constraints, and positioned it as a mediator following the suggestion of Perry and Wallace (2013) who explained that work volition can be treated as a mediating or moderating variable that presumably might operated differently based on an individual's social class world view. Furthermore, counseling interventions might focus on fostering career adaptability rather than work volition in that work volition is a psychological propensity that may require more time to change and currently there are no specific directions for its development. Moreover, from the CCT perspective, development of adaptability resources precedes and influences volition beliefs.

Career decision-making self-efficacy. The third conative mediator in the CCT adaptation model, career decision-making self-efficacy, refers to confidence about being able to perform adapting behaviors such as career exploring and decision making. The career decision-making self-efficacy construct is distinct from the related adaptability resources of career control and confidence because it explicitly denotes confidence in performing specific decision-making behaviors. CCT posits that individuals can derive career decision-making self-efficacy beliefs from the resources of Concern (i.e., a guiding vision of their career future), Control (i.e., a sense of personal responsibility to manage oneself during the decisional process), Curiosity (i.e., an interest to explore the self and occupations), and Confidence (i.e., optimism and persistence in the decisional process).

Adaptation Results

The CCT model of adaptation distinguishes variables that belong to the process of adapting from those that result from the process. Career adaptation results denote the outcomes of adapting responses to vocational development tasks, occupation transitions, and work troubles. The outcomes may involve a task accomplished, change achieved, or problem solved. The wide variety of outcomes examined by researchers will be described in subsequent chapters of this book. For now, some examples of frequently used outcomes for task accomplishment are career choice decidedness, vocational identity, occupation commitment, and work engagement; examples for a change achieved are graduating, entering a new occupational position, and getting promoted; and examples for a problem solved are reduced job stress, mastering a new skill, job success, and job satisfaction. Each of these variables indicates a level of equilibrium that has been reached.

There is a strong relation between adapting responses and adaptation results. As an example of this adapting-adaptation relation, consider possible outcomes of decision-making responses. Integrative coping may result in the outcome of decidedness, adjustive defending may result in undecidedness, and maladaptive fragmenting may result in indecisiveness. As a second example, consider possible adaptation results from exploring responses. Integrative coping may result in strategic information about long-term goals and tactical means gathered from both internal and external sources. Adjustive defending may result in tactical information about smaller steps during a shorter time-period, gathered mostly from internal sources with a few external sources being used. Maladaptive fragmenting may result in a lack of basic information and unrealistic opinions.

Interplay among Adaptivity, Adaptability, Adapting, and Adaptation

In sum, adaptive individuals draw upon their adapt-abilities to shape adapting responses that resolve significant career challenges and changes including vocational development tasks, occupation transitions, and work troubles. Higher levels of adaptation (outcome) are expected for those who are willing (adaptive) and able (adaptability) to perform behaviors (adapting) that address changing conditions. An analogy to airline travel may help readers keep in mind the distinctions between readiness, resources, responses, and results. In preparing for departure, flight attendants ask passengers seated in an exit row whether they are "willing and able" to assist in an emergency. This assistance, should it be needed, requires performance of actions that fit the situation. Passengers are asked about willingness and ability because action in an emergency requires both. Some people may be willing yet unable while other people may be unwilling yet able. In the language of CCT, the attendant is asking the passengers whether they have the readiness and resources that may be needed to act in an emergency. CCT views "willing and able" as "adaptivity and adaptability" or as "readiness and resources." To continue the analogy, the airplane emergency might require performance of some life-saving actions. Those who perceive themselves as willing and able may respond by performing the tasks needed to save lives should the situation present itself. This adapting or "doing" involves the behaviors that function to accomplish role orientation, exploration, establishment, management, and disengagement. The adapting responses, in turn, lead to some resulting outcome or adaptation, which may be judged by life and death. In career construction, the outcome is not life or death, rather it is goodness of fit or harmony as indicated by development, satisfaction, success, and stability. In a dynamic of reciprocal interaction, the passenger who performed well in an emergency may increase in adaptivity and adaptability and may be even better prepared for the next crisis.

Semantics and Pragmatics of
Terms in the Adaptation Model

Semantics considers the meaning of a term without a context. Pragmatic meaning understands the same term in a context that provides a subtext to the meaning. Thus semantics is concerned only with the exact, literal meaning of a term, whereas pragmatic usage implies meaning from the context. The terms in this text about the adaptation model are to be understood in context of CCT. A term used in CCT can have a different meaning in a different discourse about careers. For example, Inkson (2006) has explicated 24 different pragmatic meanings for the term *career*, depending on the conceptual context.

The key terms in the CCT model of adaptation (adaptivity, adaptability, adapting, and adaptation) denote subtle semantic distinctions put to pragmatic use in explaining the model. McIlveen and Midgley (2015) rightly warned that the terms may be easily conflated with one another or confused with the terminology of other theories. McIlveen and Midgley (2015) used as an example the term "preparedness" (Lent, 2013), which may be considered in CCT terms to mean a combination of adaptivity and adaptability. To reduce this possible conflation and confusion when reading a text about the CCT model of adaptation, a reader should rely on pragmatic meaning in that context. The pragmatic understanding of semantically similar terms in different discourses may differ in intended meaning. Even the same term may be taken differently in different contexts. An important example is the meaning of the word *Concern*. In many languages, including English, concern may be taken to mean "worry, uncertainty, and apprehension" rather than the *CAAS* intended meaning of "a matter of marked interest or importance to someone." A perspective from which to understand the pragmatic meaning of terms in the CCT adaptation model is their operational definitions in psychometric measures, as discussed in the next chapter.

Conclusion

In this Chapter, the Career Construction Theory model of adaptation and its components were defined and described. Distinctions were made among adaptive readiness, adaptability resources, adapting responses, adaptation outcomes, and their interplay. In addition the differences between adapting beliefs and behaviors were addressed, particularly highlighting beliefs about work volition and career decision-making self-efficacy. The Chapter ended with an admonition about semantic and pragmatic meanings of the terms in the adaptation model. The next Chapter address the operational definitions of the adaptation model constructs in terms of measurement inventories.

CHAPTER 2

CAREER ADAPTATION MEASURES

Psychometric inventories based on the Career Construction Theory (CCT) model of adaptation have been developed to operationally define adaptability resources and adapting behaviors. However, prior research has not settled on a standard operationalization of CCT adaptivity. Functioning as an abstract, global disposition (Funder, 1991), adaptivity involves a compound mixture of multiple specific personality traits that have more explanatory power across a broad range of situations and behaviors than does a single trait. This chapter begins with a discussion of adaptivity measures and then addresses, in turn, sets of measures for adaptability, adapting, and adaptation.

Adaptivity Measures

Perhaps the single most comprehensive indicator of adaptivity is the personality trait called *proactivity,* that is, a general disposition to take intentional action to effect change in one's environment (Bateman & Crant, 1993). In particular, it involves self-initiated efforts to anticipate change, seek opportunities, and prevent problems. Researchers have measured individual differences in the proactive personality trait using Seibert, Crant, and Kraimer's (1999) 10-item version of the original 17-item *Proactive Personality Scale* (Bateman & Crant, 1993). Participants respond on a 7-point Likert scale to rate the extent to which they agree with each statement (e.g., "I excel at identifying opportunities"). Highly proactive individuals show initiative in identifying opportunities, acting on them, and persevering until they bring about meaningful change. However, proactive personality disposition does not fully capture the complexity of career adaptivity as it is conceptualized in CCT. Rudolph, Lavigne, and Zacher (2017) reported that the Five Factor Model of personality traits explain significant and unique variability in adaptability above and beyond the influence of proactive personality disposition.

25

Instead of representing adaptivity as a single trait such as proactivity, many researchers represent adaptivity as a compound of existing traits, specifically the traits in the Five Factor Model (FFM) of personality traits. CCT recognizes that each of the FFM personality traits constitute plausible indicators of adaptivity. However, no single FFM trait, separately considered, adequately reflects the complexity of adaptivity. The trait interaction perspective on the FFM holds that the personality traits coexist at different levels within individuals and should be modeled as such. Savickas and Porfeli (2012) suggested the traits of Openness to Experience and Conscientiousness as a reasonable combination to indicate the characteristics of readiness and willingness to change (see also, LePine, Colquitt, & Erez, 2000).

Openness reflects *readiness* to change in that it represents a propensity to explore and consider unfamiliar ideas and new experiences required for navigating novel tasks. Rather than passively adhere to predictable routines, individuals high in Openness remain ready to explore the environment as well as their own thoughts and feelings. They actively seek, rather than avoid, new and varied situations that are novel, complex, uncertain, or unpredictable. Their openness to experience and sensitivity to context can enable them to find meaning in their actions, expand self-awareness, clarify pre-existing values and strengths, find alternative routes, and alter established views. By contrast, individuals low in Openness seem to prefer conformity, obedience, security, and stability (Kashdan & Rottenberg, 2010).

Conscientiousness reflects a *willingness* to take action that also characterizes adaptivity. Rather than procrastinate, individuals high in Conscientiousness show the initiative to set goals and are organized, persistent, and motivated in pursuing them. The initiative, striving, and perseverance characteristics displayed by conscientious individuals reflect their willingness to act in the face of disequilibrium.

In sum, while the FFM traits jointly provide a broad representation of adaptivity they may miss the dispositional flexibility to identify opportunities to engage in activities that effect career change (Perera & McIlveen, 2017). Adding together the personality trait of proactivity with the FFM traits of Conscientiousness and Openness into a compound traits may provide a more comprehensive representation of adaptive readiness.

Adaptability Measures

The standard measure of career adaptability is the *Career Adapt-Abilities Scale* (*CAAS*), which appears in Appendix A. The *CAAS* measures career adaptability as a higher-order construct that subsumes the four psychosocial resources for managing developmental tasks, occupational transitions, and work troubles. It consists of four subscales with six items each to measure the adapt-abilities of Concern, Control, Curiosity, and Confidence.

Researchers from 13 countries collaborated in constructing the *CAAS* (Savickas & Porfeli, 2012). The team worked together, communicating in the English language, to linguistically explicate and operationally define career adaptability as a meaningful construct in each of their own countries. The first step in inventory construction was to discuss cross-cultural similarities and differences as well as examine indigenous theoretical models. The International Team used the N-way approach (Brett, Tinsley, Janssens, Barsness, & Lytle, 1997) to highlight culture-specific and culture-general conceptions and aspects of adaptability. Based on four pilot studies, they field tested in each of the 13 countries a *Career Adapt-Abilities-Research Form* (*CAAS-RF*) consisting of 55 items. The *CAAS-RF* contained 11 items for five possible scales named Concern, Control, Curiosity, Confidence, and Cooperation. The resulting *Career Adapt-Abilities Scale* (*CAAS*) consists of four subscales with six items each to measure the adapt-abilities of Concern, Control, Curiosity, and Confidence. Items representing the proposed Cooperation subscale were not used in the *CAAS* because they measured interpersonal rather than intrapersonal resources.

The age of participants varied across countries. In Belgium, Dries, Van Esbroeck, van Vianen, De Cooman, and Pepermans sampled 700 high school and university students. In Brazil, Teixeira, Bardagi, Lassance, Magalhaes, and Duarte (2012) sampled 908 adults with a mean age of 29 years. In China, Hou, Leung, Li, Li, and Xu, (2012) sampled 296 university students with a mean age of 20 years. In France, Pouyaud, Vignoli, Dosnon, and Lallemand (2012) sampled 609 grade 11 students with a mean age of 16.6 years. In Iceland, Vilhjálmsdóttir, Kjartansdóttir, Smáradóttir, and Einarsdótti (2012) sampled 1566 students with a mean age of 28 years (70% of whom were between ages 14 to 30). In Italy, Soresi, Nota, and Ferrari (2012) sampled 762 adolescents with a mean age of 17 years. In Korea, Tak (2012) sampled 278 college students with a mean age of 22 years from an introductory psychology class. In The Netherlands, van Vianen, Klehe, Koen, and Dries (2012) sampled 465 college student with a mean age of 21 years. In Portugal, Duarte, Soares, Fraga, Rafael, Lima, Paredes, Agostinho, and Djaló (2012) sampled 916 participants (255 high school students with a mean age of 15 years; 395 employed adults with a mean age of 47 years; and 266 unemployed adults with a mean age of 22 years enrolled in training activities). In South Africa, Maree (2012) sampled 435 high school students with mean age 15.5 years enrolled in grades 9 and 11. In Switzerland, Rossier, Zecca, Stauffer, Maggiori, and Dauwalder (2012) sampled 391 adults with a mean age of 40 years. In Taiwan, Tien, Wang, Chu, and Huang (2012) sampled 493 adults with a mean age of 37 years. In the USA, Savickas and Porfeli (2012) sampled 460 10th and 11th grade students with a mean age of 16.5 years.

Participants indicated how strongly they had developed 24 abilities on a response scale that ranged across not strong (1), somewhat strong (2), strong (3), very strong (4), and strongest (5). Mean scores were high with Adaptability = 3.81; Concern = 3.82; Control = 3.92; Curiosity = 3.73; and Confidence = 3.87. Taiwan, China, and Iceland had the higher mean scores while France, Korea, and Italy had the lower mean scores. The differences in mean scores, or in other words the lack of scalar invariance, were expected because the subscales measure context-sensitive, psychosocial capital. The meaningfulness of the differences in scores could not be interpreted because some unknown part reflected a measurement artifact rather than a true difference. The team recommended further study to identify theoretical predictors of the mean differences between economies, cultures, and countries to determine the extent to which they explain observed differences.

The reliabilities of the *CAAS* total score and subscale scores ranged from acceptable to excellent when computed with the combined data. As expected, the reliability estimates varied across countries. Nevertheless, the internal consistency estimates for the four subscales of Concern, Control, Curiosity, and Confidence were generally acceptable to excellent across all the countries.

Confirmatory Factor Analyses of International Study Data

Savickas and Porfeli (2012) assembled the data from the partner countries into one large data set in order to conduct a confirmatory factor analysis (CFA). This analysis assessed the fit between the observed data and the *a priori* theoretical model that specified hypothesized hierarchical relations among the items, first-order factors (i.e., Concern, Control, Curiosity, and Confidence), and second-order factor (i.e., career adaptability). As shown in Figure 1, the standardized factor loading for items to first-order factors ranged from .56 to .75, with the exception of .48 for item 7 ("Keeping upbeat"). This item was shown to be a little problematic in later studies in Portugal and Iceland. Loadings for the first-order factors (i.e., career-adapt-ability dimensions) to a second-order factor (i.e., career adaptability construct) ranged from .78 to .90.

Figure 1. *CAAS* Hierarchical Confirmatory Model

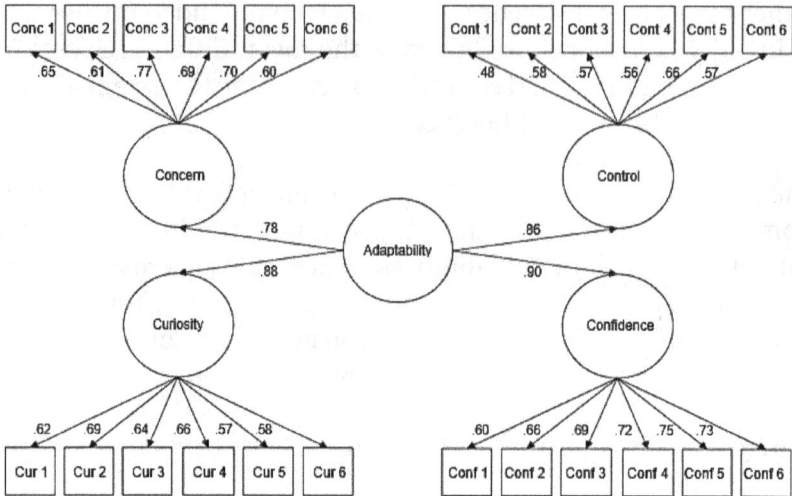

The next step involved conducting separate confirmatory factor analyses (CFA) for each country to assess the fit between the observed data and the *a priori* theoretical model. Results for each country indicated that the data adequately fit the theoretically-derived measurement model based on the established criteria of RMSEA and SRMR fit indices for the unconstrained model with unequal N. The results support structural equivalence of the model across the countries because the same factor model fit the data in each country. While the fit indices were acceptable for each country, they varied across countries. The three countries with the best fit to the model were the USA, South Africa, and Italy. Thus, the theoretically-derived measurement model of the *CAAS* worked best in these countries. The three countries with the poorest fit to the model were The Netherlands, Iceland, and Korea. Despite having the poorest indices, the fit of data to the model for those countries was adequate and acceptable. Separate articles in a special issue of the *Journal of Vocational Behavior* (Leong & Walsh, 2012) reported the psychometric characteristics of the *CAAS*, including initial validity evidence, for each of the 13 countries represented in constructing the scale.

The goodness of fit indices for eleven of the 13 countries appear in Table 2. Indices for Brazil and Portugal do not appear because they used only four items for the Control and for the Confidence subscales because of a miscommunication from the study coordinator. A model is considered to have an acceptable fit if the $\chi 2/df$ is equal to or below 3, the CFI value is about .90 or above. Good fit is indicated by RMSEA values below .08 and by SRMR values less than .05 with values less than .08 considered acceptable.

Table 2. Structural Model Fit Indices for the *CAAS* in 11 Countries

Country	χ2/df	CFI	RMSEA	SRMR
Belgium	2.02	0.90	.053	.057
China	2.14	0.86	0.64	.057
France	2.98	0.86	.056	.054
Iceland	9.57	0.87	.073	.062
Italy	3.62	0.89	.058	.049
Korea	2.33	0.89	.067	.060
Netherlands	3.00	0.85	.068	.070
South Africa	1.77	0.92	.046	.048
Switzerland	2.79	0.88	.071	.056
Taiwan	3.67	0.92	.078	.049
USA	2.24	0.94	.052	.040

Adapting Measures

Adapting during adolescence and emerging adulthood has typically been operationally defined with measures of the career choice process such as exploring, deciding, and planning. The Planning and the Exploration Scales of the *Career Development Inventory* (Super, Zelkowitz, & Thompson, 1981) are dated yet still pertinent. For adults the *Career Development Inventory–Adult Form I* is particularly pertinent. In CCT research, the most widely used specific measure of adapting responses concentrates on exploratory behavior. The *Career Exploration Survey* (Stumpf, Colarelli, & Hartman, 1983) assesses self-exploration (5 items) and environmental exploration (6 items) during the last six months. The *Career Engagement Scale* (Hirschi, Freund, & Hermann, 2014), which measures "the general degree to which an individual engages in adapting behaviors" (p. 576), is intended for both students and workers. The nine items in the scale ask about behaviors during the previous six months, with the last three items asking about networking, training, and advancement. Two sample items are: "Actively sought to design your professional future" and "Undertook things to achieve your career goals." The scale serves as a parsimonious measure of the generic construct of career adapting thoughts and behaviors at "a general level without specifically addressing differences between distinct behaviors" (p. 576). Hirschi, Freund, and Hermann (2014) advised that "Specific measures are useful if someone is interested in testing specific theories" (p. 576). This advice applies to testing the CCT career adaptation model because it requires a specific measure that assesses the distinct beliefs and behaviors that compose the adapting responses dimension of the conceptual model.

Career Futures Inventory–Adaptability Scale

The *Career Futures Inventory* (*CFI*: Rottinghaus, Day, & Borgen, 2005) includes an excellent scale with which to measure adapting responses. Although the *CFI* scale is titled the "Career Adaptability Scale," from the perspective of the CCT model of adaptation, the *CFI* measures performance of adapting behaviors. The inventory authors used Savickas (1997) article on adaptability as part of their theoretical framework for crafting the inventory. That initial conceptualization explained adaptability as having three major components: "planful attitudes, self- and environmental exploration, and informed decision making" (Savickas, 1997, p. 254). The later CCT model of adaptation (Savickas, 2013, 2020) designated planful attitudes as part of adaptability whereas exploring and deciding were designated as aspects of adapting responses. True to that 1997 conceptualization of adaptability, Rottinghaus and colleagues wrote items that concentrated on adapting behaviors for planning and adjusting to vocational development tasks and career transitions. The resulting *CFI-Career Adaptability Scale* (*CFI-CA*) uses 11 items to measure how individuals view their "capacity to cope with and capitalize on change in the future, level of comfort with new work responsibilities, and ability to recover when unforeseen events alter career plans" (Rottinghaus, Day, & Borgin, 2005, p. 11). Sample items inquire about adapting responses such as: "I am good at adapting to new work settings;" "I can adapt to change in my career plans;" "I can overcome potential barriers that may exist in my career," and "I can bounce back when my career plans don't work out quite right." In terms of pragmatic meaning in the context of CCT, the 11 *CA-CFI* items measure adapting responses, not adaptability resources. The *CFI-CA* items are about doing not about self-regulation resources. Nevertheless, many studies have used the *CFI-CA* as a measure of adaptability. The *CFI* contains two additional scales. The *Career Optimism Scale* (11 items) measures a disposition to expect positive career outcomes. In terms of CCT, career optimism as a personality disposition measures an adaptivity trait. The third *CFI* scale, *Perceived Knowledge of Job Market* (3 items) assesses how well an individual understands job market and employment trends and can also serve as a measure of an adaptation result.

As the measure that they deemed most similar to the *CAAS*, McIlveen, Perera, Hoare, and McLennan (2018) identified the Career Adaptability subscale from the *Career Futures Inventory* (*CFI-CA*; Rottinghaus, Day & Borgen, 2005). They examined the convergence of *CAAS* scores with responses to the 11-item *CFI-CA*. To compare empirically the inventories, McIlveen and colleagues administered both the *CAAS* and the *CFI-CA* to 344 pre-service teachers enrolled in a bachelor of education program at a medium-sized university in Australia. The results for comparing the *CAAS* and the *CFI-CA* indicated one general factor and two orthogonal method factors. The discrimination of the first-order career adaptability factors with the hierarchical, multi-dimensional structure provided a better fit to the data than a model positing only a unidimensional adaptability factor. The *CAAS* first-order factor loadings on the higher-order factor (Mean = .80) were larger than the loadings of the *CFI-CA* items (M = .53). The *CFI-CA* loadings themselves were sufficiently strong to suggest convergence of scores between the *CAAS* and the *CFI-CA*, accounting for measurement effects. These results suggest that the two measures

33

are related yet differ in reflecting an underlying construct. Interpreting these findings from the perspective of CCT, the underlying construct would be career adaptation, with the *CAAS* measuring adaptability resources and the *CFI-CA* measuring adapting responses.

In a second study that compared the *CFI-CA* to the *CAAS* items, Kirchknopf (2020) administered both scales to 395 apprentices (59.7% females) who attended commercial schools in Germany. The participants' ranged in age from 16 to 39 years with a mean age of 20.27 years (SD = 3.12). The squared correlation between the *CAAS* and *CFI-CA* was .57. Kirchknopf then tested two models using confirmatory factor analysis to examine the extent to which the two measures of the latent variable share variance and how they differ from each other. In the first model, both the *CAAS* and *CFI-CA* items were loaded on one factor. This model had a poor fit. In the second model, *CFI-CA* items were loaded on one factor and the *CAAS* items on four factors and on a higher-order construct. The model fit values were CFI = .943, TLI = .932, RMSEA = .054, and SRMR = .046. The author deemed this a "moderate" fit yet it met all the indicators for a good fit with CFI and TLI values .90 or above, RMSEA values below .08, and SRMR values less than .05.

To examine the overlap between the *CAAS* and *CFI-CA*, Kirchknopfer (2020) applied the Fornell-Larcker criterion that uses average variance extracted (AVE) to compare the two scales. AVE is calculated by adding the squared factor loadings of each item and then dividing by the number of items. AVE measures the level of variance captured by a construct versus the level due to measurement error. Values above 0.7 are very good and values of 0.5 or higher are considered acceptable. AVE for the *CFI-CA* was .51 and AVE for the *CAAS* was .82. The squared correlation between the *CAAS* and *CFI-CA* was .57, which was higher than the AVE for the *CFI-CA*. According to the Fornell-Larcker testing system, the levels of the AVE for each construct should be greater than the squared correlation involving the constructs. Accordingly, the degree of overlap between the *CAAS* and the *CFI-CA* does not justify a clear distinction between them. A more detailed analysis traced the overlap back to specific subscales in the *CAAS*. Applying the Fornell-Larcker criterion to the four subscales indicated that Concern (AVE Concern = .59; AVE *CFI-CA* = .51; R^2 = .24) and Curiosity (AVE Curiosity = .57; AVE *CA-CFI* = .51; R^2 = .47) could be clearly separated from the *CA-CFI*. However, Control (AVE Control = .50; AVE CA-*CFI* = .51; R^2 = .54) and Confidence (AVE Confidence = .59; AVE *CA-CFI* = .51; R^2 = .58) both missed the criterion because of their relatively high correlation to *CA-CFI*. This subscale analysis showed that the overlap between the *CAAS* and the *CFI- CA* is primarily due to the dimensions of Control and Confidence. This means that, despite lack of empirical distinctiveness in relation to the *CAAS*, the *CFI-CA* does not contain essential aspects of career adaptability, particularly Concern, which CCT positions as the most important dimension.

In 2012, Rottinghaus, Buelow, Matyja, and Schneider published a revision of the *CFI*. The *Career Futures Inventory-Revised* (*CFI-R*) contains five scales. The authors modified and refocused the Career Adaptability Scale and called it the Career Agency Scale. It contains ten items that measure the "perceived capacity for self-reflection and for forethought to intentionally initiate, control, and manage career transitions" (p. 130). Sample items read, "I can perform a successful job search," "I can adapt to changes in the world of work," "I can establish a plan for my future career," and "I will successfully mange my present career transition process." From the perspective of the CCT career adaptation model, the Career Agency Scale measures adapting responses.

Career Competencies Questionnaire

The *Career Competencies Questionnaire* crafted by Akkermans, Brenninkmeijer, Huibers, and Blonk (2013) can serve in the CCT model as an excellent measure of adapting responses. Although related, career adaptability resources and career adapting competencies are conceptually and empirically distinct. For example, they correlated .57 in a study reported by Akkermans, Paradnike, Van der Heijden, and DeVos (2019). Adaptability resources foster the development of competence in adapting to career construction challenges and changes. Akkermans and colleagues (2013) explained career competencies as knowledge, skills, and abilities that individuals can develop. In their model of career competencies, they linguistically explicated three dimensions, each with two specific competencies, and operationally define them with the *Career Competencies Questionnaire.* The Reflective dimension, or "knowing why," involves gaining self-knowledge through reflecting on motives (e.g., "I know what I like in my work") and personal characteristics (i.e., "I know my strengths in my work"). The Communicative dimension, or "knowing who," involves discussing one's career with others through networking (e.g., "I know how to ask for advice from people in my network") and self-profiling (e.g., I can clearly show others what I want to achieve in my career"). The Behavioral dimension, or "knowing how," involves constructing one's career through the actions of exploring (e.g., "I know how to find out what my options are for becoming further educated") and goal setting (e.g., "I can make clear career plans"). These competencies enable individuals to enact reflective and active adapting responses such as self-evaluation, values clarification, information seeking, generating alternatives, evaluating alternatives, and goal setting. In an insightful adaptation of the *Questionnaire*, Dumulescu, Balazsi, and Opre (2015) instructed participants to respond to the items as they performed or did not perform the action in the last six months.

In a study that used the *Career Competencies Questionnaire,* Safavi and Bouzari (2019) examined whether career adaptability mediated the relation between psychological capital and career competencies. The participants were 193 frontline employees in five-star hotels in Northern Cyprus, all of whom had direct interaction with customers. The participants ranged in age from 38 to 47 years and 58% were females. In addition to the *CAAS*, Safavi and Bouzari (2019) used the 24-item *Psychological Capital Questionnaire* (Luthans, Avolio, Avey, & Norman, 2007) to measure hope, resilience, optimism, and self-efficacy with six items each. The findings from structural equation modeling indicated direct and mediating effects. Specifically, psychological capital related to career adaptability, which in turn related to career competency. Career adaptability fully mediated the relation between psychological capital and career competency. These results support the use of the *Career Competencies Questionnaire* as measure of career adapting responses.

Student Career Construction Inventory

The *Student Career Construction Inventory (SCCI*; Savickas, M., Porfeli, Hilton, & Savickas, S., 2018) measures adapting responses, which consist of vocational thoughts and behaviors, involved in constructing a career choice. Individuals respond to the 18 items on the *SCCI* using the following five-point behavioral response scale:

5 = I have already done this
4 = I am now doing what needs to be done
3 = I know what to do about it
2 = I have thought about it but do not yet know what to do about it
1 = I have not yet thought much about it

The items are scored for four scales that assess (a) Crystallizing a vocational self-concept, (b) Exploring to gather information about occupations, (c) Deciding to commit to an occupational choice, and (d) Preparing to implement that choice. The four scales inter-relate to constitute a continuum that reflects the general factor of adapting responses during the exploration stage of a career. The *SCCI* appears in Appendix B.

Career Mastery Inventory

While the *SCCI* pertains to students, the *Career Mastery Inventory (CMAS*; Crites, 1981; Savickas, 1992) pertains to employed adults. The *CMAS* measures how well employees are adapting to six tasks for establishing themselves in an occupation. The six scales with 15 items each measure (a) fitting into an organization, (b) learning the job, (c) accepting supervision, (d) getting along with coworkers, (e) moving ahead through promotions, and (f) looking ahead by setting goals. The *CMAS* appears in the Appendix C.

Career Management Strategy Scale

An excellent measure of career adapting responses for employed adults is the *Career Management Strategy Scale* by Guthrie, Coate, and Schwoerer (1998). It measures (a) seeking a mentor or guidance (e.g., get career guidance from supervisors; get career guidance from experienced people in the organization); (b) maintaining career flexibility (e.g., look for opportunities to learn new skills; adapt to changes in my work); (c) building a broad network of contacts (e.g., get career guidance from people outside of the organization; seek development opportunities outside the organization); (d) extending involvement in work (e.g., take your work home with you; work at your job beyond normal hours;); and (e) self-presentation (e.g., work hard when you know supervisors will see results; make superiors aware of accomplishments).

Late Career Employability

To study adapting behaviors in older workers, Zacher and Griffin (2015) constructed a scale to measure "specific work- and career-related behaviors" (p. 230) associated with career adaptation. The scale consists of five items that serve as indicators of career adapting responses: (1) "Using professional networks and business contacts to develop your career;" (2) "Maintaining your knowledge of potential jobs both inside and outside of your current organization;" (3) "Regularly taking up opportunities" (e.g., courses, workshops, experiences) to develop skills you can use at work;" (4) "Keeping on top of new knowledge in your work area;" and (5) "Volunteering for roles and tasks that will expand your skills, knowledge, and values." In a group of 577 workers with a mean age of 59.56 years, the adapting scale had a coefficient alpha of .80. The results indicated that the adapting behaviors scale correlated .61 to the *CAAS* total score and .18 to job satisfaction measured by three items: "Overall, I am very satisfied in my job," "I am very interested in my job," and "I get a great deal of accomplishment from my job."

Conclusion

This Chapter began with an explanation of how the proactive personality trait and the Five Factor Model traits of openness and conscientiousness serve as preferred measures of adaptive readiness in the CCT model of adaptation. The next section concentrated on a thorough description of how the *CAAS* was constructed and initially validated by a team of researchers from 13 countries. This Chapter concluded with a discussion of measures for adapting responses, and distinguished the *CAAS* from the *Career Futures Inventory*. The next Chapter presents evidence that supports the construct validity of the *CAAS*.

CHAPTER 3

CONSTRUCT VALIDITY OF THE
CAREER ADAPT-ABILITIES SCALE

Construct validity means the extent to which an inventory measures what it purports to measure. Construct validity cannot be proven, only supported by empirical observations. Accordingly, construct validity should be demonstrated from a number of perspectives. This Chapter reports results from studies that have examined the construct validity of the *CAAS* using confirmatory factor analysis (CFA). Researchers in more than 20 different countries have used CFA to evaluate the fit of *CAAS* data to the *a priori* theoretical model. The latent factors or constructs tested in the structural model were career adaptability and its four dimensions. The results provide evidence that support the *CAAS* theoretical model and that its items truly represent their assigned constructs.

In addition to invariance of the structural model, several multiple-group confirmatory factor analyses have shown that the *CAAS* measures the same underlying construct across groups or across time. Measurement invariance means that a given measure is interpreted in a conceptually similar manner by respondents representing different genders or cultural backgrounds. Lack of measurement invariance may preclude meaningful interpretation of data. Measurement invariance is often tested with multiple-group confirmatory factor analysis (CFA). In the context of structural equation models, including CFA, factorial invariance is often termed measurement equivalence.

The *CAAS* has also demonstrated construct validity with evidence that supports its convergent and discriminant validity. Linguistic explications and operational definitions of career adaptability need to include both what it is and what it is not. In this regard, the operational definition of career adaptability must show both convergent and discriminant validity of its scores to support its construct validity, neither one alone is sufficient. Convergent validity means that *CAAS* scores must empirically correlate to theoretically-related concepts and measures. Conversely, discriminant validity means that *CAAS* scores do not correlate to theoretically-unrelated concepts and measures. These relationships are assessed using correlation coefficients. Correlations between theoretically-similar measures should be high (e.g., .50 to .70) whereas correlations between theoretically-dissimilar measures should be low or non-significant.

The following sections address the construct validity of the *CAAS* by reporting, in turn, evidence from studies of confirmatory factor analysis, multiple-group factor analysis, convergent validity, and discriminant validity.

Confirmatory Factor Analyses of the *CAAS*

More than two dozen studies conducted in at least 24 countries have evaluated the known latent structure of the *CAAS* in diverse populations. Most of these studies used hierarchical CFA to examine the relation of the four factors of Concern, Control, Curiosity, and Confidence to the higher-order construct of career adaptability. In these studies, correlations between latent variables differed across groups for a variety of reasons, including cultural issues and problems in translating the items into 20 different languages. Nevertheless, the data in each country fit the known theoretical structure.

The hierarchical structure of the *CAAS* has been supported in numerous countries including Australia (Tolentino, Garcia, Lu, Restubog, Bordia, & Plewa, 2014; McIlveen, Perera, Hoare, & McLennan, (2018).), Brazil (Audibert & Teixeira, 2015; Ambiel, Carvalho, Martins, & Tofoli, 2016; Cammarosano, Melo-Silva, & Oliveira (2019), Croatia (Šverko, Babarović, & Matić, 2015), the Czech Republic (Hlad'o, Kvaskova, Jezek, Hirschi, & Macek, 2020), Iran (McKenna, Zacher, Ardabili, & Mohebbi, 2016; Nilforooshan & Salimi, 2016), Germany (Johnston, Lucian, Maggiori, Ruch & Rossier, 2013), Hong Kong (Yuen & Yau, 2015; Hui, Yuen &, Chen, 2018a), Lithuania (Urbanaviciute, Kairys, Pociute, & Liniauskaite,

2014), Macau (Tien, Lin, Hsieh, & Jin, 2014), Papua New Guinea (de Guzman & Choice, 2013), Nigeria (Olugbade, 2016), The Phillipines (Tolentino, Garcia, Lu, Restubog, Bordia, & Tang, 2013), Portugal (Monteiro & Almeida, 2015), Romania (Negru-Subtirica & Pop, 2016), Serbia (Tolentino, Sedoglavich, Lu, Raymund, Garcia, Restubog, 2014; Mirkovic, Suvajdzic, & Dostanic (2020), Spain (Merino-Tejedor, Hontangas, & Gran, 2016), Singapore (Chan, Uy, Ho, San, Chernyshenko, & Yu, 2015), Thailand (Sibunruang, Garcia, & Tolentino, 2016), and Turkey (Kanten, 2012; Oncel, 2014). In each country the results resembled those reported by research teams in the original set of 13 countries (Savickas & Porfeli, 2012).

Data in each of these studies showed at least adequate fit to the theoretical model. The standardized loadings for the items were strong indictors of the first-order adapt-abilities which in turn were strong indicators of the second-order construct of career adaptability. As suggested by various authors (Cheung & Rensvold, 2002; Vandenberg & Lance, 2000), the researchers reported a variety of goodness-of-fit indices including $\chi2$ per degree of freedom ($\chi2/df$), goodness of fit index (GFI), comparative fit index (CFI), Tucker-Lewis index (TLI), standardized root mean square residual (SRMR), and root mean square error of approximation (RMSEA). A model is considered to have an acceptable fit if the $\chi2/df$ is equal to or below 3, while the value ≤ 5 is acceptable for the samples larger than 200 participants. Good fit is indicated by GFI, CFI, and TLI values about .90 or above; RMSEA values below .08; and SRMR values less than .05 with values less than .08 considered acceptable.

Australia

To test the hierarchical model in Australia, Tolentino, Garcia, Lu, Restubog, Bordia, and Plewa, (2014) administered the *CAAS* to 555 university students in Australia. Confirmatory factor analysis indicated a good fit to the hierarchical multi-dimensional model of career adaptability resources: RMSEA = .049 and SRMR = .041. The factor structure generally corresponded with that obtained from the *CAAS* initial validation, thus expanding its cross-national measurement equivalence. The standardized loadings for the items (.62 to .83) were strong indictors of the first-order adapt-ability factors, which in turn were strong indicators (.84 to .89) of the second-order factor of career adaptability.

In a set of studies, McIlveen, Perera, Hoare, and McLennan (2018) reported results of confirmatory factor analyses of the hierarchical model for three groups. For a group of 344 university students, the fit indices were $\chi2/df$ = 2.35 (p < .001), CFI = .966, TLI = .962, and RMSEA = .063. The loadings for the four adapt-ability factors to the higher-order adaptability factor ranged from .77 to .85. For a group of 394 retail workers, the fit indices were $\chi2/df$ = 3.50 (p <.001), CFI = .951, TLI = .945, and RMSEA = .080. The loadings from the four adapt-ability factors to the higher-order adaptability factor ranged from .74 to .90. For a group of 160 mothers engaged in full-time care-work the fit indices were $\chi2/df$ = 2.07 (p < .001), CFI = .931, TLI = .923, and RMSEA = .082. The loadings from the four adapt-ability factors to the higher-order adaptability factor ranged from ranged from .69 to .79.

Brazil

A previous study conducted by members of the International Team working in Brazil (Teixeira, Bardagi, Lassance, Magalhaes, & Duarte, 2012) confirmed the *CAAS* hierarchical factor structure with adults using 22 of the 24 *CAAS* items. The initial Brazilian version of the *CAAS* did not include two items due to changes in the wording not communicated to them by the coordinator of the International Team. Consequently, the initial scales in Portugal and Brazil contained 22 items. Nevertheless, confirmatory analyses revealed that fit indices for the model were similar to those obtained in other countries.

In 2015, Audibert and Teixeira explored the full 24-item *CAAS* in Brazil. The participants were 990 university students (64.2% females and 56.3% males) from private institutions. They ranged in age from 18 to 68 years (Mean = 25.8; *SD* = 7.45). The results showed that the higher-order factor model fit the data adequately with X^2/df = 6.794, RMSEA = .077, CFI = .951, TLI = .945. The standardized loadings for the items (.73 to .90) were strong indictors of the first-order adapt-abilities, which in turn were strong indicators (.78 to .89) of the second-order construct of career adaptability.

Also confirming the expected factor structure of the 24-item *CAAS* in Brazil, Ambiel, Carvalho, Martins, and Tofoli, (2016) used a a sample of 272 high school students and 404 adult workers. Fit indices for the confirmatory model were χ^2/df = 2.13; CFI = 0.90; AIC = 14525.252; BIC = 15.006; RMSEA = 0.069; and SRMR = 0.041. The standardized loadings for the items (.42 to .74) were strong indictors of the first-order adapt-abilities, which in turn were strong indicators (.74 to .88) of the second-order factor of career adaptability.

The hierarchical structure of the 24-item *CAAS* in Brazil was also confirmed by Cammarosano, Melo-Silva, and Oliveira (2019). They wanted to examine the *CAAS* in a sample of college graduates, check measurement invariance between males and females, and test for differences in the dimensions of adaptability between males and females. The study sample consisted of 599 professionals with university degrees. They ranged in age from 22 to 70 years old (Mean = 38; SD = 10.7). The majority of the sample was female (64.4%), married (46.7%), employed (89%), and had no children (61%). Additionally, 27.21% held a master's degree. Fit indices for the confirmatory model were χ^2/df = 2.41; CFI = 0.91; GFI = .86; RMSEA = 0.049; and SRMR = 0.06. After computing fit indices for this base model, they evaluated the invariance of the model for men and women. Results indicated that the structural model was invariant for the two groups. Additionally, they examined possible gender differences on the four subscales. The results did not differ significantly between women and men.

China

In China, four studies examined the hierarchical model for the *CAAS* and compared the results to those from the original validation study (Hou, Leung, Li, Li, & Xu, 2012). In 2013, Guan, Deng, and colleagues collected data from 697 university students who intended to seek employment rather than advanced education after graduation. Their mean age was 23.5 years (SD = 1.43); 73% were Bachelor graduates and 27% were Master graduates. The results of confirmatory factor analysis showed that all of the comparative fit indices were within the acceptable range ($\chi 2/df$ = 4.03, CFI = .920, RMSEA = .07, SRMR = .03). Also to re-examine the *CAAS* structure, Hou, Wu, and Liu (2014) collected data from 171 participants. The comparative fit indices from their confirmatory factor analysis were all within the acceptable range ($\chi 2/df$ = 4.34, CFI = .840, RMSEA = .064, SRMR = .053). Jiang (2017) tested the hierarchical model on data from 364 adult workers in China. The results showed that the higher-order factorial model fit the data adequately ($\chi 2/df$ = 2.96, RMSEA = 0.07, TLI = 0.91, CFI = 0.92). Dong, Zheng, and Wang (2020) tested the model with 218 employees in the business sector. The results showed that the hierarchical factor model fit the data adequately ($\chi 2/df$ = 2.08, RMSEA = 0.07, CFI = 0.86). The results from these four studies compared well to the results of the original CFA by Hou and her colleagues (2012) which reported RMSEA as 0.064 and SRMR as 0.057.

Croatia

In Croatia, Sverko and Babarovic (2016) tested the four-dimensional hierarchical structure using a combined sample of 339 university students and 263 employed adults. The students ranged in age from 19 to 44 years (Median = 22) and the employees ranged in age from 21 to 64 years (Median = 37). In both subsamples, the majority of respondents were female (67.6% of students and 65.8% of employees). The fit of the model was confirmed by CFA ($\chi 2/df$ = 3.70, p = .001; CFI = .86; RMSEA = .069). In an earlier study, Šverko, Babarović, and Matić, (2015, May) had strongly confirmed the four-dimensional structure of *CAAS* among 801 adolescents who ranged in age from 14 to 18 years.

Czech Republic

In the Czech Republic, Hlad'o, Kvaskova, Jezek, Hirschi, and Macek (2020) tested the hierarchical model with 3,028 full-time students (46.5% females 53.5% males) aged 18–26 (Mean = 18.97 years, SD = 1.09) attending the final year at 44 vocational upper secondary schools. The hierarchical model had acceptable fit indices ($\chi2/df$ = 1445 [p < .001], CFI = .932; RMSEA = .069; SRMR = .045). The standardized loadings for the items ranged from .43 to .83 and were strong indictors of the first-order adapt-ability constructs which in turn are strong indicators (.76 to .87) of the second-order construct of career adaptability. Additional analyses indicated that the measurement model was invariant between genders.

Germany

Using 1204 German-speaking employed adults in Switzerland, a study by Johnston, Luciano, Maggori, Ruch, and Rossier (2013) provided support for the use of the German version of the *CAAS*. They reported that a hierarchical four-factor model provided a moderate degree of fit to the data. The standardized loadings from the items to the corresponding adapt-abilities ranged from .62 to .80 (Median = .74), and the loadings from the first-order adapt-abilities to the second-order adaptability ranged from .75 to .90 (Median = .84). The fit indices were $\chi2/df$ = 8.179, p <.001, GFI = .869, CFI = .887, TLI = .875, and RMSEA = .078. They also tested a four-factor model that took into account modification indices greater than 20 associated with the co-variances between the error terms within each dimension was also tested. This model accounted for the shared variance between items within a dimension. It resulted in a significant improvement in model fit with results indicating a substantial degree of model fit. The correlations between error terms were all below .47. The standardized loadings for the items to the adapt-abilities ranged from .60 to .81 (Median = .74) and from the adapt-abilities to the second-order adaptability factor ranged from .75 to .92 (Median = .84). Finally, the hierarchical four-factor model that utilized item parceling was tested. Items with the highest correlation were paired creating three homogenous parcels per scale. The mean scores for the two items were then used in the analysis. This technique provided good model fit for the *CAAS* French-language form (Johnston et al., 2013) and thus they tested this strategy with the German-language form. The model proved to have similar fit to the model with modification indices. Standardized parcel weights ranged from .71 to .88 (Median = .78) and loadings from first-order to second-order constructs between .74 and .94 (Median = .85). The fit indices were $\chi2/df$ = 6.489 (p <.001), GFI =.957, CFI =.966, TLI = .956, and RMSEA = .068.

Due to translation reasons, the researchers wrote an alternative item for the Confidence subscale. They used "use the best of my competence" instead of "working up to my abilities." Changing just this one item improved the model fit to $\chi2/df$ = 6.52, GFI = .89, CFI = .91, TLI = .90, and RMSEA = .068. The standardized loadings from the items to the corresponding factor ranged from .62 to .79 (Median = .74), and the loadings from the first-order adapt-abilities to the second-order adaptability ranged from .75 to .90 (Median = .84). Although an improvement in model fit was gained by using this alternative item, there were no changes in scale reliability. Users of this scale in a German-speaking context may want to include both items to have congruence with the original *CAAS*.

Greece

In Athens, Sidiropoulou-Dimakakou, Mikedaki, Argyropoulou, and Kaliris (2018) tested the model fit with 452 university students. They took into account error co-variances solely within the factors and released the greatest ones that existed between items of the same factor. This practice does not imply interdependent factor modeling as factors still remained orthogonal. The fit indices were $\chi2/df$ = 2.62, GFI .90, CFI = .89, TLI = .42, and RMSEA = .062. Item loadings on the adapt-abilities ranged from .48 to .69, with the exception of .39 for item 7 ("Keeping upbeat"). The loadings of the four adapt-abilities on the second-order construct of adaptability ranged from .73 to .81.

Hong Kong

In Hong Kong, Yuen and Yau (2015) examined model fit with 543 Chinese junior secondary students from eight secondary schools in different districts of Hong Kong. The 298 males and 245 females ranged in age from 12 to 17 years (Mean = 14.92; SD = 0.82). The researchers computed confirmatory factor analysis to evaluate the fit of the data to the model. The four-factor model with one higher-order factor model provided a marginally acceptable fit to the data with χ^2 = 2.82, CFI = .926, TLI = .918, RMSEA = .058, and SRMR = .035. After revising the model to include two correlated residuals, the results showed adequate fit to the data with χ^2 = 1.99, TLI = .956, CFI = .961, RMSEA = .043, and SRMR .031. The standardized loadings for the items (.67 to .86) were strong indictors of the first-order adapt-abilities which in turn were strong indicators (.81 to .97) of the second-order construct of career adaptability.

In a second study in Hong Kong, Hui, Yuen, and Chen (2018a) examined model fit with 522 undergraduate students (69% females) who ranged in age from 18 to 24 years (Mean = 21.52; SD = 1.26). Most of the students (89.7%) were in their final year. The four-factor model with one higher-order factor model provided a good fit to the data with χ^2 = 2.82, CFI = .91, TLI = .90, RMSEA = .07, and SRMR = .05. The standardized loadings ranged from .61 to .83, indicated that that all items were strong indicators of the first-order adapt-ability constructs, which were in turn strong indicators (ranging from .78 to .91) of the second-order adaptability construct.

Iran – Persian Language

A Persian translation of the *CAAS* was produced by McKenna, Zacher, Ardabili, and Mohebbi (2016). Data were provided by 204 Persian-speaking workers in Iran. Confirmatory factor analyses indicated that the *CAAS-Iran Form* measures four distinct dimensions that can be combined into a higher-order career adaptability factor. The standardized loadings for the items ranged from .55 to .86 with the exception of .21 for item 6 which was .21 ("Concerned about my career"). The first-order adapt-ability factors were strong indicators (.80 to .93) of the second-order construct of career adaptability. Because item 6 had a factor loading of .21, they decided to exclude it from subsequent analyses. It may be that participants interpreted the verbatim Persian translation of the word "concerned" in a negative (e.g., worried) instead of a positive way (e.g., interested, involved). The fit indices for the four-factor hierarchical model, with all items including item 6, was acceptable ($\chi2/df$ = 2.31, CFI = .899, TLI = .887, RMSEA = .080). The fit indices did not change substantially when item 6 was excluded ($\chi2/df$ = 2.39, CFI = .902, TLI = .890, RMSEA = .083. Overall, consistent with previous international research, these results provide support for the hypothesized factor structure of the *CAAS— Iran Form*.

Working simultaneously and independently, Nilforooshan and Salimi (2016) also examined the fit of the Persian-language *CAAS* to the theoretical model but with university students. The participants were 201 university students (Mean age 23) at the University of Isfahan. Confirmatory factor analysis produced a $\chi2/df$ = 1.78 that indicated a good fit of the data to the model, while CFI = .91 and RMSEA = .062 indicated an acceptable fit to the hierarchical model. The standardized loadings for the items ranged from .41 to .80 with the exception of .33 again for item 6 ("Concerned about my career"). The first-order adapt-ability constructs were strong indicators (.79 to .93) of the second-order career adaptability construct.

Lithuania

In Lithuania, Urbanaviciute, Kairys, Pociute, and Liniauskaite (2014) tested the hierarchical model with 255 high school students. Their age ranged from 14 to 19 years (Mean = 16.43; SD = 1.18). The results showed a factor structure identical to that of the *CAAS*. The initial model had acceptable fit indices ($\chi2/df$ = 2.11, CFI = .91, TLI = .90, RMSEA = .066 and SRMR = .050). However, based on

49

modification indices, two item residual correlations were added to the model (item 8 with item 9 and item 23 with item 24, both pairs of items being similar in their meaning). The slightly modified model had a significantly better fit ($\chi2/df$ = 1.92, CFI = .93, TLI = .92, RMSEA = .060, and SRMR = .050. They tested this revised model with 512 different students. The results showed that the model fit the data well: $\chi2/df$ = 2.49 (p < .001), CFI = .91; TLI = .90; RMSEA = .054; SRMR = .047. The standardized loadings for the items ranged from .46 to .90 and were strong indictors of the first-order adapt-ability factors which in turn were strong indicators (.79 to .90) of the second-order factor of career adaptability.

In a second study conducted in Lithuania, Akkermans, Paradnike, Van der Heijden, and DeVos (2019) administered the *CAAS* to 672 students from nine Lithuanian universities. The participants were 68.3% females and ranged in age from 18 to 29 years (Mean = 20.62; SD = 1.70). The resulting fit indices were $\chi2/df$ = 0.44, CFI = 1.00, TLI = 1.00, RMSEA = 0.00, and SRMR = 0.01.

Macau

In Macau, Tien, Lin, Hsieh, and Jin (2014) examined the hierarchical model of the *CAAS* with 270 middle school and 188 high school students. They tested the factor structure separately for the two groups. For middle schools students, the hierarchical confirmatory factor analysis produced fit indices of $\chi2/df$ = 2.39, RMSEA = 0.072, and SRMR = 0.051. For high school students, the confirmatory factor analysis produced fit indices of $\chi2/df$ = 1.99, RMSEA = 0.053, and SRMR = 0.039. The standardized loadings for the items ranged from .46 to .81 and were strong indictors of the first-order adapt-ability constructs, which in turn were strong indicators (.86 to .96) of the second-order construct of career adaptability.

New Guinea

In Papua, New Guinea, de Guzman and Choi (2013) administered the *CAAS* to 191 participants from the Caritas Technical Secondary School in Port Moresby. Their ages ranged from 18 to 36 years

(Mean = 20.6, SD = 2.32). The fit indices from the confirmatory factor analysis were χ2/df = 1.23, CFI = .969, GFI = .895, NFI = .859, IFI = .959, and RMSEA = .035. The standardized loadings for the items ranged from .41 to .73 and were strong indictors of the first-order adapt-ability factors, which in turn were strong indicators (.71 to .95) of the second-order factor of career adaptability.

Nigeria

The hierarchical model was test in Nigeria by Olugbade (2016) who administered the *CAAS* to 143 bank and 128 hotel employees. The participants were 49.4% males and 50.6% females who ranged in age from 18 to 58 years (Mean = 29.19; SD = 6.67). The fit indices from the confirmatory factor analysis were RMSEA = .086 and SRMR = .053. The standardized loadings for the first-order adapt-ability factors to the second-order factor of career adaptability ranged from .62 to .79. The results from the confirmatory factor analysis showed a lower fit than expected to the theoretical model. The researcher suggested that this may have been due to the participants' characteristics and unpredictable labor market conditions.

The Philippines

The hierarchical model was test by two studies in The Philippines. Tolentino, Garcia, Lu, Restubog, Bordia, and Tang (2014) presented the *CAAS* in English because it is spoken by a vast majority of the population. They used a seven-point Likert scale opposed to the five-point Likert scale used in previous *CAAS* studies to provide participants with a wider range of response anchors from which to choose. In the first study, they recruited 289 undergraduate university students (Mean age = 18.64) from management courses at a large private university. Confirmatory factor analysis showed that the data fit the theoretical model very well. The fit indices were RMSEA = .074 and SRMR = .047. In the second study, they recruited 495 full-time employees who were enrolled in various post-graduate academic programs (e.g., business, education, engineering, and computer science) at a large university. The sample consisted of 56% females with a mean age of 31.71 years and an average tenure of 5.18 years. Confirmatory factor analysis showed that data also fit the theoretical model very well. The fit indices were RMSEA = .072 and SRMR = .044. The standardized loadings for the items ranged from .72 to .86 and were strong indictors of the first-order adapt-ability factors, which in turn were strong indicators (.84 to .95) of the second-order factor of career adaptability.

Portugal – Graduate Student Form

The hierarchical model for the *CAAS* was examined with graduate students in Portugal by Monteiro and Almeida (2015). Previously in Portugal, Duarte, Soares, Fraga, Rafael, Lima, Paredes, Agostinho, and Djaló (2012) had sampled 916 participants (255 high school students with a mean age of 15 years; 395 employed adults mean age of 47 years; and 266 unemployed adults enrolled in training activities with a mean age of 22 years). The study by Monteiro and Almeida (2015) sampled 406 graduate students. The internal consistency coefficient for the total scale was .92, with the reliability coefficients for the four subscales ranging from .78 to .86. The hierarchical structure fit the theoretical model with indices of $\chi2/df$ = 2.85, GFI = .87, CFI = .89, RMSEA = .07, and SRMR = .05. The results were similar to those reported by reported by Duarte and her colleagues (CFI = 0.97, RMSEA = 0.061, SRMR = 0.049). The standardized loadings for the items ranged from .42 to .80 and were strong indictors of the first-order adapt-ability factors, which in turn were strong indicators (.73 to .90) of the second-order factor of career adaptability.

Romania

In a test of the hierarchical model in Romania, Rusu, Măirean, Hojbotă, Gherasim, and Gavriloaiei (2015) administered the *CAAS* to 359 participants with a mean age of 20.9 years (SD = 2.13). The participants were 64% females and 36% males. Confirmatory factor analysis fit indices were RMSEA = .071 and SRMR = .063. The standardized loadings for the items ranged from .42 to .80 and were strong indictors of the first-order adapt-ability factors, which in turn were strong indicators (.73 to .90) of the second-order factor of career adaptability.

Serbia

In testing the hierarchical model in Serbia, Tolentino, Sedoglavich, Lu, Raymund, Garcia, and Restubog (2014) collected *CAAS* data from 380 business students. Confirmatory factor analysis showed that the data fit the theoretical model very well. The fit indices were RMSEA = .061 and SRMR = .041. The standardized loadings for the items ranged from .59 to .70 and were strong indictors of the first-order adapt-ability factors, which in turn were strong indicators (.83 to .86) of the second-order factor of career adaptability.

A second study of the *CAAS* hierarchical model was conducted in Serbia by Mirkovic, Suvajdzic, and Dostanic (2020). The sample consisted of 374 adult (57.5% females) employees in small and medium-sized enterprises. They ranged in age from 21 to 64 years (Mean = 39, *SD* = 11.35) years. The results indicated a moderate degree of model fit with $\chi2/df = 3.646$, GFI = .832, CFI = .848, TLI =.830, and RMSEA = .084. The standardized loadings for the items ranged from .50 to .82 except for item 6 which had a loading of .32. The standardized loadings of the first-order adapt-ability factors to the the second-order factor of adaptability ranged from .70 to .88.

Singapore

In testing the hierarchical model in Singapore, Chan, Uy, Ho, San, Chernyshenko, and Yu (2015) administered the *CAAS* to 854 university students with a mean age of 23.2 years. Confirmatory analysis showed that the measurement model provided a very good fit to the *CAAS* data. The fit indices were $\chi2/df$ = 2.86, CFI = .93, SRMR = .04, AIC = 44,578.80, and BIC = 44,935.62. The standardized loadings for the first-order adapt-ability factors ranged from .83 to .90, which were strong indicators of the second-order factor of career adaptability.

South Africa

In the initial studies by the International Research Team, the *CAAS* was shown to be applicable in South Africa based on a study with 435 participants from a North West province in Makikeng (Maree, 2012). A study by Albien, Kidd, Naidoo, and Maree (2020) tested its validity for use among low-resource adolescents in the isiXhosa-speaking townships of South Africa. Initially, they translated the *CAAS-South African Form* (Maree, 2012) into XhosaHence, but eventually rejected it due to regional differences in dialects, difficulty in finding equivalent words in the Xhosa language, and abstract terminology. Therefore, the researchers used the English version, with Xhosa explanations provided for items that posed potential difficulty for the participants. To collect the data, the *CAAS* was administered by field workers who acted as in-session translators to facilitate understanding with additional explanations. They answered any questions posed by the students in both English and isiXhosa, mirroring the medium of instruction followed in the school environments. The sample consisted of 396 Black township high school students (62% females and 33% males) who ranged in age from 15 to 24 years (Mean = 18; SD = 1.3).

Results showed mean scores of 3.61 for Concern, 3.68 for Control, 3.31 for Curiosity, and 3.53 for Confidence. The *CAAS* total score showed good internal consistency of .83, but internal consistency coefficients for the subscales were moderate: Concern = .64, Control = .65, Curiosity = .67, and Confidence = .71. The researchers suggested that the lower reliability coefficients could have resulted from linguistic barriers due to difficulty in finding equivalent terms in the Xhosa language or a lower literacy rate in English (as a second or third language) in township students. Confirmatory factor analysis indicated that the data fit the theoretical model well. The fit indices were $\chi2/df = 1.75$, GFI = .91, NFI = .90, RMSEA = .049, and SRMR = 0.051. The standardized loadings for the items (.38 to .58) were strong indictors of the first-order factors, which in turn were strong indicators (.78 to .98) of the second-order factor of career adaptability. The researchers concluded that the *CAAS-South African Form* seems to provide a measure of career adaptability for low-resource, Black South African township adolescents, although with moderate reliability. They recommended future research to explore the reliability and validity of *CAAS* scores with participants who come from adverse social conditions, particularly in comparison to normative samples.

Spain

In Spain, Merino-Tejedor, Hontangas-Beltran, and Boada-Grau (2016) administered the *CAAS* to 577 university students. They conducted a confirmatory factor analysis to evaluate the hierarchical model. The fit of the data to the model was deemed reasonable with indices of ($\chi 2$ /df = 4.17, NNFI = .84, CFI = .86, RMSEA = .074, and SRMR = .057. The model fit improved ($\chi 2$ /df = 3.08, NNFI = .90, CFI = .91, RMSEA = .060 and SRMR = .050) by including four error co-variances between item pairs (23–24, 1–2, 19–20, and 13–14), which represent systematic error rather than random measurement error derived from an overlap in item content. The standardized loadings for the items ranged from .52 to .73 and were strong indictors of the first-order adapt-abilities factors, which in turn were strong indicators (.80 to .90) of a second-order factor of career adaptability.

Two years later, Merino-Tejedor, Hontanga, and Petrides (2018) administered the *CAAS* to 590 Spanish university students. The confirmatory factor analysis indicated a fit to the hierarchical model that they deemed as adequate, with indices of $\chi 2$ /df =1.34, NNFI = .995, CFI = .998, and RMSEA = .024. The standardized loadings of the first-order constructs were .74 for Concern, .80 for Control, .74 for Curiosity, and .85 for Confidence.

Thailand

Working in Thailand, Sibunruang, Garcia, and Tolentino (2016) administered a translated form of the *CAAS* to 861 participants consisting of 551 students and 265 full-time employees from three different organizations (i.e., two from manufacturing and one from the hospitality industry). The fit indices (RMSEA = .055 and SRMR = .046) supported the structural validity of the *CAAS-Thailand*

Form. The standardized loadings for the items ranged from .61 to .80 and were strong indictors of the first-order adapt-ability factors, which in turn were strong indicators (.73 to .88) of the second-order factor of career adaptability.

Trinidad and Tobago

In the country of Trinidad and Tobago, Wilkins-Yel, Roach, Tracey, and Yel (2018) administered the *CAAS* to 327 students recruited from two universities in Trinidad and Tobago. The Trinbagonian sample consisted of 182 females and 145 males who ranged in age from 18 to 35 years (Mean = 24.32; SD = 4.39. The fit indices ($\chi2$ /df =1.62, CFI = 0.93, RMSEA = .05, and SRMR = .06) supported the structural validity of the *CAAS*. The standardized loadings for the items ranged from .54 to .74, suggesting that they were strong indicators of the first-order adapt-ability factors, which in turn were strong indicators of (.84 to .93) the second-order factor of career adaptability.

Turkey

Four articles reported hierarchical factor analyses of the *CAAS* in Turkey. Kanten (2012) administered the translated *CAAS* to 474 students at three schools of the Mehmet Akif Ersoy University. Confirmatory factor analysis showed that the measurement model had fit indices of $\chi2/df$ = 3.50, GFI .90, CFI = .93, and RMSEA .074. Kanten also reported a Normed Fit Index (NFI) of 0.90 and a Relative Fit Index (RFI) of .90. The NFI and RFI both range from 0 to 1, with 1 being a perfect fit. He also reported an Incremental Fit Index (IFI) of .93. IFI values that exceed .90 are acceptable although this index can exceed 1.0. Six items were removed from the *CAAS* due to low factor loadings, half of them from the Concern subscale. Confirmatory factor analysis of the remaining 18 items indicated that the standardized loadings for the items ranged from .47 to .81 and were strong indictors of the first-order adapt-ability factors, which in turn were strong indicators (.70 to .83) of the second-order factor of career adaptability.

In a subsequent study in Turkey, Buyukgoze-Kavas (2014) conducted a confirmatory factor analysis with data from 669 participants, 353 (144 males and 209 females) high school students with a mean age of 16.03 years and 316 university students (125 males and 191 females) with a mean age of 20.99 years. The fit indices for the 24 *CAAS* items were $\chi2/df$ = 3.36, CFI = .90; RMSEA = .060; and SRMR = .049. The first-order factors had standardized loadings ranging from .74 for Control to .93 for Confidence.

In a third study, Yucel and Polat (2015) tested 843 undergraduate students (57.8% females, mean age =21 years) at Erzincan University in Turkey. Confirmatory factor analysis showed that the data fit the theoretical model. The fit indices were RMSEA = 0.064 and SRMR = 0.057. The standardized loadings (ranging from .55 to .78) suggested that all the items were strong indicators of the first-order adapt-ability factors, which in turn were strong indicators (ranging from .79 to .94) of the second-order factor of adaptability.

In the fourth hierarchal factor analysis conducted in Turkey, Atac, Dirik, and Tetick (2018) used data obtained from 313 senior students from the Faculty of Economics and Administrative Sciences at a public university. The 179 females and 134 males ranged in age from 21 to 28 (Mean = 22.6; SD = 1.19). Based on the report from Kanten (2012), they used only 18 of the *CAAS* items. The goodness of fit statistics for the 18-item model were $\chi2/df$ = 2.49, CFI = .980, GFI = .904, TLI = .972, RMSEA = .06, and SRMR= .055.

In summary, the empirical results from 24 countries all supported a coherent hierarchical structure that fits the theoretical model and linguistic explication of career adaptability resources. The results are summarized in Table 3. Recall that a model is considered to have an acceptable fit if the $\chi2/df$ is equal to or below 3, the GFI, CFI, and TLI values are about .90 or above. Good fit is indicated by RMSEA values below .08 and by SRMR values less than .05 with values less than .08 considered acceptable (Cheung & Rensvold,

2002; Vandenberg & Lance, 2000).

Table 3. Fit Indices for Hierarchical Confirmatory Analyses of the *CAAS* Theoretical Model

Country	χ2/df	GFI	CFI	TLI	RMSEA	SRMS
Australia-Tolentino					.049	.041
Australia-McIlveen	2.35 3.50 2.07		.97 .95 .93	.96 .95 .92	.063 .080 .082	
Brazil-Audibert	6.07		.90		.069	.041
Brazil- Ambiel	1.79		.90		.058	.053
Brazil-Cammarosano	2.41	.86	.91		.049	.06
China–Guan	4.03		.92		.07	.03
China-Hou	4.34		.84		.064	.053
China-Jiang	2.96		.92	.91	.07	
China-Dong	2.08		.86		.07	
Croatia	3.70		.86		.069	
Czech Republic	14.45		.93		.069	.045
Francophone	8.66	.90	.86	.85	.067	
Germany	6.52	.89	.91	.90	.068	
Greece	2.62	.90	.89	.74	.062	
Hong Kong-Yuen	2.82		.93	.92	.058	.035
Hong Kong-Hui			.91	.90	.07	.05
Iceland			.97		.057	.062
Iran 1	2.31		.90	.89	.080	
Iran 2	1.78		.91		.061	
Lithuania-Akkermans	0.44		1.0	1.0	0.00	0.01

Lithuania-Urbanaviciute	2.11		.91	.90	.066	.050
Macau 1	2.39				.072	.051
Macau 2	1.99				.053	.039
New Guinea	1.23	.90	.97		.035	
Nigeria					.086	.053
Philippines 1					.074	.047
Philippines 2					.072	.044
Portugal Higher Ed	2.85	.87	.89		.07	.05
Romania					.071	.063
Serbia-Tolentino					.061	.041
Serbia-Mirkovic	3.65	.83	.85	.83	.084	
South Africa	1.75	.91			.049	.051
Singapore	2.86		.93		.04	
Spain-Tejedor 2016	4.17		.86		.074	.057
Spain-Tejedor 2018	1.34		.99		.024	
Thailand					.055	.046
Trinidad and Tobago	1.62		.93		.05	.06
Turkey-Kanten	3.50	.90	.93		.074	
Turkey-Buyukgoze-Kavas	3.36		.90		.060	.49
Turkey-Yucel					0.064	0.057
Turkey-Atac	2.49	.96	.99	.98	.060	.034

Factorial Invariance of the *CAAS*

Social or cultural factors might influence how respondents perceive inventory items. Therefore, it is important to show that the same underlying construct is being measured across groups or across time. The statistical property with which to demonstrate this measurement equivalence is called *factorial invariance* or *factor invariance*.

Some cultural or sample characteristics may influence *CAAS* scores. Savickas and Porfeli (2012) noted that "culture and context may place boundary conditions around adaptability" (p. 3). Given that the *CAAS* was developed in 13 countries, it was important to determine the measurement equivalence of the *CAAS*, that is, whether respondents from different countries and cultures interpreted the items in a conceptually similar manner. Savickas and Porfeli (2012) assessed the *CAAS* hierarchical factor model and its invariance across countries using mean and covariance structure (MACS) analysis. This approach extends the traditional covariance structure analysis within a confirmatory factor analysis (CFA) framework to include an analysis of the latent mean structure of the CFA model. First, they examined *configural invariance* to explore the basic structure of the construct "adapt-abilities" cross-nationally and determine if the same items load on the same factors across the different countries. These results largely confirm the configural invariance of the measurement model across all countries. Second, they examined the structural relationships among the construct. This more stringent form of measurement equivalence is called *metric invariance*, and means that the factor loadings associated with items are equivalent across countries. The results showed that the *CAAS* demonstrated metric invariance in that the scale items showed similar relations among the latent constructs across countries. Thus, the results suggest that the *CAAS* measures the same constructs in the same way across countries. It also had acceptable but varied reliability across all the countries. Third, they examined *scalar invariance*, that is, equivalence of mean scores across countries. They had not expected the *CAAS* to show scalar invariance because adapt-abilities are psychosocial variables, not purely psychological traits independent from context. The *CAAS* did not exhibit scalar invariance in that the subscale means, as expected, were not equal across countries. Fourth, they examined measurement precision in terms of *residual invariance* to determine whether the unexplained variance was equivalent across countries. It shows whether the random error variances of the observed items are equal across groups. The *CAAS* did not exhibit strict residual invariance, which requires an equality of the residuals of the indicators across countries. This test of the measurement precision is not required to conclude that the constructs are measured equivalently across groups. Finally, they conducted a rigorous, multi-step examination that ruled out potential threats to the accuracy of the results concerning measurement equivalence on the basis of disproportion representation of certain countries with more participants.

Five additional studies of measurement invariance tested groups within one country to examine possible differential item functioning in the relations between item responses and the construct to be quantified. To examine more closely the differences in scores obtained by adolescent students and adult workers, Ambiel, Carvalho, Martins, and Tofoli (2016) analyzed whether any of the 24 items in the *CAAS* had an increasing probability of endorsement by one group than another. Twelve items displayed differential functioning, five favoring adolescents and seven favoring adults. The content of the two sets of items that favored each group showed coherence. The five items that favored adolescents were on the Concern and Control subscales. Three of the items involved Concern about and preparing for the future as well as planning to achieve goals. The two Control items were "counting on myself" and "doing what's right for me." The items more easily endorsed by adults seemed to reflect that they already were in the world of work. Most of the items favoring adults were on the Curiosity and Confidence subscales, with the exception of one item from the Concern scale, namely "becoming aware of choices to be made." Adults were more curious about possible options and rated themselves better at problem solving and at performing tasks efficiently and well. Despite the differential item functioning, there was no psychometric evidence supporting the need for different forms of the *CAAS* for adolescents and adults.

In Macau, Tien, Lin, Hsieh, and Jin (2014) examined measurement equivalence between 270 middle school and 188 high school students. They had found that high school students scored significantly higher than did middle school students on the *CAAS* subscales. Thus, they used multiple-group second-order confirmatory factor analysis to evaluate the measurement invariance for middle and senior high school models. The factor loadings were constrained to be equal across groups and then estimated simultaneously. The fit indices were $\chi 2/df = 2.16$, $p < .05$, RMSEA = 0.071, and SRMR = 0.067. After releasing the equality restrictions on the factor loadings of the two groups, the fit indices were $\chi 2/df = 2.19$, $p < .05$, RMSEA = 0.072 and SRMR = 0.055. They used a Chi-square difference test for nested models to evaluate the measurement equivalence of the two models. The Chi-square difference test, ($\Delta\chi 2$ [24] = 33.22, $p > .05$) provided supporting evidence for second-order metric invariance for the different groups of students. The non-significant difference between the two models means that they fit the theoretical model equally well statistically. Thus, the data supported metric invariance for the different groups of students.

The third study was conducted in Lithuania. Urbanaviciute, Kairys, Pociute, and Liniauskaite (2014) followed a multiple-indicator multiple-cause model (MIMIC) to test for measurement invariance and differential item function of the *CAAS* with regard to age, gender, and place of residence. The participants were 512 high students. The analyses showed that most of the items were invariant with regard to respondent demographic characteristics. The only exception was obtained after testing the link between *CAAS* items and gender: item 10 ("Tvirtai laikytis savo įsitikinimų" / "Sticking up for my beliefs") seemed to be scored higher by girls, the rest of the items were invariant across gender groups. Age and place of residence had no effect upon the variance of the *CAAS—Lithuanian Form* factor indicators. Therefore, the items in the Lithuanian version of the *CAAS* can be considered to be valid in terms of sociodemographic variables

The fourth study examined differential item functioning in one language across four countries with similar cultures. Johnston, Broonen, Stauffer, Hamtiaux, Pouyaud, Zecca, Houssemand, and Rossier (2013) administered the CAAS to 1707 participants in France and the French-speaking regions of Belgium, Luxemberg, and Switzerland. The results of a multi-group confirmatory factor analysis indicated that the *CAAS* reached scalar equivalence and was supported by following overall model-fit statistics, $\chi 2/df$ = 3.08, CFI = .91, TLI = .91, and RMSEA = .035. They proposed that meaningful comparisons in mean scores could be made between individuals in France and French-speaking parts of Switzerland, Belgium, and Luxembourg.

In the fifth study, McIlveen, Perera, Hoare, and McLennan (2018) examined the latent structure of the *CAAS* using a factor model and estimation routine appropriate for ordinal categorical data, which are tests of full measurement invariance suitable for polytomous data. They conducted three studies, the first two with participants from an under-studied population to determine the applicability of the *CAAS* to the broader workforce. They examined the replicability of the *CAAS* factor structure among retail workers and mothers returning to work, respectively. They examined tests of invariance by comparing latent mean differences between the groups. For the first study, the participants were 394 retail workers (72.1% females) with a mean age of 25.87 years (SD = 9.51). A range of retail categories were represented, including for example stores that sold groceries, clothing, furniture, pharmaceuticals, antiques, and motor vehicles. The test of the hierarchical model resulted in an acceptable fit to the data, with χ^2 = 3.50 (p. < .001), CFI = .951, TLI = .945, and RMSEA = .080. The loadings from the four *CAAS* factors to the higher-order adaptability factor ranged from .74 to .90. The participants for the second study were 160 women who, having worked as mothers to raise their children, were aiming to enter or reenter the workforce. The age categories were 18–24 (5%), 25–34 (40.6%), 35–44 (38.1%), 45–54 (12.5%) and 55 and over (3.1%). The hierarchical, multi-dimensional model provided a largely acceptable fit to the data, with $\chi^2 = 2.07$ (p < .001), CFI = .931, TLI = .923, and RMSEA = .082. The loadings from the four *CAAS* factors to the higher-order adaptability factor ranged from .69 to .79. The third study involved as participants 344 teacher education students at a university. The confirmatory factor analysis of the hierarchical model indicated an acceptable to excellent fit to the data with fit indices of $\chi^2 = 2.35$ (p < .001), CFI = .966, TLI = .962, and RMSEA = .063. The loadings for the four *CAAS* factors to the higher-order adaptability factor ranged from .77 to .85.

To compare results for the three groups, McIlveen, Perera, Hoare, and McLennan (2018) examined the invariance of the *CAAS* responses across groups of retail workers, mothers returning to work, and pre-service teachers. The first-order configural invariance model provided an acceptable fit to the data. Next they examined the invariance of the second-order structure, with the first-order strictly invariant model serving as the baseline model from which the second-order configurally invariant model was specified. The second-order configurally invariant model provided an acceptable-to-good fit to the data. Taken together, these results (a) demonstrated the full measurement invariance of *CAAS* scores, (b) supported the multi-dimensional, hierarchical latent structure underlying responses to the *CAAS* in three different occupational groups, and (c) showed meaningful latent mean differences in adaptability with the retail workers and mothers reporting lower career adaptability than the pre-service teachers.

Convergent Validity of the *CAAS*

Convergent validity refers to the degree to which two measures of theoretically-related constructs are in fact related. In the most comprehensive study of convergent validity, Oncel (2014) administered a set of measures to 332 graduating university students to examine the convergent validity of the four *CAAS* subscale scores to theoretically-related variables from the adaptivity domain of personality traits. Related to Concern, he administered the Future Time Perspective Scale of the *Stanford Time Perspective Inventory—Short Form* (D'Alessio, Guarino,

Pascalis, & Zimbardo, 2003). An example item reads, "I believe that a person's day should be planned ahead each morning." Related to Control, he administered the eight-item Internality Subscale from the *Levenson IPC Scale* (Levenson, 1981). An example item reads, "Whether or not I get to be a leader depends mostly on my ability." Also related to Control, he administered the seven-item Neuroticism Subscale from the *Adjective Based Personality Scale* (Bacanli, Ilhan, & Aslan, 2009). Related to Curiosity, he administered the *Proactive Personality Scale* (Bateman & Crant, 1993). An example item reads, "I excel at identifying opportunities." Related to Confidence, he administered the *Core Self-Evaluation Scale* (Judge, Erez, Bono, & Thoresen, 2003). An example item reads, "I am confident I get the success I deserve in life." Also related to Confidence, he administered the *Rosenberg Self-Esteem Scale* (Rosenberg, 1965). An example item reads, "On the whole, I am satisfied with myself." And for a third scale related to Confidence, he administered the *Generalized Self-Efficacy Scale* (Schwarzer & Jerusalem, 1995). An example item reads, "Thanks to my resourcefulness, I can handle unforeseen situations."

The pattern of results support weakly the convergent validity of the *CAAS* subscales. The pattern of which constructs had the highest inter-correlation was clearly established. However, the difference between the highest and next highest construct inter-correlations were usually not significant, as can be seen in Table 2 which highlights the cells with the highest construct inter-correlations. As predicted, Concern related highest to future time perspective (.47); Control related highest to core self-evaluations (.43), self-esteem (.42), and Neuroticism (-.23); Curiosity related highest to proactivity (.46) and generalized self-efficacy (.48); and Confidence related highest to generalized self-efficacy (.53). Generalized self-efficacy had the highest correlation (.59) to the *CAAS* total score. Self-efficacy correlated consistently to all four adapt-abilities.

Table 4: Convergent Validity of *CAAS* Subscales

	Future Orient	Self-Eval	Self-Esteem	Internal Control	Neurotic	Proact-ivity	Self-Efficacy
Concern	**.47**	.37	.41	.23	-.18	.39	.42
Control	.22	**.43**	**.42**	**.25**	**-.23**	.35	.48
Curiosity	.38	.33	.29	.21	-.16	**.46**	.48
Confidence	.33	.39	.31	.21	-.19	.36	**.53**

CAAS and CMI-Form C

Two studies examined the convergent validity of the *CAAS* relative to the *Career Maturity Inventory-Form C* (*CMI-Form C*; Savickas & Porfeli, 2011). The *CMI-Form C* measures career choice readiness. Savickas and Porfeli (2011) revised the *Career Maturity Inventory-Form B-1* (Crites, 1965) by applying CCT to its 75 items. They combined (a) rational organization of the item content about forming occupational choices with (b) factor analysis to group items that reflected the adapt-abilities of Concern, Curiosity, and Confidence. Initial evidence supported the construct and concurrent validity of the *CMI-Form C* scores as indicators of readiness to engage in the process of career decision making. The *CMI-C* is presented in Appendix D.

To examine convergence between the *CAAS* and the *CMI-Form C*, Chan, Uy, Ho, San, Chernyshenko, and Yu (2015) administered both inventories at a university in Singapore to 854 students with a mean age of 23.2 years. The results showed that the two career scales were best modeled in terms of a second-order general factor that correlated .43, indicating that the scales measure two different yet related constructs. The standardized factor loading for the two scales appear in Figure 4. The results also showed that all three *CMI-Form C* subscales (Concern, Curiosity and Confidence) correlated most strongly with the Concern subscale of the *CAAS*

(r =.41, .37, and .30 respectively) rather than with the corresponding *CAAS* subscale. The researchers concluded that the *CMI-Form C* primarily measures career concern or planfulness, which is the first and most fundamental factor in adolescent career maturity and adult career adaptability. The *CMI-Form C* measures career choice readiness, not career adaptability. It may be regarded as assessing the development of adolescents' attitudes toward the career decision-making process, with higher scores indicating more mature attitudes.

Figure 4. *CAAS* and *CMI-Form C* Hierarchical Factor Loadings

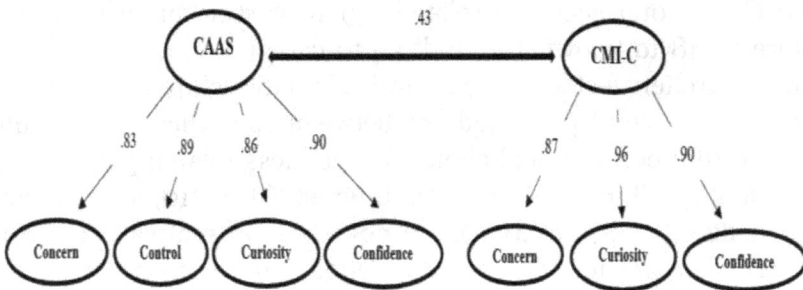

The second study examined differences between career adaptability and career maturity. Ahari, Azman, and Rasul (2019) compared the relative importance of career adaptability, career maturity, occupational knowledge, and occupational interests in contributing to degree of decidedness about occupational choice. The participants were 619 (70.9% males) full-time students at 48 Technical and Vocational Education & Training (TVET) institutions. The participants were enrolled in Malaysian Skills Certificate System programs that prepared them for technician and higher-level skill jobs. Career adaptability was measured by the *CAAS*. Career maturity, or career choice attitudes, was measured by the *Career Maturity Inventory-Form C* (Savickas & Porfeli, 2011). Career interest, knowledge, and choice were measured by subscales adapted from the *Level of Acceptance on Skills Training* (Department of Skills Development, 2012). Level of interest in skills-sector careers was measured by four items from the "Interest in TVET Stream" subscale. An example item reads "I enjoy the skills training that I am currently undergoing." Level of occupational knowledge was measured by the "Knowledge in TVET" subscale, which measures the information obtained by students in relation to the career issues in the skills sector. An example item reads, "I know the working environment in the occupation I am considering." Occupational choice was measured by four items from the "Intention to Choose" subscale, which assesses the degree to which students have decided to pursue a career in the skills sector. An example item reads, "Skills sector would be my priority when choosing a career."

The *CAAS* total score correlated .49 to career maturity, .47 to interest, .48 to knowledge, and .56 to career choice decidedness. The researchers tested the hypothesized relationships by examining the significance of path loadings between constructs. The results showed that occupational choice decidedness related positively to adaptability (β = .42, p<.001), interest (β = .10, p<.01), and knowledge (β = .13, p<.003), but not to career maturity (β = .06, p<.21). The R^2 for occupational choice decidedness was .36, indicating that together the key variables explained 36% of the variance in occupational choice decidedness.

The researchers then used importance-performance matrix analysis (IPMA: Slack, 1994) to compare the importance and performance of interest, knowledge, maturity and adaptability relative to the degree of occupational decidedness. Using IPMA, the researchers compared the salience of the attributes to the students' performance of the attributes. They then ordered the importance and performance scores to classify them into high/low categories. The results indicated that although maturity ranked high in performance (77), it ranked lowest in importance (.06). Interest (78/.11)) and knowledge (76/.14) also ranked high in performance but less important than career adaptability. Although career adaptability was the most important (.56) construct in predicting occupational choice decidedness, it ranked lowest in performance (71). This pattern means that career adaptability performance needs to be enhanced for students who have a strong degree of occupational decidedness so that they can better manage the transition from training to work. The results suggest that, in terms of intervention, focusing on maturity, interest, and knowledge would not be particularly beneficial because these variables have already played their part in the decision-making process and in determining occupational decidedness. When using the IPMA results to infer interventions, practitioners who work with decided students might concentrate on enhancing career adaptability especially in regard to the school-to-work transition, whereas interventions focused on maturity, interests, and knowledge might be considered less relevant after students have make their choice.

Work Adaptability

A fourth study of convergent validity, compared career adaptability to "work adaptability." Ployhart and Bliese (2006) defined work adaptability as "an individual's ability, skill, disposition, willingness, and/or motivation, to change or fit different task, social, and environmental features" (p. 13). They asserted that certain knowledge, skills, abilities, and other characteristics predispose workers to adapt successfully when tasks change. To understand adapting responses and performance results in this way, they conceptualized work adaptability as a compound trait characterized by eight underlying dimensions: (a) handling emergencies, (b) dealing with stressful work demands, (c) solving problems creatively, (d) learning new work duties, (e) flexibility and understanding in interpersonal relationships, (f) accepting and dealing with people with different cultural backgrounds, (g) dealing with physical or environmental conditions, and (h) coping with uncertain conditions and unpredictable situations. These dimensions of work adaptability are measured by a 55-item inventory called *I-ADAPT*. As its name suggests, work adaptability focuses on a different construct than does career adaptability.

From the perspective of CCT, work adaptability consists of adapting responses that predict effective job performance. Accordingly, career adaptability resources should predict work adaptability, meaning job performance. Hamtiaux, Houssemand, and Vrignaud

(2013) administered the *CAAS* and *I-ADAPT* to 393 students and adults who ranged in age from 16 to 75 years, with mean age of 30. The total composite score for work adaptability correlated .60 to the *CAAS* total score, and .39 to Concern, .52 to Control, .55 to Curiosity, and .61 to Confidence. The *CAAS* total score correlated to the *I-ADAPT* dimensions as follows: uncertainty (.55), learning (.50), creativity (.48), interpersonal (.47), culture (.41), crisis (.40), work stress (.33), and physical (.24). The stronger correlations for being able to deal with uncertain situations (example item reads, "I can adjust my plans to changing conditions") and willingness to learn new things (example item reads, "I am continually learning new skills for my job") support the convergent validity of the *CAAS*, as do the weaker correlations to work stress (example item reads, "I am easily rattled when my schedule is too full") and physical conditions (example item reads, "I use my muscular strength well").

Discriminant Validity of the *CAAS*

Linguistic explications and operational definitions of career adaptability must do more than show convergent validity for what the *CAAS* measures. They need to include discriminant validity concerning what the *CAAS* does not measure. Discriminant validity means that concepts or measurements that should theoretically be unrelated to *CAAS* scores are actually unrelated. This lack of relationship is demonstrated by low or non-significant correlations between theoretically-dissimilar measures. The following sections present evidence for the *CAAS* discriminant validity by reporting that career adaptability correlates to neither age, intelligence, nor interests.

Career Adaptability and Age

Four studies have shown that adults may possess stronger career adaptability than adolescents, probably because they have had more life experiences that have developed their adapt-abilities. Duarte and her colleagues (2012) reported that adults (Mean = 96.30) in Portugal scored a little higher than adolescents (Mean =

91.98), due in large part to higher scores on the Confidence and Control dimensions.

Adults showed higher scores than adolescents on all four adapt-abilities in a combined sample from France and French-speaking regions of Switzerland, Belgium, and Luxembourg (Johnston, Broonen, Stauffer, Hamtiaux, Pouyaud, Zecca, Houssemand, & Rossier, 2013). The 1707 participants (57% females, 40% males) had a mean age of 24.22 years (SD = 12.33). Age correlated significantly and positively to Concern (.06), Control (.14), Curiosity (.22), Confidence (.15), and career adaptability (.18).

In a study by Rossier, Zecca, Stauffer, Maggiori, and Dauwalder (2012), age did not relate to the *CAAS* total score yet it did relate to Concern (−.13) and Control (.14) in an adult sample of 220 women and 171 men (83% were employed) who ranged in age from 20 to 79 years (Mean = 39.65; SD 12.30). The small effect sizes suggested that adults may be slightly more focused on controlling their situations rather than planning to make future choices.

In another study, adults scored higher and had lower standard deviations than adolescents on all four *CAAS* subscales. Ambien, Carvalho, Martins, and Tofoli (2016) compared the adapt-abilities of 272 adolescent students to 404 adult workers in Brazil. For the *CAAS* total score, adolescents' mean score was 90.55 compared to adults' mean score of 97.56. To further compare the two age groups on the *CAAS*, Ambien and colleagues analyzed differential item functioning to determine if any *CAAS* items showed an increased probability of endorsement by either group. Although all the items in each of the four *CAAS* subscales assessed a unidimensional construct (e.g., Concern), it is still possible for one or more items in a subscale to have something in its content that elicits more easily an endorsement from one group than another group. Five items favored endorsement by adolescents. The items appeared on the Concern and Control subscales, including the item with the biggest difference between groups ("doing what's right for me"). The items more easily endorsed by adolescents related to future concerns. The seven items endorsed more easily by adults

71

seemed related to already being in the world of work. More specifically, three of the items were in the Confidence subscale (performing tasks efficiently, taking care to do things well, and solving problems) and two were in the Curiosity subscale (curious about new opportunities and probing into questions), with one each in the Concern subscale (becoming aware of choices) and the Control subscale (taking responsibility for my actions). Ambiel and colleagues noted that although 12 of the 24 *CAAS* items functioned differently, the effect sizes were small. They concluded that a single form of the *CAAS* works well for both adolescents and adults.

Retiree's adapt-abilities. In a study of older adults, Luke, McIveen, & Perera (2016) examined the relevance of career adaptability to retirees' experiences of re-engagement in employment. The qualitative study involved intensive interviews with 22 retirees between the ages of 56 and 78 years (Mean = 68.24) about their reasons for returning to employment. Thematic analyses of the interview transcripts extracted evidence of the four career adaptability resources. The participants expressed Concern with respect to their future; Control with respect to keeping active and engaged; Curiosity with respect to learning new skills and knowledge; and Confidence in knowing that they could make a positive contribution. This research showed that older adults may remain concerned and curious about work, in control of opportunities and resources, and confident that they may thrive and make an authentic contribution. Thus, the study provided evidence that career adaptability is not only a psychosocial resource for emerging adults and mid-career adults in the workplace. The results indicated that career adaptability may be a life-long self-regulation resource for all people interested in working.

In a study of late career planning, Fasbender, Wohrmann, Wang, and Klehe (2018) examined the post-retirement work plans of 586 people in the United Kingdom. The participants ranged in age from 50 to 79 years (Mean = 57.13; SD = 5.22). Of the participants, 360 (45.0%) were female and 304 (38.0%) held a university degree. Most participants were employed full-time (77.4%), and they worked on average 34.3 hours per week (SD = 6.6) in different industries ranging across consumer goods, technology, media, and tele-communications. Then Fasbender and colleagues measured the participants' perceptions of the time and opportunities they had remaining in their careers -- which they called "occupational future time perspective" -- with six items developed by Zacher and Frese (2009). Three items measured remaining opportunities: "Many opportunities await me in my occupational future," "I expect that I will set many new goals in my occupational future," and "My occupational future is filled with possibilities." Three items measured remaining time: "Most of my occupational life lies ahead of me," "My occupational future seems infinite to me," and "As I get older, I begin to experience time in my occupational future as limited" (reverse coded). The researchers measured post-retirement work planning with the four-item scale developed by Wohrmann, Deller, and Wang (2013). The items are "I have spoken to relevant person(s) about post-retirement work," "I have visited web sites on post-retirement work," "I have discussed my post-retirement work plans with colleagues or my supervisor," and I have discussed my post-retirement work plans with working retirees." The inventories were administered in a time-lagged design. At Time 1, the participants responded to the *CAAS*, the occupational future time perspective scale, and the career planning scale. Three months later, at Time 2, the participants responded again to the time perspective and planning measures.

The *CAAS* total score correlated to the occupational future time perspective measure .50 at Time 1 and .45 at Time 2. The stronger correlations of time perspective to the four adapt-abilities at T1 and T2 were to Concern (.58 and .52) and Curiosity (.47 and .43). The *CAAS* correlated to post-retirement work planning .20 at Time 1 and .21 at Time 2. The stronger correlations of planning activities to the four adapt-abilities were to Concern (.29 and .29) and Curiosity (.20 and .20). The structural equation model shown in Figure 5 indicated full mediation of occupational future time perspective at Time 1 between career adaptability at Time 1 and Post-retirement work planning at Time 2. Also, the indirect effect of career adaptability on late career planning at T2 via time perspective at T1 was positive and significant (.06). The cross-lagged effects between time perspective and planning supported the direction of the hypothesized relationship in that perspective at T1 affected planning at T2 but planning at T1 did not affect perspective at T2.

Figure 5. Time Perspective Mediates Relation of
Adaptability to Retirement Planning

The researchers concluded older workers' career adaptability predicted their post-retirement work planning. Yet, this relationship was indirect, as it was mediated by older workers' occupational time perspective, that is, positive beliefs about the time and opportunities left in their working lives made them more likely to engage in planning activities.

Overall, one might conclude that the career adaptability increases with age through childhood and adolescence yet does not keep developing during adulthood. Rather in adulthood, the resources may be activated and strengthened during periods of occupational transitions. Furthermore, adults score slightly higher on the *CAAS* and adolescents show larger standard deviations.

Career Adaptability and Intelligence

In explaining a concept, definitions need to include what it is not. Given the problems with the *Career Maturity Inventory's* correlation with intelligence (Savickas, 1984), it is important to show that the *CAAS* is not measuring intelligence. van Vianen, Klehe, Koen, and Dries (2012) examined the discriminant validity of the *CAAS* by investigating its relationship to general mental ability. The participants in the study were 465 university students in The Netherlands with a mean age of 21 years. van Vianen and her colleagues measured general mental ability with the *Raven Progressive Matrices* (Raven, Raven, & Court, 2000), which is a non-verbal test consisting of 60 mazes designed to measure the ability to form comparisons, reason by analogy, and organize spatial information into related wholes. Research has established the *Matrices* as one of the purest measures of general intelligence. van Vianen, Klehe, Koen, and Dries (2012) reported that the *CAAS* total score correlated .08 (non-significant) to general mental ability. The correlations between general mental ability and the four adaptability constructs were Concern = .02, Control = .09, Curiosity =.05, and Confidence = .09. These results support the discriminant validity of *CAAS* in differentiating it from a measure of general intelligence.

A study of 400 university students in Switzerland by Udayar, Fiori, Thalmayer, and Rossier (2018) found that the *CAAS* total score correlated .01 (non-significant) to fluid intelligence as measured by the *Raven Progressive Matrices*.

Although they did not correlate career adaptability to intelligence, Santilli, Nota, Ginvera, and Soresi (2014) studied the *CAAS* with a group of 120 adults who had received a primary diagnosis of mild intellectual disability measured by the *Raven Progressive Matrices*. The 60 men and 60 women (Mean age = 30.4 years; SD = 8.32) had each been working for at least six months in competitive settings as salespersons, gardeners, warehouse clerks, assistant librarians, office clerks, or door attendants. The *Adult Trait Hope Scale* (Snyder et al., 1991) was used to measure hope for the future. Career adaptability correlated .59 to hope. This study suggests that the *CAAS* works well with individuals functioning with mild intellectual disability.

Career Adaptability and Vocational Interests

To investigate the relation of career adaptability to vocational interests, Sverko and Babarovic (2016) collected data from 568 students in the final year of high school. To include variability of vocational interests and educational aspirations, they conduced the study at three different types of high schools in Croatia: general gymnasia (one third), technical schools (one third), and high schools for applied arts, medical studies, and economics and trades. They measured vocational interests with the *Personal Globe Inventory-Short* (*PGI*; Tracey, 2010). The *PGI* items present 40 different vocational activities to which respondents indicate both liking and competence on a 7-point Likert scale. These 80 items are organized into the ten vocational interest scales of Social Facilitating, Managing, Business Detail, Data Processing, Mechanical, Nature/Outdoors, Artistic, Helping, High Prestige and Low Prestige. The two Prestige scales represent the equatorial plane and along with the two poles of *People-Things* and *Data-Ideas* of Tracey's (2002), they form a sphere or globe.

The *CAAS* showed weak bivariate correlations to the 10 interest factors. Overall, the *PGI* interest scales did not relate to adaptability. The only correlations above .2 were Concern to high prestige (.20); Curiosity to high prestige (.26); Confidence to Management (.23), Business Detail (.23), Mechanical (.20), and high prestige (.22). Placing the four adaptability scores in the circumplex formed by the two vectors of People-Things and Data-Ideas showed that three of four career adaptability measures fit with R^2 values greater than .64. All three of these career adaptability facets (i.e., Concern, Control, and Confidence) were oriented toward the Data pole of circumplex and toward interest in Business Details and Managing. Sverko and Babarovic (2016) explained this association by reasoning that Business Detail activities include careful, organized, and conscientious behavior, while Managing activities require confidence, control, and assertiveness. Curiosity was oriented between the *Ideas* and *Things* pole, but due to the strength of its association with *People-Things* and *Data-Ideas* dimensions it did not fit well into two-dimensional interest space. Furthermore, the positions of vectors in circumplex space indicated that *Things* pole of interests did not associate directly with career adaptability.

The dimension of *Prestige* systematically related to the *CAAS* total score (.28), and to its subscales of Curiosity (.26), Confidence (.22), Concern (.20), and Control (.18). People who showed greater interest in highly prestigious activities tended to be at the same time more curious about possible future career options, more confident in pursuing career tasks, more concerned with their careers, and more willing to take control of preparing for their vocational future. This is not surprising as pursuing highly prestigious careers necessarily requires strong commitment to career construction, and therefore greater career adaptability. Although the four career adaptability facets showed importance for explaining highly prestigious interests (R^2 = .28), their contributions were negligible when they were included with personality traits in hierarchical regression analysis (ΔR^2 = .01).

The dimensions of *People-Things* and of *Ideas-Data* showed no substantial relations to career adaptability. A principal component analysis of the ten *PGI* interest scales produced a four-dimensional solution the explained 77.1% of variances. With no rotation, the first component resembled the general factor of interests, while the three subsequent components mainly reflected Tracey's (2002, 2010) suggested dimensions of *People-Things, Ideas-Data* and *Prestige.*

The *CAAS* total score correlated to profile elevation (.20). Confidence correlated .21 to profile elevation while Curiosity correlated .20 to profile elevation. Concern and Control showed even lower relations. The pattern of correlations was similar for the general factor of interests. The general factor of interests correlated .22 to *CAAS* total score, .23 to Confidence, and .19 to Curiosity. The finding that career adaptability correlated weakly to the general factor was consistent with the findings reported by Soresi, Nota, and Ferrari (2012). The contribution of career adaptability facets for explaining the general factor variability (R^2 = .06) dropped down when career adaptability was included in the hierarchical regression analysis in addition to personality ($\Delta R2$ = .03), but was still significant at the .01 level). This finding is in line with previous suggestions that the general factor of interests reflect to some degree the traits of curiosity, flexibility, and enthusiasm.

In a study of the prestige dimension of occupational interests, Urbanaviciute, Kairys, Pociute, and Liniauskaite (2014) administered the *Career Aspiration Scale* (Gray & O'Brien, 2007) to 255 high school students (Mean age = 16.43; SD= 1.18) in various regions of Lithuania. The ten-item scale assesses aspirations for leadership roles (e.g., "I hope to move up to a leadership position in my organization or business"), achievement (e.g., "Being outstanding at what I do at work is very important to me"), and continued education in their occupational field (e.g., "I will pursue additional training in my occupational area of interest"). The results showed that aspirations for prestigious careers correlated .39 to the *CAAS* total score, with correlations of .36 to Concern, .33 to Control, .30 to Curiosity, and .34 to Confidence.

While vocational interests themselves do not correlate to career adaptability, breadth of vocational interests has been shown to have a small relation to career adaptability. Soresi, Nota, and Ferrari (2012) investigated the relation of career adaptability to breadth of vocational interests in 762 adolescents with a mean age of 17.38 years. They measured vocational interests with the *Inventory of Children's Activities-Revised* (Tracey & Ward, 1998) which consists of five items for each of the six RIASEC themes. Breadth of interests was calculated by giving one point for each scale score that was one standard deviation above the mean and then summing the six scores, resulting in scores ranging from 0 to 6. Breadth of vocational interests correlated .25 to the total *CAAS* score, with highest subscale correlation being .25 to Curiosity.

A second study of breadth interest used the *Work Activities Questionnaire* (Nota & Soresi, 2013), which measures 11 types of work activities. The researchers calculated breadth of interests by giving one point for each subscale score that was one standard deviation above the mean and the summing the 11 scores of 0 or 1. The participants were 762 Italian adolescents (383 males and 379 females) who ranged in age from 15 to 20 years (Mean = 17.28; SD = 1.07). Results indicates that breath of interest correlated .25 to Concern, .13 to Control, .21 to Curiosity, and .16 to Confidence.

78

Conclusion

This Chapter addressed the construct validity of the *CAAS* by reporting, in turn, evidence from 37 confirmatory factor-analytic studies in 24 countries, six studies of factorial invariance, and a set of studies showing convergent and discriminant validity. The next Chapter concentrates on studies of the test-retest reliability and profile analysis of the *CAAS*.

CHAPTER 4

CAAS RELIABILITY AND PROFILE ANALYSIS

This Chapter deals with *CAAS* scores, specifically in terms of reliability and profile analysis. *Test-retest reliability* indicates the degree to which scale scores obtained from the same group of individuals remain stable over time. The time between the first and second administrations of the test are short, usually about two weeks, to mitigate against conclusions being due to age-related and experiential changes in performance, as opposed to poor test stability. *Score profile analysis* refers to examination of scale score patterns to identify if two or more groups of test takers produce significantly distinct score profiles.

Test-Retest Reliability

Five studies have examined the temporal stability of the *CAAS*. Di Maggio, Ginevra, Nota, Ferrari, and Soresi (2015) examined test-retest reliability with 239 male and 209 female middle-school students in Italy. The *CAAS* total score had a temporal stability coefficient of .93 over a three-month period. The correlation coefficients over this interval were .79 for Concern, .69 for Control, .81 for Curiosity, and .86 for Confidence. The researchers also used multiple-group second-order confirmatory factor analysis to test the measurement invariance of the *CAAS* across gender. The results supported measurement invariance for gender, with boys and girls perceiving the adaptability resources similarly.

A second study of test-retest reliability was conducted in Serbia by Tolentino, Sedoglavich, Lu, Raymund, Garcia, and Restubog (2014). They calculated test–retest reliabilities over a four-month interval for 180 students. Test–retest reliability for the overall *CAAS* was .85. Test–retest reliabilities for the subscales were .76 for Concern, .78 for Control, .75 for Curiosity, and .69 for Confidence.

A third study of test-retest reliability was conducted by Tolentino, Garcia, Lu, Restubog, Bordia, and Plewa (2014) among 555 students at two universities in Australia. Over a four-week interval, the test-retest correlation was .76 for the *CAAS* total score. Test–retest reliabilities for the subscales were .73 for Concern, .61 for Control, .66 for Curiosity, and .70 for Confidence. Coefficient alpha for internal consistency was .93 at Time 1 and .94 at Time 2.

A fourth study of test-retest reliability (Zacher, 2014a) involved a two-wave survey study with 659 full-time employees in Australia, including 322 men (49%) and 337 women (51%). The average age of participants was 48.17 years (SD = 10.87) and ranged from 20 to 69 years. In terms of education level, one participant had not finished high school (0.2%), 192 (29.1%) completed high school, 179 (27.2%) held a technical college degree, 186 (28.2%) held an undergraduate university degree, and 101 (15.3%) held a post-graduate university degree. Participants worked in a broad range of jobs, occupations, industries, and organizations across Australia. The test-retest correlations over six months were .66 for the *CAAS* total score, .66 for Concern, .56 for Control, .60 for Curiosity, and .63 for Confidence.

A fifth study of test-rest reliability tested 40 university students in Greece twice over a five-week interval (Sidiropoulou-Dimakakou1, Mikedaki, Argyropoulou, & Kaliris, 2018). The test-retest correlation was. 87 for the *CAAS* total score, with test–retest correlations of .82 for Concern, .77 for Control, .69 for Curiosity, and .64 for Confidence.

Profile Analysis

A study by Hirschi and Valero (2015) used latent profile analysis of the *CAAS* subscales to determine if they could identify sub-populations of individuals with distinct career adaptability profiles. Prior research had established that the adapt-abilities of Concern, Control, Curiosity, and Confidence are not inter-changeable representations of career adaptability and on average relate differently to diverse predictors and outcomes. In addition, several studies indicated that when variability occurred among the four subscales, Concern and Curiosity varied together as did Control and

Confidence. However, these variable-centered studies did not examine the possibility that several sub-populations within a research sample may show different combinations of the four adapt-abilities. Thus, Hirschi and Valero (2015) applied a person-centered approach to determine if they could identify groups of individuals with distinct profile shapes.

They administered the *CAAS* to 1773 students in the second and third year at a German university. In a latent profile analysis that used the four adapt-ability scores as indicators, they settled on a solution that showed five different profiles. The first profile (5% of the cases) had considerably below-average scores on all four subscales. The second profile (19%) had below-average scores for all four subscales. The third profile (52%) had scores near the mean for all four subscales. The fourth profile (3%) had mean scores for Concern and Confidence but low scores for Control and Curiosity. The fifth profile (21%) had the highest scores for all four subscales. Overall, four of the five profiles differed quantitatively, representing low to high scores on all four subscales. The fourth profile was the only one that differed qualitatively from the others. Hirschi and Valero (2015) concluded that the existence of quantitatively different adaptability profiles but did not find clear support for qualitatively different profiles.

They then conducted a second study to replicate the profiles in the first study using a different sample of 1226 German university students from the same population. Again, they chose a five-profile solution from latent analysis. The first profile (2%) had the lowest scores for all four subscales. The second profile (10%) also had low subscale scores -- although somewhat higher than the first profile. The third profile (29%) had scores slightly below the mean score for all four subscales. The fourth and most common profile (45%) had scores slightly above the mean for all four subscales. The fifth profile (15%) had the highest scores for all four subscales. Thus, all five latent profiles were quantitatively different, indicating different degrees of relatively homogeneously low to high adaptability subscale scores. No profile differed qualitatively from the others. In both studies, the researchers confirmed the external validity of the profiles by showing that the five latent profiles varied in their relation to the adapting behaviors of career exploring, decision making, and planning. The students with profiles characterized by generally higher levels of the four adaptability measures also showed higher levels of adapting behaviors.

Based on their two studies, Hirschi and Valero (2015) concluded that level effects clearly dominate shape effects in latent profiles. They explained that strong level effects are conceptually meaningful because Concern, Control, Curiosity, and Confidence are theoretically and empirically related components of the higher-order construct of career adaptability. Furthermore, they suggested that the general career adaptability level is a latent factor underlying the four adapt-abilities and may be used an alternative to the total career adaptability score. Thus, the *CAAS* total score represents overall career adaptability as an aggregate construct whereas the latent factor score represents a general adaptability level. They suggested further studies to explore the meaning of these two alternative approaches to conceptualizing the higher-order construct of career adaptability.

The results of the Hirschi and Valero (2015) studies provided strong support for the hierarchical-factor model and the variable-based approach to studying career adaptability. At the population level, different groups cluster in terms of their overall level of adaptability. These latent profile analyses results may be attributed to the inter-correlations among the four adapt-abilities. The correlations suggest rank-order stability across the four subscales. In other words, if a person scores high on one adapt-ability, then chances are that she or he will score high on the other three adapt-abilities. However, the inter-correlations are not exceptionally high so there remains the possibility for a variety of different profile shapes for people who exhibit the same level of adaptability yet achieve this level with various amounts of the four adapt-abilities. This may be particularly relevant for profiles pairing similar scores for Control and Confidence versus similar scores for Concern and Curiosity. In the majority of the profile groups reported by Hirschi and Valero (cf., top-two bar charts in their Figure 1), Control and

Confidence are more extreme (either higher in high groups or lower in low groups) than are Concern and Curiosity. The latent profile analysis probably produces results suggesting the variables that are the stronger separator of the groups (akin to factor loadings). It seems that Control and Confidence may be strong separators, as suggested in the bottom set of bar charts in terms of decision making (Control) and self-efficacy (Confidence) being generally more extreme in all the groups. Several variable-centered studies to be discussed in later sections of this book, seem to also suggest the pairing of Control with Confidence and of Concern with Curiosity. In sum, it would be useful to study variability of profile shapes among individuals with the same level of adaptability and consider nuances of interpretation for commonly occurring distinct profiles.

Conclusion

This Chapter provided evidence to support the test-retest stability of *CAAS* scores and the rank-order stability of the four subscale scores. The next Chapter describes alternative forms of the *CAAS*.

CHAPTER 5

CAAS ALTERNATIVE FORMS

Researchers have published several alternative versions of the *CAAS* for particular uses, including a short form and a behavioral form.

Career Adapt-Abilities Scale–Short Form

A brief version of the *CAAS* was produced by Maggiori, Rossier, and Savickas (2015) for possible use in lengthy surveys that include a battery of tests. They sought to reduce the number of items to three per subscale yet preserve the excellent psychometric properties of the *CAAS*. The study participants lived in Switzerland and consisted of 2,800 French- and German-speaking adults aged between 20 and 65 years (Mean = 41.2; SD 9.4). Women represented 51.0% of the sample and German-speakers represented 52.8%. Using a principal-component analysis with promax rotation, they reduced the total number of items to 12. They then tested the items for four first-order factors (Concern, Control, Curiosity, and Confidence) and a second-order factor (career adaptability). Overall, the model showed a satisfactory fit with a $\chi 2/\mathrm{df}$ of 4.18, a RMSEA lower than .04 and NFI, CFI, and TLI values all above 0.95. The loadings from the items to the corresponding factor varied between 0.63 and 0.94 and from the factors to career adaptability factor the coefficients ranged between 0.73 and 0.88. Furthermore, the 12-item and 24-item versions correlated strongly. Moreover, the 12-item *Career Adapt-Abilities–Short Form (CAAS-SF)* showed psychometric and structural properties close to those of the *CAAS*.

The researchers next tested the *CAAS-SF* for measurement equivalence between men and women and between French- and German-speaking participants. The participants consisted of 2,800 French-speaking and German-speaking adults aged between 20 and 65 years (Mean = 41.2; SD = 9.4) who lived in Switzerland. Women represented 51.0% of the sample and German speakers 52.8%. More precisely, 2,375 participants composed a representative sample from the Swiss population aged between 25 and 55 years (Mean=41.9; SD=8.6). To obtain younger participants, they added a convenience sample recruited from several high schools, vocational schools, and career service centers (N = 425; Mean age = 37.4; SD = 12.3). The researchers conducted a multi-group confirmatory factor analysis to compare (a) the two languages and (b) the women and men.

Overall, both between French- and German-speaking participants and between women and men, the configural, metric, and scalar invariance models showed acceptable to good fit to the data. The configural invariance model showed that the four-factor structure fit the data and met measurement invariance in two different linguistic regions of Switzerland and between women and men. The RMSEA was below 5 and the NFI, TLI, and CFI values were higher than 0.95. Thus, the results confirmed the configural invariance of the hierarchical four-factor model. The indices emphasized by the metric invariance model demonstrated a satisfactory model fit. The comparison between configural and metric models in terms of fit suggested negligible differences. In fact, the $\Delta\chi^2$ test was non-significant, and ΔCFI and ΔRMSEA were at 0.001. Finally, for the scalar invariance, except for the $\chi2/df$ higher than 5, the model presented a good fit. Regarding the differences in fit indices between the metric and the scalar models, the values were 0.001 and 0.003 for ΔRMSEA and ΔCFI, respectively, thus meeting the criteria of invariance. However, with a more restrictive ΔCFI threshold (0.002), they released one Curiosity item for gender to meet scalar invariance. Women scored higher on "Looking for opportunities to grow as a person." For the linguistic groups, they released two Curiosity items on the same 3-item factor to meet scalar invariance. French speakers scored higher on "Looking to grow as a person" and "Counting on myself." After analyzing the contribution of each item and according to these more restrictive criteria, the Curiosity subscale of the *CAAS-SF* did not reach full scalar invariance. Nevertheless, it is important to stress that the different subgroups showed a similar distribution overall on the total score and subscale scores, suggesting that the more restrictive threshold might be too limiting. Overall, the confirmatory factor analysis results demonstrated that the four-factor structure fit the data and met measurement invariance in two different linguistic regions of Switzerland and between women and men.

CAAS-SF in Turkey

A validity study of the *CAAS-Short Form* was conducted in Turkey by Isik, Yegin, Koyuncu, Eser, Comlekciler, and Yildirum (2018). Data were collected from 650 high school students, 327 college students, and 247 working adults with a mean age of 29.16 years (SD = 6.93). Cronbach alpha coefficients of internal consistency for the total score were .85 for high school students, .90 for college students, and .91 for working adults. Test-retest stability for 127 high school students after four weeks was satisfactory with a coefficient of .82 for the *CAAS-SF* total score, and .66 for Concern, .62 for Control, .68 for Curiosity, and .64 for Confidence. The researchers compared the 12-item and 24-item forms with the college student sample only. They reported that the 12-item *CAAS-SF* correlated .98 to the 24-item *CAAS* total score. The subscales in the two versions correlated .95 for Concern, .94 for Control, .93 for Curiosity, and .93 for Confidence.

Confirmatory factor analyses showed that the data across the three samples fit the theoretical model very well. For the high school students, the fit indices were $\chi2/df = 3.38$, GFI = .960, CFI = .947, TLI = .930, RMSEA = .061. For the college students, the $\chi2/df = 2.13$, GFI = .950, CFI = .966, TLI = .955, and RMSEA = .059. For the working adults, the $\chi2/df = 2.83$, GFI = .914, CFI. = 941, TLI = .922, and RMSEA = .082. Across the three samples, the standardized loadings from the items to the four first-order factors and from the factors to the second-order factor ranged from .59 to .96, suggesting that the items and factors were strong indicators of their respective constructs. To follow-up these findings, the researchers conducted multi-group confirmatory factor analyses to test for configural, metric, and scalar invariance across the three groups. For both gender and age groups, the data demonstrated a very good fit to the configural, metric, and scalar models. This means that the *CAAS-SF* operates in the same way and that the underlying constructs have the same theoretical pattern across gender and the three age groups.

CAAS-SF in Germany

In a study of 1477 employees in Germany, Spurk, Vomer, Orth, and Goritz (2020) assessed career adaptability with the *CAAS-SF* and a subscale of the short form *Career Futures Inventory* (*CFI-9*; McIlveen, Burton, & Beccaria, 2013). The three items were "I can adapt to change in the world of work;" "I can adjust to change in my career plans;" and "will adjust easily to shifting demands at work." At Time 1 the *CAAS-SF* total correlated .65 to the *CFI-9*, three months later they correlated .62, and six additional months later they correlated .59.

CAAS-SF in China

A validity study of the *CAAS-SF* was conducted in China by Yu, Dai, Guan, and Wang (2020). The participants totaled 3,081 individuals across three groups. The first sample consisted of 926 college students (55.6% females) in Beijing. The second sample consisted of 905 civil servants from nine Chinese government sectors in six different Provinces. The third sample consisted of 1,250 enterprise employees (57% females) from 13 companies engaged in manufacturing, information technology, and service in five Provinces. Hierarchical confirmatory factor analysis of each sample yielded acceptable model fit ($\chi2$/df = 2.37 /2.74 / 3.95; NFI = .93 /.93 /.93; IFI = .96 / .95 /.94; CFI = .96 / .95 /.94; TLI = .94 /.93 /.91; and RMSEA = .06 /.07 / .06). Standardized loadings from items to the four first-order factors and from the factors to the second-order adaptability factor ranged from 0.50 to 0.95 across the three samples, suggesting that all items and factors were strong indicators of their respective constructs. The researches concluded that the results supported the four-factor hierarchical structure of the 12-item *CAAS-SF* in all three groups. The four-factor solution for the *CAAS-SF* coincided with the 24-item *CAAS* as well as the theoretical background of career adaptability.

Models for configural, metric, and scalar invariances showed acceptable to good fit to the data collected from different social as well as gender groups. Analysis of configural equivalence across gender groups showed that the two groups shared the same factor structure. Tests of measurement invariance across the three sample groups also showed good results. Fit indices for the scalar invariance model showed a good fit, and the critical values (ΔCFI = .001 and ΔRMSEA = .001) were well below the cutoff values, suggesting that respondents who have the same score on the latent factor would obtain the same score on its indicator regardless of their group membership. In addition, the results showed that the *CAAS-SF China* accounted for even more variance (61.46%, 70.47%, and 66.28%) than the *CAAS-China* (47.66%, 60.48%, and 53.50%) across the three different groups. This indicates that the *CAAS-SF China* captures the most critical items for measuring career adaptability.

Given the measurement invariance results, the researchers compared the differences in career adaptability among the three samples. Analysis of variance tests found significant differences in the samples for all subscales except the Curiosity subscale. The enterprise employees reported the highest level of Control, while college students reported the lowest level. Civil servants reported the lowest level of Concern, but no significant difference in the scores was observed between college students and enterprise employees. College students reported the lowest level of Confidence, but no significant difference in the scores was observed between civil servants and enterprise employees.

In addition, consistent with expectations, the results showed that the *CAAS-SF* accounted for even more variance (61.46%, 70.47%, and 66.28%) than the *CAAS* China (47.66%, 60.48%, and 53.50%) across the three different groups. This indicates that the *CAAS-SF* captures the most critical items for developing career adaptability.

CAAS-SF in USA

In a lengthy survey such as envisioned by Maggori, Rossier, and Savickas (2015), Tokar, Savickas, and Kaut (2020) used the *CAAS-SF* and evaluated its hierarchical structure in a sample of 243 employed adults. Confirmatory factor analysis results indicated that the hypothesized model fit the data reasonably well, $\chi 2/df$ =3.85, $p < .001$, CFI = .90, SRMR = .070, RMSEA = .100, 90% CI = .085. However, fit index values indicated a relatively poorer fit than that reported by Maggiori, Rossier, and Savickas (2015) in their initial test of the *CAAS-SF* structure that showed CFI = .98 and RMSEA = .049. However, Maggiori, Rossier, and Savickas (2015) slightly improved the fit of their final model by allowing two sets of error terms to co-vary. In a similar manner, Tokar and colleagues re-tested the hypothesized model allowing two sets of error terms (corresponding to item pairs 1-2 and 8-9) to co-vary. They based the minor modifications on the empirical modification indices (i.e., MI > 10) as well as the conceptual and semantic similarity of the item pairs. The modified model resulted in an adequate ($\chi 2/df$ =3.16, $p < .001$, CFI = .93, SRMR = .054, RMSEA = .087, 90% CI = .071, and significantly improved fit. Factor loadings for all factors were substantial and significant ($p < .001$). Item factor loadings ranged from .52 to .81 (Median = .70), and loadings from the Control, Concern, Curiosity, and Confidence factors to the higher-order adaptability factor ranged from .68 to .99 (Median = .82). Overall, the confirmatory factor analysis results supported the hypothesized hierarchical structure of the *CAAS-SF* in this sample of workers.

CAAS-Behavioral Form

To measure *behavioral* manifestations of career adapting, Zacher (2015) changed the wording of the 24 items in the *CAAS* to the past tense. For example, "I thought about about what my future will be like" (Concern), "I made decisions by myself" (Control), "I explored my surroundings" (Curiosity), and "I overcame obstacles" (Confidence). This substantial change of item wording to the past tense converts the *CAAS* from a measure of adaptability resources to a measure of adapting behaviors. Zacher then added the word "Today" at the beginning of each item to assess daily occurrences of adapting behaviors (e.g., a Concern item became "Today, I thought about what my future will be like"). In responding to the *CAAS-Behavioral Form*, individuals indicate the extent to which they had engaged in the 24 specific behaviors that day on a 5-point scale ranging from 1 (never) to 5 (very often).

To study intra-individual variation in adapting behaviors, Zacher conducted two studies. He administered the *CAAS-Behavioral Form* to participants daily for period of five or more days and then compared the extent of adapting behaviors to job performance and other variables (e.g., Zacher, 2015; Zacher 2016). The reports of these two studies included convergent validity evidence for the *CAAS-Behavioral Form*. In the first study (Zacher, 2015), the *CAAS* total score correlated .60 to the daily adapting total score, .45 to daily Concern, .56 to daily Control, .50 to daily Curiosity, and .50 to daily Confidence. For the dimensions, the correlations between *CAAS* subscale scores and the corresponding daily adapting scores were .58 for Concern, .56 for Control, .53 for Curiosity, and .56 for Confidence. In the second study (Zacher, 2016), the *CAAS* total score correlated .66 to the daily adapting total score. For the dimensions, the correlations between *CAAS* subscale scores and daily adapting scores were .61 for Concern, .66 for Control, .66 for Curiosity, and .66 for Confidence.

A second version of the *CAAS-Behavioral Form* was devised by Kaur and Kaur (2020). They adapted the *CAAS* items to reflect levels of career adaptability monthly. Example items read, "I plan how to achieve my monthly goals" and "I investigate options before making a choice." Confirmatory factor analysis indicated that the data fit the measurement model with $\chi2/df = 1.66$, CFI = .98, TLI =.97, and RMSEA =.05. They administered the scale to 239 employees at four top-ranked banks in India. Of the respondents, 57.6% were male and the average age of the sample was 34 years old. The participants responded to the *CAAS-Behavioral Form* (monthly) three times, three months apart, along with measures of job satisfaction and job performance. The job measures were combined into one score to represent job outcomes. At Time 1 career adapting correlated .49 to job outcomes; at Time 2 the correlation was .31; and at Time 3 the correlation was .37.

CAAS+Cooperation Scale

The attempt to include a "cooperation subscale" as an *intrapersonal* dimension of the *CAAS* failed in the initial attempt by the International Research Team (Savickas & Porfeli, 2012). The Cooperation subscale itself showed excellent psychometric properties yet it did not cohere with the other four adapt-ability subscales in the *CAAS* (i.e., Concern, Control, Curiosity, and Confidence). The International Team concluded that Cooperation is an *interpersonal* resource that supports adaptability yet is not an intrapersonal resource. Nevertheless, several team members -- including Vilhjálmsdóttir, Einarsdóttir, McMahon, Watson, and Bimrose -- astutely noted that the *Cooperation Scale* may be a relevant instrument in cultures where relational support for career adaptation is an important factor. They suggested that the *CAAS* measures internal resources activated within the self, whereas the Cooperation Scale may measure external resources activated within the community. The 11-item Cooperation Scale used as part of the *CAAS Research Form* by the International Research Team appears in Table 5.

<u>Table 5. Cooperation Scale Items</u>

Becoming less self-centered
Acting friendly
Getting along with all kinds of people
Cooperating with others on group projects
Playing my part on a team
Compromising with other people
Learning to be a good listener
Contributing to my community
Going along with the group
Sharing with others
Hiding my true feelings for the good of the group

Further research needs to explore in cultural context hypotheses about the relation of career adaptability resources to cooperation as an interpersonal resource activated during times of transition. This hypothesis has only been studied by Einarsdóttir, Vilhjálmsdóttir, Smáradóttir, and Kjartansdóttir (2015). They reported two studies in Iceland that strongly supported the conceptualization of cooperation as an adapting response. In the first study, Einarsdóttir and her colleagues (2015) recruited a sample of 456 students. The participants consisted of 276 students attending 9th and 10th grade classes in six compulsory schools and 215 students attending four upper secondary schools. The mean age of participants was 17.1 years (SD = 2.8). The researchers tested the fit of the *CAAS* four-dimension model in the sample of secondary and upper secondary students only. The results showed a reasonably good fit of the four-dimensional model with CFI = 0.97, RMSEA = .057, and SRMR = .062. The researchers then added Cooperation items to test a five-dimensional model. Based on principal-components analysis with orthogonal rotation, they selected the five Cooperation items with the highest loadings on the Cooperation component and lowest cross-loadings on the other four dimensions. They also added a new item ("Understanding others point of view"). The resulting six-item scale shown in Tabled 6 had a Cronbach alpha coefficient of .83. Next, they tested the fit of the five-dimension model. The results indicated CFI = 0.97, RMSE = 0.054, and SRMR = 0.062. Thus, the fit of the five-dimensional model that included the Cooperation subscale was very similar to the fit of the four-dimensional model in Iceland.

In Study 2, they constructed a six-dimensional form of the *CAAS* that consisted of the Concern, Curiosity, Control, Confidence, and Cooperation subscales plus the addition of a new subscale measuring Contribution. The items in the Contribution subscale, shown in Table 6 express a need to be active in the community and develop a reputation for contributing to society. The researchers tested their six-dimensional model with 625 university students who ranged in age from 18 to 68 years with a mean age of 30.5 (SD = 9.3). The six-dimensional model showed a good fit with CFI = 0.98, RMSEA = 0.053, and SRMR = 0.065. The correlations between the components ranged between .46 and .75, suggesting that they measure six separate constructs because the correlations were each less than .80.

Table 6. Cooperation and Contribution Items
(Einarsdóttir et al., 2015)

Cooperation Items	Getting along with all kinds of people Cooperating with others on group projects Compromising with other people Going along with the group Sharing with others Understanding others point of view
Contribution Items	Finding purpose in my studies and work Wanting to be appreciated Wanting my work to be respected Expecting to be active in my community Wanting people to think I do good work Understanding others point of view I know I have to perform well to obtain my future goals

The results of the studies by Einarsdóttir, Vilhjálmsdóttir, Smáradóttir, and Kjartansdóttir (2015) show that special attention needs to be paid to social context and culture in the conceptual and operational definitions of career adaptability in different countries. The two dimensions labeled cooperation and contribution supported in Iceland represent aspects of career adapting responses that refer to the social context and interpersonal relations. The researchers suggested that these interpersonal dimensions in Iceland may be important in Nordic societies which value equality, have a relatively small dispersion of income, maintain a closely knit welfare system, and support a mutual social contract in relation to work as an individual's contribution to society. Based on their research, Cooperation and Contribution may be conceptualized as interpersonal dimensions of career adapting in contrast to the intrapersonal dimensions of Concern, Control, Curiosity, and Confidence. Further research needs to test this conceptualization as well as examine the six-dimensional model in various societies.

CAAS -Francophone Form

An expanded French-Language Form of the *CAAS* was produced by Johnston, Broonen, Stauffer, Hamtiaux, Pouyaud, Zecca, Houssemand, and Rossier (2013) who re-analyzed the *CAAS-Research Form*. Recall that the *Research Form* contained 11 items per subscale. Results of the International Study identified seven items per scale that worked well. In the end the *CAAS* (i.e., the standard 24-item form) uses only the best six items for each subscale because no psychometric advantage came from using the seventh item on each subscale. In their study, Johnson and her colleagues administered the *CAAS–Research Form* in France and the French-speaking regions of Switzerland, Belgium, and Luxembourg. They used the four 11-items subscales for Concern, Control, Curiosity, and Confidence. The combined sample of 1707 participants (57% females, 40% males) ranged in age from 13 to 79 years (Mean = 24.22; SD = 12.33). The Swiss sample (N = 468) consisted of 54% females and 46% males with an age range of 14 to 79 years (Mean = 35.92; SD = 13.37). Participants in the Belgian sample (N = 395) consisted of 54% females and 35% males with ages ranging from 16 to 21 years (Mean = 17.49; SD = .87). The Luxembourg sample had 181 participants ranging in age from 16 to 75 year (Mean = 33.61; SD = 12.90) with 68% female and 32% male participants. Finally, the French sample (N = 663) consisted of 42% males and 58% females with ages ranging from 13 to 21 years (Mean = 16.59; SD = .88).

The study confirmed that seven items not included in the *CAAS* functioned well in the Francophone regions, possibly because the item content reflected cultural difference. They added the seven items to the 24 items in the *CAAS* to construct the *CAAS Francophone Form*. For the Concern subscale, a general future orientation seemed to fit better than planning related directly to goals. For the Control subscale, the added items in the

Francophone Form corresponded more with learning how to improve decision making. The added items on the Curiosity subscale represented represented more specific behaviors (e.g. "searching for information about choices I must make"), rather than general ones (e.g., "exploring my surroundings"). This "searching" item was the seventh items that worked in all 13 countries but was not used in the *CAAS* because it offered little psychometric gain. Finally, on the Confidence subscale, "doing challenging things" seemed to be important. Again, this "doing" item was the seventh item for the Confidence subscale in the International Study which could have been included. The selection of these items improved reliability. The structures of both the *CAAS* and *CAAS-Fancophone Form* were replicable in the countries of Switzerland, Belgium, France, and Luxembourg.

The standardized loadings for the *CAAS-Francophone Form* ranged from .56 to .73 (Median = .61) for the items, and from .77 to .88 (Median = .81) to the second-order factor of adaptability. These loadings were comparable to and even slightly better than those obtained for the *CAAS*, which had item loadings that ranged from .46 to .72 (Median = .58) and from .69 to .89 (Median = .82) to the second-order factor. The model fit statistics for the *CAAS* ($\chi2/df$ = 6.35; GFI = 9.24, CFI = .888, TLI = .875, and RMSEA = .056) were slightly better than the model fit statistics for the Francophone form ($\chi2/df$ = 8.66. GFI = .897. CFI = .861, TLI = .846, RMSEA = .067). An additional model that utilized item parceling, with three homogenous parcels per scale, was created by pairing items with the highest correlations, and then using the mean score of the two items in the analysis. This technique provided some improvement on the model fit: $\chi2/df$ = 4.17, GFI = .980, CFI = .976, TLI = .968, and RMSEA = .043. The researchers recommended using both sets of items (31 total items with 24 from the *CAAS* and 7 added items) to allow for comparisons with measurement of adapt-abilities in different countries that use the *CAAS* as well as contribute to more accurate measurement of adapt-abilities in Francophone countries. The additional seven items appear in Table 7.

Table 7. *CAAS-Francophone Form* Seven Additional Items

Subscale	Item
Concern	Taking charge of my future
Control	Finding the strength to keep going
Control	Learning how to make better decisions
Control	Expecting the future to be good.
Curiosity	Considering my alternatives
Confidence	Doing challenging things
Confidence	Performing tasks efficiently
Subscale	**Item**
Concern	Taking charge of my future
Control	Finding the strength to keep going
Control	Learning how to make better decisions
Control	Expecting the future to be good.
Curiosity	Considering my alternatives
Confidence	Doing challenging things
Confidence	Performing tasks efficiently

Qualitative Assessment of Career Adapt-Abilities

To assess career adaptability qualitatively, rather than quantitatively with the *CAAS*, McMahon, Watson, and Bimrose (2012) developed a set of descriptors derived from the items contained in the *CAAS-Research Form*. The qualitative descriptors for the four dimensions of career adaptability were identified to provide researchers with a "coding scheme" for analyzing interview transcripts. The four sets of descriptors appear in Table 8.

Table 8. Coding Scheme Descriptors for Qualitative Assessment of Adapt-Abilities

Adapt-Abilities	Descriptors
Concern	Planful, forward thinking, connects present and future, optimistic, hopeful, prepared, ready
Control	Independent, autonomous, contemplative, accountable, trustworthy, persistent, patient, self-principled
Curiosity	Investigative, self-reflective, open, exploratory, informed, observant
Confidence	Efficient, productive, self-perceptive, reliable, proud, self-confident

A study by McMahon, Watson, and Bimrose (2012) demonstrated that career adaptability can be assessed qualitatively using their scoring scheme. Furthermore, using the descriptors of career adaptability afforded a deep and rich understanding of participants' objective and subjective experiences of career transitions. McMahon, Watson, and Bimrose (2012) reported that career adapt-abilities were present in facets of the older women's career development other than during times of transition. They demonstrated that the career adapt-abilities may have wider application in career development than only during times of transition.

A second qualitative study of career adapt-abilities was conducted in Turkey. Ozdemir (2019) examined differences between students with high and low scores on the *CAAS*. The participants were twelve male and eight female students in grades ten and eleven. On the *CAAS*, half of the students scored above the 75th percentile and half scored below the 25th percentile. Ozdemir conducted a Career Construction Interview (Savickas, 2019b) with each student and then submitted their response to content analyses. The coding scheme was similar to the themes and described by McMahon, Watson, and Bimrose (2012).

With regard to main themes, the most frequent for the high adaptability group was Curiosity, followed by Control. Within the low career adaptability group, lack of Confidence and Control were the most frequent main themes. The researchers also reported sub-themes for each of the four adapt-abilities. For Concern, pessimism appeared among the high group and lack of hope appeared among the low group. Ozdemir interpreted the unexpected finding of pessimism among the high group as possibly caused by worry about the future due to the competitive examinations and high pressure in the Turkish educational system. An alternative explanation may be word meaning. "Concern" in Turkish, and many other languages including English, may be taken to mean "worry, uncertainty and apprehension" rather than the *CAAS* intended meaning to denote "a matter of marked interest or importance to someone." The finding concerning lack of hope among the low group coincided with previous studies showing that hope is an antecedent of the Concern adapt-ability. For Control, persistence was strong in the high group and weak in the low group. The two groups also differed with the high group showing more autonomy and sense of responsibility and the low group showing more indecisiveness. For Curiosity, the two groups differed in inquisitiveness and exploratory behavior, with the high group showing greater initiative in thinking about self and possible occupations and engaging in more information-seeking activities. For Confidence, the high group showed more self-confidence, with the low group showing less self- confidence and problem-solving ability. While content emerged from each of the five Career Construction Interview questions, practitioners might be particularly attuned for the expressions of Concern in discussing role models, for Control in discussing favorite story, for Curiosity in discussing television shows, and for Confidence in discussing mottos and early recollections.

A third qualitative study interviewed 13 women in the maintenance stage of a professional career to explore the meaning that they attributed to their work and career stage (Whiston, Feldwisch, Evans, Blackman, & Gilman, 2015). The participants, all college graduates, ranged in age from 50 to 66 years (Mean = 59.62%; SD

= 4.84). The in-person interview topics included job satisfaction, influences of age and gender on work, interactions with others, and influences on career decisions. Example questions in the interview were "How do you think your age influences your current work?" and "What influences your current decisions that you make at work?" Iterative analysis of each participant's interview transcripts identified the theme of career adaptability and suppleness in adjusting to changing work issues. Although labeling this domain as career adaptability was not originally intended to mirror the dimensions of career adaptability, the similarities between the dimensions and the interview content became evident as data analysis continued. This finding reinforced McMahon, Watson and Bimrose's (2012) conclusion that career adaptability is a construct not limited to adolescents and young adults, but is also prevalent in older adult women.

Conclusion

This Chapter 5 described alternative forms of the *CAAS*, beginning with a *Short Form*. The 12-item *CAAS-Short Form* met the specifications of the the theoretical model and showed configural, metric, and scalar invariance in both Turkey and China as well as convergent validity in Germany and the USA. The second adapted form discussed was a measure of behavioral manifestations of adaptability that changes the *CAAS* items into measures of adapting behaviors rather than adaptability resources. A third adapted form was the Francophone version that adds seven additional items to the *CAAS*. The Chapter includes a discussion of a measure of Cooperation as an interpersonal resource activated within the community. The Chapter concluded with an explanation of a set of descriptors that may be used as a coding or scoring scheme in analyzing interview transcripts. The next Chapter discusses family antecedents of an individual's career adaptability resources.

CHAPTER 6

FAMILY ANTECEDENTS OF CAREER ADAPTABILITY

This chapter examines factors that may contribute to an individual's development of career adaptability resources. Children and adolescents benefit from emotional and instrumental support for their career development. Accordingly, the family environment plays an important role in fostering the development of adaptability resources in youngsters. Career-specific parental behaviors and support may prompt children to internalize the value of preparing for the future and encourage adolescents to develop career adaptability resources. This assertion has been tested in at least 14 studies that have examined the relation of the *CAAS* to career-specific parental behaviors, perceived parental career support, social support from family and significant others, career-related filial piety, and grandparents and parents' role modeling.

Career-Specific Parental Behaviors

Four studies have focused on career-specific parental behaviors. Guan, Wang, Liu, Ji, Jia, Fang, Li, Hua, and Li (2015) surveyed 244 pairs of Chinese university students and their parents to study the effects of career-specific parental behaviors (reported by parents at Time 1) on students' career exploration (reported by students at Time 2) and career adaptability (reported by students at time 3). The researchers measured career-specific parental behaviors with the 15-item *Perceived Parental Career-Related Behaviors Scale* (Dietrich & Kracke, 2009). The Scale has has three subscales of five items each that measure Parental Support (e.g., "My parents support me in getting an apprenticeship"), Lack of Parental Career Engagement (e.g., "My parents cannot support my vocational preparation because they know too little about different vocations"), and Parental Interference (e.g., "My parents have their own ideas about my future vocation and try to influence me accordingly"). The researchers measured career exploration with five self-exploration items and six environment exploration items from the *Career Exploration Survey* (Stumpf, Colarelli, &

Hartman, 1983). Because the two exploration scales correlated .69, they combined the 11 items to represent career exploration (Cronbach alpha = .92). They measured adaptability with the Chinese version of the *CAAS* (Hou et al., 2012). The results indicated that parents' supportive behaviors related positively to *CAAS* scores (.21), whereas lack of parental career engagement had a direct negative effect on career adaptability (-.27). In addition, the results supported a mediation model such that a high level of parental support and a low level of parental interference had beneficial effects on the students' career exploration, which in turn predicted positively their career adaptability. The corresponding moderated-mediation model was also supported. Significant interaction effects were found among the three types of parental behaviors such that career exploration was better predicted by less parental interference and more parental career engagement and parental support.

A second study in China also used the *Perceived Parental Career Related Behaviors Scale* (Dietrich & Kracke, 2009) to examine the relation between parental support and children's career adaptability. Liang, Dou, Li, Liang, Zhou, Cao, Wu, and Lin (2020) conducted a three-wave longitudinal study to examine how different types of career-related parental behaviors associate with adolescents' consideration of consequences, which in turn may relate to career adaptability ten months later. Participants were recruited from five high schools in Southeastern China. A total of 441 adolescents (46.3% females) who ranged in age from 15 to 19 years (Mean = 16.87; SD = 0.63) participated in the study. The researchers measured career-specific parental behaviors with three scales developed by Dietrich and Kracke (2009): Parental Support, Lack of Parental Career Engagement, and Parental Interference. To measure thinking about the future, the researchers used the *Consideration of Future Consequences Scale* (Strathman, Gleicher, Boninger, & Edwards, 1994). The scale measures the extent to which individuals consider the potential distant outcomes of their current behaviors and the extent to which these potential outcomes influence them. The items concentrate on the intrapersonal struggles between present behavior and future outcomes. Example

ample items read, "I only act to satisfy immediate concerns, figuring the future will take of itself" and "I consider how things might be in the future, and try to influence those things with my day to day behavior." The parental measure was administered at Time 1, five months later the *Consideration of Future Consequences Scale* was administered, and then another five months later the *CAAS* was administered.

The correlations for consideration of future consequences to the adapt-abilities were .23 to Concern, .17 to Control, .22 to Curiosity, and .18 to Confidence. Parental interference did not correlate significantly to any adapt-ability. Support correlated .23 to Concern, .19 to Control, .24 to Curiosity, and .25 to Confidence. Lack of engagement correlated significantly only to Control (.12). As shown in the Figure 8, confirmatory factor analysis results indicated that career-related parental support at Time 1 associated positively with adolescents' consideration of future consequences at Time 2 (β = .24, p < .001), which in turn related positively to adolescents' career adaptability at Time 3 (β = .21, p <.01). These associations were significant after controlling for the effects of child gender, child age, and parents' education. The indirect association was small in magnitude (β = .033). Perceived parental support at Time 1 still associated directly and positively with adolescents' career adaptability at Time 3 (β = .23, p < .007).

Figure 8. Parenting Behaviors and Career Adaptability

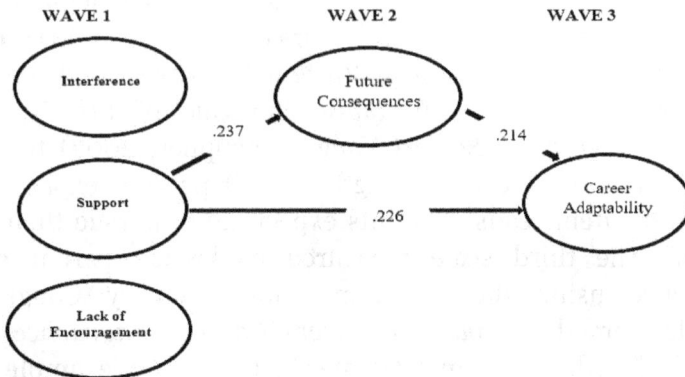

WAVE 1   WAVE 2   WAVE 3

Interference

Future
Consequences

.237

.214

Support

.226

Career
Adaptability

Lack of
Encouragement

103

The researchers concluded that the unexpected non-significant relation of parental interference to career adaptability could be because the Western conceptualization of career-related parental behaviors may not be culturally appropriate for Chinese parents, and it is necessary to understand the association between parenting practices and child development outcomes within specific cultural contexts. The researchers offered two possible explanations for why parental interference did not relate significantly and negatively to career adaptability over time. First, in China, controlling parents may engage their children in career exploration and other career-related activities. Second, parents' controlling practices encompass Chinese indigenous concepts of loving and caring and thus may not be perceived as negative by some adolescents. Chinese parents frequently use the strategies of "Guan" (to safeguard children's well-being and maintain family interdependence) and "Jiao" (to train and teach parents' expectation of excellence from children). The non-significant relation between parental lack of engagement and adolescents' career adaptability over time may be because parents might lack sufficient knowledge and skills to support their adolescent children's career development and thus seem to be disengaged.

A third study in China also used the *Perceived Parental Career-related Behaviors Scale* (Dietrich & Kracke, 2009) to measure career-related parenting practices. In a large-scale study, Zhou, Nie, Yu, Deng, Zang, Sun, Fang, Cao, Li, Liang, and Buehler (2019) administered that scale along with three other scales to 5,408 high school students in the 10th and 11th grades. The participants, who ranged in age from 13.40 to 19.67 years (Mean = 15.79; SD = 0.66), consisted of 2,587 males and 2,801 females. The second scale was the nine-item Career Expectation Subscale of the *Perceived Parental Expectation Scale* (Wang & Heppner, 2002) to which participants indicated the strength of their parents' expectations. An example item reads, "Parents expect me to pursue their ideal careers." The third scale measured adolescent–parent career congruence using the five-item Complementary Congruence Subscale from the *Adolescent-Parent Career Congruence Scale* (Sawitri, Creed, & Zimmer-Gembeck, 2012). An example item reads, "My parents encourage me to explore the career areas I am interested in." The final scale was the four-item ambivalence subscale from the *Ambivalence in Career Decision-Making Scale* (Kasperzack, Ernst, & Pinquart, 2014). An example item reads, "I have mixed feelings concerning my intended field of study/my intended professional training."

Results showed that the *CAAS* total score correlated .14 to interference, .09 to barriers to engagement, .42 to support, .36 to career expectations, .37 to congruence, and -.06 to ambivalence. To go beyond the study of individual parental processes used in variable-centered approaches, the researchers used a person-centered design to examine how the separate variables may be configured in a variety of ways within families and how such configurations may be linked to children's career development. They applied latent profile analysis to examine potential typologies based on the five parental processes: parental expectations, support, interference, barriers to engagement, and parent-child congruence. They identified three distinct profiles: (a) unsupportive but not permissive, (b) supportive but not intrusive, and (c) ambivalent and controlling. The meaningfulness of profiles was evidenced by the finding that adolescents' career adaptability and ambivalence varied as a function of profiles. The "supportive but not intrusive" profile (45.38% of the sample) showed the lowest levels of interference and barriers to engagement along with moderate levels of support, expectation, and congruence. Parents fitting this profile may actively engage in their adolescents' career development by providing support and appropriate autonomy, while not interfering too much with adolescents' career exploration, planning, and actions. The "unsupportive but not permissive" (37.84% of the sample) showed moderate levels of interference and barriers to engagement with the lowest levels of support, expectation, and congruence. Parents fitting this profiles may prioritize children's academic success believing that children's academic achievement is critical for increasing upward mobility. They are not permissive nor indifferent about their children's career development. Nevertheless, they seem unsupportive, possibly when they try to get involved they may be ineffective or inappropriate for various reasons. One reason may be that they themselves do not have sufficient knowledge regarding how to appropriately guide children to cope with career development challenges, given the rapid social changes. The "ambivalent and controlling" profile (17.28% of the sample) showed the highest levels of interference and barriers to engagement along with the highest levels of support, expectation, and congruence. Parents fitting this profile may provide substantial career guidance and resources yet at the same time present substantial career expectations, barriers, and interference. The researchers wondered if the contradictory amounts of high support, expectation, and interference might characterize "tiger parents" who pressure their children to excel in academics or other high-status activities such as music.

Overall, adolescents in the "support but not intrusion" and "ambivalent and controlling" groups reported higher levels of career adaptability and lower levels of career ambivalence than did those in the "unsupportive but not permissive" group. The researchers suggested that there are beneficial effects of parental involvement in adolescents' career development, regardless of whether the involvement is supportive or intrusive/controlling. When paired with support and congruence, parents' use of psychologically controlling strategies and high career expectation may convey concern and warmth, as well as serve as motivation and resources for Chinese adolescents. The researchers concluded that the person-oriented approach yielded unique insights for understanding the variety of ways in which different career-related parental processes may be configured within families and how such configurations may be linked to their children's career development.

A fourth study also used the *Perceived Parental Career-related Behaviors Scale* (Dietrich & Kracke, 2009) to measure career-related parenting practices. In The Philippines, Amarnani, Garcia, Restubog, Bordia, and Bordia (2018) examined whether parental engagement amplifies the influence of children's self-esteem on their career adaptability, which in turn predicts academic persistence. The researchers reasoned that perceived parental engagement confirms and verifies a child's positive sense of self. To test the hypothesis, they conducted a time-lagged study of computer science undergraduate students at a large university in Manila. The final sample of 232 students had a mean age of 17.34 years and were 34% females. At Time 1, students responded to measures of self-esteem and parental engagement. Self-esteem was measured using the *Self-Esteem Scale* (Rosenberg, 1979). Student-reported parental engagement was measured with the five-item scale developed by Dietrich and Kracke (2009). An example item reads, "My parents cannot support my vocational preparation, because they know too little about different vocations" (reverse scored). At Time 2 one year later, participants responded to the *CAAS* and a measure of intention to leave the computer science program in the next two years. The persistence measure consisted of three items: (a) "If I have my own way, I will drop from my computer science program," (b) "I am planning to drop out of my computer science program in the next 2 years," and (c) "I frequently consider dropping from my computer science program."

The *CAAS* total score correlated .24 to self-esteem, .21 to self-reported parental engagement, and .18 to career persistence. Results for the mediation model appear in Figure 9. Analysis for moderation indicated that the relationship between self-esteem and career adaptability was strong among students who perceived high levels of parental engagement (β = .25, p < .01) yet null at low levels of parental engagement (β = .004, ns). The researchers concluded that the results indicated that parental engagement -- serving as a tacit indicator of how much one is valued by very important others -- indirectly contributes to career adaptability and career persistence among STEM students.

Figure 9. Parental Engagement and Career Adaptability

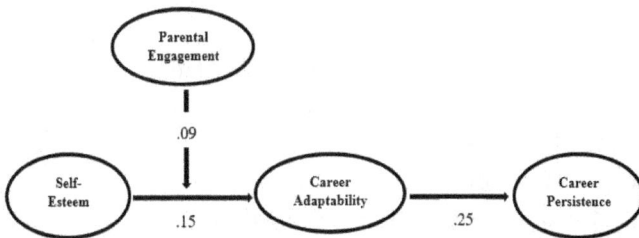

107

A fourth study in China also investigated career-specific parenting behaviors. Guan, Wang, Gong, Cai, Xu, Xiang, Wang, Chen, Hu, and Tian (2018) proposed that parents' own career development and values may influence their parenting behaviors that in turn influence their college children's career development. They tested this linkage with a mediation model in which career-specific parenting behaviors mediate the relationships of parent career adaptability and career values to the career adaptability of their undergraduate children. The students were from a university career center in Northern China. Each participant had a parent complete study surveys. The 264 students (29.5% males and 70.5% females) had a mean age of 21.00 years (SD = 1.29). Seventy-eight (29.50%) participants were men and 186 (70.50%) were women. Among the parents, 165 (62.50%) were fathers and 99 (37.50%) were mothers. The mean age of parents was 47.20 years (SD = 4.34).

Career adaptability of both parents and their children was measured with the *CAAS*. The researchers measured parents' career values with a scale developed by Zhou et al. (2013) in a Chinese context. It which consists of 21 items that measure three career values: intrinsic fulfillment (e.g., "One's talents and potential capacities are fully utilized in his or her career"), external compensation (e.g., "One can get good material compensation from one's work"), and work–life balance (e.g., "One can take care of his or her family when developing his or her career"). To measure parenting behaviors, they used the Chinese version of the *Career-Specific Parenting Behavior Scale* (Guan, Wang, et al., 2015). The scale includes five items to measure each of three types of behaviors, namely, parental support, interference, and engagement. An example item reads "I support my child in getting an apprenticeship."

Students' career adaptability correlated .21 to parents' *CAAS* total score, .22 to parents' work-life balance values, .27 to parental support, and .19 to parental engagement. The *CAAS* did not show statistically significant relations to parents' compensation values, intrinsic fulfillment values, nor parent interference. Results of a mediation analysis, as shown in Figure 10, indicated that parental support and parental engagement mediated the effects of parental career values and adaptability on students' career adaptability. When parents highly value intrinsic fulfillment and work–life balance, they tended to display more parental support behaviors such as offering useful suggestions and opportunities to their children.

Figure 10. Parenting Practices and Career Adaptability

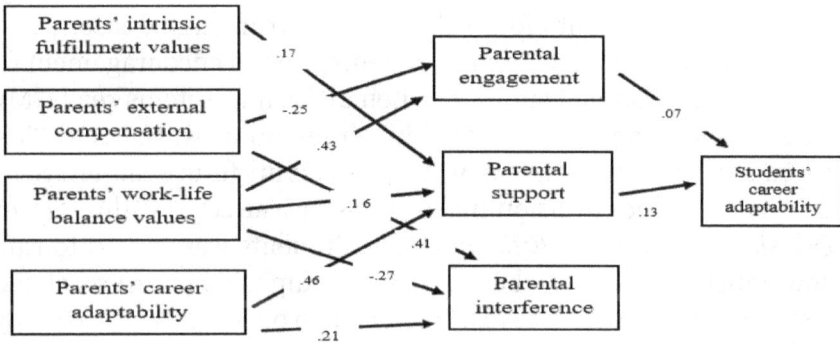

When examining whether fathers and mothers play different roles in shaping their children's career adaptability, the researchers found a three-way interaction of parents' career adaptability, parents' gender, and children's gender on children's career adaptability through the mediation of parental support. The effect of mothers' career adaptability on sons' career adaptability through parental support was stronger than its effect on daughters' career adaptability. Similarly, the effect of fathers' career adaptability on daughters' career adaptability through parental support was stronger than the effect on sons' career adaptability. They reported no other significant interactions.

Perceived Parental Support

A study in China concentrated on the relation of parental support to children's career adaptability. Guan, Capezio, Restubog, Read, Lajom, and Li (2016) examined the moderating role of traditional beliefs as an influence on the relations between parental support, career decision-making self-efficacy, and career adaptability among

731 Chinese university students. They hypothesized that parental support relates positively to both career adaptability and career decision-making self-efficacy. At Time 1, 2435 participants completed the *Career-Related Parent Support Scale* (Turner, Alliman-Brissett, Lapan, Udipi, & Ergun, 2003), the *Career Decision-Making Self-Efficacy Scale* (Betz, Klein, & Taylor, 1996), and a measure of traditional values. The *Career-Related Parental Support Scale* consists of 27 items that assess students' perceptions of parental support for educational and vocational development, which are grouped into four sub-scales: instrumental assistance (7 items), career-related modeling (7 items), verbal encouragement (6 items), and emotional support (7 items). Example items read, "My parents show me the kind of things they do at work," and "My parents talk to me when I am worried about my future career." Self-efficacy for career decision making was measured with the *Career Decision-Making Self-Efficacy Scale*. Students were asked to rate how much confidence they felt in accomplishing career-related tasks. An example item reads, "I am able to persistently work at my major or career goal even when I get frustrated." Participants rated the importance of seven traditional values (Stern, Dietz, & Guagnano, 1998) such as family, security, and obedience. The *CAAS* was administered to the same students 18 months after the Time 1 data collection.

A total of 731 cases could be matched by student ID. The final sample comprised 63.9% males and 36.1% females, with a mean age of 21.29 years (SD = 1.74). Time 2 career adaptability correlated .20 to Time 1 perceived parental support, .22 to career decision-making self-efficacy, and .20 to traditional beliefs. These results demonstrated the positive influence that parental support can exert on development of career adaptability. The direct effects of Time 1 parental support on Time 2 career adaptability were moderated by traditionality beliefs. The researchers concluded that strong beliefs in traditional values may weaken the relationship of parental support to adaptability. These findings coincide with prior research suggesting that traditionality beliefs can limit one's sense of personal agency and career choices (Hardin, Leong, & Osipow, 2001). The authors concluded that in the Chinese context, belief in traditional values may limit career choices and career exploration, thereby inhibiting personal growth.

Social Support from Family, Friends, and Significant Others

Studies in six different countries have examined the relation of career adaptability to perceptions of social support using the *Multidimensional Scale of Perceived Social Support* (*MSPSS*; Zimet, Dahlem, Zimet, & Farley, 1988). The *MSPSS* measures the subjective perception of social support adequacy from three specific sources: family (e.g., "My family really tries to help me"), friends (e.g., "I can talk about my problems with my friends"), and significant others (e.g., "There is a special person who is around when I am in need"). The 12-item instrument measures these three sources of social support with four items each.

In China, Tian and Fan (2014) used the *MSPSS* to investigate the relation of career adaptability to perceived social support among 431 student nurses. The *CAAS* total score correlated .41 to the total score for social support, with correlations of .42 to family, .38 to friends, and .36 to significant others. The correlations between the four *CAAS* subscales and the three social support subscales ranged from .28 to .36.

In Hong Kong, Hui, Yuen and Chen (2018a) used the *MSPSS* to examine the role of perceived parental support in mediating between self-esteem and career adaptability. The participants were 522 (69% females) business studies students at a university. They ranged in age from 18 to 24 years (Mean = 21.52; SD = 1.26), with 89.7% of the participants being final-year students. The participants responded to the *CAAS*, *MSPSS*, and the *Self-Esteem Scale* (Rosenberg, 1965). The *CAAS* total score correlated .30 to self-esteem and .24 to perceived social support. The findings from mediation analysis, shown in Figure 11, indicated that the total effect of self-esteem on career adaptability was significant (total effect = .32, $p < .001$). The indirect effect of self-esteem on career adaptability was also significant. With the presence of social

111

support as a mediator, the direct effect of self-esteem on career adaptability also remained significant (direct effect = .27, $p < .001$) and the absolute size was reduced. This indicated that a partial mediation relationship existed.

Figure 11. Perceived Parental Support and Career Adaptability

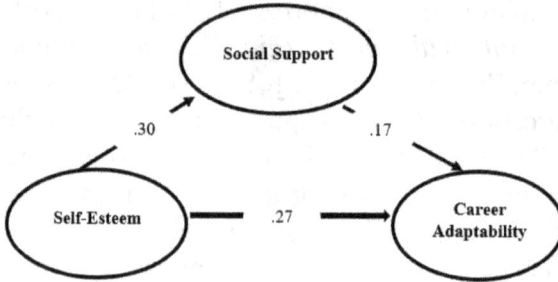

In Turkey, Atac, Dirk, and Tetik (2018) administered the *CAAS* and the *MSPSS* to 313 senior students in Economics and Administrative Sciences at a public university. The 179 females and 134 males ranged in age from 21 to 28 years with a mean of 22.6 years (SD = 1.19). The *CAAS* total score correlated .52 to the total score for social support, with correlations of .50 to family, .37 to friends, and .42 to significant others. The correlations between the *CAAS* subscales and the three social support subscales ranged from .19 to .49, with the strongest correlations to Control and Confidence.

In Nigeria, Ebenehi, Rashid, and Bakar (2016) also studied the relation of career adaptability to social support measured with the *MSPSS*. Their participants were 603 university students in Agricultural, Business, and Technical Education programs who were randomly selected from six colleges in Nigeria. The participants consisted of 58.5%, males and 41.5% females with an average age of 22 years. The *CAAS* total score correlated .36 to perceived social support.

In Serbia, Mirkovic, Suvajdzic, and Dostanic (2020) administered the *CAAS* and *MSPSS* to 374 adult employees (57.5% female) at small and medium-sized enterprises. They ranged in age from 21 to 64 years (M = 39; SD = 11.35). The *CAAS* total score correlated .28

to perceived social support, with correlations of .23 to Concern, .24 to Control, .22 to Curiosity, and .21 to Confidence.

In the USA, Ghosh and Fouad (2017) administered the *CAAS* and *MSPSS* 164 full-time students (90 females and 74 males) who were graduating from college. Their results were surprisingly opposite of the other five studies. The researchers reported a *negative* relation between career adaptability and social support. The correlations between the *MSPSS* and the *CAAS* subscales were -.22 for Concern, -.17 for Control, and -.17 for Confidence. The correlation to Curiosity was not significant (-.09). The researchers suggested that graduating seniors who are higher in career adaptability have less need for social support because they may be better equipped to consider, control, and confidently cope with the challenges of career decision making.

Although they did not use the *MSPSS*, Hlad'o, Kvaskova, Jezek, Hirschi, and Macek (2020) investigated the relation of career adaptability to four forms of social support. Working in the Czech Republic, they used a sample of 1,874 students in the final year at 44 vocational upper secondary schools. They measured parental support with the *Parent Career Behavior Checklist* (Keller & Whiston, 2008), which uses 15 items to measure psychosocial support and instrumental support. Teacher support was assessed with the *Teacher Support Scale* (Metheny, McWhirter, & O'Neil, 2008), which uses 21-items to measure perceptions of teacher support in terms of investment, positive regard, expectations, and accessibility. Peer support was measured with the seven-item *Close Friend Support Scale* (Hlad'o & Jezek, 2018).

The results indicated that perceived social support correlated .36 to the *CAAS* total score, and related significantly to all four dimensions of career adaptability. The findings indicated that diverse sources of social support contribute differently to the four adaptability dimensions. In the regression model, shown in Figure 12, parental psychosocial support had an effect on Concern (β = .22, p < .001), Control (β = .20, p < .001), and Confidence (β = .16, p < .001) but not on Curiosity (β = .06, ns). Teacher support and peer support were each found to be predictors of Concern (β = .18, p < .001 and β = .16, p < .001), Control (β = .08, p < .01 and (β = .22, p < .001), Curiosity (β = .10, p < .001 and β = .23, p < .001), and Confidence (β =.16, p < .001 and β = .17, p < .001). Parental action did not predict any of the four adapt-abilities, possibly explained as part of the individuation process that occurs during emerging adulthood. At that age, young people value emotional support linked with autonomy.

Figure 12. Sources of Social Support and Career Adaptability

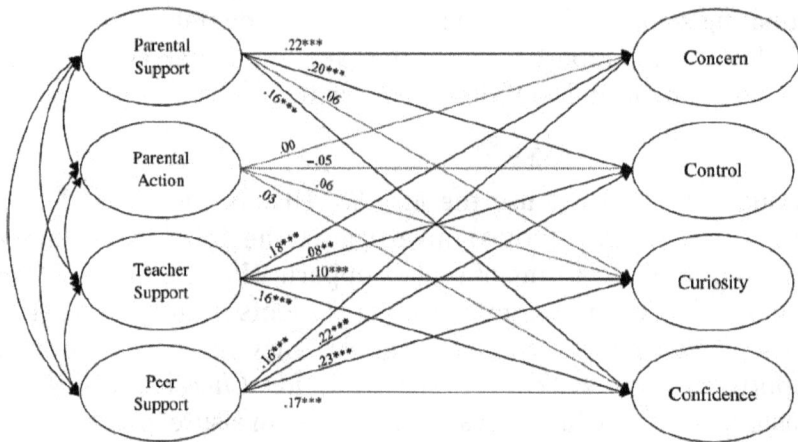

One study examined social support from a single source, namely, peers. Working in China, Wang and Fu (2015) used as participants 879 college seniors (423 males; Mean age = 21.5 years). They measured social support from "schoolmates" using the *Social Support Rating Scale* (Xiao, 1994), which consists of ten items across the three dimensions of objective support, subjective support, and support utilization. The *CAAS* total score correlated .39 to social support but not to gender (non-significant .06).

Rather than social support, Yuen and Yau (2015) studied sense of connectedness among Chinese male (298) and female (245) ninth-grade students in eight different Hong Kong schools. Connectedness refers to an individual's sense of belonging within a particular social group such as family, school, or friends. The researchers measured connectedness with the School, Teachers, Peers, and Parents Connectedness Subscales from the *Hemingway Measure of Adolescent Connectedness* (Karcher & Sass, 2010). Each subscale consists of six items. Career adaptability correlated to connectedness .31 to parents, .37 to school, .25 to peers, and .32 to teachers. The correlations between the four connectedness groups and the four adapt-abilities ranged from .25 to .37, with the exception of .12 between Concern and peer connectedness. The highest relations were between the four adapt-abilities and the connectedness groups was to school connectedness.

Career-Related Filial Piety

Filial piety offers a different perspective on parent-child relations. The Confucian concept of filial piety is an influential belief that may guide inter-generational relationships. In Chinese culture, the hierarchical parent–child relationship tends to influence academic choices, study motivation, career decisions, courtship, and psychosocial adjustment. Jin (2009) explained two different forms of filial piety relative to career development. Reciprocal filial piety involves attending to one's parents out of gratitude yet still provides opportunities for offspring to make their own choices and become self-determining. It involves talking with parents about career intentions while still choosing their own path if it enables them to repay their parents' love and nurturance once they start working. In comparison, authoritarian filial piety involves suppressing one's own ambitions and independence while submitting to parental wishes in making career decisions.

Working in Hong Kong, Hui, Yuen, and Chen (2018b) investigated the relation of career-related filial piety to career adaptability. The participants were 522 university students (69% females) who were studying business. Most of the participants (89.7%) were in their final year. The participants responded to the *Career-Related Filial Piety Scale* (Jin, 2009), which measures the two types of filial piety beliefs in the career decision-making process. Each dimension has eight items. An example item from the reciprocal beliefs dimensions reads, "I talk more with my parents to understand their thoughts and feelings about my career choices." An example item from the authoritarian beliefs dimension reads, "I take my parents' suggestions on career choices even when I do not agree with them." Results showed that the *CAAS* total score correlated .20 to reciprocal filial piety with correlations to the adapt-abilities ranging from .14 to .21. Neither the *CAAS* total score nor the four adapt-abilities scores correlated significantly to authoritarian filial piety. The findings suggest that students with reciprocal filial piety beliefs are better able to develop the self-regulation resources of adaptability.

Grandparents' and Parents' Role Modeling

In The Phillipines, Garcia, Restubogb, Ocampo, Wang, and Tang (2019) proposed that career adaptable grandparents are likely to shape the way their children's career values, skills, and knowledge. When that child grows up and becomes a parent, the grandparents in turn influence the career adaptability of their grandchildren. The researchers examined whether career adaptability can be socially learned and developed from one generation of a family to the next via role-modeling processes, as portrayed in Figure 13.

Figure 13. Inter-generational Transmission of Career Adaptability

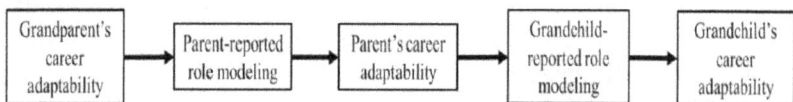

The researchers recruited 187 grandparent-parent-grandchild triads. The grandchildren were students (55.1%) with an average age of 20.57 years. The researchers measured career adaptability for each participant in a triad with the *CAAS-SF*. Student participants reported the extent to which they considered their parents as role models on a three-item scale developed by Ragins and McFarlin (1990). The items were "My parents served as a role model for me," "My parents represented who I want to be," and "My parents are people I identified with." For parent participants, role modeling was assessed retrospectively with the items written in the past tense.

116

Grandparents' career adaptability correlated .59 to parents' career adaptability and .16 to grandchildren's career adaptability. Parents' career adaptability correlated .28 to their children's career adaptability. Grandchildren's reported role modeling correlated .55 to their own career adaptability. Structural equation modeling results indicated that grandchild-reported role modeling mediated the positive relationship between parent's career adaptability and grandchild's career adaptability. This mediation also had a significant indirect effect after controlling for grandparent's career adaptability, parent-reported role modeling, and parent's and grandchild's demographic characteristics (indirect effect = .15). The direct association between parent's career adaptability and grandchild-reported career adaptability was not significant (direct effect = −.06). Results of a serial mediated effect linking grandparent's career adaptability *to* parent-reported role modeling to parent's career adaptability to grandchild-reported role modeling to grandchild's career adaptability suggested that the indirect effects were weak yet significant (indirect effect = .01), while the direct effect linking grandparent's career adaptability and grandchild's career adaptability was not significant.

Attachment Orientations during Adulthood

Attachment orientations formed during childhood usually continue throughout life and effect individuals' adaptability in meeting career challenges and changes. Three studies have examined relations between attachment orientations and career adaptability. Secure attachment to parents is though to foster exploration, decision making, and risk taking. Shin and Lee (2017) argued that secure attachment to peers may increase students' career adaptability resources and promote adapting responses. In contrast, insecure attachment may cause students to under-develop adaptability resources and adopt dysfunctional strategies to deal with vocational tasks, occupational transitions, and work troubles. To examine this idea, Shin and Lee hypothesized a mediation model in which insecure peer attachment associates with career adaptability through a sequence of career-choice pessimism and less intrinsic motivation. They tested the model in both the U.S. and

Korea to learn if the results would differ in individualistic and collectivistic cultures. They anticipated the results would be equivalent because of the similarities in the college students' career development experiences. They used the *Experiences in Close Relationship Scale–Short Form* (Wei, Russell, Mallinckrodt, & Vogel, 2007) to measure insecure attachment to peer groups along two dimensions: anxiety about abandonment (e.g., "I do not often worry about being not accepted by group of friends I have") and avoidance of closeness (e.g., "I prefer not to show a partner how I feel"). Career-choice pessimism was measured by the Pessimistic View Subscale of the *Emotional and Personality Career Difficulties Scale* (Saka & Gati, 2007). The Subscale is scored for pessimistic views about the career decision-making process (e.g., "I can't take all the relevant considerations into account when choosing a career"), the world job market (e.g., "Few careers are really interesting"), and one's general control of the process (e.g., "I have no control over the career possibilities that will be available for me in the future"). The Intrinsic Motivation Subscale of the *Career Decision-Making Autonomy Scale* (Guay, 2005) was used to measure self-determination or autonomy in decision making. A sample of 492 undergraduate students participated in the study. The U.S. sample (N = 198; 77.3% females) ranged in age from 18 to 39 years (Mean = 23.2). The Korean sample (N = 294; 42.9% females) ranged in age from 18 to 29 years (Mean = 22.26).

The hypothesized model was tested separately for the U.S.A. and Korean data. Results indicated an acceptable fit of the data to the model for both groups as shown in Figure 14 (U.S.A. sample above line, Korean sample below line). All factor loadings were significant (p < .001), thereby indicating that attachment, pessimism, intrinsic motivation, and career adaptability were well-represented by the indicators. The indirect effect of the two mediators supported the significant mediation effect of both pessimism and intrinsic motivation on the relationship between attachment and career adaptability in both the U.S.A. and Korean samples. The results provided empirical support for cross-cultural validation of the hypothesized model that links insecure attachment to career adaptability through career-choice pessimism and intrinsic motivation. In sum, participants with insecure peer attachment in

118

both cultures reported a higher level of pessimism, which decreased intrinsic motivation and led to weaker career adaptability resources.

Figure 14: Structural Model for Attachment, Motivation, and Adaptability

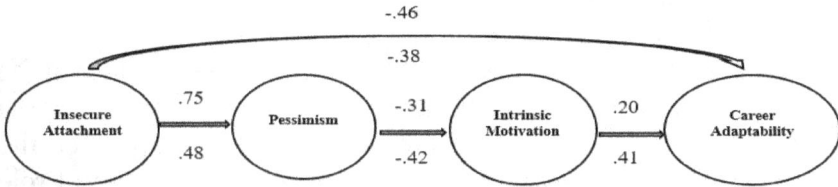

A second study that investigated attachment orientations as antecedents of career adaptability also used a version of the *Experience in Close Relationship Scale-Revised* (Fraley, Waller, & Brennan, 2000). Ramos and Lopez (2018) reasoned that secure attachment orientations facilitate the emergence and deployment of career adaptability resources during significant life transitions and lead to subjective well-being. Two groups of individuals participated in the study. The first group consisted of 298 young adults (234 females, 64 males) who were college seniors or recent graduates poised to enter the workforce. They ranged in age from 21 to 20 years (M = 23.36; SD = 2.25). The second group consisted of 169 older adults who were either contemplating retirement or recently retired. They ranged in age from 55 to 81 years (M = 64.58, SD = 5.62). Along with the *CAAS*, the participants responded to two measures of subjective well-being. The *Meaning in Life Questionnaire* (Steger, Frazier, Oishi, & Kaler, (2006), which consists of five items that measure presence of meaning (e.g., "I understand my life's meaning") and five items that measure search for meaning (e.g., "I am looking for something that makes my life feel meaningful"). For the total sample of 467 career transitioners, the *CAAS* total score correlated -.21 to attachment anxiety, -.22 to attachment avoidance, .32 to life satisfaction, .46 to presence of meaning, and .17 to search for meaning.

A series of three multiple regression analyses indicated that attachment and career adaptability each made unique contributions to markers of well-being. All three regression models confirmed that the inclusion of career adaptability after attachment orientation accounted for significant incremental variance in life satisfaction and life meaning scores. Career adaptability accounted for an additional 5% of the variance (β = .24) in life satisfaction scores, 15% of incremental variance (β = .40) in the presence of life meaning scores, and 5% of additional variance in the search for life meaning scores (β = .23). These regression results supported the idea that dispositional attachment orientations play a critical role in shaping adaptability resources for managing a career transition. The researchers concluded that being securely attached likely enhances an individual's access to internal coping resources for responding appropriately to career disequilibrium, which, in turn, positively influences their well-being during important career transitions.

A third study that related attachment orientations to career adaptability concentrated on attachment at work. Furness (2020) used a convenience sample of 210 respondents from a health-care organization (N = 92), an engineering consultancy (N = 22), and a management consultancy (N = 96). Within this sample, 53.4% were females and the mean age was 38 years old (SD =11.8). Career adaptability was measured with the *CAAS-SF*. Anxious and avoidant attachment were measured by five items each in the 10-item *Brief Attachment Questionnaire* (Leiter, Day, & Price, 2015). Example items read, "I fear that people at work will let me down" (anxious attachment) and "I don't need close relationships at work" (avoidant attachment). The *CAAS* total score correlated -.35 (p < .01) to anxious attachment and -.21 (p < .05) to avoidant attachment. A structural model, which included supervisor autonomy support and mastery goal orientation, supported the expectation that anxious attachment would negatively predict adaptability (β = -.30, p < .02). The researchers explained that anxious attachment may undermine career adaptability by limiting confidence when planning and navigating career transitions or by making people doubt whether others will provide sufficient support during career challenges and changes. Unexpectedly, avoidant attachment did not predict career adaptability (β = -.03 p < .79).

The researchers speculated that the disadvantages of avoidant attachment could be offset by its benefits. By maintaining social distance, those with high avoidant attachment may on their own somehow more successfully develop adaptability resources. Apparently each participant was given a score for both attachment orientations. It would be interesting to assign each participant to one of the two orientations and them analyze separately the results for the two groups of participants.

Conclusion

This Chapter discussed evidence that families and significant others foster the development of career adaptability in adolescents through career-specific parental behaviors and social support. The next Chapter discusses biographical antecedents of career adaptability.

CHAPTER 7

BIOGRAPHICAL ANTECEDENTS
OF CAREER ADAPTABILITY

Socio-biographical background factors influence the emergence and development of an individual's career adaptability resources. Personal niches of environmental interactions and particular activities can foster the formation of adaptability resources. Accordingly, researchers have examined the correlation between several biographical factors and career adaptability including parents' family business, work experiences, leisure activities, academic achievement, meaning life, and cultural orientation.

Family Business

The role of career adaptability in predicting entrepreneurial intentions was investigated by Tolentino, Sedoglavich, Lu, Raymund, Garcia, and Restubog (2014). They reasoned that career adaptability is instrumental in supplying the considerable self-regulative competence needed to form entrepreneurial intentions. They had business students (N = 380) in Serbia respond to the *CAAS* and indicate whether their father or mother ran their own business. Two months later, 180 of these students responded to an entrepreneurial self-efficacy scale and another two months later answered two questions about their entrepreneurial intentions. The students' *CAAS* total score correlated .17 to their family running a business and .30 to their own entrepreneurial intentions. Family business correlated .30 to entrepreneurial intentions. The researchers concluded that a family business can offer children forms of human capital that foster entrepreneurial intentions (e.g., role models, vicarious learning opportunities, feedback, support, and mentoring). Access to such resources during adolescence may foster a stronger willingness to invest time and effort in running a business.

Prior Work Experience

Student work experience refers to activities resulting from their own initiative and not related to a curricular program. Monteiro and Almeida (2015) investigated whether graduate students' work experience related to their career adaptability. In Portugal, they studied 406 graduate students (51% female, average age 25.6 years) majoring in four different fields: economics (25%); social sciences (14%); law (13%); and engineering (48%). They found no difference in total *CAAS* scores for students with and without work experience. They did report three significant but minor statistical differences on two subscales. Students who currently had a part-time job scored significantly higher on Control and Curiosity. Monteiro and Almeida also asked the students with a single item whether they anticipated any difficulties in the securing employment after graduation. Students who anticipated difficulties in this transition scored significantly lower on Control.

Leisure Activities

Monteiro and Almeida (2015) reported that there were no differences in career adaptability among Portuguese graduate students who participated in extra-curricular activities and those who did not participate. However, Celen-Demirtas, Konstam, and Tomek (2015) reported contrary findings relative to leisure activities. They hypothesized that leisure activities may be beneficial for vocational development. Celen-Demirtas and colleagues studied 184 unemployed, emerging adults (84 women, 100 men; Mean age = 25 years) to determine if frequency and quality of three types of leisure activities related to higher levels of career adaptability. The first type of leisure activity was relaxation, that is, activities that allow one to relax without doing anything physically or mentally straining (e.g., watching television). Achievement leisure activities challenge oneself (e.g., completing a puzzle, practicing a sport). And social leisure activities, the third type of leisure, involve socializing with others (e.g., talking on the phone, going out with others) no matter what people are actually doing. The relationship between *frequency* of leisure activity and adaptability was not significant. To measure *quality* of leisure activities, Celen-Demirta and colleagues assessed the degree to which each type of leisure activity satisfied the latent functions identified by Jahoda (1981): time structure, meaning, purpose, and sense of self. The quality of achievement and social leisure activities related to all four career adapt-abilities (the eight correlations ranged between .24 and .37). Relaxation related less strongly to Concern, Control, and Confidence but not to Curiosity. Multivariate analyses indicted that the emerging adults who experienced higher quality of achievement and social leisure activities reported higher levels of Concern, Control, Curiosity, and Confidence. In contrast, the quality of relaxation leisure activities did not independently contribute to career adaptability.

Academic Achievement

In a three-wave longitudinal study across one academic year, Negru-Subtirica and Pop (2016) examined how career adaptability and academic achievement influenced each other. They measured academic achievement as the mean of grades a student received for all school subjects, that is, Grade Point Average (GPA). The participants were 1,151 adolescents from seven schools in Northwestern Romania with a mean age of 16.5 years. Students in academic high schools composed 49% of the participants and 51% were students in vocational schools. All participants completed the same self-report questionnaires three times during one academic year, with an interval of 3 to 4 months between the measurement points. At Time 1, students self-reported the GPA they had achieved in the previous academic year and at Time 2 the GPA they had achieved in the first semester of the current academic year. At Time 3, the GPA for the second semester of the current academic year was collected from official school records. At Time 1 GPA correlated .26 to Concern, .08 to Control, .17 to Curiosity, and .13 to Confidence. Negru-Subtirica and Pop (2016) tested for cross-lagged associations between career adapt-abilities measured at Time 1 predicting educational achievement at Time 2 and educational achievement at Time 1 predicting career adaptability at Time 2. GPA was a strong positive predictor of Control and Confidence. They found positive unilateral links from academic achievement to career Control and Confidence. Interestingly, GPA did not significantly predict longitudinal changes in Curiosity. As expected, Concern had a significant positive effect on GPA and vice-versa. Higher GPA predicted increases in adolescents' Concern across time. These results were not moderated by adolescents' gender, age, nor school type. The pattern of results was the same for boys and girls, for adolescents enrolled in academic and vocational schools, and for early-to-middle and middle-to-late adolescents. Negru-Subtirica and Pop (2016) found no significant longitudinal links between GPA and Curiosity.

A subsequent study of career adaptability and academic performance reversed the model used by Negru-Subtirica and Pop (2016) to examine whether career adaptability predicts academic performance. To do so, Avram, Burtaverde and Zanfirescu (2019) investigated the mediation role of career adaptability in the relationship between personality dispositions (i.e., Extraversion, Conscientiousness, and Openness) and academic performance. They administered the *CAAS* together with the *IPIP-50* (Goldberg, 1992) to measure the FFM traits and the *HEXACO-60* (Ashton & Lee, 2009) to measure the six traits in the HEXACO model. Academic performance was indicated by the students' GPA obtained from school records. The participants were 437 undergraduate psychology students (85% females) in Romania. They ranged in age from 19 to 53 years (M = 22.5; *SD* = 5.85).

Results indicated that the *CAAS* total score correlated .16 to GPA, with the highest correlations to the adapt-abilities being .20 for Confidence and .16 for Concern. All the FFM personality traits related positively to career adaptability, with the strongest correlates to career adaptability being between Agreeableness (.49), Openness (.44) and Conscientiousness (.42). Four of the six traits in the HEXACO model related to career adaptability, with the CAAS total score correlating highest to Conscientiousness (.48) and Extraversion (.47).

Career adaptability mediated the relationship between FFM Extraversion, HEXACO Openness, and FFM Conscientiousness on one hand, and academic performance on the other hand. Results of mediation analyses confirmed the mediation role of career adaptability in the relationship between FFM Extraversion and academic performance (β = .04). In addition, results indicated that the direct effect of FFM Extraversion on academic performance became non-significant (β = .00) when controlling for career adaptability, suggesting full mediation. Results of mediation analyses confirmed the mediation role of career adaptability in the relationship between HEXACO Openness and academic performance (β = .03). In addition, results indicated that the direct effect of HEXACO Openness on academic performance became non-significant when controlling for career adaptability, suggesting full mediation. A third mediation analysis indicated that career adaptability mediated the relation between FFM Conscientiousness and academic performance (β = .06). The direct effect of Conscientiousness on academic performance became non-significant after controlling for career adaptability, again suggesting full mediation. The researchers concluded that these findings can be explained by assuming that academic performance is largely determined by dispositional characteristics and dynamic activation of adaptability resources.

Meaning in Life

A study of meaning in life was conducted by Yuen and Yau (2015) with Chinese male (298) and female (245) ninth-grade students in eight different Hong Kong schools. The researchers measured "presence of meaning in life' and "search for meaning in life" with the two five-item subscales in the *Meaning in Life Questionnaire* (Steger, Frazier, Oishi, & Kaler, 2006). Adaptability correlated .41 to presence of meaning and .30 to search for meaning. Among the four adapt-abilities, presence of meaning correlated highest to Concern (.50) and lowest to Curiosity (.31). Search for meaning correlated highest to Curiosity (.32) and lowest to Concern (.18). Thus the adaptability profiles differed in expected ways for those with present meaning and those searching for meaning. Present meaning related strongest to Concern with making plans, possibly to implement present meaning in career choices. Search for meaning related strongest to Curiosity, possibly to explore the world for life and career options. In sum, career adaptability resources seem strongest for individuals who experience a sense of life meaning.

Meaning as a sense of coherence was studied by Harry and Coetze (2013) among 409 early career staff employed at a call center in South Africa. The *Orientation to Life Questionnaire* (*OLQ-29*; Antonovsky, 1987), was used to measure the participants' sense of coherence. The *OLQ-29* consists of 29 Likert-type self-rating items. Respondents are required to make a choice from a seven-point semantic differential scale with two anchoring phrases. The *OLQ-29* contains three sub-dimensions: (a) comprehensibility (11 items); (b) manageability (10 items); and (c) meaningfulness (8 items).

The *CAAS-Research Form* total score correlated .30 to the *OLQ-29* total score, with correlations of .29 to Concern, .27 to Control, .15 to Curiosity, and .24 to Confidence. The *CAAS* total score correlated .45 to the meaningfulness score. That score indicates the degree to which one's life is meaningful, makes sense on an emotional level, and that life's demands are worthy of commitment. Due to the low Cronbach's alpha coefficients obtained for the *OLQ-29* comprehensibility and manageability subscales ($\alpha < .70$), they scales were omitted from the statistical analyses.

Cultural Orientation: Individualism versus Collectivism

The relationship between career adaptability and the cultural values of individualism and collectivism was studied in Malaysia by Omar and Noordin (2016). Individualism denotes being independent, competitive, and working towards personal goals. In comparison, collectivism denotes being interdependent in valuing joint effort and rewards. Within both individualism and collectivism, people can be further distinguished by emphasizing horizontal equality versus vertical inequality. Putting the constructs in a two-by-two grid results in four types. Vertical collectivism emphasizes interdependent self-construals and accepts hierarchical inequality among members of a collective. Vertical individualism emphasizes independent self-construals and accepts hierarchical inequality among members of a collective. Horizontal collectivism emphasizes interdependent self-construals and values equality among members of a collective. Horizontal individualism emphasizes independent self-construals and values equality among members of a collective. Omar and Noordin (2016) investigated whether individuals who hold these four types of cultural values differ in career adaptability. They measured the four cultural orientations with the *Horizontal and Vertical Individualism and Collectivism Scale* (Singelis, Triandis, Bhawuk, & Gelfand, 1995). Example items read, "I often do my own thing" (HI); "The well-being of my co-workers is important to me" (HC); "It annoys me when other people perform better than me" (VI); and "I would sacrifice an activity that I enjoy very much if my family did not approve of it" (VC). The researchers administered the measure of cultural orientation and the *CAAS* to 303 (43% females) information and communication technology professionals in Malaysia.

The results indicated that, overall, information and communication technology professionals in Malaysia held cultural values favoring a vertical-collectivist orientation. The researchers concluded that the positive relationships between the constructs of individualism-collectivism and the constructs of career adaptability provide evidence that cultural orientations do influence the development of career adaptability. The four cultural orientations each correlated significantly to the four adapt-abilities. The highest average correlation of the four adapt-abilities was to horizontal individualism (Mean = .44). The other three cultural orientations average correlation to the adapt-abilities were .30 to horizontal collectivism, .29 to vertical individualism, and .26 to vertical collectivism. The findings suggest that cultural values oriented toward individual autonomy among equals relates to stronger development of career adaptability.

Conclusion

This Chapter addressed socio-biographical background factors that influence the emergence and development of an individual's career adaptability resources. These factors included significant experiences, activities, and achievements that may foster development of adaptability resources during adolescence. The next Chapter concentrates on the relation between career adaptability and employment status.

CHAPTER 8

CAREER ADAPTABILITY AND EMPLOYMENT STATUS

The adaptations required by seeking and maintaining a job trigger the use of self-regulatory capacities to shape responses to changes in employment status and the challenges of job insecurity. Several researchers have examined the relation of career adaptability resources to employability, unemployment, job insecurity, and refugee resettlement.

Employability

The term *employability* refers to the general and non-technical competencies required for getting, keeping, and doing well on a job, regardless of type. Employers have identified three foundational employability skills that enable workers to meet the demands of ever-changing occupational situations: (a) communication, (b) problem solving, and (c) teamwork. To study the relation of employment skills to adaptability, De Guzman and Choi (2013) constructed a measure consisting of ten-items for each of the three key skills. An example communication item reads, "I have the ability to express ideas verbally to others." An example problem-solving item reads, "I have the ability to gather information to solve problems." An example teamwork item reads, "I have the ability to understand the needs of others." In a group of 183 female students in the 12th grade in Papua, New Guinea, the *CAAS* total score correlated .59 to the employability skills total score, with correlation of 67 to teamwork, .48 to communication, and .44 to problem solving. Canonical correlation analysis between the three skills and the four adapt-abilities produced one significant function defined by teamwork skills and concern. The researchers concluded that teamwork skills may a useful indicator for career adaptability in the culture of New Guinea.

In a study of 196 early career professional in the field of human resources, Coetzee, Ferreira, and Potgieter (2015) examined the relation between employment skills and adaptability resources. They defined employability as the ability to gain and maintain employment and manage transitions between jobs and roles in the same organization. They measured employability skills with the *Graduate Skills and Attributes Scale (GSAS;* Coetzee, 2012). The *GSAS* is a multi-factorial measure of generic attributes that add to the "graduateness" of university graduates. It consists of 64 items on eight subscales: (a) problem solving and decision-making skills (eight items; e.g., 'I consider the complexities of the larger cultural, business, and economic reality when approaching a problem or situation'), (b) enterprising skills (nine items; e.g., 'I find it easy to identify business opportunities for myself, my community or organization'), (c) analytical thinking skills (four items; e.g., 'I can make a rational judgment from analyzing information and data'), (d) interactive skills (16 items; e.g., 'I find it easy to communicate effectively with people from different cultures, backgrounds and authority levels'), (e) presenting and applying information skills (five items; e.g., 'The solutions I offer make a positive difference in my personal life, community or workplace'); (f) ethical and responsible behavior (five items; e.g., 'I uphold the ethics and values of my profession, community or workplace in all I do'), (g) goal-directed behavior (10 items; e.g., 'I develop plans for specific goals and tasks') and (h) continuous learning orientation (seven items; e.g., 'I make sure that I keep myself up to date on technical knowledge and new developments in my field'). Individuals respond to the 64 items on a six-point Likert scale.

The *CAAS* total score correlated .46 to the *GSAS* total score. Zero-order correlation coefficients between the *CAAS* total score and the eight *GSAS* subscales ranged from .38 for enterprising skills to .45 for continuous learning, with the single exception of .19 for analytical thinking skills. A canonical correlation analysis between the four *CAAS* subscales and the eight *GSAS* subscales resulted in one significant function that explained 43% of the variance between the two variates. *CAAS* subscale loadings on the function were the lowest for Concern (Rc = .43) in comparison with Control (Rc = .83), Curiosity (Rc = .83), and Confidence (Rc = .90). Loadings for the *GSAS* subscales were highest for goal-directed behavior (Rc = .90) and continuous learning (Rc = .90), followed by problem solving and decision-making skills (Rc = .83) and interactive skills

(Rc = .82). The career adaptability variables contributed positively in explaining the variance in especially goal-directed behaviour (Rc = .48; 23%), continuous learning orientation (Rc = .48; 23%), problem-solving and decision-making skills (Rc = .44; 19%), interactive skills (Rc = .44; 19%) and enterprising skills (Rc = .40; 16%). These findings showed that the three adapt-abilities of Control, Curiosity, and Confidence contributed the most to explaining higher levels of goal-directed behavior and continuous learning orientation that helps individuals adapt to unexpected changes in the labor market or working conditions.

Unemployment

Career adaptability resources shape search strategies for re-employment following job loss (Koen, Klehe, Van Vianen, Zikic, & Nauta, 2010). Unemployed individuals typically (re)activate and upgrade these resources in order to manage the job search process. Accordingly, career adaptability resources increase after the first months of unemployment and then tend to remain stable. This explains why unemployed individuals generally score higher on the *CAAS* than do employed individuals. For example, Duarte, Soares, Fraga, Lima, Paredes, Agostinho, and Djaló. (2012) reported that in Portugal 266 unemployed adults scored significantly higher than 395 employed adults on career Concern, Control, and Curiosity. Duarte and her colleagues concluded that unemployed adults may be more aware of the importance and need to improve their adaptability resources in order to obtain new employment opportunities. Maggori, Johnston, Krings, Massoudi, and Rossier (2013) reported results similar to those of Duarte and her colleagues (2012) in showing that unemployed participants had higher total scores and stronger adapt-abilities resources.

In a study with similar findings, Johnston, Maggiori, and Rossier (2016) examined whether career adapt-abilities could be considered as resources that individuals activate when needed. The researchers used data from a representative sample of workers in Switzerland to find whether levels of career adaptability varied according to their professional situations during one year. At Time

1, an initial sample of 2,469 (49.3% male) employed and unemployed participants aged between 26 and 56 years (Mean age = 42.5) was obtained. At Time 2 one year later, all participants who started the research protocol at Time 1 were invited to participate in the study again. Of these, 1,944 participants (49.4% males) aged between 27 and 57 years (Mean age = 43.5) responded. The final group of participants included the 1,608 individuals (48.5% males) aged between 27 and 57 years (Mean age = 43.4) who responded to all the protocols in both waves. The researchers categorized the participants into four groups. The first group (no change active group, N=1,041) had no change in employment during the year. The second group remained employed yet experienced a change of employer or change in role while remaining with the same employer (change-active group, N=217). The third group moved from unemployment to employment (employment active group, N=189). And, the fourth group was unemployed and remained unemployed (unemployed-unemployed group, N=161). One-way analysis of covariance showed significant differences in *CAAS* scores between the four professional groups (F = 12.96, p < .001). The unemployed-active group had the highest levels of adaptability (3.91), followed by the unemployed-unemployed (3.86), change-active (3.83), and no change-active groups (3.74). This result confirmed and extended previous cross-sectional findings (Maggori et al., 2013) concerning group differences in adaptability and showed, with a longitudinal perspective, that adaptability is a resource that individuals can activate in response to the professional environment and may be an important element in career development.

Interestingly, the studies by Duarte et al. and Maggori et al. both reported an increase in Concern, Control, and Curiosity, but not Confidence. Maggori and colleagues agreed with Duarte and colleagues that unemployed individuals (re)activate and upgrade some resources to conduct a job search and gain reemployment. Furthermore, this interpretation seems to be supported by the differences in terms of adapt-abilities resources highlighted in relation to the length of unemployment. The data from Maggori and colleagues showed that after the first months of unemployment adapt-ability resources increased and tended to remain stable. In their sample, the *CAAS* total score was 3.6 in the first one-to-three months of unemployment but increased to 4.0 in months four to ten, and for those unemployed for eleven or more months was 3.8. In sum, the studies in both Portugal and Switzerland indicated that adapt-ability resources are in varying states of activation depending on contextual contingencies.

Underemployment

Unemployed means that an individual does not have a job; while underemployment means that the person has higher levels of skill, knowledge, ability, education, and experience than the job requires. Woo (2020) addressed the concern that employees who perceive themselves as being over-qualified tend to experience lower job satisfaction and higher turnover intention. He speculated that alternatively they may use job crafting to proactively redesign and reinterpret their job. Job crafting is defined as the physical and cognitive behavior employees used to initiate job-relevant changes in their work and relationships. Woo (2020) hypothesized that career adaptability may be a factor that moderates the relationship between perceived over-qualification and job crafting. Depending on the level of career adaptability, perceptions of over-qualification can lead either to frustration or opportunities for a challenge.

To test his hypothesis, Woo (2020) conducted a study with 257 employees who worked in call centers at three Korean telecom companies. The employees had five or less years of work experience. He measured perceived over-qualification using nine items that assess the level of perceived over-qualification based on education, experience, knowledge, skills, and ability (Maynard, Joseph, & Maynard, 2006). An example item reads, "I feel confident in designing new procedures for my work area." Job crafting was measured using the *Job Crafting Questionnaire* (Slemp & Vella-Brodrick, 2013), which has 15 questions, with five questions being allocated to each of the three sub-factors of job crafting identified by Wrzesniewski and Dutton (2001): task crafting, relational crafting, and cognitive crafting. Career adaptability was measured using the *CAAS*.

Results showed that the *CAAS* total score correlated .37 (p < .01) to job crafting. Perceived over-qualification did not correlate significantly to career adaptability (r = .03) nor job crafting (r = .09). The hypothesis that perceived over-qualification has a significant non-linear influence with an inverted U-shape on job crafting was supported. Career adaptability moderated the relation of perceived over-qualification to job crafting (R^2 = .20). Higher career adaptability led to strengthening of the inverted U-shaped relationship between perceived over-qualification and job crafting. However, lower career adaptability associated with a weaker curved relationship between perceived over-qualification and job crafting. Woo (2020) concluded that for individuals with average or high levels of career adaptability, an appropriate level of perceived over-qualification prompts job crafting.

Job Insecurity

While unemployed individuals seem to activate and increase their adaptability resources, so do employed individuals who experience job insecurity. Workers who face career circumstances such as new job demands, reduced work hours, or potential job loss tend to activate or increase their adaptability resources. Maggori, Johnston, Krings, Massoudi, and Rossier (2013) evaluated the impact of job insecurity (past and future) on career adaptability. They used a representative sample of 2002 employed adults (Mean age = 41.99 years) who lived in the French- and German-speaking regions of Switzerland. They measured general professional insecurity with two items. The first item asked participants how many times during the last year they faced the risk of losing their job. The second item asked how they evaluated the risk of losing their current job in the next year. The *CAAS* total score correlated .50 to past job insecurity and .17 to future job insecurity. Employed individuals who felt low future job insecurity showed greater adaptability resources than did employed individuals who felt high job insecurity. Maggori and colleagues speculated that greater adaptability resources may even help workers remain in more stable professional situations.

In a related study, Urbanaviciute, Udayar, Maggori, and Rossier (2020) examined the role of career adaptability in counter-acting job insecurity, which they defined as the perceived threat of losing one's job. To compare job insecurity among different groups of employees, the researchers constructed precariousness profiles by combining the two vulnerability indicators of perceived income difficulties and lack of employability. The participants were 799 employed adults (49.2% females; Mean age at Time 1 = 45.13; SD = 8.10) from a wide variety of occupations. Data were drawn from three yearly waves (2014–2016) of a longitudinal survey on professional paths. The participants indicated their perceived difficulty to find a similar job to the one that they had at the time (1 = very difficult, 4 = very easy). Second, they rated how easy or difficult it was to survive with their household income (1 = very easy, 4 = very difficult). Using this information from Time 1, the researchers clustered the participants into three precariousness profiles: (a) a precarious profile of high financial difficulties and low employability (N = 271); (b) a non-precarious profile with below-average financial difficulties and high employability (N = 273); a partially-precarious profile with low financial difficulties and low employability (N = 255). Career adaptability was measured at Time 1 with the *CAAS–SF*. Job insecurity was measured at all three occasions with three items specifically designed for the study. The first item measured satisfaction with job security (1 = very satisfied, 4 = very dissatisfied), the second item measured fear of job loss in the upcoming 12 months (1 = do not fear, 4 = highly fear), and the third item measured cognitive evaluation of good job security (1 = totally agree, 4 = totally disagree). A composite indicator of job insecurity was derived based on the mean score of these items.

To begin the analyses, Urbanaviciute and colleagues calculated bivariate correlations between the study variables. The *CAAS* total score at Time 1 correlated to job insecurity -.21 at Time 1, -.19 at Time 2, and -.17 at Time 3. Among the adapt-abilities, Concern (-.21, -.22, -.18) and Control (-.20. -.18, -.15) had stronger correlations to job insecurity than did Curiosity (-.11, -.09, -.10) and Confidence (-15, -.10, -.13). The researchers continued the analyses by investigating career adaptability as a predictor of mean levels of job insecurity. The results showed a negative relationship between career adaptability and the levels of job insecurity in the precarious and the non-precarious profiles, the link being insignificant in the partially precarious profile. While both overall adaptability and the four adapt-abilities individually were generally linked with lower levels of job insecurity, the adapt-abilities did seem to be equally relevant in job-insecure situations. For the precarious profile, Concern was the only significant predictor, suggesting that in vulnerable populations maintaining Concern and interest in developing one's career may help cope with insecurity. For the non-precarious profile, Control was the only adapt-ability that significantly predicted levels of job insecurity, with a higher score relating to reduced levels of job insecurity. Looking at the growth of job insecurity across the three measurement periods, the researchers found that in the precarious profile higher Control related to higher rates of growth in job insecurity. This finding may imply that a precarious situation restricts one's opportunities to apply control-oriented resources, which results in increased job insecurity.

Refugee Resettlement

In a conceptual article, Campion (2018) explained that the strong positive relationship of career adaptability to objective markers of success (e.g., pay and job quality) does not necessarily generalize to refugees who likely experience downward occupational mobility. Vulnerable refugees may concentrate first on building social networks and then on employment by seeking jobs occupied by those in their social network. Campion proposed that career adaptability relates positively to the generation of a social network in the refugee job-search process. Subsequently, the use of social ties may mediate the relationship between career adaptability and both objective and subjective resettlement success.

Drawing from Career Construction Theory, Pajic, Ulcelsue, Kismihok, Mol, and den Hartong (2018) hypothesized that adaptive readiness in terms of psychological capital relates positively to job-search self-efficacy through career adaptability. They also examined two sets of career barriers that might strain refugees' self-regulatory mechanisms, weakening the effects of career adaptability on desirable outcomes. Administrative barriers include immigration policies and bureaucratic rules whereas social barriers include differences in cultural backgrounds and social practices. The researchers tested their model with refugees from Syria because Syria represents the most common origin country of approved asylum applicants within the European Union. The participants consisted of 330 refugees who had settled in The Netherlands (59.4%) or Greece (40.6%). They had an average age of 31.72 years (SD = 8.33), with 30.6% being females. The majority of participants held a bachelor's degree (36.4%) or high school diploma (30.9%). Psychological capital was measured with the 12-item *Compound-Psychological-Capital Questionnaire* (Lorenz, Beer, Pütz, & Heinitz, 2016). The scale consists of four subscales that measure hope (e.g., "If I should find myself in a jam, I could think of many ways to get out of it"), resilience (e.g., It's okay if there are people who don't like me"), optimism ("The future holds a lot of good in store for me"), and self-efficacy ("I can remain calm when facing difficulties because I can rely on my coping abilities). Self-efficacy about job- search behaviors was measured using Saks, Zikic, and Koen's (2015) 10-item scale. An example item reads, "Plan and organize a weekly job search schedule." Administrative barriers were measured by five items (e.g., "Not having my qualifications recognized") as were social barriers (e.g., "Not fitting in the local culture") obtained from Bloch (2002).

The results showed that the *CAAS* total score correlated .53 to psychological capital and .43 to job-search self-efficacy. The *CAAS* did not correlate significantly to social barriers (-.08) nor administrative barriers (-.08). The path model shown in Figure 15 indicates that career adaptability resources provided critical self-regulatory strengths for adapting to occupational transition within the destination country. Hope, optimism, resilience, and self-efficacy together related positively to career adaptability resources, which in turn related to higher confidence in performing behaviors relevant for finding a job in the destination country. Psychological capital related indirectly to job search self-efficacy through career adaptability.

Figure 15. Adaptability and Refugee Job-Search Self-Efficacy

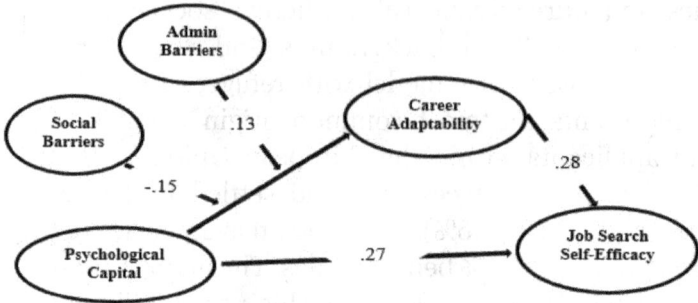

To further examine the mediation model, the researchers tested the role of both social and administrative career barriers as external contingencies that condition the positive relationships among psychological capital, career adaptability, and job-search self-efficacy. Unexpectedly, the social and administrative barriers differed in their consequences. As expected, the relationship between psychological capital and career adaptability was moderated negatively by social career barriers ($\beta = -.15$). When experienced social barriers were lower, the positive indirect relationship between psychological capital and job-search self-efficacy was stronger than when experienced social barriers were higher. The researchers suggested that the experience of not fitting into the culture of the destination country seems to create feelings of misfit between a person and the local environment, thereby weakening the positive self-regulatory mechanisms related to psychological capital and, at a high level of social barriers, even diminishing the strength of these relationships.

Administrative barriers also moderated the indirect effect of psychological capital on job-search self-efficacy but in a positive direction ($\beta = .13$). Contrary to expectations, when experienced administrative barriers were higher, the positive indirect relationship between psychological capital and job-search self-efficacy was stronger than when such barriers were lower. High administrative barriers, although negatively related to job-search self-efficacy, did not appear to compromise the positive role of adaptive readiness or adaptability resources in job-search self-efficacy. The researchers suggested that individuals may experience administrative barriers as inevitable hassles that probably disappear once handled, whereas overcoming social barriers may present long-term challenges.

Cultural contexts can either impede or facilitate individuals' adaptability resources and their use. Most research on the CCT model of adaptation has concentrated on the person with little attention to the role of context. However, understanding the adaptation process is incomplete without considering contextual factors. In a qualitative study, Wehrle, Kira, and Klehe (2019) investigated the content of the four adapt-abilities and their adapting enactment in refugees' adaptation to the host country's labor market. The researchers conducted semi-structured interviews with 36 individuals who were making involuntary career transitions to resettle in Germany. The refugees held a work permit and had sought or secured employment. The participants came from seven different countries and were mostly male (30 men), young (Mean age = 32 years), and single (23).

Through analysis of the interview transcripts, the researchers unraveled the constraining and enabling influences of the context on refugees' career adaptability resources and adapting responses after resettlement. Deficits in adapt-abilities combined with contextual barriers to cause career transition problems. Contextual factors seemed to stifle the Control and Confidence adapt-abilities, resulting respectively in feeling helpless and doubting their ability to overcome obstacles. The researchers indicated that the Concern and Curiosity adapt-abilities remained strong in themselves yet the context restricted their implementation in terms of adapting behaviors. Although being Concerned and Curious, the participants could not enact associated adapting responses such as making plans and exploring themselves and the environment. The researchers related this finding to the CCT proposition that setting only present and proximal goals indicates a lack of Concern. They explained that when facing uncertainties and feeling pressured to quickly get a job, many refugees oriented their planning to short-term goals, just to stabilize their situations by taking immediate opportunities available in the context. Although long-term planning was often difficult, the participants still showed intense Concern about their futures. In the end, the researchers identified two overarching contextual enablers particularly relevant to Confidence and Curiosity. First, social connections that led to feeling understood and supported bolstered the adapt-ability of Confidence. Second, opportunities offered by the educational system and by employers bolstered the adapt-ability of Curiosity. Furthermore, two adaptive characteristics also strengthened refugees' adapt-abilities of Concern and Control, namely, a '"can do" personality and an optimistic attitude.

In a study of 267 refugees (Mean age =27.5 years; 78.1% males) newly arrived in Germany mostly from Syria about for months previously, Obschonka, Hahn, and Bajwa (2018) studied personal agency in the early integration process. In particular, they examined personality factors relevant for agentic processes in the early stage of the integration process among newly arrived refuges. They defined three aspects of adaptive readiness as background factors in adaptive readiness: risk taking, resilience, and self-efficacy. They hypothesized that these factors predict entrepreneurial alertness, which is a proximal predictor of career adaptability and entrepreneurial intentions. In the CCT model of adaptation, entrepreneurial alertness consists of cognitions that shape career adaptability resources. Alertness to opportunities should foster adaptability in respect to entrepreneurial opportunities. The researchers measured career adaptability with the *CAAS*. They measured entrepreneurial alertness in pursuit of new opportunities with a 13-item scale (Tang, Kacmar, & Busenitz (2012) that assesses three types of cognitions, namely scanning and searching, association and connection, and evaluation and judgment. Cognitions about intentions to become an entrepreneur and start one's own firm were measured by a six-item scale (Linan, & Chen, 2009).

Results indicated that the three dimensions of entrepreneurial alertness correlated to the four adapt-abilities ranging from .40

(Concern to Evaluation and Judgment) to .57 (Confidence to Evaluation and Judgment), with a mean correlation of .48. Entrepreneurial intentions correlated .36 to Concern, .25 to Control, .29 to Curiosity, and .30 to Confidence. Structural equation modeling showed that entrepreneurial alertness had substantial effects on both career adaptability (β = .56) and entrepreneurial intentions (β = .59), but unexpectedly there was not a significant effect between the two despite their bivariate correlation. Based on their findings, the researchers suggested that newly arrived refugees with entrepreneurial cognitions may unlock their entrepreneurial spirit and career adaptability to cope with uncertainties and barriers in the early stage of the integration process.

Conclusion

This chapter discussed how the adaptations required by seeking and maintaining a job activate the use of self-regulatory resources to deal with employability, unemployment, job insecurity, and refugee resettlement. The next Chapter begins a set of seven Chapters that each examine the relation of career adaptability to the other components in the CCT model of adaptation. Chapter 9 begins the set of Chapters by describing the relation of adaptive readiness to adaptability resources.

CHAPTER 9

ADAPTIVE READINESS RELATES
TO ADAPTABILITY RESOURCES

In the Career Construction Theory (CCT) model of adaptation, adaptive readiness precedes and activates adaptability resources as portrayed in Figure 16. The model conceptualizes adaptivity in terms of personality as a point of view or perspective from which individuals interpret the environment and, when needed, activate career adaptability resources to better adjust to that environment. The current chapter begins with an explanation of adaptivity as a compound trait of personality and then discusses how researchers have investigated the relation of adaptability resources to three different models of personality organization – single trait models, hierarchical trait models, and motivation models. The career adaptation model distinguishes between traits as indicators of *readiness* to activate adaptability responses and motivation as *willingness*. This is relevant to developing and activating career adapt-abilities because personality traits describe attributes, but they are not as good as motivational variable in predicting performance.

Figure 16. Adaptivity Relates to Adaptability in CCT Model

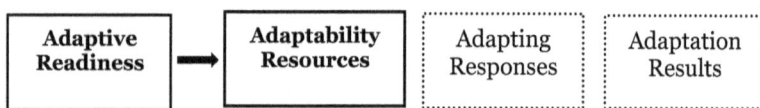

Adaptive Readiness as a Compound Trait

Personality acts as a filter through which individuals interpret the environment and, when needed, activate self-regulation processes to better deal with transitions (Rossier, Zecca, Stauffer, Maggiori, & Dauwalder, 2012). When encountering career changes and challenges, individuals differ in the quickness with which they perceive a need to change and the promptness in which they engage adaptability resources and enact adapting responses. This individual difference variable is denoted in CCT as adaptivity, or readiness and willingness to respond to change. The CCT adaptation model views adaptivity as a relatively stable and general personality trait or behavioral pattern that disposes an individual to be ready and willing to change to meet the demands of new situations. In comparison, career adaptability encompasses individual differences that are neither embedded in personality nor dispositional. Career adaptability resources are more dynamic, subject to change, and intermittently activated. Adaptivity and adaptability interrelate to the degree that an adaptivity trait includes encodings, expectations, beliefs, goals, and values pertinent to the dynamics of adaptability in the career context. Accordingly, career adaptability resources may correlate to particular adaptive readiness dispositions of personality such as proactivity, Conscientiousness, and Openness, yet adaptivity is not a narrow personality trait.

Adaptive readiness itself is a compound or global trait that contains multiple specific traits and motivations that relate broadly to patterns of behavior over time and across situations (Funder, 1991). As a complex amalgam of individual traits that function together, adaptivity constitutes an action orientation that prompts responses to changing circumstances and maintains movement across transitions. Compound traits have greater explanatory power across a wider range of situations and behaviors than does an elemental trait, which relates narrowly to one or two specific behaviors. A narrow trait such as proactivity may increase correlations when predicting behavior, but it decreases the range of behaviors that can be predicted.

To understand how personality traits are organized in the compound trait of adaptivity, researchers have investigated three different structures. The structures each concentrate on three different elements as central constructs in personality organization. The first structure consists of *single trait models* that represent adaptivity with one personality traits. The second structure consists of hierarchical trait models. And, the third structure consists of *motivational systems models* that concentrate on basic dimensions of approach and avoidance in goal pursuit. Each of these three structures have been used in research to represent adaptivity. The three models are discussed separately in the following three sections of this Chapter, beginning with a discussion of single traits used to represent adaptive readiness.

Single Trait Models of Adaptive Readiness

This section reports studies that used single personality traits as proxies for adaptive readiness and examined their relationships to career adaptability. Elemental traits examined in this section include proactivity, time perspective, emotional intelligence, attention control, self-esteem, and core self-evaluations.

Proactivity

The most single personality trait used most frequently by researchers to represent the construct of adaptive readiness is *proactivity*, defined as "a dispositional tendency to take initiative across a range of situations and activities" (Crant, 2000). Proactivity as a personality trait indicates "an effort to build-up general resources that facilitate promotion toward challenging goals and personal growth" (Luszczynska, Diehl, Gutiérrez-Doña, Kuusinen, & Schwarzer, 2004, p. 558). In the CCT model of adaptation, this means striving to improve one's career circumstances and developing the career adaptability resources to do so. Thus, highly proactive people tend to develop their career adapt-abilities and readily use them to form adapting responses that accomplish developmental tasks, bridge occupational transitions, and resolve work troubles. Fourteen studies that used proactivity as a proxy for adaptivity have confirmed its relationship to adaptability. Twelve of the fourteen studies measured proactive personality with the original 17-item *Proactive Personality Scale* (Bateman & Crant, 1993) or the 10-item *Proactive Personality Scale-Short Form* (Seibert, Crant, & Kraimer, 1999). Three example items read, "No matter what the odds, if I believe in something I will make it happen;" "I am constantly on the lookout for ways to improve myself;" and "I always look for better ways to do things."

The relationship between proactivity and adaptability was examined by Cai, Guan, Li, Shi, Guo, Liu, Li, Han, Jiang, Fang, and Hua (2015) in a two-wave study conducted with Chinese university students (N = 305). They measured proactive personality with the *Proactive Personality Scale* (Bateman & Crant, 1993). Self-esteem was measured with the 10-item *Self-Esteem Scale* (Rosenberg, 1965). An example item reads, "On the whole, I am satisfied with myself." The results showed that both self-esteem and proactive personality measured at Time 1 predicted career adaptability measured at Time 2. Career adaptability correlated .32 to proactivity and .30 to self-esteem. Both proactivity and self-esteem correlated the strongest to the adapt-ability of Confidence (r = .38). Through bootstrapping tests, the researchers confirmed that at higher levels of the proactive personality trait, the indirect effect of self-esteem on career adaptability was stronger.

Also in China, Gao, Xin, Zhou, and Jepsen (2019) examined the relationships between the *CAAS* and proactive personality as measured by the *Proactive Personality Scale-Short Form* (Seibert, Crant, & Kraimer, 1999). They collected data from 232 employees who worked for a Chinese manufacturing company with branches in Beijing, Tianjin, Shanghai and Shenzhen. Of the participants, 40% were females and 60% were males, with an average age of 32.7 years (SD = 5.27). Bivariate correlation coefficients indicated that proactive personality correlated .73 to the *CAAS* total score, with correlations of .60 to Concern, .61 to Control, .66 to Curiosity, and .69 to Confidence.

Using the *Proactive Personality Scale-Short Form* (Seibert, Crant, & Kraimer, 1999) and the *Self-Esteem Scale* (Rosenberg, 1965), Oncel (2014) studied 332 college seniors in Turkey. Self-esteem correlated .44 to the *CAAS* total score with the highest correlation being .43 to the adapt-ability of Control. Proactive personality correlated .49 to the *CAAS* total score with the single highest correlation being .46 to the adapt-ability of Confidence.

Self-esteem correlated to proactive personality .36. The difference in results from Cai and colleagues (2015) might be due to cultural differences between Turkey and China.

Using the *Proactive Personality Scale* (Bateman & Crant, 1993) in Singapore, Uy, Chan, Sam, Ho, and Chernyshenko (2015) tested 750 college students (45% females) with a mean age of 23.25 years (SD = 1.51). Proactivity correlated .63 to the *CAAS* total score, and .46 to Concern, .52 to Control, .59 to Curiosity, and .53 to Confidence.

In a fifth study of proactivity, Hou, Wu, and Liu (2014) examined its relation to career adaptability among 810 senior students (males = 367, females = 443; Mean age = 22.90 years; SD = 0.82) at four 4-year comprehensive universities in China. They reported a correlation of .62 between the *CAAS* total score and the *Proactive Personality Scale* (Seibert, Crant, & Kraimer, 1999).

A unique study by Jiang (2017) informed an early empirical explanation of how the personality trait of proactivity may influence adaptability. Jiang (2017) reasoned that "thriving at work" may be a process or mechanism through which proactive personality shapes career adaptability. Thriving at work has been defined as a "psychological state in which individuals experience both a sense of vitality and learning" (Porath, Spreitzer, Gibson, & Garnett (2012, p. 250). People who are thriving experience growth and momentum marked by both a sense of feeling energized and alive (vitality) and a sense that they are continually improving and getting better at what they do (learning). Proactive individuals may be more likely to thrive at work and, as a result, they may be better able to develop career adaptability resources. The energy, vitality, and learning that constitute thriving may explain in part the continuous development of adaptability resources during a career. The research model in Figure 17 displays how Jiang positioned thriving at work as a mediator between proactivity and adaptability. As a mediator, thriving transmits the influence of proactive personality to the development of career adaptability. While proactive personality and thriving both can drive career construction, they are conceptually and empirically distinct. Jiang conceptualized proactivity as an indicator of adaptivity because it appears to be a stable personality trait whereas he conceptualized thriving as a dynamic state that may bring out the effects of proactivity on adaptability.

Figure 17. Thriving Mediates Between Proactivity and Adaptability

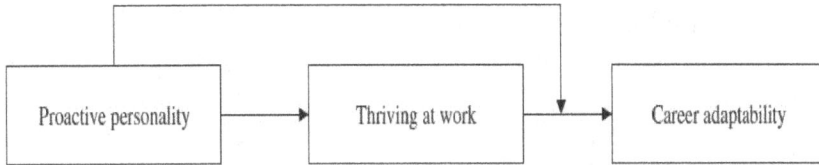

Four items from Bateman and Crant (1993) were used to measure proactive personality: "Nothing is more exciting than seeing my ideas turn into reality"; "If I see something I don't like, I fix it"; "I am always looking for better ways to do things"; and "If I believe in an idea, no obstacle will prevent me from making it happen." These four items were chosen because they had consistently demonstrated the highest factor loadings across different samples (Bateman & Crant, 1993). Thriving at work was measured with ten items about learning orientation (e.g., "I find myself learning often") and vitality (e.g., "I am looking forward to each new day") each measured by five items from Porath, Spreitzer, Gibson, and Garnett (2012). The *CAAS* was used to measure career adaptability. Participants in the study were 364 (45% females) adult workers in China. They differed in age categories: 18–25 years (N = 42, 11.54%), 26–30 years (N = 105, 28.85%), 31–40 years (N = 149, 40.93%), 41–50 years (N = 48, 13.19%), and over 50 years (N = 20, 5.49%). Most held a bachelors degree (N = 217, 59.60%), followed by those with a tertiary diploma (N = 87, 23.90%).

Zero-order correlations indicated that the *CAAS* total score correlated .70 to proactive personality and .78 to thriving. Structural analysis indicated that thriving mediated the relationship between proactivity and adaptability. This result supports the viewpoint by Porath and colleagues (2012) that

147

proactive personality involves internal constructive and positive changes that sustain thriving at work and foster further career development.

Results from a moderated-mediation analysis showed that the indirect effect of proactive personality on career adaptability via thriving was stronger for those with lower rather than higher proactivity. Thus, thriving demonstrated differential effects on career adaptability between high and low proactive groups. This finding suggests that although in general thriving tends to increase the level of career adaptability, this tendency may be attenuated by individuals' proactive efforts. In explaining the differential effects of thriving, Jiang (20170 suggested that highly proactive people tend to develop adaptability resources because they are intrinsically motivated. Given that low proactive individuals display less intrinsic motivation and are more passive in response to change, they may need additional psychological motivators such as thriving to drive them to develop career adaptability resources.

Although the main study focused on global career adaptability, a series of supplementary analyses were performed to examine the four adapt-abilities. Results showed that the indirect effect of proactive personality on the adapt-abilities of Concern, Control, Curiosity, and Confidence were each significant, indicating that thriving could mediate the relationships between proactive personality and the four career adapt-abilities. Supplementary moderation analyses demonstrated that proactive personality moderated the relationship of thriving with Concern, but not with the other three adapt-abilities.

The relation of proactivity and social support to career adaptability was studied in Malaysia by Fawehinmi and Yahya (2018). The participants were 188 students (76.6% females) in the final semester of a Bachelor in Business Administration program. Proactive personality was measured with the *Proactive Personality Scale* (Seibert, Crant, & Kraimer, 1999) and social support was measured with the *Multidimensional Scale of Perceived Social Support* (Zimet, Dahlem, Zimet, & Farley, 1988). The *CAAS* total score correlated .60 to proactive personality and .53 to social support. Multiple regression analysis produced $R = .67$, indicating that 44.7% of the variance in career adaptability was explained by proactive personality and social support. Proactive personality ($\beta = 0.45$, $p < .01$) was more significant than social support ($\beta = 0.33$, $p < .01$) in influencing career adaptability.

In an eighth study of the relation between proactive personality and career adaptability, Stauffer, Abessolo, Zecca, and Rossier (2019) studied 234 employees in Switzerland. The *CAAS* total score correlated .51 to the *Proactive Personality Scale* (Bateman & Crant, 1993), with correlations of .39 to Concern, .39 to Control, .44 to Curiosity, and .29 to Confidence.

In a ninth study that reported correlations between proactive personality and career adaptability, Tokar, Savickas, and Kaut (2020) examined the correlations between the *CAAS* and proactive personality using the *Proactive Personality Scale* (Seibert, Crant, & Kraimer, 1999) among 243 employed adults. The results indicated that proactive personality correlated .43 to the *CAAS* total score and .26 to Concern, .28 to Control, .42 to Curiosity, and .39 to Confidence.

A tenth study of proactivity concentrated on learning. Tolentino, Garcia, Lu, Restubog, Bordia, and Plewa, (2014) examined the relation of *CAAS* scores to adaptivity among a sample of Australian university students (N = 447) enrolled in business and management courses. They also measured learning goal orientation and career optimism, considering them to also represent aspects of the global adaptivity. Proactive personality was measured with the *Proactive Personality Scale* (Seibert, Crant, & Kraimer, 1999). Learning goal orientation refers to a disposition to develop or demonstrate ability in achievement situations. The researchers measured it using an 8-item scale (VandeWalle, Cron, & Slocum, 2001). Participants indicated how strongly they agreed with statements such as: "The opportunity to extend the range of my abilities is important to me" and "I prefer to work on tasks that force me to learn new things." Career optimism was defined as a disposition to expect the best possible outcome in relation to one's future career development (Rottinghaus, Day & Borgen, 2005). It was measured with ten items from the Career Optimism Scale of the *Career Futures Inventory* (Rottinghaus, Day, & Borgen, 2005), which was slightly modified to reflect optimism regarding the students' future business ventures. One item (i.e., "It is difficult for me to set career goals") was dropped because it was too general to be modified in relation to future business ventures. Example items read, "Thinking about my future business venture inspires me" and "I am eager to pursue my business dreams." Participants first responded to the adaptivity measures of proactive personality, learning orientation, and career optimism and then four weeks later took the *CAAS*. Adaptability correlated .45 to proactive personality, .37 to learning goal orientation, and .33 to career optimism. The results suggest that people with a proactive personality disposition, learning orientation, and career optimism are more likely to develop career adapt-abilities.

Two additional studies computed the correlations of the *CAAS* to the 17-item *Proactive Personality Scale* (Bateman & Crant, 1993). Ma, Chen, and Zeng (2020) reported a correlation of .60 among 1062 college nursing students in Northwest China while Green, Noor, and Hashemi (2020) reported that the *CAAS* correlated .32 to Concern, .29 to Control, .23 to Curiosity, and .34 to Confidence for 49 college business students in a control group for a study at Islama University.

In a 13th study of proactivity as a key trait in global adaptivity, Hirschi, Hermann, and Keller (2015) measured proactive personality with the seven-item personal initiative questionnaire developed by Frese, Fay, Hilburfer, Leng, and Tag (1997). Items in the questionnaire addresses self-starting, proactivity, and persistence. An example item reads, "I actively attack problems." Proactivity measured as personal initiative correlated .47 to Concern, .45 to Control, .44 to Curiosity, and .53 to Confidence.

A 14th study on the relation of proactive personality to career adaptivity took a different perspective. Coetzee and Schreuder

(2018) viewed proactive self-management of career as including the traits of proactive personality, Openness to experience, flexibility, and intrinsic motivation. To examine the relation of proactive self-management of career to adaptability, Coetzee and Schreuder (2018) administered the *Psychological Career Resources Inventory* (Coetzee, 2008) and the *CAAS* to 248 participants employed in a South African organization. The sample consisted of 63% females and 37% males between the ages of 18 and 49 years old, and who mostly occupied management positions (75%). The *Psychological Career Resources Inventory* (Coetzee, 2008) measures eleven variables: growth/development career value (three items; e.g., "I like to help others grow and develop"), authority/influence career value (three items; e.g., "I like to have the power to make important things happen"), practical/creative skills (four items; e.g., "I am good at putting my ideas into practical plans and making it work for me"), self/other skills (four items; e.g., "I am good at analyzing situations and data to create new solutions"), career purpose (five items; e.g., "I feel confident I my ability to achieve my career goals"), career directedness (three items; e.g., "I am clear about what I would like to become career wise"), career venturing (four items; e.g., "I am willing to go out and test new career experiences"), self-esteem (five items; e.g., "I feel as worthwhile as anyone else'), behavioral adaptability (six items; e.g., "It is easy for me to adapt to new things and situations in my life"), and emotional literacy (five items; e.g., "I find it easy to express my feelings and needs clearly and directly") and social connectivity (five items; e.g., "I find it easy to ask others for or accept their help or support").

Coetzee and Schreuder (2018) used canonical correlation to analyze the relation between the adaptivity and adaptability variates. Three functions were significant, yet the first function explained 77% of the shared variance between the two variates. The redundancy index (squared canonical correlation) was .63. The researchers considered the first function as practically sufficient for interpreting the links between the two variates. The canonical cross-loadings showed the strongest links between, on the one hand, behavioral adaptability (rc = .68), self-esteem (rc = .65), career directedness (rc = .64) and, on the other hand, career Concern (rc = .75), Control (rc = .65), Curiosity (rc = .62), and Confidence (rc = .58). The results suggest that those who scored higher on career adaptability described themselves as flexible in adapting to change, clear about their career goals, and self-confident. The researchers suggested that career adaptivity as measured by proactive self-management of career involves conscientiousness in setting and implementing clear goals.

In summary, the proactive personality trait shows fairly consistent correlations to career adaptability as shown in Table 8, suggesting that the two variables share about 25 % variance. It is worth testing in future research that uses longitudinal designs whether individuals who display a proactive personality develop, in particular, strong adapt-ability resources of Curiosity and Confidence. The cumulative results support the use of Seibert, Crant, and Kraimer's (1999) 10-item version of the original 17-item *Proactive Personality Scale* (Bateman & Crant, 1993) as an excellent indicator of career adaptivity in studies of the CCT model of adaptation.

Table 8: Correlations of Proactivity to CAAS in 11 Studies

	CAAS Total	Concern	Control	Curiosity	Confidence
Cai	.32	.24	.22	.30	.33
Fawehinmi	.60				
Gao	.73	.60	.66	.66	.69
Hou	.62				
Jiang	.70				
Oncel	.49	.39	.35	.46	.36
Stauffer	.51	.39	.39	.44	.29
Tokar	.61	.46	.28	.42	.39
Tolentino	.45	.36	.37	.36	.44
Uy	.43	.26	.52	.59	.53
Ma	.60				
Mean of 7	**.51**	**.38**	**.40**	**.46**	**.43**
Mean of 11	**.55**				

Psychological Hardiness

Hardiness refers to an adaptive readiness characteristic that may be considered alongside proactivity in that it motivates an individual to engage in effortful coping. When an individual encounters a difficult situation, hardiness decreases feelings of threat, enhances stress tolerance, and increases the expectancy of overcoming difficulties. Kobasa (1979) conceptualized psychological hardiness as a meta-construct constituted by three personality traits: control, challenge, and commitment. Hardy control disposes individuals to view stressors as changeable and manageable, thus prompting coping efforts. Hardy challenge inclines individuals to view change as a growth opportunity rather than a threat. Hardy commitment inclines individuals to dedicate themselves to their work and engage in purposeful activities.

In the first study to relate psychological hardiness to career adaptability, Coetzee and Harry (2015) measured the three dimensions of hardiness with Maddi's (1987) *Personal Views Survey II* (*PVS-II*), which consists of 50 items across three scales: commitment–alienation (e.g., "I often wake up eager to take up my life where I left it off the day before;" "Most of my life gets wasted doing things that don't mean anything"), control–powerlessness (e.g., "Planning ahead can help avoid most future problems;" "No matter how hard I try, my efforts will accomplish nothing"), and challenge–threat (e.g., "I enjoy being with people who are unpredictable;" "I want to be sure someone will take care of me when I get old"). Coetzee and Harry (2015) administered the *PVS-II* along with the *CAAS* to 409 (66% females and 34% males) out-sourced financial call-center agents in South Africa, who ranged in age from 25 to 40 years (Mean age = 32 years). The *CAAS* total score correlated .12 to hardiness. The Challenge scale did not correlate significantly to any of the adapt-abilities. The Control scale correlated to all the adapt-abilities, namely .21 to Concern, .23 to Control, .16 to Curiosity, and .26 to Confidence. The Commitment subscale did not correlate significantly to Curiosity and ranged between .14 and .20 for the remaining three adapt-abilities. The researchers concluded that hardy control, or being highly motivated to engage in effortful coping, may lead to strengthening career adaptability resources.

In a second study of psychological hardiness, Ndlovu and Ferreira (2019), examined college students' hardiness in relation to career adaptability. The study participants were 198 engineering students (57.6% females) enrolled at a university in South Africa. They assessed hardiness using the *Personal Views Survey III-R*, which includes only the best 30 items from the 50-item *Personal Views Survey-II* (Maddi, 1987). The *CAAS* total score correlated .28 to hardiness, with correlations of .25 to both the Control and Challenge scales but did not correlate significantly to the Commitment subscale. Hardiness correlated .25 to Concern, .08 (not significant) to Control, .30 to Curiosity, and .24 to Confidence. The Control adapt-ability did not correlate significantly to any of the hardiness dimensions. Note that hardiness Control did not correlate significantly to Adapt-ability Control (.03), indicating they are distinct constructs with the same name. The Concern adapt-ability had the highest correlations to the hardiness scales of Commitment (.25), Control (.23), and Challenge (.21). The researchers suggested that psychological hardiness significantly contributes to students' development of career adaptability resources. They concluded that psychological hardiness and career adaptability are both career resilience enhancers.

Psychological hardiness was also examined in a study by Ferreira, Coetzee, and Masenge (2013). They created two variates and assessed their relationships using canonical correlational analysis. The first variate, "psychological career meta-capacities," included three sets of personal resources that enable individuals to adapt to career changes and challenges. The career resources were assessed with *The Psychological Career Resources Inventory* (Coetzee, 2008); psychological hardiness was measured with the *Personal Views Inventory II* (Maddi, 1987); and career adaptability was measured with the *CAAS*. The job-retention variate included commitment as measured by the *Organizational Commitment Scale* (Meyer & Allen, 1997) and embeddedness measured by *The Job Embeddedness Scale* (Mitchell, Holtom & Lee, 2001). The participants were 355 (76% female and 55% single) adults employed at managerial and staff levels in a South African service industry. Results indicated that the first canonical function was statistically significant (Rc = 0.45; Rc^2 = .21). The researchers did not report zero-order correlation coefficients. Among the *CAAS* subscales, canonical coefficients for the first variate were .20 for Control and .18 for Concern. Overall, the results suggested that the psychological career meta-capacities significantly contributed to explaining the participants' sense of fit with their work group, job and organization as well as commitment to their organizations. Their overall career adaptability related significantly to their sense of fit with the job and organization.

One study generally related to resilience examined the relationship of career adaptability to pathological personality traits. Carvalho, Moreira, and Ambiel (2017) administered the *Dimensional Clinical Personality Inventory* (Carvalho & Pianowski, 2015) to 342 individuals who ranged in age from 17 to 59 years old (Mean = 26.5; SD= 9.13). In general, the idea of the negative relationship between adaptive capacity in a career context and pathological personality traits was supported.

Protean Career Orientation

Strong correlations have been reported between proactive personality and protean career attitudes because both incline individual to be flexible and adaptive in facing transitions, challenges, personal development, and self-fulfillment. Proactivity and a protean orientation are both based on values that dispose people to take initiative in identifying and acting on opportunities. They differ in that proactive personality represents a general personality trait whereas protean orientation pertains specifically to the career domain. Based on the results of a meta-analytic study, Wiernik and Kostal (2019) suggested that a protean orientation may have advantages over broad personality traits for understanding careers.

155

Douglas Hall (2004) explained that the *protean* attitudes dispose individuals to use their own values ("values driven") and take an independent role ("self-directing") in managing their vocational behavior. Previously, Hall and Mirvis (1995) had suggested that two meta-competencies sustain the development of a protean career orientation, namely, career adaptability and career identity. For Hall (2004), adaptability refers to the motivation and capacity to learn to adapt to a changing environment and identity refers to the motivation and capacity to formulate accurate self-conceptions and change one's self-concept as appropriate" (Briscoe & Hall, 1999). Protean-oriented individuals, with their self-directed and value driven career attitudes, employ these meta-capacities to construct their careers. CCT deems Hall's description of the meta-competencies of adaptability and identity as adaptive readiness characteristics. Following Hall's lead, CCT (Savickas, 2011) proposed that the effects of the protean orientation as adaptive readiness on career success and satisfaction are mediated by career adaptability. Four studies have examined this CCT proposition.

The relation of protean adaptivity to career adaptability was investigated by Chan, Uy, Ho, San, Chernyshenko, and Yu (2015) in Singapore with a sample of 854 university students (Mean age = 23.2 years). The researchers measured protean career orientation with the *Protean Career Attitudes Scale* (Briscoe, Hall, & DeMuth, 2006), which consists of 14 items that measure the two distinct yet related dimensions of a self-directed career (eight items; e.g., "I am responsible for my success or failure in my career") and values-driven career (six items; e.g., "I navigate my own career, based on my personal priorities, as opposed to my employer's priorities"). Protean career orientation correlated .56 to the *CAAS* total score, and correlated from .46 to .54 with the four adapt-abilities. In addition, using the *Leadership Motivation Scale* (Chan, Ho, Chernyshenko, Bedford, Uy, Gomulya, et al., 2012), they reported that leadership motivation correlated .44 to the *CAAS* total score and had correlations ranging from .34 to .41 with the four adapt-abilities.

In 2015, Uy, Chan, Sam, Ho, and Chernyshenko published a second study about the relation between career adaptability and protean orientation. They administered the *Protean Career Attitudes Scale* (Briscoe, Hall, & DeMuth, 2006) to 750 college students (45% females; Mean age = 23.25 years; SD = 1.51). Protean career attitudes correlated .56 to the *CAAS* total score, and .46 to Concern, .54 to Control, .50 to Curiosity, and .46 to Confidence.

In a study that investigated both career adaptability and career identity, Haibo, Xiaoyu, Xiaoming, and Zhihin (2018) examined the interaction between the two meta-competencies by examining the possible effects of career identity on the relationship of career adaptability to success and satisfaction as shown Figure 18.

Figure 18. Identity Mediates between Adaptability & Employee Outcomes

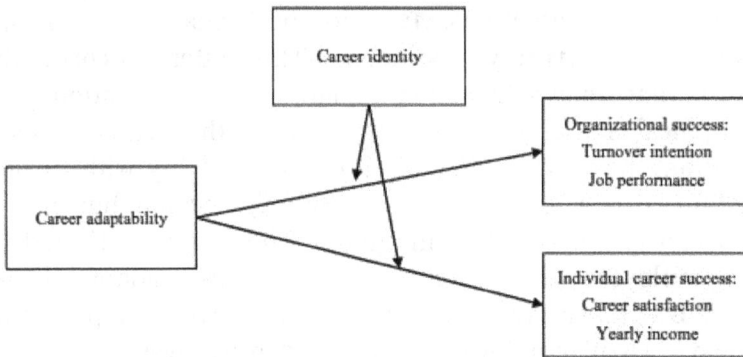

Haibo and colleagues recruited participants from 20 enterprises located in five different provinces of China. In total, 2,000 employees and 190 managers participated in the survey. The researchers used the time-lag technique to reduce common method bias. Career adaptability of employees was measured first, and then two weeks later supervisors rated the employees' job performance and employees reported their yearly income and evaluated their career satisfaction, turnover intention, and career identity. Data collection resulted in a match of 1,652 employee–supervisor dyads. Of the employees, 60.6% had a college education, 43.3% were males, and 61.3% had less than three years of tenure. Career identity was measured with five items adapted from the dimension

157

"identity with career commitment" of the *Vocational Identity Status Inventory* (Porfeli, Lee, Vondracek, & Weigold, 2011). A sample item reads, "My career will help me satisfy deeply personal goals." Turnover intention was measured by three items developed by Konovsky and Cropanzano (1991). An example item reads, "I will look for a job outside of this organization during the next year." Career satisfaction was measured by the *Career Satisfaction Scale* (Greenhaus, Parasuraman, & Wormley, 1990). An example item reads, "I am satisfied with the progress I have made toward meeting my goals for advancement." Yearly income was measured by one item: "How much is your current average yearly income?"

The *CAAS* total score correlated .27 to career identity, -.12 to turnover intention, .16 to job performance, .28 to career satisfaction, and .16 to yearly income. Career identity correlated -.20 to turnover intentions, .12 to job performance, .50 to career satisfaction, and .11 to yearly income. This pattern of correlations suggests that when satisfaction is high, turnover intention is low. Hierarchical regression analysis showed that career identity moderated the relationships of career adaptability with turnover intention, career satisfaction, and yearly income but not job performance. For turnover intentions, the results indicated that when employees' career identity was high, career adaptability did not relate significantly to turnover intentions (β = .09, p < .27). In contrast, when employees' career identity was low, career adaptability related significantly to higher turnover intention (β = .18, p < .05). This contrast suggests that some individuals with relatively high career adaptability yet lower career identity may choose to cope with their career-related difficulties by leaving their current organization. For career satisfaction, career identity did moderate the relation to career adaptability. Career adaptability and career satisfaction related significantly for employees with high career identity (β = .26, p < .01) and stronger than for employees with low career identity (β = .22, p < .01). For yearly income, career identity moderated the relationship with career adaptability for employees with high levels of career identity (β = .15, p < .05) but not for employees with low career identity (β = .09, p = .20). Career identity did not moderate the relationship between career adaptability and job performance. Hierarchical regression analysis showed that employees' career adaptability related significantly to their job performance (β = .15, p < .01) yet the moderating effect was not significant (β = .02). In short, the results of this study showed that career adaptability related positively to both career satisfaction and yearly income and that career identity moderated these relationships.

Boundaryless Career Orientation

A construct frequently studied in combination with protean career orientation is *boundaryless* career orientation. To address discontinuous and fragmented work contexts with frequent occupational transitions, Arthur (1994) proposed a new career model as an alternative to the traditional organizational model. The boundaryless career model addresses a life course in which individuals make frequent transitions and their resulting occupational positions span different organizations, sectors, and domains rather than a single organization. Managing a boundaryless career requires flexibility, preference for mobility, self-management of career trajectory, and development of knowledge networks. According to Arthur, Claman, and DeFillippi (1995), success in making transitions during a boundaryless career is eased by competence at "knowing why," "knowing whom," and "knowing how."

In a study of both protean and boundaryless career orientations, Stauffer, Abessolo, Zecca, and Rossier (2019) investigated whether the orientations indirectly influence career satisfaction through career adaptability. Participants for the study consisted of 234 undergraduate students enrolled in a research methods class. They participants were 55% females with a mean age of 35.62 years old (SD = 13.27) and had a mean organizational tenure of 6.99 years (SD = 3.0) with 73% working full time. Career adaptability was measured with the *CAAS-SF*. The *Career Satisfaction Scale* (Greenhaus, Parasuraman, & Wormley, 1990) was used to assess the degree to which employees felt satisfied with their career. Protean career orientation was measured with the *Protean Career*

Attitudes Scale (Briscoe, Hall, & DeMuth, 2006), with its two subscales of self-directed career and values-driven career. Boundaryless career orientation was measured with the *Boundaryless Career Attitudes Scale* (Briscoe, Hall, & DeMuth, 2006), which consists of 13 items measuring the two inter-related dimensions of boundary mindset (eight items; e.g., "I seek job assignments that allow me to learn something new") and mobility preference (five reverse-scored items; e.g., "In my ideal career I would work for only one organization").

The *CAAS* total score correlated .30 to career satisfaction, .40 to the *Protean Career Attitude Scale* (self-directed = .44 and values-driven = .23), and .30 to the *Boundaryless Career Attitude Scale* (boundaryless mindset = .31 and mobility preference = .19). Relative to the adapt-abilities, protean orientation correlated .26 to Concern, .46 to Control, .26 to Curiosity, and .23 to Confidence. Correlations of the adapt-abilities were stronger across the board to the self-directed subscale than to the values- driven subscale. Both the self-directed (.44) and values- driven (.33) subscales had their strongest correlations to Control. The boundarlyes orientation correlated .19 to Concern, .21 to Control, .25 to Curiosity, and. 25 to Confidence. The strongest correlations were for the boundaryless mindset were .29 to Confidence and .26 to Curiosity. The adapt-abilities correlated more strongly to the boundaryless mindset subscale than to the mobility preference subscale. This pattern coincides with the conclusion by Wiernik and Kostal (2019) in their meta-analytic review of the two career orientations that the self-directed, value driven, and boundaryless mindset subscales all load on a single general factor, and relate only weakly to mobility preferences.

As shown in Figure 19, the results confirmed that protean and boundaryless orientations predict career satisfaction beyond the effect of career adaptability, and that career adaptability mediated the relationship, albeit partially, of protean and boundaryless orientations to career satisfaction. Protean and boundaryless orientations significantly explained 20% of the variance in career adaptability. Additionally, protean and boundaryless orientations, mediated by adaptability, significantly explained 15% of the variance in career satisfaction. The researchers concluded that individuals with protean and boundaryless orientations are satisfied with their career direction because they have developed psychological resources to cope with occupational changes and challenges.

Figure 19. Adaptability Mediates between
Career Orientations and Satisfaction

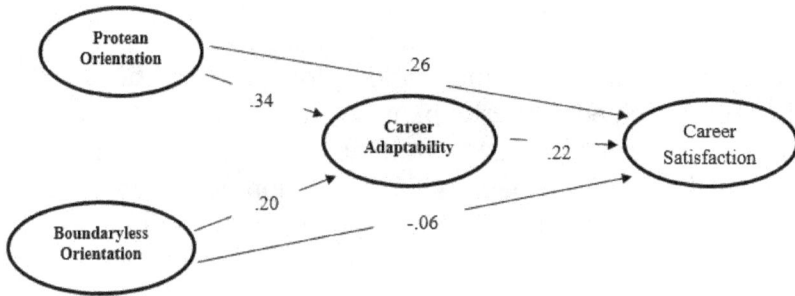

Hypothesizing that seeking challenge on the job may be a protean value, Yang, Guan, Lai, She, and Lockwood (2015) examined the relation of career adaptability to valuing work opportunities that strongly challenge one's competitiveness and problem-solving skills. They measured valuing challenge with three items from Schein's (1990) *Career Anchor Scale*. In a sample of 220 Chinese full-time human resource management professionals, the scale has a coefficient alpha of .90. The results showed that the *CAAS* total score correlated .38 to the career anchor of challenge. Valuing challenge had its highest correlation of .41 to the adapt-ability of Curiosity, with correlations to the other three adapt-abilities ranging between .26 and .30.

Learning Orientation

As just noted from Tolentino, Garcia, Lu, Restubog, Bordia, and Plewa, (2014), a positive learning orientation seems to foster the

161

development of career adaptability resources. Given a changing environment, life-long learning is critical to meeting career changes and challenges. In a qualitative study, of 64 mid-career changers, Brown, Bimrose, Barnes, and Hughes (2012) concluded that adaptive adults used both formal and informal learning to develop career adapt-abilities, both over time and across occupations. They emphasized that career adapt-abilities at mid-life can be developed through learning, particularly through engaging in challenging work and updating a substantive knowledge base. Specific beneficial actions included asking questions, getting information, finding key people to provide support, listening and observing, learning from mistakes, giving and receiving feedback, trying things out, independent study, and working for a qualification. In turn, adaptability helped the participants to effect positive career change. Bimrose and Hearne (2012), studying the same 64 participants, concluded that resilient individuals develop career adaptabilities over time. They defined resilience as personal attributes such as being tenacious, determined, single-minded, and flexible when faced with difficult circumstances. In CCT, resilience pertains to applying the general model of adaptation to dealing with adversity and trauma.

A qualitative study conducted by Brown (2016) identified three different career patterns among individuals employed in low-skill work. The informants were 105 low-skilled individuals mainly between 25 and 40 years old, who began their career with few qualifications. Brown concluded that individuals with few initial qualifications by early to mid-career differ in how they envision the future (Concern), the extent to which they take responsibility for their own development (Control), explore visions of possible future selves (Curiosity), and believe in their ability to solve problems and to succeed (Confidence). The group who passed through low-skilled work and moved to more highly skilled employment were committed to "getting on." They valued further learning and were proactive in combining their experience and skills to progress. Their career adaptability resources developed in tandem with a commitment to learning. The other two groups showed less adaptability. The group considered as "getting by" remained in low skill-employment. They found it difficult to take control of their career and were hanging on to their jobs. They were more hesitant about their learning, being reactive in responding only to employers' requirements for further learning. Their career adaptability resources were under-developed. The third group perceived themselves as "going nowhere." They struggled to even just get by in their current work. They lacked direction and had a poor outlook on the future, even feeling helpless and fatalistic. They reported negative attitudes toward re-engaging in formal education or participating in some other form of learning. They lacked career adaptability resources and a support network. In many ways, the three groups seemed to each represent one of Super's (1980) maintenance stage strategies of breaking new ground, keeping up, and holding on.

Entrepreneurial Orientation

In 2015, Uy, Chan, Sam, Ho, and Chernyshenko published a study showing the relation of career adaptability to entrepreneurial alertness, that is, quickness in identifying unexploited opportunities for career investment. They administered the *Entrepreneurial Alertness Scale* (Tang, Kacmar, & Busenitz, 2012) to 750 college students (45% females) with a mean age of 23.25 years (SD = 1.51). The scale has three dimensions: scanning and search (e.g., "I am avid information seeker"), association and connection (e.g., "I see links between seemingly unrelated pieces of information"), and evaluation and judgment (e.g., "I have a gut feeling for potential opportunities"). Entrepreneurial alertness correlated .57 to the *CAAS* total score, and .43 to Concern, .45 to Control, .60 to Curiosity, and .48 to Confidence.

Entrepreneurship was defined by Ispir, Elibol, and Sonmez (2019) as the ability to turn ideas into action using creativity, innovation, risk taking, and planning. They explained that in nursing, entrepreneurship means developing creative and innovative methods for patient care as well as dealing with the uncertainty and complexity associated with their job. They investigated entrepreneurship among junior and senior students in the nursing faculty of a state university in Istanbul (N=265). The participants were 85.3% females with a mean age of 21.04 years (SD = 1.29). Along with the *CAAS*, they administered the *Scale of University Students Entrepreneurship* (Yılmaz & Sünbül, 2009), which consists of 36 items that load on a single factor. Entrepreneurship correlated .60 to the *CAAS* total score, with correlations of .48 to Concern, .49 to Control, .52 to Curiosity, and .47 to Confidence.

The role of career adaptability in predicting entrepreneurial intentions was investigated by Tolentino, Sedoglavich, Lu, Raymund, Garcia, and Restubog (2014). They posited that individuals rely on their adaptability resources and entrepreneurial self-efficacy as they form entrepreneurial intentions. Career adaptability, as a self-regulatory resource, is further strengthened by prior exposure to a family business. To test their model, they collected data from 380 Serbian business students over three measurement periods. At Time 1, they administered the *CAAS* to the 380 participants. At Time 2, two months after the Time 1, they asked the same 380 participants to answer a questionnaire assessing their entrepreneurial self-efficacy. A total of 200 surveys were retrieved yielding a response rate of 52.63%. Entrepreneurial self-efficacy was measured by six items that asked about solving problems, managing money, being creative, getting people to agree, being a leader, and making decisions. At Time 3, two months after the Time 2 data collection, they asked the remaining 200 participants to answer a questionnaire assessing entrepreneurial intentions. Entrepreneurial intentions were measured using two items: "I have always wanted to work for myself" and "If I have the opportunity, I would start my own business venture." A total of 180 completed questionnaires were retrieved. They also asked "Does your father or mother run their own business?" (no or yes). The final sample of 180 matched responses over the three measurement periods comprised of 56% males with a mean age of 24.38 years (SD = 2.82).

The results showed that the *CAAS* total score correlated .43 to Time 2 entrepreneurial self-efficacy, .30 to Time 3 entrepreneurial intentions, and .17 to family business ownership. The authors concluded that career adaptability predicted entrepreneurial self-efficacy and entrepreneurial intentions over time. Thus, career adaptability is instrumental in entrepreneurial intention formation because it necessitates the enactment of considerable self-regulative competencies. The indirect effect of .20 between career adaptability and Time 3 entrepreneurial intentions was significant. The .42 direct effect of career adaptability on Time 3 entrepreneurial intentions indicated partial mediation. They then examined whether the strength of this mediated relationship depends on the presence or absence of a family business. With family business as a moderator, the significant indirect relationship was stronger for those with prior exposure to a family business, possibly because a family business can offer role models, vicarious learning opportunities, feedback, support, and mentoring. The conditional indirect effect between Time 1 career adaptability and Time 3 entrepreneurial intentions through Time 2 entrepreneurial self-efficacy was significantly stronger for those with a family business (indirect effect = .34) compared to those without a family business (indirect effect = .10). The observed pattern of relationships supporting the model was robust in light of the time-lagged data collection which emphasizes the change process and time elements necessary to test antecedents of entrepreneurial intentions.

Future Time Perspective

Time perspective refers to individuals' perceptions of the past, present, and future. It is important because it affects how people incorporate past experiences, current situations, and future expectations into their attitudes, cognitions, and behavior. Ringle and Savickas (1983) reviewed the extensive research on time perspective and organized its network of constructs into three dimensions of perspective, differentiation, and integration.

The relation of future time perspective to career adaptability was investigated with 609 eleventh-grade students in France. Pouyaud, Vignoli, Dosnon, and Lallemand (2012) measured future time perspective, or present anticipation of future goals, with a 25-item scale in the *Motivation Formation Questionnaire* (Forner, 2005). In addition, the researchers measured (a) general anxiety with the French version of the *Trait Anxiety Inventory* (Bruchon-Schweizer & Paulhan, 1993;) and (b) Fear of Failing scale from the *Future School and Career Anxiety Inventory* (Vignoli, Croity-Blez, Chapeland, DeFillipis, & Garcia, 2005). The *CAAS* total score correlated .42 to future time perspective. Concern, which involves a planful attitude toward the future, correlated .62 to future time perspective, much stronger than to the other three scales (.15 to both Control and Curiosity and .30 to Confidence). The correlation matrix also provided information regarding the concurrent validity of the *CAAS* Control subscale. Internal locus of control correlated more highly to Concern (.41) and Confidence (.33) but only .29 to the Control subscale. However, the Control subscale did have the strongest inverse relation to fear of failing (-.25) and general anxiety (-.39), which can be caused by a sense of lack of control.

An aspect of future time perspective has been conceptualized as temporal focus, that is, the extent to which people characteristically direct their attention to perceptions of the past, present, and future. Zacher (2014a) compared career adaptability to focus on these three time zones. He measured past, current, and future temporal focus dimensions with the *Temporal Focus Scale* (Shipp, Edwards, & Lambert, 2009), which has four items for each time zone. Example items read, "I reflect on what has happened in my life" (past temporal focus); "I focus on what is currently happening in my life" (present temporal focus); and "I think about what my future has in store" (future temporal focus). The results indicated that the *CAAS* total score correlated .18 to the past focus, .37 to the present focus, and .41 to the future focus. Among the subscales an interesting pattern emerged. Concern correlated .48 to a focus on the future but .17 to a focus on the Present. This finding was as expected for Concern because it involves forward thinking and attitudes toward planning. The pattern reversed for Control and Confidence in that both dimensions correlated .40 to a present focus and .27 to a future focus. As one might expect, Curiosity correlated stronger to the present (.31) and to future (.36) than to the past (.17). In short, the future maps onto Concern and the Present maps onto Control and Confidence.

A second study that correlated the *CAAS* to the *Temporal Focus Scale* (Shipp, Edwards, & Lambert, 2009) used only the future focus subscale. Future temporal focus was examined as a mediator between inspirational motivation by supervisors and career adaptability. Inspirational motivation refers to supervisors who envision the future and present images of it. Through this future focus, leader visioning fosters a future temporal focus among employees. Schuesslbauer, Volmer, and Goritz (2018) measured this future envisioning by supervisors with the Inspirational Motivation subscale of the *Multifactor Leadership Questionnaire* (Bass, 1985). The subscale consists of four statements to which participants rate their supervisors. An example item reads, "talks optimistically about the future." Future temporal focus was measured with the future subscale of the *Temporal Focus Scale* (Shipp, Edwards, & Lambert, 2009) and the *CAAS* was used to measure career adaptability. Data were collected, via a German online panel, from 776 (56.7% women) employees with a mean age of 46.3 years (SD = 10.4). Inspirational motivation and future temporal focus were measured at Time 1 and career adaptability was measured at Time 2, three months later.

Time 1 future focus correlated .32 to the Time 2 *CAAS* total score, with correlations of .44 to Concern, .15 to Control, .27 to Curiosity, and .21 to Confidence. Time 1 inspirational motivation correlated to the Time 2 CAAS total score .32, with correlations of .28 to concern and Curiosity, .26 to control, and .24 to Confidence. Linear regression analyses were calculated with age, gender, education, working hours, tenure, and managerial position entered on the first step. The results are shown in Figure 20. Inspirational motivation predicted overall career adaptability (β = .30, p < .001). Inspection of the four dimensions of career adaptability showed positive associations between inspirational motivation and Concern (β = .27, p < .001), Control (β = .25, p < .001), Curiosity (β = .26, p < .001), and Confidence (β = .23, p < .001), respectively. Mediation analyses, as shown in Figure 20, indicated significant indirect effects of inspirational motivation via future temporal focus on career adaptability (indirect effect, $\beta = .03$, 95% CI [.019, .048]) and all of career adaptability's dimensions, namely, Concern (indirect effect, $\beta = .06$, 95% CI [.034, .084]), Control (indirect effect, $\beta = .01$, 95% CI [.004, .028]), Curiosity (indirect effect, $\beta = .03$, 95% CI [.015, .051]), and Confidence (indirect effect, $\beta = .02$, 95% CI [.010, .037]). The findings suggest that supervisors who convey an attractive vision of the future, who are optimistic about the future, and who signal trust in the attainability of the communicated goals contribute to the development of their employees' career adaptability.

Figure 20. Future Focus Mediates between
Motivation and Adaptability

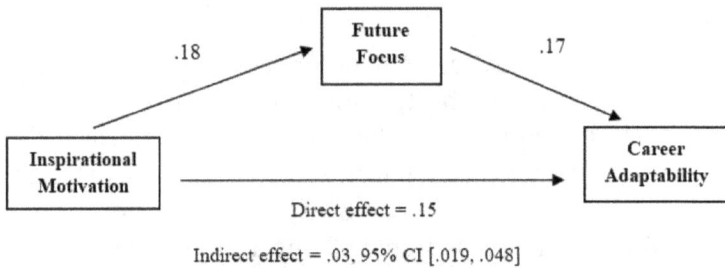

Another study of adaptability and future time perspective was conducted by Santilli, Marcionetti, Rochat, Rossier, and Nota (2017). They administered the *CAAS* and the *Visions of the Future Scale* (Ginevra, 2013) to 726 Italian and 533 Swiss adolescents between the ages of 12 and 16 years. The *CAAS* total score correlated .53 to future orientation among the Swiss adolescents yet only .19 among Italian adolescents.

A second study of Italian adolescents using a different measure of future orientation found results similar to the Swiss adolescents. Ginevra, Annovazzi, Santilli, DiMaggio, and Camussi (2018) administered the *CAAS* and the 11-item *Future Orientation Subscale* (e.g., "Thinking about the future excites me") from the *Design My Future Scale* (DiMaggio, Ginevra, Nota, & Soresi, 2016) to 762 Italian adolescents (383 males and 379 females) who ranged in age from 15 to 20 years (M =17.28, SD =1.07). Results indicated that future orientation correlated .56 to Concern, .44 to Control .45 to Curiosity, and .44 to Confidence.

A summary of correlations between future time perspective and the career adapt-abilities appears in Table 9. The strongest correlation, by far, is the correlation between future time perspective and the adapt-ability of Concern. This finding confirms theoretical expectations and adds concurrent validity evidence for the Concern subscale. Simply stated, individuals with a future orientation are more likely to demonstrate Concern about their future careers.

Table 9. Relation of Future Time Perspective to *CAAS* Dimensions

Future Perspective	Concern	Control	Curiosity	Confidence	*CAAS* Total
Ginevra	.56	.44	.45	.44	
Oncel	.47	.22	.28	.33	.44
Pouyaud .	.62	.35	.15	.30	.42
Santilli					.53 / .19
Schuesslbauer	.44	.15	.27	.21	.32
Zacher	.48	.27	.36	.27	.41
Mean *r*	.53	.29	.30	.31	.35

Hope and Optimism

Two constructs in the integration dimension of time perspective are hope and optimism. Three studies in Italy related career adaptability to hope and optimism. Santilli, Nota, Ginvera, and Soresi (2014) investigated their relations among 120 adults with a primary diagnosis of mild intellectual disability. The participants consisted of 60 men and 60 women with a mean age of 30.4 years (SD = 8.32). They had each been working for at least six months in competitive settings as salespersons, gardeners, warehouse clerks, assistant librarians, office clerks, or door attendants. The *Adult Trait Hope Scale* (Snyder et al., 1991) was used to assess agency or willpower (four items; e.g., "I energetically pursue my goals") and pathway thinking or way power (four items; e.g. "I can think of many ways to get the things in life that are important to me"). The *CAAS* total score correlated .59 to the total score for hope. Concern correlated .50 to agency and .40 to pathways. Control correlated .36 to agency and .28 to pathways. Curiosity correlated .38 to both agency and pathways. Confidence correlated .45 to agency and .37 to pathways.

In a second study in Italy of the relation of career adaptability to hope and optimism, Di Maggio, Ginevra, Nota, Ferrari, and Soresi (2015) administered the *CAAS* and the *Visions of the Future Scale* (Ginevra, 2013) to 838 middle school pre-adolescents Italy. The *Scale* measures the orientation toward hope (seven items; e.g. "In the future I will be involved in very important projects"), optimism (four items; e.g., "I consider myself as a person who thinks positively"), and pessimism (five items; e.g., "It is useless to hope in the future: I will not be able to do what I have in mind") Hope correlated .56 to the *CAAS* total score, with correlations to the four subscales ranging from .44 for Concern to .52 for Confidence. Optimism correlated .49 to the *CAAS* total score, with correlations to the four subscales ranging from .36 for Concern to .46 for Confidence. The correlation between the *CAAS* total score and pessimism was not significant but pessimism correlated -.08 to Control and -.10 to Confidence.

In a third study of the relation of career adaptability to hope and optimism, Ginevra, Pallini, Vecchio, Nota, & Soresi (2016) investigated the relation of career adaptability to career decidedness and dimensions of future time perspective. The participants in the study were 408 males and 366 females who ranged in age from 14 to 21 years (M = 17.45; SD = 0.93). In addition to measuring optimism, pessimism, and hope with the published version of the *Visions About the Future Scale* (Ginevra, Sgaramella, Ferrari, Nota, Santilli, & Soresi, 2017) that include three extra items, the researchers measured career adaptability with the *CAAS*. Also, they measured future orientation with the *Future Orientation Subscale* (11 items; e.g., "Thinking about the future excites me") from the *Design My Future Scale* (DiMaggio, Ginevra, Nota, &

Soresi, 2016). They measured career decidedness with the *Level of Decision and Assurance Related to One's School/Career Future* subscale (10 items; e.g., "I don't know what to think when I have to decide which is the best school for me") from the *Ideas and Attitudes on School/Career Future Scale* (Soresi & Nota, 2003). The results indicated that future orientation correlated from .54 with Concern to .36 with Control. Optimism correlated from .39 with Concern to .23 with Control and Confidence. Hope correlated from .48 with Confidence to to .36 to Curiosity. Pessimism correlated from -.18 with Control to -.10 with Curiosity. Decidedness correlated .37 with Concern, .19 with Control, .12 with Curiosity, and .24 with Confidence.

Another study of the relation of career adaptability to hope and optimism was conducted in Turkey by Buyukgoze-Kavas (2014). The sample of the study consisted of 669 participants: 353 high school students (144 males and 209 females) with a mean age of 16.03 years (SD = .75) and 316 university students (125 males and 191 females) with a mean age of 18.38 years (SD = 2.87). They measured hope with the *Dispositional Hope Scale* (Snyder et al., 1991) and optimism with the *Life Orientation Test-Revised* (Scheier, Carver, & Bridges, 1994), which assesses generalized expectations for positive (three items; e.g., "I'm always optimistic about my future") versus negative outcomes (three items; e.g., "I hardly ever expect things to go my way"). The results indicated that the *CAAS* total score correlated .61 to hope, with the adapt-abilities ranging from .46 for Concern to .53 for Confidence. The *CAAS* total score correlated .35 to optimism, with coefficients for the adapt-abilities ranging from .25 for Concern to .34 for Control.

In study by Cabras and Mondo (2018), future time perspective was conceptualized as a sense of continuity and as affective optimism. Cognitive beliefs about connections among past, present, and future behaviors were measured by the *Long-Term Personal Direction Scale* (Wessman, 1973). Example items read, "I am aware of a sense of continuity in my life" and "I feel my life is a series of starts and stops—stuck, moving, then stuck again." Affective evaluation of the future was measured with the *Achievability of Future Goals Scale*

171

(Heimberg, 1961). Example items read, "I look forward to the future with hope and enthusiasm" and "I am afraid of getting older." The sample comprised 373 university students enrolled in the first and second years of humanities courses at an Italian university (197 students) and at a Spanish university (176 students). Sense of continuity correlate .48 to Concern, .41 to Control, .32 to Curiosity, and .38 to Confidence. Optimism about achievability of future goals correlated .41 to Concern, .28 to Control, .34 to Curiosity, and .38 to Confidence.

In another study that positioned temporal continuity as an antecedent of career adaptability, Liang, Dou, Li, Liang, Zhou, Cao, Wu, and Lin (2020) studied 441 high school students (Mean age = 16.87; SD = 0.63; 46.3% females). First, they administered the *Consideration of Future Consequences Scale* (Strathman, Gleicher, Boninger, & Edwards, 1994). The items inquire about linking present behavior to future outcomes. Sample items read, "I only act to satisfy immediate concerns, figuring the future will take of itself" and "I consider how things might be in the future, and try to influence those things with my day to day behavior." Five weeks later, they administered the *CAAS*. Continuity correlated .23 to Concern, .17 to Control, .22 to Curiosity, and .18 to Confidence.

Emotional Intelligence

Emotional intelligence, as an exemplar of an adaptive readiness characteristic, relates to adaptability. CCT asserts that emotional intelligence increases adaptive readiness for dealing with vocational tasks, occupational transitions, and work troubles. Furthermore, emotional intelligence fosters the development and activation of career adaptability resources, which in turn leads to better adapting responses and adaptation results. The original ability–trait mixed-model (Salovey & Mayer, 1990) espoused emotional intelligence as a set of information-processing skills that individuals use to construct reality from emotional stimuli for the purpose of managing life in an adaptive manner (Puffer, 2011). Salovey and Mayer's (1990) original model proposed that emotional intelligence consists of four dimensions: (a) appraisal of emotion in the self and others, (b) expression of emotion, (c) regulation of emotion in the self and others, and (d) utilization of emotion in solving problems. Subsumed under these dimensions are functions such as verbal and non-verbal appraisal and expression of emotion and using emotions to motivate oneself. Salovey and Mayer (1990) also explained that emotional intelligence helps individuals to generate plans, motivate self to achieve success, improve decision-making processes, and enhance persistence in mastering challenging tasks.

In the literature on emotional intelligence, two streams of research reflect distinct conceptualizations and measurement approaches. The mental-ability models of emotional intelligence define emotional intelligence as a set of emotion-processing skills (e.g., Mayer, Caruso, & Salovey, 1999; Mayer & Geher, 1996). The mixed models of emotional intelligence conceptualize it as a diverse construct and adopt a trait approach. The mixed models emphasize the ability to perceive, assimilate, understand, and manage emotions yet also include in emotional intelligence aspects of personality, motivational, and affective dispositions such as self-concept, assertiveness, and empathy (Bar-On, 1997; Goleman, 1995). In research relating emotional intelligence to career adaptability, investigators have adopted the trait model of emotional intelligence.

Based on the Salovey and Mayer (1990) model of emotional intelligence, Schutte, Malouff, and Bhullar (2009) constructed the 33-item *Assessing Emotions Scale* as a mixed model self-report inventory to measure the following four emotional intelligence traits: perception of emotion (10 items; e.g., "I am aware of my emotions as I experience them"), managing own emotions (9 items; e.g., "When I am faced with obstacles, I remember times I faced similar obstacles and overcame them."), managing others' emotions (8 items; e.g., "I know when to speak about my personal problems to others"), and use of emotions (6 items; e.g., "Some of the major events of my life have led me to re-evaluate what is important and not important").

173

To study the relation of career adaptability to emotional intelligence, Coetzee and Harry (2014) administered the *Assessing Emotions Scale* (Schutte, Malouff, & Bhullar, 2009) to 409 call center agents, who had a mean age of 32 years. The correlation between the *CAAS* total score and overall emotional intelligence was .52, with correlations of .53 to Concern, .47 to Curiosity, and .43 to both Control and Confidence. Canonical correlation analysis produced two significant functions, but the second function accounted for only 3% additional variance. The redundancy index indicated that emotional intelligence explained a large practical effect of 31% of the variance in career adaptability. The first function indicated that managing ones' own emotions was the strongest predictor of career adaptability and that career concern was the best predictor of emotional intelligence. Managing one's own emotions refers to confidence in the ability to control one's personal emotions, using positive mood to persevere in spite of obstacles, motivate the self to achieve success, engage in problem solving, and deal positively with career challenges (Schutte et al., 2009). The results suggest that well-developed emotional intelligence provides energy and readiness for developing career adaptability resources, particularly the willingness to plan one's future.

Initial studies concerning the influence of emotional intelligence on career adaptability relied on cross-sectional designs and samples of university students (e.g., Celik & Storme, 2017; Coetzee & Harry, 2014; Merino-Tejedor, Hontangas, & Petrides, 2018; Udayar et al., 2018). Results from these studies were used to draw causal inferences yet they could not be used to draw causal conclusions. To establish causal conclusions about the CCT hypothesis requires longitudinal evidence. Accordingly, Parmentier, Pirsoul, and Nils (2019) used a longitudinal, cross-lagged design to investigate the causal hypothesis about the impact of emotional intelligence on career adaptability. They collected data at Time 1 from 282 participants of which 208 responded six months later. The participants were adults (Mean age = 34.22; SD = 9.06; 72.3% females) enrolled in Educational Sciences programs at a university in Belgium with goals of earning a salary increase, becoming a school principal, managing a major career change in education, or becoming a teacher or adult trainer. Dropout analyses indicated that there were no differences in age, gender, educational attainment, tenure, marital status, number of children, nor in mean levels of emotional intelligence and career adaptability,

At both Time 1 and 2, the participants responded to the *CAAS* and the *Profile of Emotional Competence* (Brasseur, Gregoire, Bourdu, & Mikolajczak, 2013). The self-report inventory measures five dimensions (i.e., identification, understanding, expression, regulation, and use) relative to the two targets own/intrapersonal vs. others'/interpersonal emotions. The researchers used only the 25 items for the intrapersonal dimension. Example items read, "I am aware of my emotions as soon as they arise" (identification), "When I am sad, I often don't know why" (reversed; understanding), "I am good at describing my feelings" (expression), "I find it difficult to handle my emotions" (reversed; regulation) and "I use my feelings to improve my choices in life" (use). The *CAAS* total score correlated .36 to emotional intelligence at Time 1 and .38 at Time 2. The emotional intelligence scores at Times 1 and 2 correlated .76. In comparison, the *CAAS* total scores at Times 1 and 2 correlated only .40, suggesting the development and activation of career adaptability resources over six months among individuals advancing their careers by enrolling in university programs.

To test the causal hypothesis, the researchers examined data fit in several competing cross-lagged models. First, they tested a stability model that contained only the autoregressive effects. After comparing several models, they concluded that, compared to the stability model, the causality model provided a significantly better fit to the data. The standardized estimates of the causality model appear in Figure 21. Time 1 emotional intelligence positively predicted Time 2 career adaptability levels ($\beta = 0.24, p < .05$) while controlling for the prior levels of career adaptability ($\beta = 0.33, p < .001$). The causality model explained a substantial part of the variance of career adaptability ($R^2 = .23$). When including the control variables in the analysis, results were identical and did not change the interpretation of the findings.

Figure 21. Cross-Lagged Relations between Emotional Competence and Career Adaptability

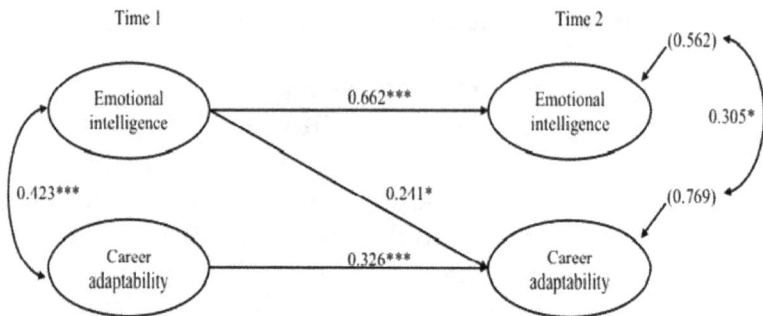

In an alternative model, the researchers reversed causality to examine the influence of career adaptability at Time 1 on emotional intelligence at Time 2. The path was not significant (β= 0.04, p = .523) and the model fit did not improve ($\Delta\chi2$ = 0.40, p = .526). Finally, they tested a reciprocal causality model. Results did not improve the model fit compared to the causality model ($\Delta\chi2$ = 0.06, p = .81). The researchers thereby retained the causality model as the best fitting model. They concluded that the results supported the causal relationship between emotional intelligence and career adaptability. Furthermore, they stressed the importance of considering emotional intelligence as a factor of general adaptive readiness that individuals may rely upon to develop and mobilize their career adaptability resources, and lead to better adapting responses.

Prior research has shown that emotional intelligence is a set of dispositional characteristics that contribute to flexibility, readiness, and willingness to adapt. Going a step further, Celik and Storme (2018), hypothesized that the trait of emotional intelligence predicts academic satisfaction through career adaptability. They reasoned that understanding and regulating one's own and others' emotions to obtain one's goals should foster career adaptability in one's academic life and lead to higher academic satisfaction. The researchers followed Petrides and Furnham (2006) in conceptualizing trait emotional intelligence as a set of personality characteristics and self-perceptions related to the management of emotions, self-control, and optimism. To measure emotional intelligence, they used the short form of the *Trait Emotional Intelligence Questionnaire* (*TEIQue-SF*; Petrides, 2009), which consists of 30 items designed to measure emotional intelligence as a global trait. The items address four dimensions: (a) well-being or the tendency to feel fulfilled and satisfied with life (e.g., "I generally don't find life enjoyable), (b) self-control over urges and impulses (e.g., "I usually find it difficult to regulate my emotions"), (c) emotionality or the ability to recognize and express emotions (e.g., "Expressing my emotions with words is not a problem for me"), and (d) sociability or the ability to use efficiently emotions when interacting with others (e.g., "I'm usually able to influence the way other people feel"). The researchers measured the degree to which students were satisfied with their academic lives using the seven-item scale devised by Lent, Singley, Sheu, Schmidt, and Schmidt (2007). Two example items read, "I am generally satisfied with my academic life" and "For the most part, I am enjoying my coursework." The participants were 410 students enrolled in an introductory course on human resource management at a university in Belgium. Data were collected in three phases to avoid common-method bias. Participants responded a week apart to the *TEIQue*, *CAAS*, and the academic satisfaction items. Between the first and last data collection point, the drop-out rate was 8%.

Results indicated that trait emotional intelligence correlated .45 to academic satisfaction and .49 to the *CAAS* total score, with correlations of .40 to Concern, .50 to Control, .32 to curiosity, and .41 to confidence. The estimates of the structural model appear in Figure 22. The total effect of trait emotional intelligence on academic satisfaction was positive and significant (β = .43, p < .001). The direct effect of emotional intelligence on academic satisfaction was still significant when controlling for career adaptability (β = .18, p < .05) but significantly reduced (β = .25, p < .001) because emotional intelligence predicts career adaptability (β = .62, p < .001), which in turn predicts academic satisfaction (β = .41, p < .001). This pattern of results indicated that career adaptability significantly mediated the relationship between trait emotional intelligence and academic satisfaction.

Figure 22. Adaptability Mediates between Emotional Intelligence and Satisfaction

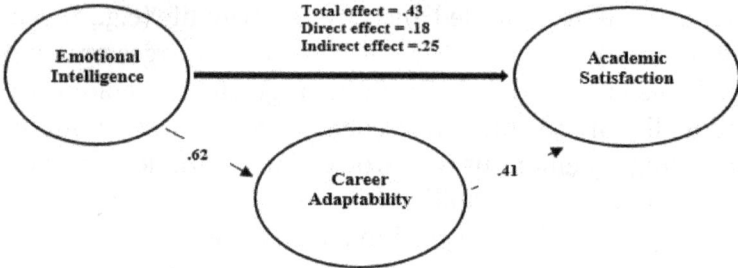

In another study of the adaptivity-adaptability-adaptation path, Merino-Tejedor, Hontanga, and Petrides (2018) tested the mediating role of career adaptability on the relation between trait emotional intelligence and academic engagement. Career adaptability was measured with the *CAAS*. The researchers assessed emotional intelligence with the short form of the *Trait Emotional Intelligence Questionnaire* (*TEIQue-SF*; Petrides, 2009). They measured academic engagement with a 24-item version of the *Utrecht Work Engagement Scale* adapted for university students (Schaufelie al., 2002). It consists of three dimensions: dedication (e.g., "To me, my studies are challenging"), absorption (e.g., "I get carried away when I am studying"), and vigor (e.g., "When I'm doing my work as a student, I feel bursting with energy").

The participants were 590 undergraduate students (35.2% males) with a mean age of 21.66 (SD = 4.24) in Spain. The students majored in social science (46.9%), health sciences (33.6%), engineering (8.8%), arts and humanities (6.4%), and physical sciences at 4.2%. The participants were in their first year (36.9%), second year (18%), third year (28.5%), fourth year (15.1%), or final year (1.6%). Most of the participants (71.5%) were full-time students, while the rest attended part-time (28.5%).

Emotional intelligence correlated .50 to the *CAAS* total score, with correlations of .32 to Concern, .55 to Control, .35 to Curiosity, and .47 to Confidence. Academic engagement correlated .39 to the *CAAS* total score, with correlations of .52 to Concern, .45 to Control, .47 to Curiosity, and .61 to Confidence. These results shown in Figure 23 supported the full mediation model in which adaptability mediated between the adaptive readiness characteristic of emotional intelligence and the adaptation outcome of academic engagement. The direct effect of emotional intelligence on academic engagement was not significant.

<u>Figure 23. Career Adaptability Mediates</u>
<u>Emotional Intelligence and Engagement</u>

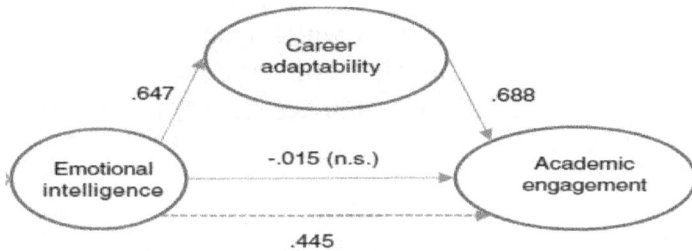

The two studies (Celik & Storme, 2018; Merino-Tejedor, Hontanga, & Petrides, 2018) that correlated the *CAAS* to the *Trait Emotional Intelligence Questionnaire* (Petrides, 2009) reported similar results. Emotional intelligence correlated strongest to Control (.50 and .55), followed by Confidence (.41 and .57), and then Concern (.40 and .32) and Curiosity (.32 and .35). This pattern of correlations supports the interpretation of the *CAAS* Control subscale as a measure related to managing life and making decisions.

A third study that used the *Trait Emotional Intelligence Questionnaire* (Petrides, 2009) did not report *CAAS* subscale scores. Udayar, Fiori, Thalmayer, and Rossier (2018) conducted the study in Switzerland to look at career adaptability as a process that may explain the strong association between emotional intelligence and career indecision. They examined the indirect effect of trait emotional intelligence on career indecision and on self-perceived employability through career adaptability, controlling for personality traits, fluid intelligence, and sex. They operationally defined career indecision with the *Career Decision-Making Difficulties Questionnaire* (Gati, Krausz, & Osipow, 1996). They also measured a more positive aspect of the college-to-work transition called self-perceived employability, which is defined as the characteristics needed to secure a job that corresponds to one's interests and goals. They measured employability self-perceptions and expectations with a 16-item scale developed by Rothwell and Arnold (2007). An example item reads, "The skills and abilities that I possess are what employers are looking for." They measured two control variables, namely, fluid intelligence with the *Raven's Standard Progressive Matrices* (Raven, J., Raven, J. C., & Court, J. H. (2000) and personality traits with the *Brief HEXACO Inventory* (Ashton & Lee, 2009). The 400 participants (46% female) university students who ranged in age from 17 to 48 years (Mean = 21.39; SD = 3.27)

The *CAAS* total score correlated .60 to trait emotional intelligence, -.38 to career indecision, .44 to perceived employability, .22 to Extraversion, -.06 to Agreeableness, .41 to Conscientiousness, .19 to Openness, -.20 to Emotionality, and a non-significant .01 to fluid intelligence. In the test of the structural model, career adaptability fully mediated the relationship between trait emotional intelligence and career decision-making difficulties, after controlling for the effect of sex, intelligence, and personality traits on emotional intelligence and career adaptability. In addition, tests of three different models showed that career adaptability fully mediated the direct relationship between trait emotional intelligence and each of the decision-making difficulties subscales (i.e., lack of readiness, lack of information, and inconsistent information). Individuals with high emotional intelligence displayed fewer difficulties related to a lack of willingness to make a decision, to a general difficulty in making decision, or to dysfunctional beliefs about the career decision-making process. Career adaptability had a significant indirect effect on the relationship between emotional intelligence on both lack of information and inconsistent information, but not on lack of readiness to enter the career decision-making process.

They also tested a model in which career adaptability fully mediated the relationship between emotional intelligence and self-perceived employability, after controlling for the effect of Conscientiousness on career adaptability. The fully mediated model, shown in Figure 24, indicated satisfactory fit. Emotional intelligence also had a significant indirect effect on self-perceived employability through career adaptability. They concluded that the ability to deal with emotions may activate the adaptability resources, which in turn raises confidence in finding a future employment.

Figure 24. Career Adaptability Mediates between
Emotional Intelligence and Employability

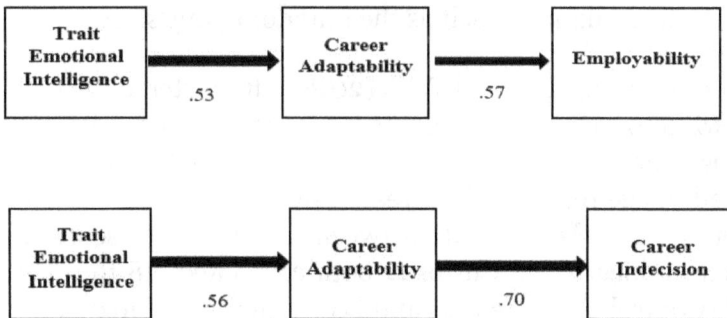

| Trait Emotional Intelligence | → .53 | Career Adaptability | → .57 | Employability |

| Trait Emotional Intelligence | → .56 | Career Adaptability | → .70 | Career Indecision |

Self-Esteem

In two of the proactive personality studies, the researchers used the *Rosenberg Self-Esteem Scale* (*RSES*; Rosenberg, 1965), which is a global measure of self-reported self-esteem. It contains ten items related to overall feelings of self-worth and self-acceptance. An example item reads, "On the whole, I am satisfied with myself." As already noted, Cai, Guan, Li, Shi, Guo, Liu, Li, Han, Jiang, Fang, and Hua (2015) reported that, among Chinese university students (N = 305), self-esteem correlated to career adaptability .30, with the highest correlation to the adapt-ability of Confidence (r = .33). Oncel (2014) reported that for 332 college seniors in Turkey, self-esteem correlated .44 to *CAAS* total score, with highest adaptability correlation to the adapt-ability of Control at .43. Also in study discussed previously Hui, Yuen, and Chen (2018a) reported that the *RSES* correlated .30 to the *CAAS* total score.

Four additional investigations have also examined the relation of the *CAAS* to the *RSES*. van Vianen, Klehe, Koen, and Dries (2012) were the first to study the relation of self-esteem to adaptability using the *RSES*. The participants were university students in the Netherlands (N = 465; 74% females) with a mean age of 20.77 years. All correlations between self-esteem and the adapt-abilities were positive and significant (p<.01). Self-esteem correlated .17 to Concern, .52 to Control, .23 to Curiosity, and .29 to Confidence. The researchers concluded that self-esteem correlated particularly with career Control because that scale includes items such as "Counting on myself," and "Sticking up for my beliefs," which refer to self-reliance and taking the self as the initiator of one's actions.

In Turkey, Atac, Dirk, and Tetik (2018) administered the *CAAS* and the *RSES* to 313 senior students in Economics and Administrative Sciences at a public university. The 179 females and 134 males ranged in age from 21 to 28 years (Mean = 22.6; SD = 1.19). They reported a correlation of .42 between the *CAAS* total score and self-esteem. Concern and Curiosity both correlated .28 to self-esteem while Control correlated .45 and Confidence correlated .36.

In Greece, Sidiropoulou-Dimakakou1, Mikedaki, Argyropoulou, and Kaliris (2018) compared scores on the *CAAS* and the *RSES* using as participants 452 university students. They reported that the *RSES* correlated .44 to the *CAAS* total score, with correlations of .12 to both Concern and Curiosity, .30 to Control, and .21 to Confidence.

Scores on the *CAAS* were correlated to the *RSES* for 212 undergraduate psychology students (Mean age = 20.7; 50% females) in Romania. Rusu, Măirean, Hojbotă, Gherasim, and Gavriloaiei (2015) reported that the *RSES* correlated .40 to the *CAAS* total score, as well as .29 to Concern, .41 to Control, .26 to

Curiosity, and .32 to Confidence. In addition, as predictors of adaptability they compared implicit self-esteem to explicit self-esteem as measured by the *RSES*. Implicit self-esteem is less accessible to introspection and results from implicit processes that are fast, automatic, and reliant on early socialization experiences, while explicit self-esteem results from rational deliberations. Research has separated, both conceptually and operationally, the explicit and implicit aspects of self-esteem to examine how a discrepancy between the two affects mental health. There are two major types of discrepancy. Fragile self-esteem combines high explicit self-esteem with low implicit self-esteem. Damaged self-esteem combines high implicit self-esteem with low explicit self-esteem. Both fragile and damaged self-esteem related to vulnerability. Rusu, Măirean, Hojbotă, Gherasim, and Gavriloaiei (2015) measured implicit self-esteem with the *Name-Letter Task* (Nuttin, 1987). Participants rated their liking from one to seven for each letter of the alphabet. High implicit self-esteem was indexed by the extent to which a person prefers his or her initials to other letters of the alphabet. Scores for implicit self-esteem did not correlate significantly to *CAAS* total or any of it dimensions.

Rusu and colleagues (2015) also examined two types of associative patterns between implicit and explicit self-esteem: additive and multiplicative. An *additive* model tests whether an implicit measure increases prediction of a criterion beyond just explicit self-esteem. They computed a hierarchical regression to test whether implicit self-esteem can explain significant variance in adaptability and its dimensions over and above explicit self-esteem. It did not. The *multiplicative* model tested whether implicit and explicit self-esteem interact in predicting adaptability. Congruence between implicit and explicit self-esteem should lead to an increased predictability of adaptability, while conflict between them should reduce their predictive capacity. The results for the multiplicative model indicated that the implicit and explicit measures of self-esteem related to Control, Confidence, and overall adaptability. Specifically, implicit self-esteem significantly moderated the relationship between explicit self-esteem and Control, Confidence, and overall adaptability. The multiplicative model results suggested that participants with high explicit self-esteem and low implicit self-esteem declared themselves as being more in control, more confident, and with higher overall adaptability than all other participants. These findings are in line with previous research showing that individuals with discrepant high self-esteem make more favorable self-evaluations regarding personal attributes, exhibit more unrealistic optimism than the ones with congruent self-esteem, and score higher on narcissism. From this perspective, the particularly positive valence of Control and Confidence as personal attributes with social impact, unlike Concern and Curiosity, could represent the reason for the participants' self-enhancement tendencies. In the end, the researchers concluded that adaptability is, at most, weakly influenced by the automatic processing based on the associative structures of self-esteem.

As summarized in Table 10, self-esteem correlated more strongly to the adapt-ability of Control, followed by Confidence then Concern and Curiosity. This suggests that individuals with higher self-esteem display stronger regulatory resources for taking responsibility and having faith in their abilities to perform tasks.

Table 10. Correlations between the *Rosenberg Self-Esteem Scale* and the *CAAS* in 8 Studies

	CAAS Total	Concern	Control	Curiosity	Confidence
Amarnani et al. Phillipines	.24	.27	.21	.13	.15
Atec et al. Turkey	.42	.28	.45	.28	.36
Cai et al. China	.30	.24	.23	.32	.33
Hui et al. Hong Kong	.30				
Oncel Turkey	.44	.41	.42	.29	.31
Rusu et al. Romania	.40	.29	.41	.26	.32

Sidiropoulou-Dimakakoul Greece	.24	.12	.30	,12	.21
vanVianen et al. – The Netherlands	.38	.17	.52	.23	.29
Mean r	.33	.25	.36	.23	.28

Core Self-Evaluations

Although researchers usually study self-esteem as single trait, Judge, Locke, and Durham (1997) integrated self-esteem into a broader construct called "core self-evaluations." Their original purpose was to formulate propositions regarding dispositional factors that affect job satisfaction. After reviewing the literature, they identified four lower-order personality dimensions that were relatively powerful predictors of job satisfaction: self-esteem, generalized self-efficacy, locus of control, and emotional stability. Then they integrated the four traits into a compound trait that they named core self-evaluations. They defined this stable personality trait as encompassing an individual's fundamental appraisals of themselves, their abilities, and their control. The broad trait is typically measured with the *Core Self-Evaluations Scale* (*CSES*; Judge, Erez, Bono, & Thoresen, 2003) which has 12 items, including "I am confident I get the success I deserve in life" and "I do not feel in control of my success in my career."

The *CSES* was used to study the relation of core self-evaluations to career adaptability by Ma, Chen, and Zeng (2020), Zacher (2014a), and Hirschi, Herrmann, and Keller (2015). In a study of 1,062 college nursing student in Northwest China. Ma, Chen, and Zeng (2020) reported that career adaptability correlated .59 to core self-evaluation. Among a heterogeneous sample of 1723 employees in Australia, Zacher (2014a) reported that core self-evaluations correlated .41 to the *CAAS* total score, with correlations of .21 to Concern, .48 to Control, .30 to Curiosity, and .43 to Confidence. He concluded that individuals with positive core self-evaluations were more likely to take an interest in and responsibility for their career development. In addition, employees with high core self-evaluations should be more likely to be confident in their abilities to overlap address career challenges and to realize their personal career goals. For 1260 university students in Germany, Hirschi, Herrmann, and Keller (2015) reported correlations of .34 to Concern, .61 to Control, .29 to Curiosity, and .46 to Confidence. The pattern of correlations of core self-evaluation to the four adapt-abilities was the same as that of self-esteem. Core self-evaluation relates more strongly to Control and Confidence than to Concern and Curiosity.

Self-Reflection

Self-reflection is a cognitive process with which individuals intentionally make sense of and reconstruct the meaning of experiences. Research based in on CCT usually studies self-reflection as a meaning-making process engaged in by an autobiographical author (Savickas, 2016). Only two studies have investigated self-reflection relative to a motivated agent's career adaptability. The first study to link career adaptability to self-reflection concentrated more broadly on self-focused attention, that is, awareness directed internally to thoughts, emotions, beliefs, and attitudes (Shin & Li, 2019). There are two types of dispositional self-focus. Self-reflection, which is adaptive, attends to inner experience that in the career domain leads to greater authenticity, exploration, and satisfaction. Self-rumination, which is maladaptive, involves a self-absorption that in the career domain leads to anxiety, negativity, and self-doubt. Self-focused attention may serve as an adaptive readiness that motivates individuals to use their adaptability resources to deal with career tasks, transitions, and troubles.

Using this reasoning, Shin and Lee (2019) examined the effects of self-focused attention, as a measure of adaptive readiness, on career anxiety via career adaptability. Participants consisted of 326 undergraduate students (375 females) who were enrolled in introductory psychology classes at a large university in South Korea. Self-focused attention was measured by the *Scale for*

Dispositional Self-Focused Attention in Social Situations (Lee & Kwon, 2005), which assesses two types of self-focused attention: (a) the general, natural, and adaptive tendency to pay attention to the self and to monitor and regulate one's thoughts and behaviors (self-reflection) and (b) maladaptive and negative self-absorbed attention (self-rumination. Career anxiety was measured by the Anxiety Scale of the *Emotional and Personality-Related Career Difficulties Questionnaire* (Saka & Gati, 2007).

Results indicated that the *CAAS* total score correlated .36 to reflection, with the highest subscale correlation being .40 to Concern. The *CAAS* total score correlated -.15 to rumination, with the highest subscale correlation of -22 to Control. The *CAAS* total score correlated significantly and negatively to (-.27) to career anxiety. Results of the structural model shown in Figure 25 were subjected to mediation analysis.

Figure 25. Adaptability Mediates between Reflection and Anxiety

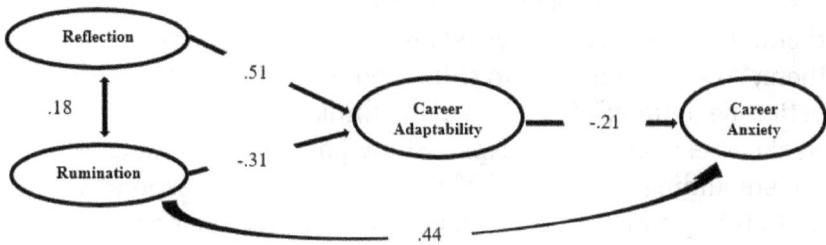

The direct effect of reflection on career anxiety was not significant (β = -.05) whereas the direct effect of rumination was significant (β = .44). The indirect effect of reflection and adaptability on anxiety was significant (β = -.11) as was the indirect effect of rumination (β = .07). Thus, career adaptability partly mediated the association between self-reflection and career anxiety as well as the association between self-rumination and career anxiety. The researchers concluded that in-depth self-reflection may foster development of adaptability resources to cope with career changes and challenges, which in turn decreases career anxiety. In contrast, rumination could cause individuals to exaggerate negative self-evaluation and emotions that impede the development and use of adaptability resources, which in turn increases career anxiety.

In a study that examined both core self-evaluation and self-reflection, Son (2018) proposed that self-reflection mediates between adaptive characteristics and career adaptability. He selected two operational definitions of adaptivity, namely learning goal orientation and core self-evaluations. Learning goal orientation in the work domain was assessed with a five-item scale (VandeWalle, 1997) that measures the disposition to develop self at work by acquiring new skills, mastering new situations, and improving one's competence. Example items read, "I often look for opportunities to develop new skills and knowledge" and "I enjoy challenging and difficult tasks at work where I'll learn new skills. To measure the broad personality trait involving fundamental evaluations about one's self, abilities, and control, the researchers used the *Core Self-Evaluation Scale* (Judge, Erez, Bono, & Thoresen, 2003). A five-item instrument developed by Peltier, Hay, and Drago (2006) was used to measure self-reflection. The items read, (a) "I often reflect on my actions to see whether I can improve them;" (b) "I often reappraised my experiences so I could learn from them;" (c) "I often tried to think about how I could do something better next time;" (d) "I tried to think about my strengths and weaknesses;" and (e) "I explored my past experiences as a way of understanding new ideas." The participants also responded yes or no to the question "Do you have a mentor (someone who actively assists your career growth and provides career-related and interpersonal support)?" Three months after the initial data collection, the *CAAS* was administered to the participants.

The *CAAS* total score at T2 correlated .44 to core self-evaluation at T1 and .44 to learning goal orientation at T1, and .38 to self-reflection at T1. As shown in Figure 26, core self-evaluation related directly to both self-reflection (β = .24) and career adaptability (β = .33). Learning goal orientation related directly to self-reflection (β = .21) and career adaptability (β = .35). Self-reflection related indirectly to career adaptability. 35. There were indirect effects of both core self-evaluation (indirect effect = .07) and learning goal orientation (indirect effect = 0.05) on career adaptability through self-reflection.

Figure 26. Self-Reflection Mediates between Core Self-Evaluation and Adaptability

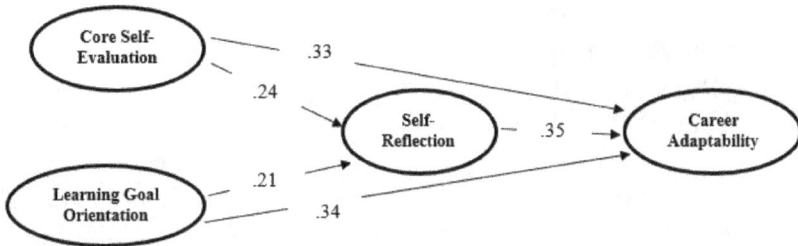

Moderation analyses indicated that having a mentor strengthens the relationship between self-reflection and career adaptability. The relation was stronger for individuals with mentors (β = .53, p < .01) than for those without (β = .24, p < .01). This finding supports the view that a mentor is a source of self-reflection and suggests that having a mentor provides more chances for individuals to reflect, which, in turn, increases their career adaptability. The researchers concluded that individuals' reflection plays a significant role in the process of making meaning in vocational and occupational experience. Following this section that concentrated on element traits plus core self-evaluations, the next section deals with traits in three hierarchical taxonomic models.

Hierarchical Trait Models of Adaptive Readiness

Taxonomies of personality traits are hierarchical models that assert three to six broad dimensions concisely and adequately describe personality. This second section of Chapter 9 examines relations of adaptability to adaptive readiness represented by the Five Factor Model, Alternative Five Factor Model, and HEXACO model.

Five Factor Model

The best known and most commonly accepted hierarchical model is the Five-Factor Model (FFM) that uses five broad dimensions to describe stable dispositions in human personality (McCrae & Costa, 1999): Openness, Conscientiousness, Extraversion, Agreeableness, and Neuroticism. Openness to experience denotes a tendency to be intellectually curiosity, creative, and to prefer novelty and variety. Conscientiousness denotes a tendency to be organized and dependable, show self-discipline, act dutifully, strive to achieve, and prefer planned rather than spontaneous behavior. Extraversion denotes a tendency to be energetic, sociable, assertive, and talkative. Agreeableness denotes the tendency to be compassionate and cooperative, trusting and helpful. And finally, Neuroticism denotes poor impulse control and the tendency to easily experience unpleasant emotions such as anger, anxiety, and depression. Neuroticism has also been labeled by its inverse, namely, Emotional Stability.

The five dimensions in the FFM of personality traits constitute plausible indicators of adaptivity. However, no single FFM dimension, separately considered, adequately reflects the complexity of adaptivity. The Life Design International Research Group (2008) suggested the dimensions of Openness to Experience and Conscientiousness as a reasonable combination to indicate the characteristics of readiness and willingness to change. Openness reflects readiness to change in that it represents a propensity to explore and consider new and unfamiliar ideas and experiences required for navigating unfamiliar tasks. Rather than passively adhere to predictable routines, individuals high in Openness more readily seek new and varied experiences. In facing career transitions, individuals more open to experience may more promptly activate adaptability resources, especially Curiosity, because of the six characteristic facets of Openness: intellectual curiosity, active imagination, aesthetic sensitivity, attentiveness to inner feelings, and preference for variety. Conscientiousness reflects the willingness or initiative to take action that also characterizes adaptive readiness. Rather than procrastinate, individuals high in Conscientiousness show the initiative to set goals and are organized, persistent, and motivated in achieving them. Indeed, the initiative, striving, and perseverance characteristics of conscientious individuals reflect their willingness to act in the face of disequilibrium. In confronting career transitions, individuals high in Conscientiousness may be more willing to activate adaptability resources because of the characteristic facets of Conscientiousness: thorough, careful, organized, deliberate, planful, systematic, achievement striving, and self-disciplined. Thirteen studies that compared the FFM personality traits to career adaptability indicate that Conscientiousness is the trait most related to adaptability, having the highest correlation to the *CAAS* total score in nine of the thirteen studies. In 12 of the 13 studies that measured Openness to Experience, it had the second strongest correlation to the *CAAS* total score.

FFM in Australia

In Australia, Perera and McIlveen (2017) examined the relation of the FFM to career adaptability in two studies. Both studies operationally defined the FFM traits with the *NEO-Five Factor Inventory* (Costa & MacCrae, 1992). In one study with 1566 (66.5% females) the *CAAS* total correlated .26 to Openness, .44 to Conscientiousness, .37 to Extraversion, .34 to Agreeableness, and -.43 to Neuroticism. In the other study with 546 university students and recent graduates (76% females; Mean age = 31.66; SD = 11.13), the *CAAS* total score correlated -.14 to Neuroticism, .17 to Extraversion, .14 to Openness, .11 to Agreeableness, and .36 to Conscientiousness. Regarding the adapt-abilities, the strongest correlations were Conscientiousness to Concern (.36), Control (.30), Curiosity (.22), and Confidence (31). With the exception of a correlation of -.21 between Neuroticism and Control and .18 between Extraversion and Concern, all the other correlations between the adapt-abilities and FFM traits were .15 or less.

FFM in Brazil

In Brazil, Teixeira, Bardagi, Lassance, Magalhaes, and Duarte (2012) examined the relation of the FFM traits to career adaptability. The participants consisted of 908 adults (71.5% females) with a mean age of 28.6 years (SD = 9.7). The majority of the sample had completed higher education (50.8%) or were taking a university degree (46.3%), and 57.3% were employed. The researchers measured the FFM traits with the *Brazilian Five-Factor Personality Markers* (Hutz, Nunes, Silveira, Serra, Anton, & Wieczorek, 1998). The inventory is a self-report instrument composed of 64 adjectives. Conscientiousness (.48) and Openness (.47) were the strongest correlates of the *CAAS* total score, followed by Extraversion at .32 and Agreeableness at .27. Neuroticism correlated -.36 to career adaptability. For the subscales, the highest correlations to a personality factor were as follows: Concern correlated .39 to Conscientiousness, Control .38 to Openness, Curiosity .46 to Openness, and Confidence .53 to Conscientiousness.

FFM in China

In North China, Li, Guan, Wang, Zhou, Guo, Jiang, Mo, Li, and Fang (2015) examined the relation of the FFM to career adaptability among 264 undergraduates enrolled in a management course at a university. The mean age of the participants (71% females) was 20.97 years (SD = 1.32). The researchers measured the FFM traits with the *GSOEP Big Five Inventory* (Hahn, Gottschling, & Spinath, 2012). The results showed that career adaptability associated with all five factors of personality. Openness to experience (.44), Conscientiousness (.41) and Agreeableness (.33) were the strongest correlates of the *CAAS* total score. Extraversion correlated .25 to career adaptability and Neuroticism correlated -.24 to career adaptability. For the subscales, Concern correlated .39 to Conscientiousness; Control .34 to Openness; Curiosity .41 to Openness; and Confidence .41 to Openness and .40 to Conscientiousness.

In a second study in China, Zhuang, She, Cai, Huang, Xiang, Wang, and Zhu (2018) administered the *CAAS* and the *Chinese Big-Five Personality Scale – Short Form* (Li, Guan, Wang, Zhou, Guo, Jiang, et al., 2015) to 165 Chinese university students. The results indicated that the *CAAS* total score correlated .38 to Openness, .28 to Extraversion, .22 to Agreeableness, .40 to Conscientiousness, and -.39 to Neuroticism.

In a third study in China, Guan, Liu, Guo, Li, Wu, Chen, Xu, and Tian (2018) compared the *CAAS* total score to the FFM traits using the *GSOEP Big Five Inventory* (Hahn, Gottschling, & Spinath, 2012) which measures each factor with three items. The participants were 222 students (62 males and 160 females) from mainland China who were enrolled in undergraduate (37.8%), Masters (43.7%), and Doctoral (18.5%) programs at overseas universities. The results indicated that the *CAAS* total score correlated .31 to Openness, .18 to Extraversion, .31 to Agreeableness, .38 to Conscientiousness, and -.29 to Neuroticism.

FFM in France

In examining the relation of career adaptability to the FFM, Storme, Celik, and Myszkowski (2020) took a unique approach by examining the relation in terms of within-person variability in the five personality factors. The degree of behavioral consistency of an individual across situations is a personality trait in itself, independent of average trait levels. This means that the five factors of personality can be considered in terms of both a set of stable traits across situations as well as a set of dynamic traits that can be expressed differently depending on the characteristics of situations. A technique has been developed to assess individuals on the FFM in terms of both consistent cross-situational behavioral tendencies and a stable tendency to vary FFM behaviors across situations (Lang, Lievens, De Fruyt, Zettler, & Tackett, 2019). For example, overall a more conscientious attitude is beneficial, yet as CCT suggests being selectively conscientious could be an additional advantage. Storme and colleagues argued that being flexible rather than rigid in FFM behavioral tendencies is advantageous because some situations could call for different behavioral tendencies than the ones that are usually adaptive. As an example, they explained that displaying Openness-related behaviors can be adaptive or maladaptive depending on the context. Many studies have shown that trait levels of Extraversion, Agreeableness, Conscientiousness, Emotional Stability, and Openness relate to career adaptability because in most situations they facilitate career adapting. Storme and colleagues argued that, in addition, within-person variability in these traits may associate with career adaptability as well. Thus, they hypothesized that career adaptability is predicted by within-person variability in personality, over and beyond average trait levels. They measured the FFM traits using the *Big Five Inventory* (John & Srivastava, 1999) to assessed overall trait levels as usual and then estimated intra-individual variability across the traits with the Trait Variability Tree Model (Lang et al., 2019). The participants from the Paris area of France were 452 third-year undergraduate students (53.7% females) in business administration who ranged in age from from 18 to 25 years (Mean = 20.71, SD =.97). To reduce common-method bias, participants completed the *Big Five Inventory* in a first session and then the *CAAS* a week later.

Bivariate correlations showed that the *CAAS* total score correlated .33 to Extraversion and .34 to Extraversion variability; .23 to Agreeableness and .24 to Agreeableness variability; .32 to Conscientiousness and .32 to Conscientiousness variability; .32 to Emotional Stability and .16 to emotional stability variability; and .25 to Openness and .24 to Openness variability. Overall personality variability correlated .31 to career adaptability. Furthermore, each of the four adapt-abilities correlated with with-in person variability ranging between .21 and .34. The magnitudes of correlations to career adaptability were similar overall to those of the average trait levels. In addition, results of five separate hierarchical regressions showed that within-person variability had incremental predictive power over and beyond average trait levels when predicting the four adapt-abilities and the overall level of career adaptability. The researchers concluded that personality should no longer be considered only as a set of stable and invariable traits across situations, but as a set of dynamic traits that can be expressed differently depending on the characteristics of situations.

FFM in Romania

In Romania, Rusu, Măirean, Hojbotă, Gherasim, and Gavriloaiei (2015) studied 212 undergraduate psychology students with a mean age of 20.7 years. They measured Extraversion, Conscientiousness, and Emotional Stability with the Romanian version (Rusu, Maricuțoiu, Macsinga, Vîrgă, & Sava, 2012) of the IPIP 50 questionnaire (Goldberg, 1992). Results showed that *CAAS* total score correlated .36 to Conscientiousness, .26 to Extraversion, and -.15 to Neuroticism. Regarding correlations to the adapt-abilities, Concern correlated .42 to Conscientiousness; Control correlated .25 to Conscientiousness; Curiosity correlated .21 to Extraversion and .20 to Conscientiousness; and Confidence correlated .29 to Conscientiousness.

A second study of FFM and adaptability was conducted in Romania by Avram, Burtaverde, and Zanfirescu (2019) who also used the *IPIP 50* questionnaire (Goldberg, 1992). Results for 437 university students showed that *CAAS* total score correlated .42 to Conscientiousness, .36 to Extraversion, .44 to Openness, .49 to Agreeableness, and -.23 to Neuroticism. Regarding correlations to the adapt-abilities, Concern correlated .35 to Conscientiousness and .34 to Agreeableness. Control correlated .42 to Openness, .40 to Agreeableness, and .38 to Conscientiousness. Curiosity correlated .45 to Agreeableness .43 to Openness, and .38 to Conscientiousness. Confidence correlated .47 to Agreeableness, .42 to Openness, and .43 to Conscientiousness.

FFM in Switzerland

In French-speaking Switzerland, Rossier, Zecca, Stauffer, Maggiori, and Dauwalder (2012) examined the relation of the FFM to career adaptability. They studied 391 participants (220 females, 171 males) with ages ranging from 20 to 79 years (M = 39.6; SD = 12.3). The sample consisted largely of employed people (81.84%), with the remainder of the participants being unemployed people seeking employment (2.30%), students (11.25%), and retired people with a private income or those that didn't indicate their professional status (4.61%). The researchers measured the FFM traits with a brief version of the French-language *NEO-FFI-R* (McCrae & Costa, 2004). The *CAAS* total score correlated .43 to Conscientiousness, .33 to Extraversion, -.33 to Neuroticism, .17 to Openness, -24 to Agreeableness. Regarding correlations to the adapt-abilities, Concern correlated .37 to Conscientiousness; Control correlated -.50 to Neuroticism and .38 to Conscientiousness; Curiosity correlated .28 to Conscientiousness and -.28 to Agreeableness; and Confidence correlated .41 to Conscientiousness. The strength of relation to Neuroticism, being much higher than that reported in the prior four studies, might have been due to the use of a brief inventory for assessing the FFM traits. So too might the unusual negative correlations of Agreeableness (-.28) to the *CAAS* total score and from -.12 to -.28 for the adapt-abilities.

The University of Lasuanne research team (Johnston, Maggiori, & Rossier, 2016) also reported FFM correlations to the *CAAS* total score for 1,447 employed adults and 161 unemployed adults in Switzerland. The researchers measured the big-five personality traits with a brief version of the French-language *NEO-FFI-R* (McCrae & Costa, 2004).). The *CAAS* total score correlated .50 to Conscientiousness, .40 to Extraversion, -.36 to Neuroticism, .34 to Openness, -.04 to Agreeableness.

FFM in The Netherlands

In The Netherlands, van Vianen, Klehe, Koen, and Dries (2012) examined the relation of the FFM to career adaptability among 465 university students. The FFM was measured with the *Dutch 5-Factor Personality Test* (Elshout & Akkermans, 1975). Each scale consisted of 14 items measured on a 7-point response scale. The *CAAS* total correlated .39 to Openness, .37 to Conscientiousness, .33 to Extraversion, .22 to Agreeableness, and -.18 to Neuroticism. The highest correlation for Concern was .39 with Conscientiousness; Control correlated .38 to Extraversion;

Curiosity correlated .41 to Openness; and, Confidence correlated .38 to Conscientiousness and .35 to Openness.

FFM in Turkey

In Turkey, Ispir, Elibol, and Sonmez (2019) examined the relationships of career adaptability to the FFM among 265 junior and senior students in the nursing faculty at a state university in Istanbul. The participants were 85.3% females with a mean age of 21.04 years (SD = 1.29). They assessed the FFM traits with the *Ten Item Personality Inventory* (Gosling, Rentfrow, & Swann Jr., 2003), which uses one positive and one negative item to measure each of the FFM traits. The *CAAS* total score correlated .32 to Extraversion, .05 (non-significant) to Agreeableness, .24 to Conscientiousness, .16 to emotional stability, and .33 to Openness. The highest correlation for Concern was .30 with Openness: Control correlated .34 to Extraversion and .33 to Openness; Curiosity correlated .23 to Openness; and, Confidence correlated .31 to Extraversion.

Summary of Correlations between the CAAS and FFM

According to the results from the 13 studies, Conscientiousness and Openness to Experience are the broad dimensions of personality more strongly related to adaptive readiness. The mean correlations between the FFM traits and the *CAAS* total score ranged from .17 for Agreeableness to a high of .40 for Conscientiousness. A recap of the correlations between the FFM traits and the *CAAS* subscales appears in Table 11.

Table 11: Correlations between the *CAAS* and FFM Personality Traits

FFM Trait	Study	CAAS Total	Concern	Control	Curiosity	Confidence
Openness						
	Perera	.26				
	Perera	.14	.08	.10	.13	.12
	Li	.44	.33	.34	.41	.41
	Zhuang	.38				
	Guan	.31				
	Teixeira	.47	.27	.38	.46	.40
	van Vianen	.39	.22	.26	.41	.35
	Rossier	.17	.13	.06	.24	.14
	Johnston	.34				
	Avram	.44	.20	.42	.43	.42
	Storme	.16	.09	.13	.15	.16
	Isipir	.33	.30	.33	.23	.24
Mean r		**.32**	**.20**	**.25**	**.31**	**.28**

	Study	CAAS Total	Concern	Control	Curiosity	Confidence
Extraversion						
	Perera	.37				
	Perera	.17	.18	.11	.11	.14
	Li	.25	.15	.21	.23	.25
	Zhuang	.28				
	Guan	.18				
	Teixeira	.32	.17	.32	.27	.28
	van Vianen	.33	.18	.38	.25	.24
	Rossier	.33	.27	.31	.22	.30
	Johnston	.40				
	Avram	.36	.22	.33	.33	.36
	Storme	.33	.26	.30	.21	.33

	Study	CAAS Total	Concern	Control	Curiosity	Confidence
	Rusu	.26	.17	.21	.21	.24
	Isipir	.32	.21	.34	.19	.34
Mean r		**.30**	**.20**	**.28**	**.22**	**.28**

Agreeableness						
	Perera	.14				
	Perera	.11	ns	ns	.14	.15
	Li	.33	.30	.27	.21	.35
	Zhuang	.22				
	Guan	.31				
	Teixeria	.27	.20	.18	.25	.25
	van Vianen	.22	.16	.18	.16	.18
	Rossier	-.23	-20	-.12	-.28	-.20
	Johnston	-.04				
	Avram	.49	.34	.40	.45	.47
	Storme	.23	.17	.21	.19	.20
	Isipir	ns	ns	ns	ns	ns
Mean r		**.17**	**.16**	**.19**	**.16**	**.20**

Emotional Stability						
	Perera	.43				
	Perera	.14	.08	.21	.08	.09
	Li	.24	.21	.19	.17	.18
	Zhuang	.39				
	Guan	.29				
	Teixeira	.36	.19	.35	.27	.34
	van Vianen	.18	ns	.40	ns	.13
	Rossier	.43	.37	.38	.28	.41
	Johnston	.36				
	Avram	.23	ns	.37	.19	.20
	Storme	.25	.19	.29	.15	.18
	Rusu	.15	ns	.23	.16	ns
	Isipir	.16	.20	.24	ns	ns
Mean r		**.28**	**.21**	**.30**	**.19**	**.22**

Conscientiousness						
	Perera	.44				
	Perera	.36	.31	.30	.22	.29
	Li	.41	.39	.31	.27	.40
	Zhuang	.40				
	Guan	.38				
	Teixeira	.32	.17	.32	.27	.28
	van Vianen	.37	.39	.12	.23	.38
	Rossier	.43	.37	.38	.28	.41
	Johnston	.50				
	Avram	.49	.34	.40	.45	.47
	Storme	.32	.29	.27	.18	.32
	Rusu	.36	.42	.25	.20	.29
	Isipir	.24	.21	.28	.15	.25
Mean r		**.40**	**.32**	**.29**	**.26**	**.34**

In the thirteen studies that related the *CAAS* to the FFM traits, the bivariate correlations between Conscientiousness and the *CAAS* total score were the highest. As shown in Table 12, the correlations ranged from .24 to .50, with a mean correlation of .40. Moreover, in nine of the thirteen studies, Conscientious had the strongest correlation to adaptability. Table 12 highlights for each study the FFM personality trait with the strongest correlation to the CAAS total score. Overall, the results suggest that the "will to achieve" characteristic of Conscientiousness may in fact predispose people to develop and activate adaptability resources.

Table 12: Correlations between *CAAS* Total Score
and FFM Personality Traits

	Openness	Extraversion	Agreeableness	Conscientiousness	ES
Perera	.26	.37	.14	.44	.43
Perera	.14	.17	.11	.36	.14
Li	.44	.25	.33	.41	.24
Zhuang	.38	.28	.22	.40	.39
Guan	.31	.18	.31	.38	.29
Teixeira	.47	.32	.27	.32	.36
van Vianen	.39	.33	.22	.37	.18
Rossier	.17	.33	-.23	.43	.43
Johnston	.34	.40	-.04	.50	.36
Avram	.44	.36	**.49**	.49	.23
Storme	.16	.33	.23	.32	.25
Rusu		.26		.36	.15
Isipir	.33	.32	ns	.24	.16
Mean *r*	**.32**	**.30**	**.17**	**.40**	**.28**

In 12 of the 13 studies that measured Openness to Experience (the Romanian study did not), it had the second strongest correlation to adaptability, with a mean of .32 and values ranging from .14 to .47. In four of the twelve studies, Openness had the strongest correlation to adaptability. Openness to experience involves not only an exploratory attitude but also a more sophisticated intellectual functioning and cultural awareness. As a consequence, individuals highly open to their own experiences may be more likely to develop and activate adaptability resources. Furthermore, rather than just responding to change, the facets of imagination, adventure, and curiosity may prompt change.

The adaptability dimension of Curiosity was expected by CCT to have its strong relationship to Openness, and as shown in Table 13 it did with a mean correlation of .31. In four of the nine studies (highlighted in Table 13) that reported subscale scores for the *CAAS*, Curiosity (compared to Concern, Control, and Confidence) had the highest correlations to Openness (.42, .46, .41. and .23). In three of the studies (highlighted in Table 12), Curiosity correlated most strongly to Conscientiousness (.22, .28, and .45). The pattern of correlations shown in Table 13 support the concurrent validity of the *CAAS* Curiosity subscale.

Table 13: Correlations between *CAAS Curiosity Subscale* and FFM Personality Traits

CAAS Curiosity	Openness	Extraversion	Agreeablenes s	Conscientiousnes s	ES
Perera	.13	.11	.14	**.22**	.08
Li	**.41**	.23	.21	.27	.17
Teixeira	**.46**	.27	.25	.27	.27
van Vianen	**.41**	.25	.16	.23	ns
Rossier	.24	.22	-.28	**.28**	.28
Avram	.43	.33	**.45**	**.45**	.19
Storme	.15	**.21**	.19	.18	.15
Rusu		**.21**		.20	.16
Isipir	**.23**	.19	ns	.15	ns
Mean r	**.31**	**.22**	**.16**	**.26**	**.19**

Alternative Five Factor Model

An Alternative Five-Factor Model (AFFM) based on psychobiology has been presented by Zuckerman (1999). He reasoned that the basic factors of personality should each show a biological-evolutionary basis, one evidenced by comparable traits in non-humans. The five dimensions in the AFFM each include four facets. The Extraversion dimension, which is very similar to FFM Extraversion, contains the facets of positive emotions, social warmth, exhibitionism, and sociability. The Neuroticism-Anxiety dimension, which is basically identical to FFM Neuroticism, contains the facets of anxiety, depression, dependency, and low self-esteem. The Aggressiveness dimension, contains the facets of physical aggression, verbal aggression, anger, and hostility. It is the inverse of FFM Agreeableness. The Activity dimension, which is similar to FFM Conscientiousness, contains the facets of work compulsion, general activity, restlessness, and work energy. The Sensation-seeking dimension contains the facets of thrill and adventure seeking, experience seeking, disinhibition, and boredom susceptibility/impulsivity. It is to some degree the inverse of FFM Conscientiousness but it is more behavioral in content. The most obvious difference between the FFM and the AFFM is that AFFM does not include a dimension similar to FFM Openness to Experience. Reasoning that indicators of culture, aesthetics, and intellect are absent in non-human species, Zuckerman deliberately excluded Openness as a dimension.

The relation of the AFFM to career adaptability in French-speaking areas of Switzerland was studied by Rossier, Zecca, Stauffer, Maggiori, and Dauwalder (2012). Their sample consisted of 391 participants (220 females and 171 males) who ranged in age from 20 to 79 years (M = 39.59; SD = 12.30). Most of the sample consisted of employed people (81.84%), unemployed people seeking employment (2.30%), students (11.25%), or retired people with a private income or those that did not indicate their professional status (4.61%). The researchers used the French version of the *Zuckerman–Kuhlman–Aluja Personality Questionnaire (ZKA-PQ*; Rossier, Hansenne, Baudin, & Merizot, 2012) to measure the five dimensions in the AFFM. Each 20 facet-scale includes 10 items.

The *CAAS* total score correlated positively with AFFM Activity (.31) and Extraversion (.32); slightly with Sensation-seeking (.16);

negatively with Neuroticism (-.42); but not Aggressiveness (-.04). The *CAAS* total score and several *ZKA-PQ* facet-scales associated with a large or medium effect size. Positive correlations were observed between career adaptability and work energy (.39), positive emotions (.34), and exhibitionism (.30). Negative correlations were observed between career adaptability and depression (-.37), dependency (-.37), and low self-esteem (-.45). Concern correlated .34 to Extraversion, -.34 to Neuroticism, .28 to Activity, .09 to Sensation-seeking, and -.03 to Aggression. Control correlated -.53 to Neuroticism, .34 to Extraversion, .28 to Activity, .21 to Sensation-seeking, and -.02 to Aggression. Curiosity correlated -.16 to Neuroticism, .14 to Extraversion, .12 to Activity, .11 to Sensation-seeking, and -.05 to Aggression. Confidence correlated -.38 to Neuroticism, .35 to Activity, .22 to Extraversion, .12 to Sensation-seeking, and -.03 to Aggression.

Nilforooshan and Salimi (2016) also examined the relation of career adaptability to the AFFM using the *Zuckerman–Kuhlman–Aluja Personality Questionnaire* (Aluja, Kuhlman, & Zuckerman, 2010). The participants were 201 students (50% female) at a large university in Iran, with 64% being undergraduate students and the remainder being graduate students. They had a mean age of 23 years. The *CAAS* total score correlated positively with AFFM Activity (.39) and Extraversion (.37); slightly with Sensation-seeking (.12); negatively with Neuroticism (-.40); Aggressiveness (-.22). Concern correlated .43 to Activity, 36 to Extraversion, -.29 to Neuroticism, -.20 to Aggression, and .06 (NS) to Sensation-seeking. Control correlated -.41 to Neuroticism, .35 to Extraversion, .32 to Activity, -.26 to Aggression, and .08 (NS) to Sensation-seeking. Curiosity correlated -.35 to Neuroticism, .29 to Extraversion, .29 to Activity, .18 to Sensation-seeking, and .13 to Aggression. Confidence correlated -.30 to Neuroticism, .30 to Activity, .26 to Extraversion, -.17 to Aggression, and .08 (NS) to Sensation seeking.

As shown in Table 14, the results from the two studies that examined the AFFM, low Neuroticism, high Activity, and high Extraversion are broad dimensions of personality more related to adaptability resources. The results obtained from the two studies produced quite similar correlations of AFFM to career adaptability (Activity .31 and .39; Extraversion .32 and .37; Aggressiveness -.04 and -.22; Sensation-seeking .16 and .12; Neuroticism -.42 and -.40). The results suggest that career adaptivity may combine lower dependence and higher self-esteem, work energy, work compulsion, positive emotions, and high self-esteem. It is difficult to compare the FFM results to the AFFM results because the AFFM lacks an Openness dimension and Conscientiousness is measured more as Activity. This may be why Neuroticism and Extraversion played a stronger role in the AFFM relations to adaptability. Given the evidence at hand, Openness and Conscientiousness seem to be more important in career adaptability.

Table 14: Correlations between *CAAS* Scores
and AFFM Personality Traits

Trait	Study	CAAS Total	Concern	Control	Curiosity	Confidence
Activity	Rossier	.39	.43	.32	.29	.30
	Nilforooshan	.38	.28	.25	.12	.35
Aggression	Rossier	ns	ns	ns	ns	ns
	Nilforooshan	-.22	-.20	-.26	ns	-.17
Extraversion	Rossier	.32	.34	.32	.14	.22
	Nilforooshan	.37	.36	.35	.29	.26
Sensation	Rossier	.16	ns	.22	ns	ns
	Nilforooshan	ns	ns	ns	.18	ns
Neuroticism	Rossier	-.42	-.34	-.53	-.16	-.38
	Nilforooshan	-.40	-.29	-.41	-.35	-.30

HEXACO Model

The third taxonomic model of personality structure is the HEXACO model created by Ashton and Lee (2009) based on a series of lexical studies of several European and Asian languages. The model identifies six broad dimensions of personality based on factor-analyses of adjectives found in language that describe behaviors and tendencies among individuals. In the HEXACO model, Extraversion, Conscientiousness, and Openness resemble the dimensions included in the FFM. Agreeableness and

Neuroticism/Emotionality differ somewhat from those in the FFM. Humility-Honesty is unique to the HEXACO model.

The first study to examine the relation of the HEXACO model to career adaptability was conducted in Switzerland by Udayar, Fiori, Thalmayer, and Rossier (2018) who administered the brief 24-item version of the *HEXACO Inventory* (De Vries, 2013) to 400 university students (46% female) who ranged in age from 17 to 48 year (Mean = 21.39; SD = 3.27). Results showed that *CAAS* total score correlated .41 to Conscientiousness, .22 to Extraversion, .19 to Openness, and -.20 to Emotionality, and -.06 to Agreeableness but not to Humility.

In a second study that examined the relation of the HEXACO model to career adaptability, Sverko and Babarovic (2019) used only the Conscientiousness, Extraversion, and Openness scales from the *HEXACO Inventory* (Ashton & Lee, 2009). The researchers collected data from 299 (73.9% females), generally 17 or 18 years old and in the last year of secondary school. Results indicated that Extraversion correlated .27 to Concern, .42 to Control, .21 to Curiosity, and .31 to Confidence. Conscientiousness correlated .40 to Concern, .20 to Control, .18 to Curiosity, and .44 to Confidence. Openness correlated .10 to Concern and .27 to Curiosity but not to Control nor Confidence.

A third study of the the HEXACO model relative to adaptability was conducted in Romania by Avram, Burtaverde, and Zanfirescu (2019) who also used the *HEXACO Inventory* (Ashton & Lee, 2009). Results for 437 university students showed that *CAAS* total score correlated .48 to Conscientiousness, .47 to Extraversion, .26 to Openness, and -.20 to Emotionality but not to Humility nor Agreeableness.

The HEXACO results resemble those from the AFFM in highlighting Conscientiousness and Extraversion, and not Openness. The strongest correlations to the *CAAS* total score were with Conscientiousness (.41, .48, .41) followed by Extraversion as a distant second (.19, .42, .22). Conscientiousness and Extraversion were generally moderately correlated to the four adapt-abilities. Openness correlated weakly to the *CAAS* total score (.14, .19, .26) but did show the expected stronger relation to Curiosity (.30 and .29).

Comparisons of Individual + FFM Traits
Relations to Adaptability

Two studies compared the relation of individual traits (i.e., proactivity and core self-evaluations) and the FFM to career adaptability. In a meta-analysis of the relation of career adaptability to individual traits and the FFM, Rudolph, Lavigne, and Zacher (2017) reported that FFM personality dimensions could explain significant, unique variability in adaptability above and beyond the influence of proactive personality disposition. Conscientiousness and Openness seem to be the more salient FFM dimensions relative to developing and activating adaptability resources as well as managing a career. Openness to Experience provides the imagination to dream about possible futures and the Curiosity to explore current situations and form creative plans. Conscientious individuals with their high need for achievement seem more motivated to prepare to execute the plans and then implement the plans with self-discipline, effort, problem solving, and persistence.

In a second study, Zacher (2014a) investigated the effects of demographic characteristics and three sets of individual difference variables (i.e., FFM personality traits, core self-evaluations, and temporal focus) on changes in employees' career adaptability over a period of six months. He concentrated on the extent to which certain individual differences prompted employees to experience increases or decreases in career adaptability over time.

Data for this two-wave survey study came from 659 full-time employees in Australia, including 322 men (48.9%) and 337 women (51.1%). The average age of participants was 48.17 years (SD = 10.87) and ranged from 20 to 69 years. In terms of highest level of education achieved, one participant had not finished high school (0.2%), 192 (29.1%) had finished high school, 179 (27.2%) held a technical college degree, 186 (28.2%) held an undergraduate university degree, and 101 (15.3%) held a postgraduate university degree. Participants worked in a broad range of jobs, occupations, industries, and organizations across Australia.

The FFM was assessed with five 4-item scales developed by Donnellan, Oswald, Baird and Luca (2006). Core self-evaluations were measured at Time 1 with a 12-item scale developed by Judge, Erez, Bono, and Thoresen (2002). Past, current, and future temporal focus dimensions were assessed at Time 1 with four items each (Shipp. Edwards, & Lambert, 2009). Example items read, "I replay memories of the past in my mind" (past temporal focus); "I focus on what is currently happening in my life" (current temporal focus; and "I think about what my future has in store" (future temporal focus.

Of all individual difference predictors investigated in this study, future temporal focus had the most consistent effects on changes in career adaptability variables over time, as it predicted changes in overall career adaptability as well as in Concern, Control, and Curiosity but not Confidence. The positive effects are consistent with theorizing in the vocational psychology literature, which has characterized future temporal focus as a key predictor of career adaptability. The results suggested that a future temporal focus may be more important in preparing for future career tasks (Concern), taking responsibility for influencing one's development and work environment (Control), and exploring future possibilities (Curiosity) than for employees' beliefs that they can turn their career goals into reality (Confidence). With regard to the FFM, Extraversion positively predicted change in Concern, Neuroticism negatively predicted change in Control, Openness to Experience positively predicted change in Curiosity, and core self-evaluations positively predicted change in Confidence over time.

Conclusions about Adaptivity as Personality Traits

Prior research has not settled on a standard operational definition of adaptivity. Perhaps the most conceptually comprehensive single indicator of adaptivity is proactive personality, that is, a general disposition to take intentional action to effect change in one's environment (Bateman & Crant, 1993). Highly proactive individuals show initiative in identifying opportunities, acting on them, and persevering until they bring about meaningful change. However, proactive personality disposition does not fully capture the complexity of career adaptivity from the CCT perspective. Overall, the research that has examined adaptivity in terms of personality traits indicates that further research might concentrate on crafting a precise measure of career adaptivity that is a compound of proactivity, conscientiousness, and openness.

Adaptivity as Willingness:
Motivational Orientation Models

This section discusses studies that relate three different models of motivational orientation to career adaptability. Following the trait models, the second dominant approach to understanding personality structure involves motivational systems models. The career adaptation model distinguishes between traits as indicators of *readiness* to activate adaptability responses and motivation as *willingness*. This is relevant to developing and activating career adapt-abilities because personality traits describe attributes, yet they are not as good as motivational variables in predicting performance.

Recent models for the study of human motivation, particularly those that include the approach-avoidance dichotomy, are highly relevant to the aspect of career adaptivity denoted as willingness to approach goals. This is because an individual's chronic orientation to approach or avoid may be viewed as an organizing force for personality expression (Manczak, Zapata-Gietl, & McAdams, 2014). Motivational theories begin by positing a higher-order motivational state that directs focus of attention and evaluation on approach goals or avoidance goals and, in due course, also directs approach and avoidance behaviors. Viewing these models of *regulatory focus* as part of adaptivity fits well with the CCT conceptualization of adaptability as self-regulation resources. Self-regulation focus (i.e., adaptivity orientation) activates and directs the use of self-regulation resources (adapt-abilities).

Approach and avoidance are essential structures for adaptive functioning because they move organisms toward beneficial stimuli and away from harmful stimuli. Because approach and avoidance are the two must elemental reactions with which an organism may react to environmental stimuli, some theorists have argued that they are the most fundamental dimensions of personality (Elliot, & Thrash, 2010). Simply stated, the basic principle is that people approach pleasure and avoid pain. Consequently, motivational orientation models focus on the two different ways that people pursue their goals. With a focus on approach, individuals pursue goals for growth and advancement. They tend to explore, expand, articulate, discover, and fulfill the self. In contrast, individuals who focus on avoidance look to not making mistakes and remaining safe. They tend to control, tame, discipline, or subdue the self. Note that motivational systems models do not address need satisfaction, instead they concentrate on the manner of pursuing goals. Elliot and Thrasher (2010) called the two dimensions "instigators" (p. 868) that orient individuals' goals and behavior. The notion of motivational systems as instigator fits well with the view that adaptivity instigates or activates adaptability resources.

Contemporary models of motivational orientation have updated the traditional hedonic principle that people act to maximize pleasure and minimize pain. Four different models have been studied as indicators of adaptivity. Each model conceptualizes motivational orientation as stable, dispositional tendencies toward approach and avoidance. The first model (Gray, 1970) concentrates on the neurophysiological substrates of these two motivational systems. A second model (Elliot & Thrash, 2002) extends Gray's bio-behavioral model. And a third model (Higgins, 1997) concentrates on how social and cognitive development shape the internalization of promotion and prevention goal representation systems. The fourth model is Brandtstadter and Renner's (1990)) dual-strategies model of coping when goal attainment is blocked. They posit two distinct yet complementary adaptivity styles in the face of blocked goals: the assimilative tenacity to continue pursuing blocked goals in the face of obstacles and the accommodative flexibility to adjust blocked goals. Both assimilative tenacity and accommodative flexibility constitute trait-like dispositions for coping that are activated by adaptive strain. Both holding on and letting go may produce adaptive strategies, with more adaptive individuals dynamically balancing the two coping styles. Each of these four models of motivational orientation have been investigated as indicators of adaptivity in terms of their relation to adaptability resources.

Behavioral Activation and Inhibition Orientations

Reinforcement Sensitivity Theory (Gray, 1970; Gray & McNaughton, 2008) takes a physiological perspective on self-regulation focus. The model conceptualizes two neural motivational systems that condition behavior by regulating sensitivity to reward and punishment. The behavioral activation system (BAS) is sensitive to rewarding stimuli and fosters approach behaviors that dispose individuals to pursue goals. It moves individual to approach potentially rewarding situations. BAS pertains to wanting and pursuing rather than getting (McAdams, 2015). Thus it may be particularly important in activating career adapt-abilities during times of transition and goal pursuit. In comparison, the Behavioral Inhibition System (BIS) is sensitive to negative stimuli and inhibits behavior in order to avoid negative or painful outcomes during times of threat, uncertainty, conflict, and social risk. According to McAdams (2015), anxiety results from activating the BIS in situations that are vaguely defined, ambiguous, strange, or unpredictable. In turn, BIS produces passive and cautious behaviors to avoid punishment, reduce uncertainty, and resolve conflicts

Because BAS moves people to approach goals, it should have a positive relationship to career adaptability. BIS may have a negative relationship to career adaptability because it may inhibit its development. Li, Guan, Wang, Zhou, Guo, Jiang, Mo, Li, and Fang (2015) examined the relation of the BAS/BIS model to career adaptability. On one hand, they reasoned that BAS may foster development of psychosocial resources through prompting positive affect and approach behaviors that develop psychosocial resources. On the other hand, BIS may inhibit development of career adaptability resources through prompting negative affect and avoiding behaviors that develop psychosocial resources. They administered the *BIS/BAS Scales* (Carver & White, 1994) to 246 undergraduates (71% females, Mean age = 20.9 years) enrolled in a management course at a university in North China. The *BIS/BAS Scales* contain 20 items. The *BIS* contains seven items (e.g., "I worry about making mistakes"). The *BAS* contains 13 items (e.g., "I go out of my way to get things that I want"). After controlling for the effects of gender, age, and grade, the results indicated that *BAS* correlated .52 to the *CAAS* total score, with correlations of .42 to Concern, .39 to Control, .49 to Curiosity, and .46 to Confidence. *BIS* correlated -.12 to the *CAAS* total score. Clearly, an orientation toward approach and achievement related much more strongly to adaptability whereas an orientation toward avoidance and safety actually correlated negatively to adaptability.

Approach/Avoidance Temperament

The Approach and Avoidance Temperament (AAT) framework proposed by Elliot and Thrash (2002) extends the BAS and BIS constructs. They reasoned that Gray (1970) linked BAS and BIS to a rather constrained set of neuroanatomical structures and neurophysiological processes (see Gray, 1990), whereas AAT links these temperament constructs to a broader network of neuroanatomical structures and neurochemical processes across the central nervous system, including yet not limited to those detailed by Gray (Elliot, & Thrash, 2002).

Working in the AAT framework, Bipp, Kleingeld, and van Dam (2018) hypothesized that individuals with a strong approach temperament seek positive stimuli, such as career success and personal development. Individuals with a strong avoidance temperament tend to avoid task-based or normative incompetence and try to minimize hindering work demands. Although they may be concerned with their vocational future, they are mainly interested in keeping the status quo and not losing competence instead of developing themselves and adapting to change. Therefore, they may be less able to effectively deal with unfamiliar, complex, or high-risk problems as well as tend to move away from negative stimuli regarding their careers.

In their study of 290 Dutch college seniors from five academic programs, Bipp and colleagues measured AAT with the 12-item *Approach-Avoidance Temperament Questionnaire* (Elliot & Thrash, 2010). Six items each measured approach temperament (e.g., "I'm always on the lookout for positive opportunities and experiences") and avoidance temperament (e.g., "It is easy for me to imagine bad things that might happen to me"). The *CAAS* total score correlated .56 to approach temperament and -.13 to avoidance temperament. Furthermore, they investigated the mediating role of career adaptability for the effects of approach and avoidance temperament on work engagement, which they measured with the Dutch version of the 9-item short scale of the *Utrecht Work Engagement Scale for Students* (Schaufeli, Bakker, & Salanova, 2006) (e.g., "I get carried away when I'm studying"). Items were rated on a 7-point Likert scale (0 = never, 6 = always/every day). Bipp and colleagues reported a significant indirect effect of both temperament dimensions on engagement through career adaptability. thus supporting the mediation hypothesis. They also agreed with van Vianen et al (2012) in concluding that people pursuing avoidance motivation (a chronic prevention focus) display lower career adaptability.

In another study of the approach-avoidance framework, Zhuang, She, Cai, Huang, Xiang, Wang, and Zhu (2018) also administered the *CAAS* and the *Approach-Avoidance Temperament Questionnaire* (Elliot & Thrash, 2010) to 165 Chinese university students. The results indicated that the *CAAS* total score correlated .43 to approach and -.43 to avoidance. Approach and avoidance correlated -.04.

In yet another study of the approach-avoidance framework, Guan, Liu, Guo, Li, Wu, Chen, Xu, and Tian (2018) (2018) also administered the *CAAS* and the *Approach-Avoidance Temperament Questionnaire* (Elliot & Thrash, 2010) to Chinese university students. The participants in the study were 222 students (62 males and 160 females) from mainland China who were enrolled in undergraduate (37.8%), Masters (43.7%), and Doctoral (18.5%) programs at overseas universities. The results indicated that the *CAAS* total score correlated .52 to approach and -.24 to avoidance. Approach and avoidance correlated -.26.

In a model similar to the ATT framework, VandeWalle, Cron, and Slocum Jr. (2001) proposed that goal orientation is better conceptualized as a three-factor construct with goal orientations of learning, proving, and avoiding. In Nigeria, Ebenehi, Rashid, and Bakar (2016) studied the relation of career adaptability to learning goal orientation, which refers to developing one's competence by learning new skills, mastering new situation, and learning from experience. They measured it with the 5-item learning goal orientation from the *Goal Orientation Scale* (VandeWalle, Cron, & Slocum, 2001). An example item reads, "I truly enjoy learning for the sake of learning." They collected data from 603 university students in Agricultural, Business, and Technical Education programs who were randomly selected from six colleges in Nigeria. The participants consisted of 58.5%, males and 41.5% females with an average age of 22 years. The *CAAS* total score correlated .36 to learning goal orientation.

Promotion vs. Prevention Orientations

Regulatory focus is a motivational theory that posits two independent foci to describe the way individuals pursue goals (Higgins, 1997). A focus on promotion moves toward achievement, hopes, and advancement whereas a focus on prevention moves toward safety, responsibility, and security. While the approach/avoidance dichotomy coincided with Gray's (1970) BAS/BIS model, it does not as closely match Higgin's promotion/prevention model. Higgins (1997) begins with the same hedonic principle yet asserts that promotion and prevention each have approach and avoidance impulses. Promotion goals move toward opportunities for rewards and away from the absence of rewards. In comparison, prevention goals move away from the presence of negative outcomes and toward the preservation of their absence. An individual's tendency to pursue promotion and prevention goals can be conceptualized as a stable and persistent preference across time and situations. They differ in that promotion focus directs behavior toward what one wants to do while prevention focus directs behavior toward what one ought to do -- a difference between playing to win and playing not to lose.

Because promotion focus directs people to seek personal growth and opportunities in the environment, it should have a moderate correlation to career adaptability. Similar to BIS, one would expect prevention focus to have a negative correlation to career adaptability. In The Netherlands, van Vianen, Klehe, Koen, and Dries (2012) studied how promotion and prevention foci related to career adaptability with a sample of 466 university students. Promotion focus and prevention focus were measured with Lockwood, Jordon, and Kunda's (2002) regulatory focus measure. Both scales consisted of nine items on a Likert scale to which participants indicated how strongly they agreed with statements such as: "I typically focus on the success I hope to achieve in the future" (promotion focus), and "In general, I am focused on preventing negative events in my life" (prevention focus). The researchers reported that promotion focus correlated .41 to the *CAAS* total score, along with .47 to Concern, .16 to Control, .31 to Curiosity, and .29 to Confidence. Prevention focus correlated -.21 to the *CAAS* total score, along with -.40 to Control and -.20 to Confidence. The correlations to Concern and Curiosity were not significant. The researchers concluded that individuals who focus on their hopes and aspirations tend to rate themselves higher in terms of career adaptability resources. In contrast, people with a prevention focus tend to be particularly concerned about the possible negative outcomes of their actions which may impair their confidence that they can overcome obstacles.

Promotion focus may also be linked to an internal locus of control with a prevention focus connected to an external locus of control. Career locus of control refers to one's beliefs about important factors that determine career success, which include: (a) internal factors such as personal motives, capabilities and effort, (b) external factors such as social or organizational determinants, and (c) chance factor such as luck or chance events (Guan, Wang, et al., 2013). Rotter (1966) suggested that individuals with an internal locus of control attribute behavioral consequences to their personal characteristics such as ability and effort. Therefore, they are more likely to proactively develop relevant competencies and skills to achieve positive career outcomes.

Although not linked to promotion/prevention orientations by the authors, a study of perfectionism seems relevant here. The literature on perfectionism highlights two basic orientations. One orientation is toward self-established high standards for achievement, resembling to some degree a promotion focus. The second orientation involves a concern with mistakes, evaluation, and comparison to the standards of others in conjunction with discrepancy between self-standards and actual performance, resembling to some degree a prevention focus. Crossing these two orientations produces a 2 x 2 matrix of four types of perfectionism as shown in table 15.

Table 15. Four Types of Perfectionism

Non-Perfectionism (NP) Low standards and Low discrepancy	*Pure Discrepancy* (PD) Low standards and High discrepancy
Pure High Standards (PHS) High standards and Low discrepancy	*Mixed Perfectionism* (MP) High standards and High discrepancy

Working in China, Wang, Hou, Ni, Tian, Zhang, Chi, and Zhao (2020) investigated the relationship of the four perfectionism subtypes to career adaptability and career decision-making difficulties. The participants consisted of 672 sophomore and junior

215

students (60.57% females) at five universities. The researchers measured career adaptability with the *CAAS*. Decisional difficulties were measured with the *Emotional and Personality-Related Career Decision-Making Difficulties Scale – Short Form* (Saka, Gati, & Kelly, 2008), which contains three subscales: pessimistic views (6 items), anxiety (8 items), and self-concept and identity (6 items). Perfectionism was assessed with the High Standards (7 items) and Discrepancy (12 items) subscales from *Almost Perfect Scale – Revised* (Slaney, Rice, Mobley, Trippi, & Ashby, 2001).

Results indicated that the *CAAS* total score correlated -.17 to decisional difficulties, .50 to high standards, and -.22 to discrepancy evaluations. The two perfectionism scores were submitted to latent profile analysis to locate participants in the four subtypes of perfectionism, resulting in placement of 65 Non-Perfectionism, 122 Pure High Standards, 247 Pure Discrepancy, and 214 Mixed Perfectionism. The researchers then calculated for each subtype mean scores on indices representing the latent variables of career adaptability and decisional difficulties. The Pure High Standards subtype (promotion focus) with indices of the highest career adaptability (.82) and lowest decision-making difficulty (.00) was deemed the healthiest perfectionism subtype. The Pure Discrepancy subtype (prevention focus) with indices of low career adaptability (.19) and high career decision-making difficulty (1.20) was deemed the unhealthiest subtype of perfectionism. The Mixed Perfectionism subtype (high promotion and prevention) had the second highest index for career adaptability (.71) but the highest index for decisional difficulties (1.27). While individuals of the Mixed Perfectionism subtype possess the capacity to activate adaptability resources, they seem to be at significant risk of career decision-making difficulties. And finally, the Non-Perfectionism (low promotion/moderate prevention) subtype was deemed the most detrimental one with the lowest index for career adaptability (.00) combined with a moderate index for decisional difficulties (.41). The researchers suggested that individuals in this group may be somewhat apathetic. In sum, perfectionism subtypes vary systematically in career adaptability resources and decisional difficulties.

Assimilative Tenacity and Accommodative Flexibility

In two studies of regulatory focus in coping with blocked goals and adjusting to life circumstances, Tolentino, Garcia, Lu, Restubog, Bordia, and Tang (2014) examined two distinct yet complementary motivational orientations that individuals may use when encountering obstacles to goal attainment. Assimilative tenacity remains focused on achieving a difficult goal by trying harder or by looking for alternative means. In contrast, accommodative flexibility entails changing the goal and moving on. Both adaptive orientations involve negotiating transitions, adjusting to new circumstances, and activating adaptability resources.

In both studies, the researchers administered the *Tenacious Goal Pursuit Scale* (e.g., "I stick to my goals and projects even in face of great difficulties") and the *Flexible Goal Adjustment Scale* (e.g., "After a serious setback, I soon turn to new tasks"), each scale consisting of 15-items (Brandtstadter & Renner, 1990). Data for the first study was obtained from 289 undergraduate university students (Mean age = 18.64) enrolled in management courses at a large private university in The Philippines. Data for the second study was obtained from 495 full-time employees who were enrolled in various post-graduate academic programs at the university. The employed sample consisted of 56% females with a mean age of 31.71 years and an average tenure of 5.18 years. In study 1, the *CAAS* total score correlated .40 to flexible goal adjustment and .38 to tenacious goal pursuit. In study 2, the *CAAS* total score correlated .48 to flexible goal adjustment and .28 to tenacious goal pursuit.

Attention Control in Goal Pursuit

Attentional control denotes a relatively stable characteristic of an individual that facilitates exercising control over actions by means of focusing attention on goal pursuit and avoiding distractions. Dispositional self-regulation of attention implicates an action orientation as a component of adaptivity. Merino-Tejedor, Hontangas-Beltran, and Boada-Grau (2016) studied the relation of attentional control to adaptability among 577 university students in Spain. They reported that dispositional attention control, as measured by the *Self-Regulation Scale* (Luszczynska, Diehl, Gutiérrez-Doña, Kuusinen, & Schwarzer, 2004) correlated .46 to *CAAS* total score and, as one might expect, it had the highest correlation of .47 to Control, followed by correlations of .40 to Confidence, .34 to Concern, and .31 to Curiosity.

Intrinsic vs. Extrinsic Reward Orientations

The rewarding power of an activity may be inherent in the activity itself or as an outcome of doing it. Motivational focus may be used to derive predictions concerning the preference for intrinsic or extrinsic work values. Intrinsic values or goals may arise from a promotion focus whereas extrinsic values may arise from a prevention focus. For example, Sassenberg and Scholl (2013) hypothesized and confirmed that a promotion focus correlates to valuing power and opportunities for self-direction. In contrast, a prevention focus correlates to valuing security. However, McAdams (2015) pointed out that although promotion focus and intrinsic goals may be highly correlated, they are not identical. A promotion focus could also concentrate on an extrinsic goal such as becoming rich.

The relation of career adaptability to work values was examined in India by Sharma, Sunny, & Parmar (2017). Work values were measured with the *Work Values Inventory* (Super, 1970). Twelve items measured intrinsic values such as challenging work, creativity in work, and new opportunities. Nine items measured extrinsic values such as income, promotion opportunities, and pleasant lifestyle. The participants were 129 undergraduate and graduate students from private universities in Himachal Pradesh, India. Career adaptability correlated .43 to intrinsic values and .24 to extrinsic values. What is most interesting about the results is the pattern of correlation of the *CAAS* adapt-abilities to work values. Extrinsic work values correlated .38 to Career Concern yet correlated no more than .18 to the three other adapt-abilities. In comparison, intrinsic work values correlated .46 to Control, .38 to

Confidence, and .19 to Curiosity. This pattern suggests that Career Concern might relate to perceptions of employment insecurity. Two additional studies that examined the relation of career adaptability to work values did not shed light on this question.

Two studies investigated the relation of career adaptability to both reward orientation and locus of control. Zhou, Guan, Xin, Mak, and Deng (2016) studied these goal orientations in terms of criteria for career success. They used the 21-item scale developed by Zhou, Sun, Guan, Li, and Pan (2013) to measure three motives for career success: (a) fulfillment of intrinsic psychological needs such as achievement, autonomy and joy; (b) extrinsic rewards such as monetary or material compensation; and (c) balance between work and non-work lives. Zhou and colleagues also measured career locus of control beliefs about three important factors that determine career success: (a) internal factors such as capabilities and effort, (b) external factors such as social or organizational determinants, and (c) chance factor such as luck. Career locus of control was measured with a 15-item multi-dimensional scale developed by Guan, Wang et al. (2013). Data were collected from 431 undergraduate students at a university in Beijng, China. Results showed that intrinsic criteria related .40 to the *CAAS* total score. Correlations to the *CAAS* subscales ranged from .28 for Concern to .36 for Confidence. The correlation between career adaptability and extrinsic motives was only .04.

Internal career locus of control related .36 to the *CAAS* total score, and related to the four *CAAS* subscales ranging from .23 for Curiosity to .35 for Confidence. Intrinsic criteria related .41 to internal control, demonstrating the difference between motives and attributions for outcomes. There were no significant correlations between career adaptability and the chance factor of career locus of control (-.02) nor external locus of control (.08). It appears that an internal locus of control may prompt proactive efforts to develop adaptability resources. And finally, the goal of balancing work and non-work roles may move individuals to develop adaptability resources. The career goal of work-life balance related .27 to the

CAAS total score, with *CAAS* subscales ranging from .14 for Concern to .30 for Control.

The other study that investigated the relation of career adaptability to both reward orientation and locus of control was conducted in France with 609 eleventh-grade students. Pouyaud, Vignoli, Dosnon, and Lallemand (2012). Measured these two variables with 25-item scales in the *Motivation Formation Questionnaire* (Forner, 2005). Reward orientation was defined as need for achievement or desire for significant accomplishment, mastering of skills, control, or high standards. The second scale measured internal locus of control. The *CAAS* total score correlated .40 to need for achievement and .41 to internal locus of control.

A unique approach to motivation concentrates on passions, that is, strong dispositions to invest time and effort engaging in highly meaningful activities on a regular basis. Vallerand and colleagues (2003) classified passions into two types. He characterized obsessive passion toward an activity as only partially and incompletely internalizing that activity into one's identity, making it less volitional, more rigid, and dependent on external rewards and social acceptance. In contrast, Vallerand characterized harmonious passion toward an activity as completely integrated into one's identity, making it more volitional, flexible, and enjoyable for their own sake. The term "harmonious" is used to indicate that the passions for work activities are not overpowering but in harmony with other life roles.

Amarnani, Lajohm, Restubog, and Capezio (2020) reasoned that career adaptability buffers obsessive passion against emotional exhaustion. Career adaptability enables individuals to more flexibly regulate obsessive passions in order to maintain a high level of work performance despite the inclination toward intense and rigid work behaviors that would otherwise drain resources and lead to emotional exhaustion. With regard to harmonious passions, Amarnani and colleagues hypothesized that career adaptability does not influence the relation of harmonious passions to work performance because these passions cause minimal resource loss and promote strong performance regardless of career adaptability resources. With regard to obsessive passions, they reasoned that career adaptability helps mitigate resource loss by optimizing how employees allocate their resources. The researchers tested a model in which the indirect effect of obsessive passion through emotional exhaustion on performance is conditional on career adaptability at both the first- and second-stages. The indirect effect of harmonious passion through emotional exhaustion on performance is conditional on career adaptability at the second stage. As shown in Figure 18, the model developed by Amarnani and colleagues (2020) represented adaptive readiness by passions, career adaptability resources by career adaptability, (mal)adapting responses by emotional exhaustion, and an adaptation result by job performance.

Figure 27. Structural Model of Passion, Adaptability, and Job Performance

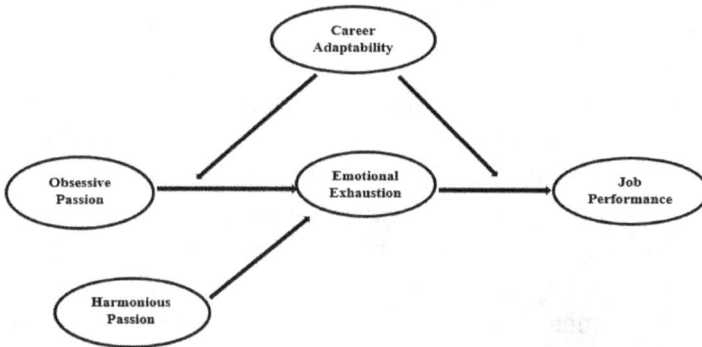

The researchers tested the proposed model with two samples in The Philippines, one cross-sectional and the other time-lagged by two weeks. Sample 1 consisted of 139 employee-supervisor dyads of business professionals, whereas Sample 2 consisted of 156 employee-peer dyads of nurses. In Sample 1, the participants had a mean age of 30 years (SD = 8.9) and 63% were females. In Sample 2, the participants had a mean age of 28 years (SD = 5.7) and 71% were females. Obsessive and harmonious passions toward activities were measured with a scale developed by Vallerand and his colleagues (2003). An example item for harmonious passion reads, ""My work allows me to live a variety of experiences." An example item for obsessive passion reads, "I am emotionally dependent on my work." Emotional exhaustion was measured with a nine-item scale from the *Maslach Burnout Inventory* (Maslach & Jackson, 1981). Example items read: "I feel emotionally drained from work" and "I feel I'm working too hard on my job." Performance was assessed with a four-item measure of job performance (Williams & Anderson, 1991) completed for Sample 1 by supervisors and Sample 2 by peers. Example items read, "This person adequately completes assigned duties" and "This person fulfills responsibilities specified in his/her job description."

In Sample 1, the *CAAS* total score correlated .71 to harmonious passion, -.38 to emotional exhaustion, and .54 to supervisor-rated performance. The correlation to obsessive passion (.09) was not significant. In Sample 2, the *CAAS* total score correlated .45 to harmonious passion, -.23 to emotional exhaustion, and .56 to peer-rated performance rated two weeks later. Again the correlation to obsessive passion (-.03) was not significant. The relationship between emotional exhaustion and informant-rated performance was moderated by career adaptability. The regression estimates were $B = .16$ in Sample 1 and $B = .21$ in Sample 2. As expected, only among workers with low career adaptability was emotional exhaustion negatively related to performance (Sample 1 $B = -.27$ and Sample 2 $B = -.41$). Emotional exhaustion was not associated with performance at high levels of career adaptability (Sample 1 $B = .02$ and Sample 2 $B = .04$). A test of the full conditional indirect effects model for obsessive passion showed that the indirect effects model was conditional on low levels of career adaptability in both samples (Sample 1 indirect effect = -.12,; Sample 2 indirect effect = -.23). No indirect effect was found in either sample for employees with high levels of career adaptability. The researchers tested the conditional indirect effect of harmonious passion on informant-rated performance through emotional exhaustion conditional on career adaptability in the second stage only. As predicted, the indirect effects were conditional on low levels of career adaptability in both samples (Sample 1 indirect effect = .11 and Sample 2 indirect effect = .18). No indirect effect was observed for employees with high career adaptability. No evidence was observed for an interaction between career adaptability and harmonious passion.

Overall, Amarnani and colleagues concluded that career adaptability buffers the relationship between obsessive passion and emotional exhaustion. Whether obsessive passion has counter-productive consequences for performance depends on the level of career adaptability. By comparison, the relationship between harmonious passion and emotional exhaustion did not need a buffer because harmoniously passionate employees already tend to allocate their scarce resources more fluidly by dint of their intrinsic, agentic motivation towards their occupational pursuits. For both groups, career adaptability buffers the relationship between emotional exhaustion and job performance. Finally, they emphasized that the the relationship between career adaptability and job performance, which was not inflated by common method variance in their study, appears to be real and substantive.

Conclusion

This chapter described how researchers have investigated the relation of adaptability resources to three different models of personality organization -- single trait models, hierarchical trait models, and motivation orientation models. Included was a explanation that the career adaptation model distinguishes between traits as indicators of *readiness* to activate adaptability responses and motivation as *willingness*. This was relevant to developing and activating career adapt-abilities because personality traits describe attributes, but they are not as good as motivational variable in predicting performance.

CHAPTER 10

ADAPTABILITY RESOURCES RELATE
TO ADAPTING RESPONSES

The previous Chapter reviewed studies that investigated the relation of adaptive readiness to adaptability resources. This Chapter reviews research that investigated the relation of adaptability resources to consequent adapting responses as portrayed in Figure 28. The studies each examined the relation of the self-regulatory *psychosocial resources* of adaptability to the actual adapting *responses*, both behaviors and beliefs, used to construct a career and manage transitions.

Figure 28. Adaptability Relates to Adapting

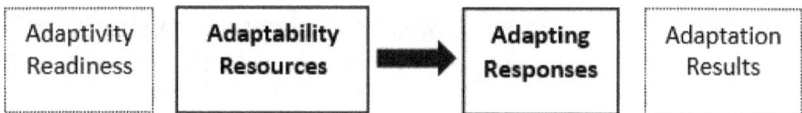

Adaptability Resources Relate
to Adapting Response Behaviors

The first section of this Chapter addresses adapting behaviors and the second section addresses adapting beliefs. Adapting behaviors have been represented in terms of enacting behaviors such as exploring, deciding, planning, initiating personal growth, transitioning, job search, engagement, and coping with stress.

Exploring

Career exploration refers to purposive behavior and reflection that add to an individuals' fund of knowledge about occupations, jobs, or organizations. The most frequently used measure of exploratory behavior is the *Career Exploration Survey* (*CES*; Stumpf, Colareli, & Hartman, 1983), which has five scales. Researchers typically use only two of the scales. The *Environmental Exploration Scale* contains six items that ask about the extent to which the respondent has behaved in that way over the last three months. An example item reads, "Sought information on specific career areas of interest." The *Self-Exploration Scale* contains five items that ask about the extent to which the respondent has behaved in that way over the last three months. An example item reads, "Been retrospective in thinking about my career." In general, it appears that career adaptability correlates to both types of exploration yet somewhat stronger to self-exploration which deals with reflection than to environment exploration which deals with doing.

In a study of 305 Chinese university students, Cai, Guan, Li, Shi, Guo, Liu, Li, Han, Jiang, Fang, and Hua (2015) reported that the *CAAS* total score correlated .30 to *CES* self-exploration and .33 to *CES* environmental exploration. In a second study Guan, Wang, Liu, Ji, Jia. Fang, Li, and Li (2015) combined five self-exploration and six environment exploration items from the *CES* into one score (coefficient alpha = .92). They reported that for 244 Chinese university students the CES 11-items score correlated .32 to the *CAAS* total score and .25 to Concern, .19 to Control, .35 to Curiosity, and .32 to Confidence. Note that the highest correlation of career exploration was to Curiosity.

Career exploration was also studied by Yu, Daik Guan, and Wang (2020) using the *CAAS-SF*. The participants were 937 college students (55.6% females) from four universities in Beijing. Career exploration was measured by the nine-item scale developed by Werbel (2000), which contains four items for self-exploration (e.g., "been retrospective in thinking about my career") and five items for environment exploration (e.g., "went to various career orientation programs"). Career exploration correlated .44 to the *CAAS* total score, and .40 to Concern, .26 to Control, .33 to Curiosity, and .35 to Confidence.

All prior studies of career exploration followed the CCT model of adaption in which career adaptability precedes adapting responses. With regard to students attending school in foreign countries, Guan, Liu, Guo, Li, Wu, Chen, Xu, and Tian (2018) deduced that the opposite relationship from career exploration to career adaptability could also be true for sojourners who reside temporarily in a new culture. They reasoned that when encountering novel elements in a foreign culture, sojourners need to explore the environment, which then provides experiential learning with which to develop and enhance career adapt-abilities. The participants in the study were 222 students (62 males and 160 females) from mainland China who were enrolled in undergraduate (37.8%), Masters (43.7%), and Doctoral (18.5%) programs at overseas universities. Exploration during the previous six months was measured with the the *Career Exploration Survey* (Stumpf, Colarelli, & Hartman, 1983). Career adaptability was measured with the *CAAS*-SF.

Results indicated that the *CAAS-SF* total score correlated .37 to environmental exploration and .45 to self-exploration. The researchers used path analyses to compare three different models: one where career exploration predicted career adaptability, one where career adaptability predicted career exploration, and one where career exploration and adaptability co-varied. In short, the results supported only the model in which exploration preceded career adaptability, but only environmental exploration not self-exploration. They concluded that sojourners in a new cultural context, environmental exploration fosters career adaptability. This finding for sojourners raises the question of whether career adaptability and career adapting have a reciprocal relationship rather than the sequential one as portrayed in the CCT model of career adaptation, and if so, for whom and when.

Deciding

The studies that related adaptability to deciding concentrated on difficulties in the decision-making process. In the CCT model of adaptation, these decision-making difficulties represent adapting responses (i.e., thoughts and behaviors) whereas the outcome of career indecision represents an adaptation result. The best measure of decisional difficulties is the *Career Decision-Making Difficulties Questionnaire* (CDDQ-R; Gati, Krausz, & Osipow, 1996), which measures ten categories of difficulties grouped into three dimensions. The first dimension. "lack of readiness," involves difficulties prior to beginning the decisional process, namely, lack of motivation, general indecisiveness, and dysfunctional beliefs. The second and third dimensions involve difficulties encountered during the decisional process. The second dimension involves "lack of information" about the decision-making process, self, occupations, and information seeking. The the third dimension involves "inconsistent information" due to unreliable observations, internal conflicts, and external conflicts. The studies that relate career adaptability to decision-making difficulties report interesting and coherent patterns of relations between the four adapt-abilities and the different types of decisional difficulties.

In a study that examined the relationship between the four career adapt-abilities and the three dimensions of decision-making difficulties, Karacan-Ozdemir (2019) administered the *CAAS* and the *CDDQ* to a sample of 702 students (55% females) in grades nine (38%), ten (34%), and eleven (28%) from five high schools in Turkey. Bivariate correlation showed that the *CAAS* total score correlated -.21 to the *CDDQ* total score, with correlations of -.04 (non-significant) to lack of readiness, -.22 to lack of information, and -.20 to inconsistent information. Karacan-Ozdemir (2019) then analyzed the data using structural equation modeling to investigate the relation between the adapt-abilities and difficulties. As portrayed in Figure 29, not all dimensions of career adaptability predicted the three dimensions of decision-making difficulties.

Figure 29. Adapt-Abilities and Decision-Making Difficulties

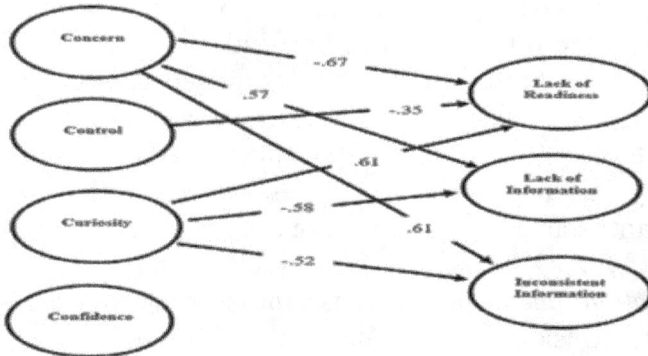

Confidence did not relate significantly to any of the difficulty dimensions. Concern negatively predicted lack of readiness (β = −.67) suggesting that being future oriented increases motivation for career planning. In contrast, Concern positively predicted lack of information (β = .57) and inconsistent information (β = .61), suggesting that anxiety about career planning may be higher among individuals who lack consistent information. Control negatively predicted only lack of readiness (β = −.35), suggesting that that individuals with higher Control show more motivation for in career planning. Curiosity positively predicted lack of readiness (β = .61), suggesting that inquisitiveness may be increased by general indecisiveness and dysfunctional beliefs. In contrast, Curiosity negatively predicted lack of information (β = −.58) and inconsistent information (β = −.52), suggesting that inquisitiveness and information seeking may produce useful information. The researchers highlighted the pattern of correlations in which a higher level of Curiosity resulted in a decrease in difficulties of lack of information and inconsistent information, yet an increase in difficulties due to a lack of readiness. They interpreted this pattern as suggesting that exploring oneself is harder than exploring occupations. This implies that a higher level of occupation information without a corresponding high level of self-knowledge, may relate to a higher level of difficulties experienced prior to making career decisions, including difficulty in integrating self-knowledge with occupational knowledge.

A third study that related career adaptability to decision-making difficulties measured with the *CDDQ* was conducted by Oztemel and Akyo (2021). They recruited a group of 251 participants enrolled in the 9th, 10th, 11th, and 12th grades in five different Turkish high schools. The sample comprised 112 (44.6%) female and 139 (55.4%) male students. The mean age of the participants was 15.16 years (SD = 1.04). While 161 (64.1%) participants stated that they had decided which profession to choose, 90 (35.9%) participants stated that they had not decided yet. In addition to the *CAAS* and *CDDQ*, the participants responded to the *Student Career Construction Inventory (SCCI)* as a measure of adapting behaviors related to decision making. The results of the correlation analysis showed that the *CAAS* total score correlated .71 to the *SCCI* and -.37 to the *CDDQ*. .The *CAAS* total score correlated to the SCCI scales .68 to Crystallizing, .53 to Exploring, .61 to Deciding, .56 to Preparing.

A second measure of decision-making difficulties is the *Career Indecision Profile - 65* (Brown, Hacker, Abrams, Carr, Rector, Lamp, Telander, & Siena (2012), which measures four underlying sources of indecision: (a) Neuroticism/Negative Affectivity measures general anxiety and neuroticism (e.g., "Hard to make decisions without help"); (b) Choice/Commitment Anxiety measures difficulty and anxiety in committing to a single career choice (e.g., "Can't commit, don't know other options"); (c) Lack of Readiness measures difficulty in initiating a career decision-making process, which involves self-efficacy and identity issues (e.g., "I am quite confident that I will be able to find a career in which I'll perform well"); and (d) Interpersonal Conflicts measures decision-making difficulty resulting from disagreement with important people in their life (e.g., "Important people disagree with plans" – reverse scored). Xu (2020b) constructed a 20-item short form of the inventory, which uses five items per scale.

The relation of career adapt-abilities to decision-making difficulties among both students and employees recruited through Amazon's Mechanical Turk was conducted by Xu (2020b). The student sample consisted of 330 individuals (43.3% females) who ranged in age from 18 to 45 years (M = 25.47; SD = 5.05). The employee sample consisted of 436 individuals (50.9% females) who ranged in age from 18 to 45 years (M = 29.40; SD = 6.80). In addition to the *CAAS* and the *Career Indecision Profile*, the participants responded to the Aversion subscale of the *Career Decision Ambiguity Tolerance Scale–Revised* (Xu & Tracey, 2015), which measures the tendency to find ambiguity anxiety-provoking and to avoid and withdraw from it in career decision-making (e.g., "I want to avoid processing conflictual information about a career"). The *CAAS* total score correlated to (a) Neuroticism/Negative Affectivity -.37 for students and -.45 for employees; (b) Choice/Commitment Anxiety -.33 for students and -.28 for employees; (c) Lack of Readiness -.51

for students and -.59 for employees; (d) Interpersonal Conflicts -.34 for students and -.33 for employees, and (e) Aversion -.17 for students and -.19 for employees. Of note, the strongest correlations to the *CAAS* total score for both students and employees were to Lack of Readiness, which involves difficulty in initiating a career decision-making process --- possibly because of limited career adaptability resources.

In a validity study of the *Career Decision Ambiguity Tolerance Scale* (Xu & Tracey, 2015), Storme, Celik, and Myszkowski (2019) used the *Career Decision-Making Self-Efficacy Scale* (Betz, Klein, and Taylor, 1996) and the *CAAS* as criterion measures. The participants were 246 French undergraduate students in their first year of business administrations studies. They ranged in age from 18 to 23 years (M = 18.36, SD = .85) and 48.37% were females. The *Career Decision Ambiguity Tolerance Scale* measures comfort and confidence with career informational ambiguity while making career decisions. It consists of three subscales: Preference, Tolerance, and Aversion. Preference refers to positive cognitive appraisals of ambiguous information in career decision making, especially in the exploratory phase of the career decision-making process. Preference correlated to the four adapt-adaptabilities from .20 to .27. Tolerance refers to the confidence in one's ability to cope with informational ambiguity in the career decision-making process. Tolerance correlated to the four adaptabilities from .28 to .33. Aversion refers to the behavioral tendency to avoid career informational ambiguity. Aversion correlated to the four adapt-abilities from -.22 to -.33. The *Career Decision-Making Self-Efficacy Scale* (Betz, Klein, & Taylor, 1996) correlated .61 to Concern, .56 to Control, .55 to Curiosity, and .62 to Confidence.

Planning

Following a decision to commit to goal, planning behaviors involve identifying and sequencing the steps that move from a currently experience situation to a currently desired situation. The relation of planning to exploratory behaviors may be strong or weak. A strong relationship develops when exploration leads to plans. A weak relationship occurs when exploration is occurring in service of later planning. For examples, Hirschi, Hermann, and Keller (2015) reported that high levels of Curiosity linked to lower levels of career planning after six months. Their study indicated that in the span of one academic year, adolescents' career Curiosity was not stimulated by their level of academic achievement. It may be that other types of career-relevant activities (e.g., extra-curricular activities, volunteering, direct work experiences) are more valuable for fostering this specific adapt-ability.

In a study of planning behaviors, Taber and Blankemeyer (2015) investigated how these adapting responses related to career adaptability resources in a sample of 114 undergraduate students. The measured planning behaviors with the *Career Planning Scale* (Gould, 1979) which uses six items to assess the extent to which individuals change plans, plans exist, plans are clear, and strategy exists for achieving career-related goals. The total score for the *Career Planning Scale* correlated .61 to Concern, .31 to Control, .32 to Curiosity, and .33 to Confidence. This pattern of concurrent correlations supported the anticipated link between the adapt-ability of Concern and the behaviors of planning.

In the same study, Taber and Blankemeyer (2015) measured career networking behaviors with a three-item scale: (1) "I am building a network of contacts to obtain information about how to get the job that I want;" (2) "I am building a network of contacts to provide me with help that will increase my chances of getting the job that I want;" and (3) "I am building a network of contacts I can call on for advice on how to be successful in the job I want." The three items had a coefficient alpha of .89. Career networking correlated .37 to Curiosity and .33 to Concern. The researchers also used two items to measure proactive skill development: "I gain experience in a variety of areas to increase my knowledge and skills" and "I develop knowledge and skills in tasks critical to my future work life." The two items correlated .63. Skill development correlated .44 to Confidence and .38 to Concern. These results indicated a link between the degree to which people possess the confidence to build skills and curiosity to network.

Initiating Personal Growth

A different marker of adapting response is *personal growth initiative*, which Robitschek (2003) "defined as active and intentional involvement in the self-change process" (p. 496). Robitschek (1997) developed the *Personal Growth Initiative Scale* (*PGIS*) to evaluate the effectiveness of a one-year life/career renewal program intended to enhance active involvement of 68 individuals aged 28 to 66 years in the process of personal growth. The *PGIS* (Robitschek, 1998) consists of nine items. An example item reads, "I have a specific action plan to help me reach my goals."

In a study that examined the relation of career adaptability to personal growth initiative, Wang, Tien, and Wu (2018) positioned career adaptability resources as a mediator between adaptivity represented as work-family experience and adapting response represented by personal growth initiative. The participants consisted of 598 adults who worked more than 40 hours per week and who had children under the age of 18. The participants were 37.6% males and 62.4% females who were between 20 and 58 years of age (M = 13.75; SD = 6.23). In addition to the *CAAS* and the *PGIS* (Robitschek, 2003), participants responded to two work-family experience scales: the *Work-Family Conflict Scale* (Wang, 2011; e.g., "Because of my family, I missed possible development or promotion opportunities at work") and the *Work-Family Strengths Scale* (Wang, Wu, & Li, 2014; e.g., "Work life helps me switch role-playing and helps me temporarily escape concerns related to my family life").

Bivariate correlations indicated that personal growth initiative correlated .65 to Concern, .72 to Control, .67 to Curiosity, and .69 to Confidence. The correlations of the four adapt-abilities to work-family strength ranged between .50 and .61 and for work-family conflict between -.13 and -.27. The direct effect of work-family strength on personal growth initiative was β = .47 (p < .01). After being mediated by career adaptability, the direct effect coefficient decreased to .02 (p > .05), and the difference using the mediating variable was β =.45. After the estimation using the bootstrapping method, the total-effect coefficient (.44) significantly differed from zero (95% confidence interval excluding zero), which indicated a mediation effect of career adaptability on personal growth initiative. As shown in Figure 30, after controlling for gender and age, the adapt-abilities of Concern, Control, and Confidence showed a significant mediation effect. A paired comparison between the direct effect coefficients of the four adapt-abilities indicated that Control (β =.35) and Confidence (β =.26) had stronger mediation effects that did Concern (β = .11). and Curiosity (β =.08). Accordingly, individuals with more adaptability resources probably display more adapting responses as indicated by personal growth initiative.

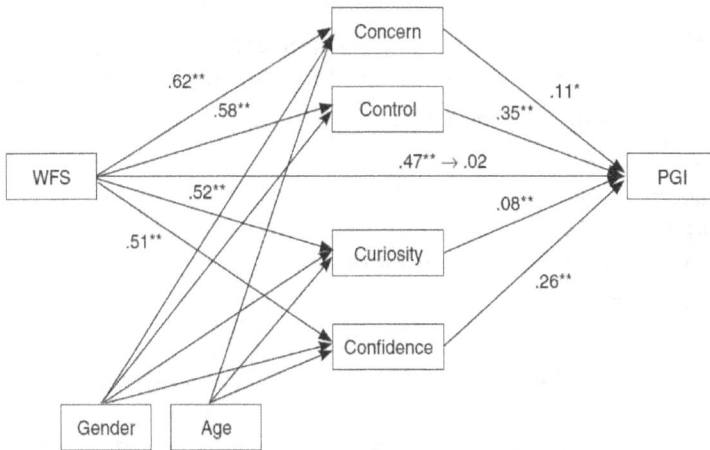

Figure 30. Adaptability Mediates between
Work-Family Strengths and Personal Growth

In 2012, Robitschek and colleagues published a new inventory derived directly from personal growth initiative theory. Although the new inventory has the same name with II added, it is quite a different measure. Whereas the 9-item *PGIS* was unidimensional, the 16 item *PGIS-II* has four factors: readiness for change, planfulness, using resources, and intentional behavior. Unlike the *PGIS*, which is a measure of adapting response, the *PGIS-II* measures both adaptive readiness and adaptability resources for the process of personal growth across life domains. Personal growth initiative as a personal resource encompasses a set of skills that contribute to making changes that promote positive development in people (Weigold & Robitschek, 2011). These resources are intrinsic and are characterized as independent dimensions that can be developed and are influenced by changes in the environment. (Weigold & Robitschek, 2011). Example items read, "I look for opportunities to grow as a person," "I am constantly trying to grow as a person," "I can tell when I am ready to make specific changes in myself," and "I use resources when I try to grow." Conceptually, the *PGIS-II* seems to have some overlap with the *Proactive Personality Scale* (Bateman & Crant, 1993) in that both scales measure initiative in identifying opportunities, acting on them, and persevering until they bring about meaningful change. Because the *PGIS-II* measures readiness, it should precede career adaptability in causal models.

In a study of the relation of personal growth initiative to career adaptability Gregor, Weigold, Wolfe, Campbell-Halfaker, Martin-Fernandez, and Del Pino (2021) positioned career adaptability as a causal outcome of personal growth initiative. They administered the *PGIS-II* and the *CAAS*, along with measures of coping and grit, to 309 students at a large mid-Atlantic community college. The participants had an average age of 22 years (SD = 6.71), and the majority were female (66%). The *CAAS* total score correlated .47 to coping with barriers, .39 to grit, and .69 to personal growth initiative. In a structural model, the strongest path was from *PGIS-II* to *CAAS* (b =.51). Based on these results, the *PGIS-II* may be an alternative to proactivity when researchers want to represent readiness with a short scale that measures a single trait.

Adapting Competencies

In a study that related adaptability resources to adapting responses Dumulescu, Balazsi, and Opre (2015) positioned adaptability as a mediator between calling as adaptive readiness and career competencies as adapting responses. The participants were 458 Romanian undergraduate and graduate students (70.6% females) with a mean age of 21.92 years (SD = 4.5). The participants responded to the *Multidimensional Calling Measure* (Hagmaier & Abele, 2012), a measure of adaptive readiness which consists of three subscales with three items each: (a) transcendent guiding force (e.g., "I follow an inner call that guides me on my career path"), (b) sense of meaning and value-driven behavior (e.g., "My job helps to make the world a better place"), and (c) identification and person-environment-fit (e.g., "Doing my job, I can realize my full potential"). Adapting responses were measured by three subscales from *Career Competencies Questionnaire* (Akkermans, Brenninkmeijer, Huibers, & Blonk, 2013): work exploring (three items; e.g., "I can actively search for the developments in my area of work"), self-profiling (three items; e.g., "I can clearly show others what my strengths are in my work); and networking (four items; e.g., "I know how to ask for advice from members of my network"). The participants were instructed to answer whether or not they performed performed the action during the last six months. The *CAAS* was used to measure adaptability resources.

The *CAAS* total score correlated .47 to calling, .50 to self-profiling, .64 to networking, and .38 to work exploring. The results of mediation analysis supported the hypothesis that career adaptability partially mediated the path between calling and the career competencies of work exploring, self-profiling and networking as shown in Figure 31. Calling had a significant positive direct effect ($B = .47$) on career adaptability which in turn had a significant direct effect on career competencies ($B = .61$). Calling had a direct effect ($B = .22$) on competencies.

Figure 31. Adaptability Mediates between Calling and Adapting Competencies

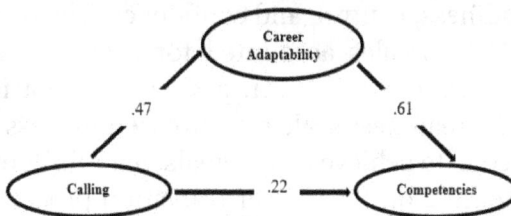

More than a half of the variance (54%) in career competencies was explained by the model. The results showed that students with a

sense of calling had more communicative and behavioral career competencies and this relation may be partially explained by career adaptability. Students with higher levels of calling developed more responsible and future-oriented perspectives that enabled them to acquire personal competencies for effectively managing their career. In particular, students who perceive their career as a calling were better able to expand their career network, communicate about their competencies, and explore more actively the career opportunities, in part because of their stronger career adaptability resources.

Transitioning

In a study of readiness to make a career transition, Ghosh and Fouad (2016) recruited 100 military veterans (65 males and 35 females) enrolled at a large public Midwestern university. They ranged in age from 19 to 50 years (M = 30.89; SD = 7.52. The participants responded to the *CAAS* as well as the *Career Transitions Inventory* (Heppner, 1998), which contains 40 items across five scales: readiness (13 items), confidence (11 items), control (6 items), support (5 items), and independence (5 items). Their response to the *CAAS* subscales, which can range from 1 to 5, were remarkably low: Concern = 2.14, Control = 2.20, Curiosity = 2.41, and Confidence = 2.07. The researchers did not report bivariate correlation coefficients. Before conducting multiple regression analyses, the researchers eliminated the support scale and independence scales due to not meeting normality assumptions and low reliability estimates. Three multiple regression analyses were used to test separately if the career adapt-abilities predicted transition readiness, control, and confidence. The results indicated that the *CAAS* subscales accounted for a significant amount of variability in readiness (R^2 = .21, p < .01) but not in control nor confidence. The readiness scale measures willingness to actually do the things needed to achieve career goals. Sample items read, "Each day I do something on this career transition process. I would say I'm motivated" and "Some would say that this career transition is a risky venture, but the risk doesn't bother me." The results suggest that the readiness scale is an indicator of adapting responses.

In a follow-up study of just transition readiness, Ghosh, Kessler, Heyrman, Opelt, Carbonelli, and Fouad (2019) examined 100 male and 34 female veterans who were university students. They ranged in age for 19 to 65 years (M = 32) and 56 were graduate students. Transition readiness was measured with the 13-item Readiness Scale from the *Career Transitions Inventory* (Heppner, 1998). Along with the *CAAS*, the participants also responded to the *Academic Satisfaction Scale* (Lent, Singley, Sheu, Gainor, Brenner, Treistman & Ades, 2005) and the 5-item *Satisfaction with Life Scale* (Diener, Emmons, Larsen, & Griffin, 1985), which measures the cognitive-judgmental component of subjective well-being (e.g., "I am satisfied with my life" and "In most ways my life is close to my ideal"). The *CAAS* total score correlated .64 to transition readiness, .68 to satisfaction with life, and .21 to academic satisfaction. Regression analyses indicated that career transition readiness and career adaptability significantly predicted satisfaction with life (R^2 = .47, $p < .05$), but not academic satisfaction. In sum, military veterans who evince more career adaptability resources showed greater readiness to make career transitions and more satisfaction with their lives.

The process of transitioning from university to employment among college students from the perspective of the CCT model of adaptation was examined by Soares, Taveira, de Oliveira, et al. (2021). They tested the invariance of the model for gender and in Portuguese and Brazilian cultural contexts. Participants included 638 students (69% females, 66.1% Brazilian), aged 18 to 56 (M = 23.78, SD = 20.33). Individuals' adaptability resources, adapting responses, and adaptation results were assessed. Multi-group path analysis results indicated invariance of the model for contexts, indicating that the adaptation process, in university to employment transition, is equivalent in Portugal and Brazil.

College Students' Job Search

Two studies of college seniors about to make the school-to-work transition were conducted in China. Hou, Wu and Liu (2014) focused on employment pressures measured with a 36-item unpublished scale. The participants were 810 senior students (367 males and 443 females; Mean age = 22.90 years; *SD* = 0.82) at four 4-year comprehensive universities in China. The *CAAS* total score correlated -.18 to job-hunting stress.

Guan and his colleagues (2013) correlated the *CAAS* to the *Jobs Search Self-Efficacy Scale* (Wanberg, Zhang, & Diehn, 2010), which consists of 11 items concerning beliefs about one's ability to perform well in job search tasks, such as writing a good resume, finding information about companies before an interview, and presenting themselves well in an interview. The participants were 697 students (340 male and 3357 female) in their final year in a Bachelors degree (73%) or Masters degree (27%) programs and who intended to seek employment rather than advanced education after graduation. Their average age was 23.5 years (SD = 1.43). Job search self-efficacy correlated .44 to the *CAAS* total score, with correlations of .39 to both Concern and Control, .38 to Curiosity, and .32 to Confidence.

In Nigeria, Ebenehi, Rashid, and Bakar (2016) studied the relation of career adaptability to sources of job-search self-efficacy measured with *Career Self-Efficacy Sources Scale* (Nastam, 2007). The five subscales each have four items to measure a source of job search self-efficacy: vicarious learning (e.g., "I see other students like me get good jobs after college"), verbal persuasion (e.g., "People tell me that I should find a job easily"), emotional arousal positive (e.g., "I feel great when I think about going to find a career"), emotional arousal negative (e.g., "I get a sinking feeling when I think of working on my job search"), performance accomplishments (e.g., "I have done well in the past in finding jobs"). Their participants were 603 university students in Agricultural, Business, and Technical Education programs who were randomly selected from six colleges in Nigeria. The participants consisted of 58.5%, males and 41.5% females with an average age of 22 years. The *CAAS* total score correlated .48 to job search self-efficacy.

A unique study on the relation of career adaptability to job-search beliefs and behaviors considered the role of self-monitoring. Tolentino, Sibunruang, and Garcia (2019) explained self-monitoring as an interpersonal flexibility that enables individuals to adjust their behavior to fit a social situation. They reasoned that career adaptability shapes the adapting response of self-monitoring that in turn shapes job-search beliefs and behaviors during the school-to-work transition. They tested this mediation model with two studies. The participants in the first study were 340 business students in their final year at a university in Thailand. The students had a mean age of 22.16 years (SD = 1.21) and 59% were females. Career adaptability was measured using the *CAAS-SF* (Maggiori, Rossier, & Savickas, 2015). Self-monitoring was measured using a 4-item version of the scale developed by Warech, Smither, Reilly, Millsap, and Reilly (1998). Two example item read, "I have found that I can adjust my behavior to meet the requirements of any situation I find myself in" and "In social situations, I have the ability to alter my behavior if I feel that something else is called for." Job-search self-efficacy beliefs were measured using the 10-item scale developed by Ellis and Taylor (1983). Participants rated the extent to which they feel confident with their general job-search ability, knowledge, and skills. Sample items read, "I am confident of my ability to make a good impression in job interviews" and "I know exactly how to find the kind of job I am looking for."

Results indicated that the *CAAS* total score correlated .48 to self-monitoring and .48 to job search self-efficacy beliefs. Mediation analysis indicated that the relationship between career adaptability and job-search self-efficacy was mediated by self-monitoring. As shown in Figure 32, the total effect was .40, with a direct effect of .31, and an indirect effect of .09.

Figure 32. Self-Monitoring Mediates between Adaptability and Job Search Self-Efficacy

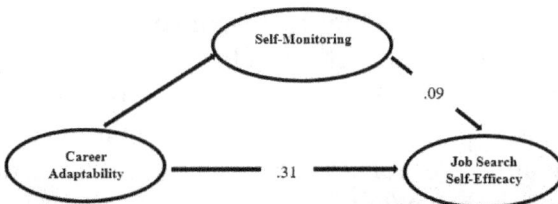

Then Tolentino and his colleagues conducted a second study to replicate the results and test a moderated-mediation hypothesis, which stated that the indirect effect of career adaptability in predicting job-search self-efficacy via self-monitoring is moderated by academic effort, such that the indirect relationship is stronger for individuals with high as opposed to low levels of academic effort. To measure academic effort they adapted three items from the *Intrinsic Motivation Scale* (Deci & Ryan, 2003) to fit schoolwork activities. The items used were "I put a lot of effort in my schoolwork," "It is important to me to perform my schoolwork well," and "I try as hard as I can to perform my schoolwork well." The participants were 547 university students in Thailand with a mean age of 20.64 years (SD =1.76) and who were 58% females. Results indicated that the *CAAS* total score correlated .20 to self-monitoring, .37 to job search self-efficacy, and .44 to academic effort. Mediation analysis again indicated that the relationship between career adaptability and job-search self-efficacy was influenced by self-monitoring. The total effect was .43, with a direct effect of .31, and an indirect effect of .12. The cross-product term between self-monitoring and academic effort in predicting job-search self-efficacy was significant (.08). The indirect effect of career adaptability on job search self-efficacy via self-monitoring was stronger at high (indirect effect = .13) as opposed to low levels of academic effort (indirect effect = .09). The researchers concluded that academic effort acts as a second-stage moderator strengthening the positive relationship between self-monitoring and job search self-efficacy. Together, the two studies provided new insights on the adapting response component of the CCT model of adaptation by examining the role of self-monitoring behaviors.

Career Engagement

Career engagement as an adapting response means "the degree to which somebody is proactively developing his or her career as expressed by diverse career behaviors" (Hirschi, Freund, & Herrmann, 2014, p. 577). Career engagement is an excellent indicator of adapting responses because it concentrates on specific, overt vocational behaviors that improve career adaptation outcomes. It does not refer to a state of mind, identity, readiness, attitude, nor aspirations. To investigate the relation of adaptability resources to adapting responses, Nilforooshan and Salimi (2016) constructed a measure called the *Career Engagement Scale* on which participants indicated the extent to which during the last six months they had engaged in vocational coping behaviors such as career planning, career self-exploration, environmental career exploration, networking, human capital/skill development, and positioning behavior. The results of their study indicated that the *CAAS* total score correlated .66 to career engagement. Moreover, engagement correlated to .67 to Concern, .47 to Control, .60 to Curiosity, and .44 to Confidence. Note that Concern and Curiosity related best to engagement.

To examine the dynamic interdependence of career adaptability and career engagement, Spurk, Volmer, Orth, and Goritz (2020) used latent growth curve analysis on data collected at three measurement points over nine months. In particular, they investigated examined whether (a) intra-individual changes of career adaptability and proactive career behaviors related positively; (b) higher initial levels of career adaptability led to stronger intra-individual decreases in proactive career behaviors; and (c) individuals with stronger intra-individual increases in career adaptability and proactive career behaviors showed higher levels of career satisfaction at the end of the developmental process. Data came from 1,477 participants (56.2% females) with the majority living in Germany (96.8%) and the remainder living in Austria or Switzerland. The participants had a mean age of 46.9 years (SD = 10.6) and a mean organizational tenure of 12 years (SD = 10.2). Data were collected with a time lag of three months between Time 1 (T1) and Time 2 (T2), and about 6 months between T2 and Time 3 (T3). Proactive career and career adaptability were measured three times with the *CAAS*-SF and the *Career Engagement Scale* (Hirschi, Freund, & Herrmann, 2014). At T3, the participants responded to the *Career Satisfaction Scale* (Greenhaus, Parasuraman, & Wormley, 1990). The researchers controlled for stable individual differences by measuring adaptivity in terms of positive affectivity and future temporal focus. Positive affectivity was measured with the four emotional adjectives of happy, proud, grateful, and content (Watson, Clark, & Tellegen, 1988). Future temporal focus was measured with a 14-scale (Shipp, Edwards, & Lambert, 2009).

Bivariate correlations at T1 showed that the *CAAS* total score correlated .42 to career engagement behaviors and .34 to career satisfaction. Also, the T1 *CAAS* total score correlated to T3 career engagement behaviors .27 and .24 to career satisfaction. Regarding the control variables, the *CAAS* total score correlated to future temporal focus .41 at T1, .32 at T2, and .30 at T3 and to positive affect .42 at T1, .35 at T2 and, .30 at T3. Latent growth curve analysis indicated that the intra-individual development of both career adaptability resources and career engagement behaviors went along with each other over time. The steeper a person's growth trajectory in career adaptability, the steeper was her or his growth trajectory in engagement behaviors, and vice versa. The slopes of career adaptability related positively to career satisfaction beyond the initial levels of career adaptability and career engagement behaviors. The researchers concluded that their parallel development fosters career satisfaction. Also, the results indicated that the initial level of career adaptability related negatively to the slope of developmental trajectories of career engagement behaviors over time. The researchers concluded that intermittent phases with decreased or not increased career engagement behaviors might not necessarily be detrimental for career development.

Analysis of the control variables of future temporal focus and positive affect suggested that the identified relationships were not spurious due to third variables of adaptivity. The results supported CCT in showing that adaptability resources and adapting engagement develop conjointly over time -- independently from the stable adaptivity factors of future temporal focus and positive affect. The findings suggest that across time spans of several months, career management constructs emerge in an interrelated rather than isolated manner. Consequently, practitioners who wish to bolster their clients' capacity to manage their careers trajectories

242

may use synergies in the development of adaptability resources and enactment of adapting responses.

Coping with Adversity and Stress

Coping with adversity can stand as an indicator of adapting behavior. Adversity refers to an unfortunate event or circumstance or the state of serious and continued difficulty. Tian and Fan (2014) studied the relation of career adaptability to self-ratings of coping with adversity in a sample of 431 student nurses in China. The student nurses were in the final year of their program and in the fifth month after entering clinical settings. The researchers used the *Adversity Response Profile* (Stoltz, 2000) to measure the participants' adversity quotient, that is, how well an individual may respond when misfortune occurs. Individuals with a high adversity quotient are better able to cope with setbacks and choose constructive responses that turn obstacles into opportunities. The *Adversity Response Profile* (*ARP*) describes 20 scenarios, each followed by two questions answered on a five-point bipolar scale. Each answer is scored on four different subscales: control, ownership, reach, and endurance. Control refers to degree of perceived ability to alter the adverse situation. Ownership refers to degree of willingness to take responsibility for improving the situation. Reach refers to the degree to which a person perceives bad events extending into other areas of life. Endurance means the perceived length of time the adversity will last.

The *CAAS* total correlated .24 to the adversity quotient. The strongest relation of the *CAAS* subscales to the four dimensions in the adversity quotient by far was to the *ARP* control scale: Concern correlated .31, Control .25, Curiosity .17, and Confidence 20. Furthermore, student nurses who had served as student leaders had higher scores than those who did not have this experience ($p < .001$). Student leaders may have been more involved in curricular and extra-curricular activities that enhanced their career adaptability resources

The relation of career adaptability to coping with stress was also investigated by Stoltz, Wolff, Monroe, Farris, and Mazahreh (2013). They explored relationships among Adlerian life-style attributes, stress coping resources, and career adaptability. The participants consisted of 207 undergraduate teacher education students with a mean age of 22.24 years at a mid-sized university in the southern United States. The researchers measured perceived resources for coping with stress using the six scales (12 subscales) in the *Coping Resources Inventory for Stress–Short Form* (*CRIS-SF;* Matheny & Curlette, 2010). They measured Adlerian life-style attributes with the *Basic Adlerian Scales for Interpersonal Success* (*BASIS-A;* Wheeler, Kern, & Curlette, 1993), which assesses life-style attributes using 65 items in five scales: Social Interest, Going Along, Taking Charge, Wanting Recognition, and Being Cautious.

Two of the *CRIS-SF* scales correlated significantly to the *CAAS* subscales of Concern, Control, and Curiosity. *CRIS-SF* Structuring and both of its subscales of Making Plans (five items) and Carrying Out Plans (five items) correlated significantly to the three CAAS adapt-abilities. And, the *CRIS-SF* scale of Confidence and its subscales of Situational Control and Emotional Control related significantly to the three *CAAS* adapt-abilities. The authors did not report a zero-order correlation matrix. They did report a canonical correlation analysis that resulted in three significant canonical variates. The first variate consisted of stress coping resources (R^2 = 44%) and the second variate consisted or life-style variables (R^2 = 28%). They interpreted the third variate as a career adaptability dimension (R^2 = 20%). Three of the four *CAAS* scales loaded significantly on this third latent dimension (Concern .46, Control .42, and Curiosity .51). Two variables from the measure of coping resources, Confidence and Structuring, loaded significantly on this variate. The Confidence subscale of Situational Control loaded .45 on the variate and the subscale of Emotional Control loaded .35 on the variate. The Structuring subscale of Making Plans loaded .43 on the variate and the subscale of Carrying-Out Plans loaded .42 on the variate. A fifth subscale from the coping resources measure – Asserting One's Rights -- loaded .58 on the variate. Two variables from the *BASIS* loaded significantly on the variate: Taking Charge loaded .73 and Wanting Recognition loaded .56. The single highest loading on the variate was .73 for the variable of Taking Charge, a scale that examines an individual's need for control and power in social situations. Overall, these dimensional characteristics of the canonical variate suggested that the career adapt-abilities of Concern, Control, and Curiosity related to taking charge of one's career by making plans and carrying them out, as well as using coping resources to control situations and emotions when facing a challenge.

Resilience refers to the process of adapting well in the face of adversity and trauma. To elaborate career adaptability's relation to life outcomes, Xu, Gong, Fu, Xu, Xu, Chen, and Li (2020) examined the association of career adaptability to mental health problems. The participants were 372 adolescents (37.9% males and 62.1% females) from two high schools in China. The participants ranged in age from 14 to 19 years (M = 17.25; SD = .53). In addition to the *CAAS*, the participants responded to measures of mental health problems and resilience. Thee researchers assessed overall mental health problems of their adolescent participants with the *Mental Health Diagnostics Test* (Zhou, 1991), which consists of 100 items across eight content areas. The researchers explained resilience as a behavioral process of coping with disruptions. In relation to the career adaptation model, they positioned resilience as an adapting response, which involves using coping behaviors to overcome barriers and progress toward current career goals. They measured the participants' self-perceived resilience with the 27-item *Resilience Scale* (Hu & Gan, 2008).

The results indicated that the *CAAS* total score correlated .51 to resilience and -.32 to mental health problems. Resilience correlated -.53 to mental health problems. The researchers tested the mediating effects or resilience after controlling for gender, age, and only-child status. The results showed that resilience was a path through which career adaptability reduced mental health problems. As shown in Figure 33, the total direct effect of career adaptability on mental health problems was significant ($\beta = -0.33$). In the mediation model, the direct effect of resilience was statistically non-significant, yet the predictive effects of career adaptability on resilience (β = .46) and resilience on mental health problems (β = -.61) were both significant. The findings confirm that, in the CCT model of adaptation, resilience is an adaptive response that links career adaptability to adaptation results.

Figure 33. Career Adaptability Relates to Mental Health

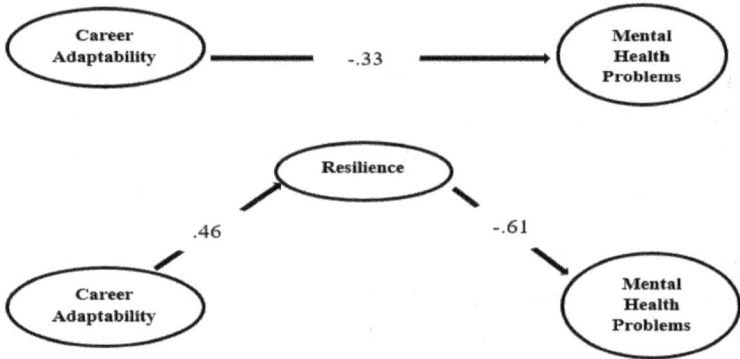

In a second study that examined the relation of career adaptability to resilience, Santilli, Grossen, and Nota (2020) noted that resilience is an ability that individuals can develop. Accordingly, they proposed that individuals with greater career adaptability resources would develop stronger resilience. They hypothesized that career adaptability, directly and indirectly through resilience, predicts life satisfaction among middle school students. The participants in the study consisted of 316 middle school students, including 158 Italian participants (83 boys, 75 girls; Mean age = 13.73 years, SD = 0.60) and 158 Belgian (Flemish) participants (83 boys, 75 girls; Mean age = 13.82 years; SD = 0.59). In addition to administering the *CAAS*, they measured resilience with the *Design My Future* (Santilli, Ginevra, Sgaramella, Nota, Ferrari, & Soresi, 2015). A sample item reads, "I think I'm able to challenge the difficult situations that may arise in the future for me. Global life satisfaction was measured with the *Satisfaction with Life Scale* (Diener, Emmons, Larsen, & Griffin, 1985).

Results for the Italian sample indicated that career adaptability correlated .60 to resilience and and .44 to life satisfaction. Results for the Belgian sample indicated that career adaptability correlated .73 to resilience and .27 to life satisfaction. Structural equation modeling indicated a significant effect for mediation, showing that career adaptability related directly and indirectly through resilience to life satisfaction for both Italian and Belgian middle school students. Bootstrapping analysis revealed that career adaptability (β = .30) had an essential indirect link (i.e., did not include zero) with life satisfaction through the mediating role of resilience. The researchers surmised that career adaptability (a) contributes positively to the ability to face future challenges associated with difficulties regarding social and work uncertainties and (b) leads to higher levels of life satisfaction.

In a study of individuals who had experienced trauma, Prescod and Zeligman (2018) hypothesized that trauma symptomatology would relate negatively to career adaptability, whereas post-traumatic growth would relate positively. Post-traumatic growth refers to positive psychological changes that follow an experience of trauma. Post-traumatic growth differs from resiliency because it denotes improved functioning from the previous baseline of functioning after struggling with adversity or trauma.

The participants in the study were college students (N= 215) who self-identified as trauma survivors. The participants (77% females) ranged in age from 18 to 55 years (M = 35; SD =7.89). They responded to the *Post-Traumatic Growth Inventory* (Tedeschi & Calhoun, 1996), which measures positive outcomes experienced following a traumatic or highly stressful event. Sample items read, "I changed my priorities about what is important in life" and "I am more likely to try to change things which need changing." To measure the perceived emotional impact of trauma experience, the researchers used the *Impact of Event Scale–Revised* (Weiss & Marmar, 1996). Example items read, "I had trouble falling asleep" and "I was jumpy and easily startled." The scale can be scored for total impact as well as for the three subscales of Intrusion, Avoidance, and Hyperarousal.

247

Impact of trauma had a moderate relationship (.30) to post-traumatic growth and a weak relationship (.14) to career adaptability. To explore the predictive nature of trauma symptoms and post-traumatic growth on career adaptability, they used regression models. Results indicated that both intrusion (β = .22, p < .002) and post-traumatic growth (β = -.20, p<.01) demonstrated significant effects on career adaptability scores. Together they accounted for 6% of variance in career adaptability. The researchers also explored whether post-traumatic growth moderated the relationship between trauma symptoms and career adaptability. Results showed that post-traumatic growth was a significant moderator, suggesting that the effect of trauma symptoms on career adaptability was tied to levels of post-traumatic growth. They concluded that growth after trauma plays a significant role in enabling trauma survivors to become more adaptable in their careers.

Adaptability Resources Relate to Adapting Response Beliefs

Beliefs about enacting adapting behaviors are included in the adapting responses dimension of the CCT model as portrayed in Figure 34. The previous section of this Chapter concentrated on the relation of adaptability resources to adapting responses only in terms of enacting behaviors. This section concentrates on the relation of adaptability to adapting beliefs, in particular contextual beliefs about work volition and personal beliefs about career decision-making self-efficacy and occupational self-efficacy.

Figure 34. Adaptability Resources Relate to Adapting Response Beliefs

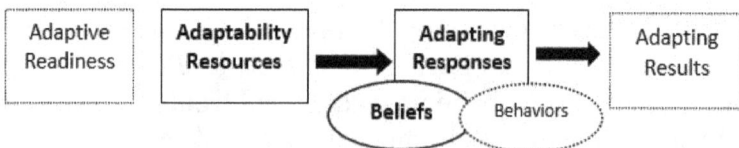

248

Research suggests that adapting beliefs actually mediate between adaptability resources and adapting responses, including both thoughts and behaviors. The CCT model of adaptation considers both beliefs and behaviors to be adapting responses, with conative beliefs shaping cognitive and behavioral responses. For CCT, a belief is mental acceptance of claim as probably true based on repeated experiences and expectations. Beliefs can serve as principles that guide and even control thinking and behaving. In contrast to a belief, a thought is created in the mind of the individual when considering something. Thus for CCT, beliefs may shape thoughts and behaviors.

CCT concentrates on two patterns of beliefs, namely, those that refer (a) to one's sense of freedom and (b) to the degree of confidence in being able to effectively perform specific adapting behaviors. These two belief patterns are conceptualized as conative variables that mediate the relation between adaptability resources and adapting behaviors. Conation refers to the connection of knowledge and affect to behavior and involves desire, volition, and striving. Its etymology traces to the Latin *conatio*, meaning "attempting to act." The CCT model of adaptation highlights two conative connectors between adaptability resources and adapting behaviors, namely *work volition* and *self-efficacy*. Work volition means one's perceived freedom to make future work choices despite constraints (Blustein, 2006). It involves a perception of control in career decision making relative to *contextual constraints*. As they grow up, individuals form understandings of their context and a set of beliefs about they can move in it. Contextual beliefs about the world and their place in it come, in large part, from the context itself. These contextual antecedents of career mentation often set structural boundaries and social barriers. During the deconstruction stage of Career Construction Counseling, practitioners focus clients' critical reflection and action on any consequential limitations arising from their beliefs and assumptions about the context in which they live (cf., Kenny, Blustein, Ling, Klein, & Etchie, 2019).

Whereas volition refers to beliefs about the context, career decision-making self-efficacy -- the second conative connector -- refers to beliefs about one's own capability to organize and execute courses of action required to perform tasks. Positive beliefs promote vocational adapting behaviors (Lent & Brown, 2013). Perceptions of volitional control and efficacious confidence are related to yet distinct from the adapt-abilities of Control and Confidence. Volition and efficacy are situation-specific evaluations of the self-perceived capacity to perform certain adapting behaviors in cultural context rather than being self-regulatory resources.

Work Volition Beliefs

Four studies have examined the relation of career adaptability to conative beliefs concerning work volition. Autin, Douglass, Duffy, England, and Allan (2017) studied the relation between career adaptability and work volition among 432 undergraduate college students. They measured work volition with the 7-item volition subscale of the *Work Volition Scale-Student Version* (Duffy, Diemer, & Jadidian, 2012). Two sample items read, "I will be able to choose the jobs that I want" and "I feel total control over my future job choices." The correlation between the *CAAS* total score and work volition was .33.

In a test of conative beliefs as mediators, Duffy, Douglas, and Autin (2015) hypothesized that both volitional control and efficacious confidence beliefs about enacting behaviors mediate the links between career adaptability resources and the adaptation result of academic satisfaction. They did not study actual adapting responses, just beliefs about being able to enact behaviors. To test their hypotheses, Duffy and his colleagues examined career decision-making self-efficacy and work choice volition as mediators between career adaptability and the adaptation outcome of academic satisfaction among 412 undergraduate students (70% females) with a mean age of 18.9 years (SD = 1.5 years). They measured self-efficacy with the 25-item *Career Decision-Making Self-Efficacy Scale* (*CDMSE*; Betz, Klein, & Taylor, 1996), which measures an individual's belief that he or she can successfully complete tasks necessary to making career decisions. A sample items reads, "How much confidence do you have that you could decide what you value most in an occupation?" The researchers measured work volition with the 7-item volition subscale of the *Work Volition Scale-Student Version* (Duffy, Diemer, & Jadidian, 2012). They measured the degree to which students were satisfied with their academic lives using a 7-item scale devised by Lent, Singley, Sheu, Schmidt, and Schmidt (2007). Two example items read, "I am generally satisfied with my academic life" and "For the most part, I am enjoying my coursework."

The results showed that the *CAAS* total score correlated .65 to *CDMSE*, .39 to work volition, and .44 to academic satisfaction. Regarding the four adapt-abilities, self-efficacy correlated highest to Confidence (.59) and volition correlated highest to Control (.40), with both correlations supporting the criterion-related validity of the two *CAAS* subscales. Work volition correlated .51 to *CDMSE*. The researchers tested a structural model, shown in Figure 35, to examine how the four adapt-abilities link with academic satisfaction and the degree to which these links are mediated by work volition and decisional self-efficacy. Both volition and self-efficacy were direct, significant predictors of academic satisfaction. Decision-making self-efficacy was the more robust mediator variable, having a stronger relation to academic satisfaction, being predicted by three adapt-abilities (i.e., Concern, Control, and Confidence), and serving as a significant mediator for each of these variables to academic satisfaction. The links of these variables make conceptual sense. The adapt-ability resources of Concern, Control, and Confidence would likely be predictive of feeling confident about one's career decision-making capabilities. When students feel confident in their career decisions, satisfaction within the academic domain to prepare one for that career likely follows. Work volition was also found to be a significant mediator, but only with the Control adapt-ability. It is important to note that although both of these variables denote feelings of control, their correlation was .40, indicating that the Control adapt-ability relates to, but is distinct from, beliefs about volitional control in career decision making. In the full model portrayed below, the Control adapt-ability was the strongest of the four significant relations from adaptability to the mediator variables, which implies that work volition may be particularly important in explaining the link between career Control and academic satisfaction. Specifically, the adapt-ability resource of Control may predict higher levels of academic satisfaction in part due to increased perceptions of the freedom to choose one's future career. Note that Confidence related only to self-efficacy, which coincides with CCT model expectations in that self-efficacy is in some part confidence about being able to execute behaviors. This adds to understanding differences between efficacy and volition.

Figure 35. Adapting Mediates between Adaptability and Academic Satisfaction

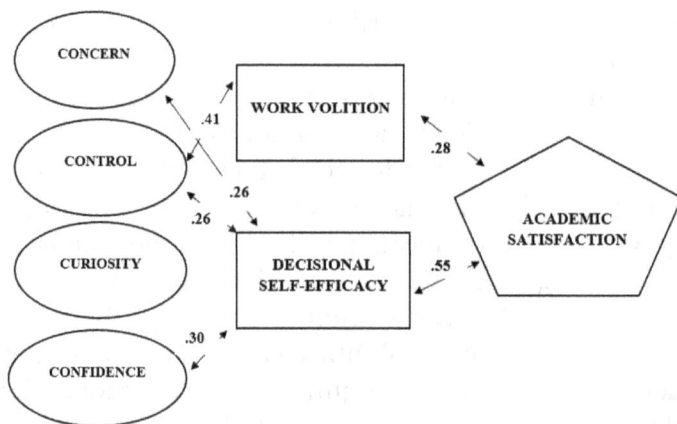

A third study of adaptability and volition positioned employability as an outcome. The term "employability" refers to the capacity to maintain a state of preparedness that makes employment feasible. Kwon (2019) investigated the roles of work volition and career adaptability in influencing university students' perceptions of their own employability. The 251 participants (36.2% females) were in their senior (84.4%) or junior (15.6%) year at three universities in South Korea. Perceived employability was measured by the *Perceived Employability Scale* (Rothwell & Arnold, 2007). Example questions read, "I can easily find out about opportunities in my chosen field" and "I am generally confident of success in job interviews and selection events." The participants also responded to the *CAAS* and the *Work Volition Scale-Student Version* (Duffy, Deimer, & Jadidan, 2011).

Results indicated that the *CAAS* total score correlated .49 to perceived employability and .26 to work volition. Work volition correlated .33 to perceived employability. In a hierarchical regression analysis, as shown in Figure 36, the researchers positioned volition before adaptability. Nevertheless, they suggested viewing work volition and career adaptability in terms of a complex interaction rather than of separate variables. Results indicated that work volition served as a significant and positive predictor for career adaptability (β = .24) and perceived employability (β = .29). Career adaptability also had a significant impact on perceived employability (β = .42). These significant relationships indicated career adaptability was a partial mediator between work volition and perceived employability. In terms of moderation, the interaction term multiplying work volition by career adaptability was significant (β = .22), indicating that work volition exerted a moderating effect on the relation between career adaptability and perceived employability. The indirect impact on perceived employability via career adaptability was stronger at higher levels of work volition (β = .15) than at a lower levels of work volition (β = .04). This result indicates that the effect of work volition on employability is more strongly mediated by career adaptability for those with higher rather than lower levels of work volition.

Figure 36: Structural Model of Adaptability, Volition, and Employability

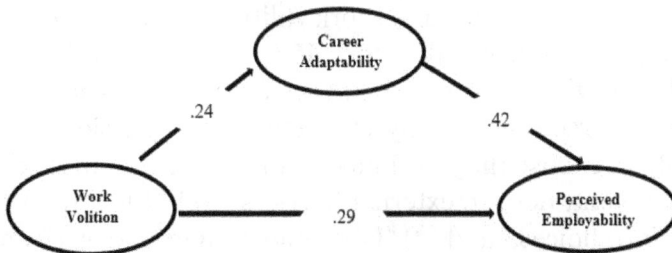

253

The researchers suggested viewing the relation of work volition and career adaptability as a complex interaction rather than of separate variables. Furthermore, they suggested that interventions to increase perceived employability might focus on fostering career adaptability because work volition is a psychological propensity that may require more time to change and currently there are no specific directions for its development. Based on the study's results, they concluded that focusing on career adaptability is a more effective direction for improving the effects of work volition on perceived employability.

A fourth study was framed from the perspective of the psychology of working model. (Duffy et al., 2016). Kozan, Isik, and Blustein (2019) examined relationships among social class, work volition, and career adaptability in determining access to decent work, work fulfillment, and overall well-being in a sample of low-income employees. The participants consisted of 401 employees (47.1% females) from diverse industries in Turkey. They ranged in age from 18 to 59 years (Mean = 28.9; SD = 8.9). The majority (91.7%) of the participants were employed full-time, with the remaining 8.3% in seasonal or part-time employment. Social class was assessed with both objective and subjective indices. Objective social class was measured by personal income and educational attainment. Subjective social class was measured by two items. The first item asked respondents how they would describe their current social class using a five-point Likert scale. The second item asked participants to indicate their perceived position in their society on a 10-rung ladder representing their social status with reference to income, education, and occupation levels. The two objective items as formative indicators and the two subjective items as reflective indicators were combined into a multiple-indicators multiple-causes variable of social class. Work volition was assessed using the Volition Subscale from the *Work Volition Scale* (Duffy, Diemer, Perry, Laurenzi, & Torrey, 2012). The subscale uses four items to assess the perceived capacity to make career decisions: (a) "I've been able to choose the jobs I have wanted," (b) "I can do the kind of work I want, despite external barriers," (c) "I feel total control over my job choices," and (d) "I feel able to change jobs if I want to."

Decent work was measured by the *Decent Work Scale* (Duffy, Allen, England, Blustein, Autin, Douglasss, & Santos, 2017), which consists of five subscales: safe working conditions, access to health care, adequate compensation, free time and rest, and complementary values. Example items from each scale read, "I feel emotionally safe interacting with people at work," "I get good health-care benefits from my job," "I am rewarded adequately for my work," "I have free time during the work week," and "The values of my organization match my family values." The *CAAS–SF* was used to measure career adaptability. Job satisfaction was indicated by one item that reads, "All in all, I am satisfied with my job." The participants also responded to the *Satisfaction with Life Scale* (Diener, Emmons, Larsen, & Griffin, 1985).

Bivariate correlations showed that the *CAAS-SF* total score correlated .28 to social class, .44 to work volition, .34 to decent work, .45 to job satisfaction, and .51 to life satisfaction. Results for model testing shown in Figure 37 indicated that social class predicted work volition (β =.39), career adaptability (β = .38), and decent work (β = .17). Work volition and career adaptability correlated significantly (r = .48), and work volition (β = .66) and career adaptability (β = .23) significantly predicted decent work. Decent work significantly predicted job satisfaction (β = .85) and life satisfaction (β = .80). Lastly, the correlation between job satisfaction and life satisfaction was significant (r = .58). Together, the set of predictors accounted for 78% of the variance in decent work, 72% of the variance in job satisfaction, and 64% of the variance in life satisfaction. The indirect effects of social class on decent work via work volition (B = .35) and career adaptability (B = .11) were both significant. The researchers concluded that work volition and career adaptability are factors that predict access to decent and fulfilling work among people with limited economic resources.

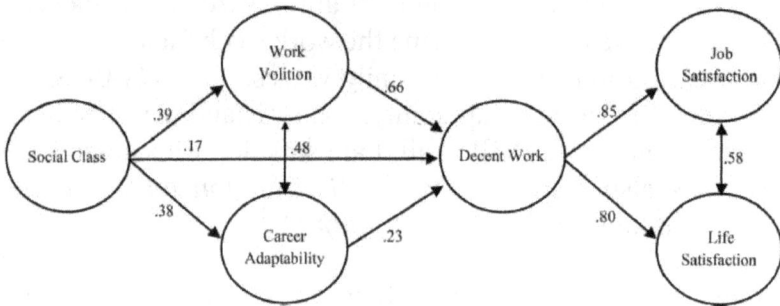

Figure 37. Structural Model of Volition, Adaptability, and Decent Work

Career Decision-Making Self-Efficacy Beliefs

The most frequently used measure of beliefs about decisional self-efficacy is the *Career Decision-Making Self-Efficacy Scale-Short Form* (*CDMSE*; Betz, Klein, & Taylor, 1996). The instrument measures an individual's degree of belief that she or he can successfully complete tasks necessary to making significant career decisions. The scale consists of five 5-item subscales that measure the career choice competencies of evaluating self-attributes, gathering occupational information, selecting goals, making plans, and solving problems in implementing plans.

Working in Beijing, China, Zhou, Guan, Xin, Kuan, and Deng (2016) examined the relation between career adaptability and career decision-making self-efficacy among 431 college students. The *CAAS* total score correlated .44 to the *CDMSE* total score, with subscale correlations ranging between .31 for Control to .41 for Confidence. In the studies by Duffy Douglas, and Autin (2015) and by Zhou and colleagues (2016), self-efficacy had the highest correlation to the adapt-ability of Confidence, fitting with a view of career decision-making self-efficacy as a confidence about being able to perform decisional tasks.

Working in South Korea, Shin, Lee, and Seo (2019) investigated the correlation of the *CAAS* to the *CDMSE* (Betz, Klein, & Taylor, 1996) among 291 students (138 females, 153 males) who were enrolled in Introduction to Psychology and Introductory Business courses at a public university. The participants ranged in age from 19 to 31 years (M = 21.34; SD = 2.54); 81 (27.8%) were first-year students, 70 (24.1%) were sophomores, 65 (22.3%) were juniors, and 75 (25.7%) were seniors. Males scored significantly higher on the *CAAS* (3.38 vs 3.16) but there was not a significant difference in *CDSME* scores (males 6.42 vs females 6.11). The *CAAS* total score correlated to the *CDMSE* for males .65 and for females .61.

In a validity study of the 12-item *CAAS–SF*, Isik and his colleagues (2018) reported that for 336 college students in Turkey, the *CDMSE* (Betz, Klein, & Taylor, 1996) correlated .66 to the *CAAS-SF* total score, with correlations of .56 to Concern, .49 to Control, .57 to Curiosity, and .56 to Confidence.

In a study that examined the relation between calling and career decision-making self-efficacy, Douglas and Duffy (2015) examined career adaptability as a mediator in a sample of 330 undergraduate students with a mean age of 19.14 years (SD = 1.43). Presence of calling, as an indicator of adaptivity, was assessed with two items: "I have a calling to a particular kind of work" and "I have a good understanding of my calling as it applies to my career." Decisional self-efficacy was measure with the *CDMSE* (Betz, Klein, & Taylor, 1996). The *CAAS* was used to measure career adaptability. The results showed that the *CAAS* total score correlated .59 to *CDMSE* and .35 to calling. In a mediator analysis, calling was entered as the independent variable, *CDMSE* as the dependent variable, and the four adapt-abilities as mediators. Presence of calling had significant direct effects on Concern (β = .38), Control (β = .32), Curiosity (β = .21), Confidence (β = .31), and *CDMSE* (β = .42). Additionally, Concern (β = .18) and Confidence (β = .14) were each significant predictors of *CDMSE* after accounting for the shared variance among these variables and calling. Calling also had significant indirect effects on *CDMSE* as mediated through Concern (β = .10) and Confidence (β = .09). Lastly, the relation between presence of calling and *CDMSE* (β = .14) weakened, yet was still significant after including Concern and Confidence into the model. These results indicated partial mediation. The researchers concluded that higher levels of calling may promote greater career adaptability which in turn promotes greater *CDMSE*. The findings of this study support viewing adaptability as a resource that fosters career decision-making self-efficacy.

In another study that examined the relation between career adaptability and career decision-making self-efficacy beliefs, Zhou, Guan, Xin, Kuan, and Deng (2016) collected data from 431 undergraduate students at a university in Beijng, China. Zero-order correlations showed that the *CAAS* total score correlated .44 to career decision-making self-efficacy.

The *CAAS* has been examined in relation to a measure partially similar to the *CDMSE*. In Brazil, Ambiel and Noronha (2012) built the *Professional Choice Self-Efficacy Scale* (*PCSES*) based on the *CDMSE*. Similar to the *CDSME*, the *PCSES* has subscales for Self-Appraisal, Occupational Information Gathering, and Future Planning. It does not measure Goal Selection nor Problem Solving. Instead, its fourth subscale measures Practical Professional Information Search with items that relate to using interpersonal contacts to get information about the professions or courses. The sample consisted of 272 adolescents who ranged in age from 14 to 19 years (*M* = 16.34, *SD* = 0.99) and was 52% females and 48% males. Participants attended high school in the interior of the state of São Paulo. They consisted of 36.6% in the first year, 32.1% in the second year, and 31.3% in the third year. The 16 correlations between the four scales on the *PCSES* and the *CAAS* ranged from .39 to .56 with a median value of .46. The highest correlations were observed between the *PCSES* Self-Appraisal subscale and the *CAAS*. The researchers concluded that thinking about one's own characteristics also helps adolescents think about their careers and prepares them to deal with the challenges that they may encounter.

In comparing career adaptability and career decision-making self-efficacy, Li, Ngo, and Cheung (2019) positioned them as mediators between protean career orientation and career decidedness. From the perspective of CCT, it would have been preferable to examine career adaptability resources as an antecedent to self-efficacy for the adapting behavior of decision making. Nevertheless, the study makes an interesting contribution to understanding the difference between career adaptability resources and self-efficacy for career decision making. The researchers measured protean career orientation with a six-item scale developed by Baruch (2014). An example item reads, "I am in charge of my own career." Career decision-making self-efficacy was measured with the eight-item *Career and Educational Decision Self-Efficacy Inventory for Secondary Students* (Ho & Sum, 2018). Five of the items inquire abut future career (e.g., "I am able to choose a career that will fit my ability"). Three of the items inquire about future planning (e.g., "I am able to make a plan of my educational and career goals for the next three years"). The *CAAS-SF* was used to measure career adaptability. Career decidedness was measured with the six-item *Career Decidedness Scale* (Lounsbury, Hutchens, Loveland, 2006). Example items read, "I have made a definite decision about a career for myself"; "I am not sure what type of work I want to do when I get out of college" (reverse-scored); and "I am having a difficult time choosing among different careers" (reverse scored). The researches examined the relationships in two different samples. The Hong Kong sample consisted of 376 university students (62.5% females) while the U.S. sample consisted of 408 university students (51.5% females).

Results showed that the *CAAS-SF* total score correlated to protean career orientation .60 in U.S. and .47 in Hong Kong. The *CAAS-SF* total score correlated to career decision-making self-efficacy .61 in U.S. and .48 in Hong Kong. The *CAAS-SF* total score correlated to career decidedness .43 in U.S. and .32 in Hong Kong. Note that the *CAAS-SF* total score correlated much higher in both samples to career decision self-efficacy than to decidedness, as would be expected based on CCT. Furthermore, career decision-making self-efficacy correlated much higher to decidedness (.49 in Hong Kong and .55 in U.S.) than did career adaptability (.32 in Hong Kong and .43 in U.S.). The stronger relation of career decision-making self-efficacy to decidedness is expected by CCT because, as a proximal antecedent of career decidedness, career decision-making self-efficacy directly enhances students' confidence in making choices. Accordingly, it should relate more strongly to decidedness than career adaptability, which is a psychosocial resource that influences decidedness indirectly via some adapting beliefs (e.g., self-efficacy) and behaviors (e.g., deciding and planning). Consistent with this modeling, the path coefficients presented by Li, Ngo, and Cheung (2019), shown in Figure 38, indicated that career decision self-efficacy, but not career adaptability, acted as a significant mediator in the relationship between protean career orientation and career decidedness. The path coefficients can be viewed as indicating discriminant validity between the *CAAS-SF* and the *Career and Educational Decision Self-Efficacy Inventory for Secondary Students*.

Figure 38. Structural Model of Decision-Making Self-Efficacy and Adaptability

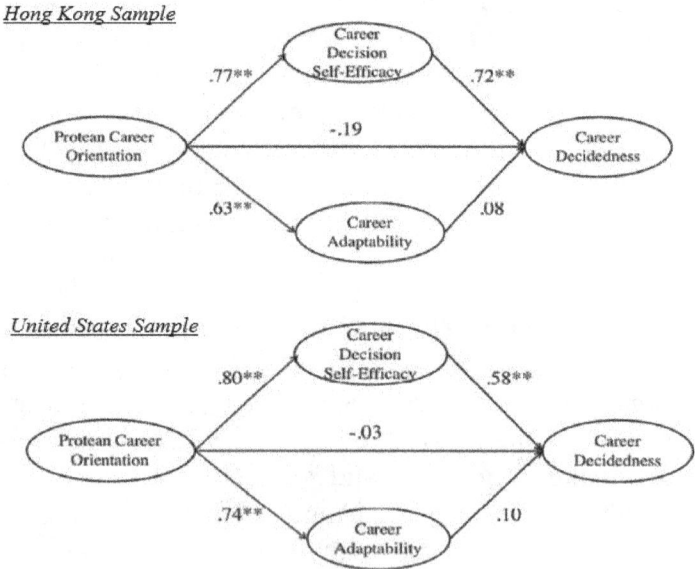

Overall, the studies of volitional control and decision-making self efficacy suggest stronger relations between career adaptability and self-efficacy. The four studies that correlated career adaptability to work volition reported coefficients of .33, .39, .26, and .44 whereas the four studies that correlated career adaptability to career decision-making self-efficacy reported coefficients of .44, .66, .59, .44, and .65 for males/.61 for females.

Occupational Self-Efficacy

While the prior studies considered self-efficacy beliefs about performing decision-making behaviors, McIlveen, Perera, Hoare, and McLennan (2018) examined self-efficacy beliefs about performing work behaviors, that is, occupational self-efficacy. For CCT, occupational self-efficacy refers to individuals' beliefs about their abilities to effectively perform work tasks and develop skills. The participants were 344 students in a teacher education program at an Australian university. They were 85.5% females with a mean age of 31.84 years (SD = 9.45). The researchers assessed occupational self-efficacy with the *Teachers' Sense of Efficacy Scale* (Tschannen-Moran & Hoy, 2001), which measures a broad range of capabilities that teachers consider important to good teaching without regard to specific contexts, levels, and subjects. The 24 items are spread across the three subscales of (a) efficacy for using effective instructional strategies (e.g., "To what extent can you use a variety of assessment strategies?"), (b) efficacy for managing student conduct and behaviors (e.g., "How much can you do to control disruptive behavior in the classroom?"), and (c) efficacy for engaging students in learning (e.g., "How much can you do to help your students value learning?"). The results indicated that career adaptability associated strongly with teacher self-efficacy efficacy for instructional strategies (r = .52), classroom management (r =.42), and student engagement (r = .57).

In a different study, McLennan, McIlveen, and Perera (2017) added career optimism as an adapting behavior. They investigated whether self-efficacy mediates between career adaptability

261

resources and an adapting behavioral response called career optimism. The researchers again administered the *Teachers' Sense of Efficacy Scale* (Tschannen-Moran & Hoy, 2001). The participants' adapting behaviors were measured by the 11-item Career Optimism scale from the *Career Futures Inventory* (Rottinghaus, Day & Borgen, 2005), Example items inquire about adapting responses such as: "I am good at adapting to new work settings;" "I can adapt to change in my career plans;" "I can overcome potential barriers that may exist in my career," and "I can bounce back when my career plans don't work out quite right." Participants in the study were 402 pre-service teachers (Mean age = 31.78; SD = 0.29; 85.8% females) enrolled in a compulsory course about classroom management. All participants had recently completed a practicum in a school at which they taught classes under the supervision of a designated mentor teacher.

Results showed that the *CAAS* total score correlated .43 to teacher self-efficacy and .67 to the adapting behaviors of career optimism. Self-efficacy beliefs correlated .47 to adapting behaviors of career optimism. Additional analyses, as shown in Figure 39, indicated that teacher self-efficacy partially mediated the relation between career adaptability resources and the adapting behaviors of career optimism. This result coincides with the CCT proposition that adapting beliefs mediate between adaptability and adapting behaviors.

Figure 39. Adapting Beliefs Mediate between Adaptability and Adapting Behaviors

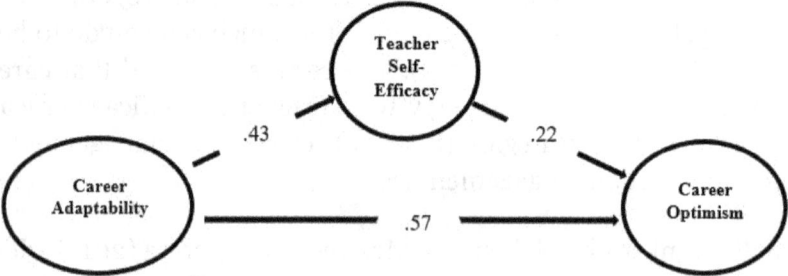

Conclusion

This Chapter described studies that examined the relation of the self-regulatory *psychosocial resources* of adaptability to the actual adapting *responses*, both behaviors and beliefs, used to construct a career and manage transitions. The first section of the Chapter addresses adapting behaviors that have been represented in terms of exploring, deciding, planning, initiating personal growth, transitioning, job search, engagement, and coping with stress. The second half of the Chapter addressed adapting beliefs represented as contextual beliefs about work volition and personal beliefs about career decision-making self-efficacy. The next Chapter reviews the relation of adaptability resources directly to adaptation results, independent of adapting behaviors.

CHAPTER 11

ADAPTABILITY RESOURCES RELATE
TO ADAPTATION RESULTS

The previous Chapter reviewed studies that examined the relation of adaptability resources to adapting behaviors and beliefs. In this Chapter, the studies reviewed concentrate on the relation of adaptability resources directly to adaptation results, independent of adapting behaviors as portrayed in Figure 40.

Figure 40. Adaptability Resources Relate to Adaptation Results

This Chapter organizes adaptation results into three sections. The first section addresses outcomes that pertain to individuals, namely vocational identity, professional identity, personal growth, quality of life, and career exploration and plans. The second section addresses the adaptation results that pertain to the job, namely work engagement, job performance, job plateauing, and work-family conflict. The third section address adaptation results that pertain to contentment, namely academic satisfaction, career satisfaction and success, entrenchment, and life satisfaction.

Adaptability Relates to Identity as an Adaptation Result

This first section of this Chapter addresses the relation of career adaptability resources to adaptation results that pertain to the individual, specifically the outcomes of vocational identity, professional identity, personal growth, quality of life, and career exploration and plans.

Vocational Identity

Positioning vocational identity as an adaptation outcome, Savickas and Porfeli (2012) examined its relation to adaptability among 460 tenth- and eleventh-grade students with a mean age of 16.5 years (SD = .97). They assessed vocational identity with the *Vocational Identity Status Assessment* (*VISA*; Porfeli, Lee, Vondracek, & Weigold, 2011), which is composed of three dimensions indicated by six 5-item subscales assessing vocational processes known to indicate progress toward an identity (Crocetti, Rubini, & Meeus, 2008). The career commitment dimension is indicated by subscales for career commitment making and career commitment identification. Making commitments means a sense of certainty about a choice that has been made whereas commitment identification means investing one's self in that choice. The career exploration dimension is indicated by subscales for in-depth and in-breadth career exploration. In-breadth exploration involves activities that lead to crystallizing preferences for occupational fields and ability levels while in-depth exploration involves activities that lead to specifying an occupational choice. The career reconsideration dimension is indicated by subscales for commitment flexibility and commitment. Commitment flexibility means sensitivity and openness to changes in occupation interests and jobs while commitment self-doubt means feeling anxious and uncertain regarding career planning.

As would be expected, career adaptability showed strong relations with in-depth career exploration and identification with career commitments. Career adaptability shared 27% variance with in-depth exploration to identify personal strengths relative to a specific occupation. It also shared 18% variance with commitment identification, or in other words, a deep personal identification with a meaningful career that will manifest one's self-concept in work activities. Higher levels of adaptability thus align with seeking and making career choices that implement one's identity. Thus, a more coherent identity may result from applying the adaptability resources of Concern, Control, Curiosity, and Confidence. In contrast, career adaptability associated inversely with the two reconsideration dimensions of identity. The significant negative relation of adaptability to self-doubt suggests that lower levels of career adaptability resources align with higher levels of anxiety and uncertainty concerning one's career choices and commitments. The lack of an association between flexibility and adaptability was expected in that the *CAAS* measures adaptability resources not adaptivity nor the willingness to adapt. The *VISA* flexibility scale appears to measure adaptivity in terms of willingness to adapt rather than the resources that condition adapting behaviors.

In addition to scores for identity-formation dimensions, the *VISA* may be scored to place individuals in one of six identity statuses. Four of the statuses are the ones identified by Marcia's (1966) foundational work that articulated four statuses produced by different combinations of exploration and commitment. The statuses are achieved (commitment based on exploration), foreclosed (commitment without exploration), moratorium (exploration without commitment), and diffused (little exploration or commitment). The *VISA* scores provide differentiation of exploration (in-depth versus in-breadth) and commitment (making and identifying). Using these differentiation scored can indicate a fifth status that has been repeatedly found in identity status research. The fifth status is typically labeled "searching moratorium," yet it could just as easily be labeled "tentative commitment" because it falls between the achieved and moratorium statuses. While there are differences among the statuses in the two exploration dimensions, there is substantial difference in the commitment dimensions. A continuum begins with the achieved status having high commitment making and low flexibility. Next comes the searching status with high commitment and very high flexibility. Finally comes the moratorium status with low commitment making and medium flexibility. The foreclosed status is characterized by low in-breadth exploration, while the diffused status is characterized by low exploration and commitment. About 20% of individuals cannot be classified into one of these five statuses by *VISA* scores; they are called undifferentiated.

266

Examining the scale mean scores for individuals placed in the identity statuses showed that career adaptability related strongly, consistently, and as expected to identity status assignment. The adaptability scores increased across the statuses arranged as diffused, moratorium, searching moratorium, foreclosed, and achieved. The results were even more striking when comparing just the achieved to the foreclosed. These two statuses are often difficult to distinguish using scores from career inventories because both statuses show strong commitment, one with exploration and one without exploration (Brisbin & Savickas, 1994). The profile of career adaptability resources clearly distinguished the two groups with the achieved status scoring higher on each of the four subscales. Even more importantly, the largest difference occurred on the Curiosity subscale with achieved scoring 4.15 and foreclosed scoring 3.85. Thus, the achieved and foreclosed statuses differed across the board on Concern, Control, and Confidence, yet the telling difference was on Curiosity. Curiosity fuels in-breadth exploration, which is the major characteristic lacking among foreclosed individuals who commit to conferred rather than self-chosen goals.

In a validation study of their translation of the *VISA* scale (Porfeli et al., 2011) into Chinese, Zhang, Chen, and Yuen (2019) also administered the *CAAS-SF* along with two six-item subscales from the *Career and Talent Development Self-Efficacy Scales* (*CTDSES*; Fan, Hao, & Yuen, 2013). The Talent Development subscale measures self-efficacy for transforming potential into ability. An example item reads, "Actively participate in different kinds of activities and contests to enrich my experience." A sample item from the Career Exploration Subscale reads, "Explore my career path and goal." The response scale ranges from "extremely lacking confidence" to "extremely confident." The participants were 495 students (61% males) from three technical school. They ranged in aged from 15 to 23 years (Mean age = 18.7 years; SD = 1.7).

Results indicated that the *CAAS* total score correlated .32 to the *VISA* total score, with correlations of .33 to Career Commitment Making, .36 to Identification with Career Commitment, .24 to In-Breadth Exploration, .35 to In-Depth Exploration, .32 to

Commitment Flexibility, and -.20 to Career Self-Doubt. Talent development self-efficacy correlated .49 to the *CAAS* total score, with correlations to the four adapt-abilities ranging from .43 to .49. Career exploration self-efficacy correlated .53 to the *CAAS* total score, with correlations to the four adapt-abilities ranging from .44 to .50. The data in this study could have been used to test the relations among adaptability (i.e., *CAAS-SF*), adapting (i.e., *CTDSES*), and adaptation (i.e., *VISA*). The pattern of bivariate correlations showed, as expected by CCT, that career adaptability correlated higher to the self-efficacy (.53) and talent development (.52) subscales than to the Identity scales (.32).

In another study of the relation between adaptability and vocational identity, Pociūtė, Kairys, Urbanavičiūtė, and Liniauskaitė (2014) examined the relation of career adaptability to in-depth exploration, commitment, and reconsideration. In-depth exploration indicates investigating current commitments without questioning them. Commitment refers to being committed to one's identity choice. Reconsideration of commitment means reevaluating commitments by comparing present commitments to possible alternative commitments. To measure the identity constructions, the researchers administered the *Utrecht Management of Identity Commitments Scales* (Crocetti Rubini, &Meeus, 2008) in Lithuania to 518 high school students (60% female) with a mean age of 16.5 years. In-depth exploration correlated .40 to the *CAAS* total score, with the highest correlation on the *CAAS* subscales being .41 to Curiosity. Commitment correlated .44 to the *CAAS* total score, with highest correlation to *CAAS* subscales being to Concern .45. Reconsideration correlated to the *CAAS* total score a non-significant .008, as well as non-significantly to all four adapt-abilities.

A variable related to vocational identity achievement is one's image of a future work self. Taber and Blankemeyer (2015) administered the *CAAS* and the *Future Work Self Salience Rating Scale* (Strauss, Griffin, & Parker, 2012) to 114 undergraduate students (97 females, 15 males, 1 not declared) at a Midwestern university. The participants were instructed to imagine their hoped for work self in terms of the kind of work they hope to be doing and what they will be like at their hoped for job. Keeping that image in mind, participants were instructed to rate how strongly they agreed or disagreed with statements such as "I am very clear about who and what I want to become in my future work" and "What type of future I want in relation to my work is very clear in my mind." Future work self salience related .58 to Concern, followed by .46 to Control, .31 to Curiosity, and .35 to Confidence. The highest correlation being to Concern, fits with the results of the study by Pociūtė, Kairys, Urbanavičiūtė, and Liniauskaitė (2014) which reported that identity commitment has the highest correlation to Concern. It also coincides with the results of the study by Porfeli and Savickas (2012) in which vocational commitment making and identification both had the highest correlations to Concern.

A second study that examined the relation of the *CAAS* to future work self was conducted in China by Guan, Guo, Bond, Cai, Zhou, Xu, Zhu, Fu, Liu, Wang, Hu, and Ye (2014). They administered the *Future Work Self Salience Rating Scale* (Strauss, Griffin, & Parker, 2012) to 340 males and 357 females (Mean age = 23.50; SD = 1.43), 73% of whom held a Bachelors degree and 27% held a Masters degrees. The *CAAS* total score correlated .62 to future work salience.

Professional identity as a social worker. Although not using a measure of vocational identity per se, the relation of career adaptability to identification with the profession of social work was studied by Guo, Guan, Yang, XU, Zhou, She, et al (2014) among 270 Chinese undergraduate students majoring in social work. Identification with the field, or vocational identity as a social worker, was defined as professional competence and assessed by the following 10 items: (a) identifying as a professional social worker and conducting oneself accordingly, (b) applying social work ethical principles to guide professional practice, (c) applying critical thinking to inform and communicate professional judgments, (d) engaging diversity and difference in practice, (e) advancing human rights as well as social and economic justice, (f) engaging in research-informed practice and practice-informed

269

research, (g) applying knowledge of human behavior and the social environment, (h) engaging in policy practice to advance social and economic well-being and to deliver effective social work services, (i) responding to contexts that shape practice, and (j) engaging, assessing, intervening, and evaluating with individuals, families, groups, organizations, and communities. The total score for these ten items correlated to all four adapt-abilities ranging from .32 to .43, with highest correlation being to Concern.

Professional identity as a counselor. A unique scale for measuring career adaptation results in terms of achieving a professional identity as a psychological counselor was devised by Eryilmaz and Ahmet (2017) in Turkey. They titled the inventory the *Career Adaptability Scale for Psychological Counselors.* From the perspective of CCT, the scale measures career adaptation results from exploration and planning rather than career adaptability resources. A more descriptive title might be the "Psychological Counselors' Career Exploration and Plans Scale." To write items for the new scale, the researchers studied the *CAAS,* the *Career Futures Inventory-Revised* (Rottinghaus, Buelow, Matyja, & Schneider, 2012), and the *Career Exploration Scale* (Stumpf, Colarelli & Hatman, 1983). They also conducted interviews with 15 counselors in which they asked three open-ended questions: (a) "How appropriate do you evaluate yourself for this vocation? (b) "What do you think about your career plan as a psychological counselor? and (c) "When and after which activities did your adaptation increase toward this vocation?" Clearly these questions inquire about adaptation results not adaptability resources. The process of scale development resulted in 17 items that composed three subscales concerning exploration and one subscale concerning planning. The Exploration of Educational Counselling subscale had three items (e.g., "I learned how to approach students who were lack of motivation" and "I learned how to help an individual who had learning difficulties"). The Exploration of Individual and Group Counseling subscale also had three items (e.g., "I know which therapeutics skills are used in psychological counseling" and "I learned which problem solving steps are used in psychological counseling"). The Career-related Self-exploration subscale had three items (e.g., "I love psychological counseling and guidance vocation" and "Seeing the process of psychological counselling increased my concern"). The Career Planning subscale had four items (e.g., "I learned how to make progress in my vocation in the future" and "I chose the institutions in which I would work"). Note that these items state adaptation results signified by verbs such as "learned," "know," "chose," "seeing," and "love" rather than adaptability resources. The total scale had a coefficient alpha of .78 and a test-retest reliability over 30 days of .93. Validity evidence was provided by the total score correlating .48 to the *Career Futures Inventory-Revised* (*CFI-R*; Rottinghaus, Buelow, Matyja, & Schneider, 2012). The *CFI-R* total score correlated .38 to exploration of individual counseling, .39 to exploration of educational counseling. .41 to self-exploration, and .49 to career planning. The highest correlation being to career planning which supports the differential validity of the subscale in that the *CFI-R* assesses aspects of career planning, outcome expectations, and personal agency. Then Eryilmaz and Ahmet (2017) administered their scale to 251 participants (65.7% females). They consisted of 88 (35.1 %) psychological counselors in government agencies who ranged in age from 22 to 28 years old and 163 undergraduate students in a psychological counseling and guidance program who ranged in age between 18 and 21 years old. The *CAAS* total score correlated .62 to the planning scale total score, with correlations of .61 or .63 to the three exploration subscales and .48 to the career planning subscale.

Adaptability Relates to Job Outcomes as Adaptation Results

This second section of Chapter 11 continues the discussion of the relation of career adaptability resources to adaptation results, specifically the job outcomes of work engagement, job performance, job plateauing, and work-family conflict.

Work Engagement

Engagement with one's work is yet another indicator of adaptation outcomes. It is conceptualized as the opposite of burnout. Work engagement refers to the degree to which employees experience their work as stimulating and energizing (vigor), significant and meaningful (dedication), and engrossing and engaging (absorption). The most frequently used measure of work engagement is the *Utrecht Work Engagement Scale-9* (Schaufeli, Salanova, González-Romá, & Bakker, 2002). It consists of three 3-item subscales: vigor (e.g., "At work, I feel bursting with energy"), absorption (e.g., "I feel happy when I am working intensely"), and dedication (e.g., "I am enthusiastic about my job").

Rossier, Zecca, Stauffer, Maggiori, and Dauwalder (2012) correlated results from the *Utrecht Work Engagement Scale-9* and the *CAAS* for 391 adults with a mean age of 40 years. Analyses showed that the *CAAS* total score correlated .40 to the work engagement total score, with correlations of .40 to vigor, .35 to dedication, and .36 to absorption. The work engagement total score correlated .33 to both Concern and Control, .25 to Curiosity, and .41 to Confidence.

In another study of work engagement, Tokar, Savickas, and Kaut (2020) examined the correlations between the *CAAS-SF* and *Utrecht Work Engagement Scale-9* among 243 employed adults. The results indicated that work engagement correlated .34 to the *CAAS-SF* total score and .25 to Concern, .23 to Control, .25 to Curiosity, and .35 to Confidence.

To measure academic engagement among university students, Schaufeli, Bakker, and Salanova (2006) adapted the *Utrecht Work Engagement Scale-9* (Schaufeli, Salanova, González-Romá, & Bakker, 2002). Sample items read, "To me, my studies are challenging" (dedication), "I get carried away when I am studying" (absorption), and "When I'm doing my work as a student, I feel bursting with energy" (vigor). Merino-Tejedor, Hontangas, and Boada-Grau (2016) administered that inventory along with the

CAAS to 577 university students in Spain. Academic engagement correlated .55 to the *CAAS* total score, as well as .46 to Concern, .38 to Control, .40 to Curiosity, and .56 to Confidence.

A study by Akkermans, Paradnike, Van der Heijden, and DeVos (2019) also compared the *CAAS* to the *Utrecht Work Engagement Scale for Students* (Schaufeli, Bakker, & Salanova, 2006). The participants were 672 students (68% females with a mean age of 20.62 years) from nine Lithuanian colleges and universities. The *CAAS* correlated .39 to study engagement.

In a study conducted in China, Yang, Feng, Yuchen, and Yong (2019) examined the role of work engagement as a mediator between career adaptability and employee well-being. In addition to the mediation model, they tested a moderated-mediation model, conceptualizing guanxi as a contextual factor that may moderate the effects of career adaptability on work engagement. The defined guanxi as an informal, non-work, personal relationship between a subordinate and a supervisor involving social exchange of favors and obligations that promote progress through work and life.

The researchers measured guanxi with a four-item scale developed by Chen, Friedman, Yu, Fang, and Lu (2009) to assess the private relationship between a supervisor and subordinate (e.g., "My supervisor would ask me to help him/her deal with some family errands"). They measured career adaptability with the *CAAS-SF* and work engagement with the *Utrecht Work Engagement Scale* (Schaufeli et al., 2006). They used the *Employee Well-Being Scale* (Zheng, Zhu, Zhao. & Zang, 2015) to measure employees' overall satisfaction with their life well-being (e.g., I feel satisfied with my life"), workplace well-being (e.g., "Work is a meaningful experience for me"), and psychological well-being (e.g., "I generally feel good about myself, and I'm confident"). Data were collected from employees in four organizations at three time points over two months to minimize potential common-method biases. The final sample consisted of 338 participants (72% males) with averages of 38.28 years (SD = 9.66) in age, 7.75 years (SD = 7.84) in organizational tenure, and 4.98 years (SD = 5.77) in position tenure. The majority of the participants had at least a bachelor's degree (53.8%).

The results indicated that the CAAS-SF total score correlated .58 to work engagement, .38 to guanxi, and .43 to employee well-being. The researchers tested the direct effect of career adaptability on employee well-being and the indirect effect of career adaptability on employee well-being via work engagement. After controlling for the effects of gender, age, education, organizational tenure, and job tenure, the results showed that career adaptability (β = .69) was a significant direct predictor of work engagement. Next, after controlling for the effects of career adaptability, work engagement had a significant effect on employee well-being (β = .50), and career adaptability had a reduced relationship with employee well-being (β = .19). Therefore, work engagement partially mediated between career adaptability and employee well-being.

In support of the moderated-mediation model, the indirect effects varied at different levels of the moderator. After controlling for the effects of gender, age, education, organizational tenure, and job tenure, the results showed that the effect of the interaction between career adaptability and guanxi on work engagement (β = .16) was significant. The indirect effect of career adaptability on employee well-being was smaller at a high level of guanxi than the indirect effect at a low level of guanxi. When guanxi was low, the relationship between career adaptability and work engagement was significant, (β = .64). When guanxi was high, the effect was diminished, (β = .35). These results suggest that guanxi weakens the effect of career adaptability on work engagement and its indirect effect on employee well-being via work engagement. This result is contrary to expectations because Chinese employees are thought to particularly value relationships. The researchers suggested that adaptable employees with low guanxi may believe that to be valued by the organization, rather than personal relationship with superiors, they need to master new skills, complete challenging tasks, and take greater responsibility.

Job Performance

Job performance has been characterized to include both in-role performance of core tasks and extra-role performance of tasks that cannot be prescribed or required. Sattar, Rasheed, Khan, Tariq, and Iqbal (2017) investigated the relation of career adaptability to both types of job performance among 360 Pakistani hospitality industry workers from six 5-star hotels situated in three different cities in Pakistan. They were (71%) men and (29%) women with a mean age of 33 years old (SD = 16) who had an average length of employment of 8.4 years (SD = 4.2). The researchers measured in-role performance with the 5-item *In-Role Performance Scale* (Williams & Anderson, 1991). Sample items read, "I fulfill responsibilities specified in job description" and "I meet formal performance requirements of the job." They measured extra-role performance with the 14-item *Extra-Role Performance Scale* (Lee & Allen, 2002). Sample items read, "I adhere to informal rules devised to maintain order" and "I assist my supervisor with his/her work (when not asked"). The *CAAS* total score correlated to .62 to in-role performance and .26 to extra-role performance. The researchers suggested that mechanisms such as happiness orientation may mediate the relation between career adaptability and extra-role job performance.

The relation of career adaptability to the job outcomes of performance and satisfaction, through Person-Job P-J) fit, were examined by Kaur and Kaur (2020). P–J fit was operationally defined to include both demand–ability fit and need–supply fit. To measure adaptability, they used the *CAAS-Behavioral Form*, which modifies the *CAAS* items to reflect levels of career adaptability monthly. Sample items read, "I plan how to achieve my monthly goals" and "I investigate options before making a choice." Technically, this form measures adapting behaviors rather than adaptability resources. In a three-wave study, the researchers hypothesized that career adaptability at Time 1 relates to both types of fit at Time 2, which in turn relate to job outcomes at Time 3. Moreover, they hypothesized that fit functions as a mediator between adaptability and outcomes in that career adaptability enables individuals to achieve better demand–ability fit by adapting to job requirements which leads individuals to perform more effectively.

P–J fit was measured using a 6-item scale (Cable & DeRue, 2002) to assess both need–supply fit (three items) and demand–ability fit (three items). Items were modified to assess monthly experienced fit. Sample items read, "Every month, there is a good fit between what my job offers me and what I am looking for in a job" (need–supply fit) and "My abilities and training are a good fit with the requirements of my job" (demand–ability fit). Job outcomes were modeled as one latent variable measured by two scales. A 5-item measure (Wood, Chonko, & Hunt, 1986) was used to assess participants' job satisfaction levels. The scale was adapted to measure monthly job satisfaction levels. Sample items read, "Overall, I am satisfied with my job" and "I am satisfied with the variety of activities my job offers me each month." A 5-item scale (Williams &Anderson, 1991) was used to assess job performance. It was adapted to reflect the monthly job performance level of participants. A sample item reads, "I can competently complete monthly assigned work."

The participants were 239 employees at high-ranked banks in India. Data were collected at three time points with three months between each measurement occasion. At each measurement occasion, 300 questionnaires were distributed. At the first wave (T1), 272 employees responded; at the second wave (T2), 254 employees responded; and at the third wave (T3), 247 employees responded. A total of 239 respondents (57.6% males) participated in all three surveys (response rate = 79.5%). The average age of the participants was 34 years.

Results indicated that at T1 career adaptability correlated .12 to demand-ability fit, .19 to need-supply fit, and .49 to job outcomes. T1 career adaptability correlated at T3 to demand-ability fit .19, need-supply fit .27, and job outcomes .38. Additional analysis found a significant mediating effect of career adaptability on job outcomes through P-J fit. The researchers concluded that career adaptability positively influenced job outcomes because it positively influenced P–J fit. They suggested that adaptability enables individuals to deal with work-related changes and circumstances by proactively regulating their needs and competencies to better fit their job.

A second study of the relation of career adaptability to job outcomes, through P-J fit, was reported by Yen, Cheng, Hsu, and Yen (2020). The results of a two-wave data collection from 234 full-time workers indicated that employees with stronger career adaptability were more likely to report career satisfaction. They found a full mediating effect for P-J fit, in which career adaptability enhanced person–job fit that resulted in greater career satisfaction.

Job-Content Plateau

Job-content plateauing occurs when employees have mastered their job responsibilities and perceive work tasks to be routine, boring, and unchallenging. Jiang (2016) asserted that adaptability may forestall job-content plateaus, reasoning that employees can use adaptability resources to keep updating their job tasks, build their careers, and cope with stagnating conditions. Furthermore, he argued that that career adaptability may prevent job-content plateaus through its influence on employees' perceptions of their fit with the job and the organization. He reasoned that individuals with high levels of career adaptability negotiate and shape environments to achieve greater fit of their needs and abilities to resources in the environment. Thus, he also examined the mediating roles of P-J fit and Person-Organization (P-O) fit between adaptability and plateauing.

Jiang (2016) collected data from 270 workers (46.7% females) in several age groups: 34 (12.6%) were 18–25 years old, 92 (34.1%) were 26–30 years old, 97 (35.9%) were 31–40 years old, 39 (14.4%) were 41–50 years old, 5 (1.9%) were 51–60 years old, and three (1.1%) were over 60 years old. He measured career adaptability with the *CAAS*. The fit constructs were measured with items developed by Cable and Judge (1996). P-E fit was measured by four items (e.g., "My knowledge, skills, and abilities match the requirements of the job"). P-O fit was measured by three items (e.g., "The values and personality of my organization reflect my own values and personality"). Job-content plateau was measured by two items (e.g., "I am challenged by my job" – reverse coded) developed by Milliman (1992).

The *CAAS* total score correlated .53 to P-J fit, .55 to person-organization fit, and -.48 to job-content plateau. Mediation analysis results, as shown in Figure 41, indicated that P-J fit and P-O fit partially mediated the relation between career adaptability and job-content plateau. The indirect effect of career adaptability on job-content plateau via person-job fit was statistically significant, as was the indirect effect via person-organization fit. Jiang (2016) concluded that career adaptability fosters coping with work-role and that career adaptability helps employees alleviate perceptions of job-content plateauing.

Figure 41. P-J Fit Mediates between Adaptability and Plateau

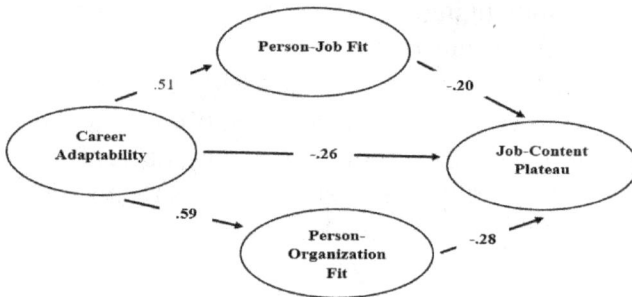

In the previous study, Jiang (2016) measured overall person–job fit perceptions. To offer a more refined examination of fit perceptions, Shabeer, Mohammed, Jawahar, and Bilal (2019) measured both components of person–job fit, namely, needs–supply fit and demands–ability fit. In addition to job-content plateauing, he studied hierarchical plateauing, that is, the likelihood of additional promotions is low. They used six items developed by Kristof (1996) to measure the two aspects of person-job fit. Three items were used to measure needs–supply fit (e.g., "There is a good fit between what my job offers me and what I am looking for in a job") and three items to measure demands–ability fit (e.g., "The match is very good between the demands on my job and my personal skills"). They measured plateauing with the 12-item scale developed by Milliman (1992). Six items measure job-content plateau (e.g., "I am challenged by my job" - reverse scored) and six items measure hierarchical plateau (e.g., "I expect to advance to a higher level in my company in the near future" - reverse scored). The participants were 294 bank employees (28% females) in the career establishment stage and worked in Pakistan.

Bivariate correlations showed that the *CAAS* total score correlated .35 to needs-supply fit, .30 to demand-ability fit, -.38 to job content plateau, and -.31 to hierarchical plateau. Mediation model analysis showed that career adaptability negatively related to both job content plateau and hierarchical plateau. Furthermore, needs–supply fit mediated the influence of career adaptability on job content and hierarchical plateaus. In comparison, demands–ability fit mediated the influence of career adaptability on job content plateau but not on hierarchical plateau.

A third study that examined job-content plateauing (Jiang, Hu, & Wang, 2018) focused on the moderating roles of job tenure and job self-efficacy. Career adaptability was measured with the *CAAS* and job-content plateauing was measured with the three items developed by Milliman (1992). An example item reads, "My job requires me to continually extend my abilities and knowledge" (reverse coded). They measured job self-efficacy by adapting three items from the 8-item *Generalized Self-Efficacy Scale* (Chen, Gully, & Eden, 2001). Job tenure was reported in months. The participants consisted of 154 full-time adult workers (53.9% females) from various occupations. They had a mean age of 33.83 years (SD = 6.57) and a mean tenure of 76.05 months (SD = 81.46). Results indicated that the *CAAS* total score correlated .67 to job self-efficacy and -.51 to job-content plateauing. The researchers used hierarchical moderated regression analyses to examine both job tenure and job self-efficacy as potential moderators of the relationship between career adaptability and job-content plateau, as shown in Figure 42.

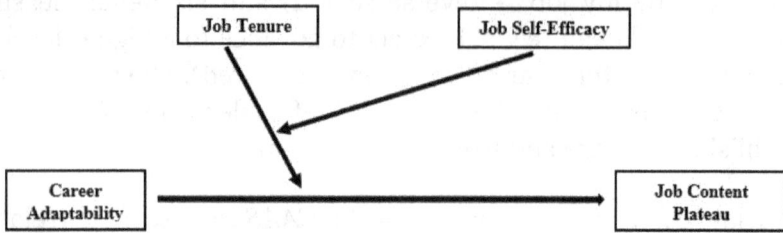

Figure 42. Job Tenure Mediates between Adaptability and Job Plateau

Results indicated a significant three-way interaction of career adaptability, job tenure, and job self-efficacy in predicting the job content plateau (β = .27). The moderating effect of job tenure was stronger when job self-efficacy was low rather than high. In contrast, when job self-efficacy was high, the relationship between career adaptability and the job-content plateau did not statistically differ across low-tenure and high-tenure groups. The researchers concluded that career adaptability is particularly important for longer-tenured employees with low job self-efficacy in dealing with job-content plateaus. Adaptability resources can foster self-regulation that reinforces motivation to keep up with changes and break new ground as they enter the maintenance stage of their careers.

Work-Family Conflict

One study reported the correlation of the *CAAS* to the adaptation outcome of work-family conflict. Amarnani, Lajohm, Restubog, and Capezio (2020) examine the relationship in two samples. Sample 1 consisted of 139 business professionals with a mean age of 30 years (SD = 8.9) and 63% were females. Sample 2 consisted of 156 nurses who had a mean age of 28 years (SD = 5.7) and 71% were females. Work–family conflict was measured using a 5-item scale developed by Netemeyer, Boles, and McMurrian (1996). In Sample 1, work-family conflict correlated -.34 to the *CAAS* total score, with correlations of -.34 to Concern, -.38 to Control, -.28 to curiosity, and -.28 to Confidence. In Sample 2, work-family conflict did not correlate significantly to the *CAAS* total score nor to any of the four subscales.

Adaptability Relates to Contentment as an Adaptation Result

This third section of Chapter 11 continues the discussion of the relation of career adaptability to adaptation results, specifically the contentment outcomes of satisfaction with school, job, career, and life.

Academic Satisfaction

High school students. The relation of career adaptability to satisfaction with school among 762 students aged 15 to 19 years (Mean = 17.38 years) was examined by Soresi, Nota, and Ferrari (2012). Along with the *CAAS*, they administered *My Life as a Student* (Soresi & Nota, 2003), which consists of 26 items that describe the students usual way of thinking and behaving. The scale domains comprise satisfaction with the School Experience (7 items; e.g., "I am really happy with the school I am attending," α = .86); Opportunities to Make Decisions Autonomously (empowerment) (5 items; e.g., "I am a free individual who can actually plan his/her own life in an autonomous way," α = .65); Relationships with Classmates (3 items; e.g., "My school friends behave very well toward me," α = .75); Current Life Conditions (3 items; e.g., "I think things are working out better for me than for my classmates," α = .74); Relationships with Family Members (4 items; e.g., "My family makes me feel important," α = .84); Praise Received when Due (2 items; e.g., "At school my diligence is appreciated," α = .71); and Help Availability (2 items; e.g., "I know who to count on in moments of need and discouragement," α =.80). Correlations results showed that the total score for *My Life as a Student* correlated .21 to the *CAAS* total score. As expected, analyses of variance showed that adolescents with higher adaptability reported a higher quality of life.

College students. Three studies of the relation between academic satisfaction and career adaptability among college students measured satisfaction with the 7-item *Academic Satisfaction Scale* (Lent, Singley, Sheu, Schmidt, & Schmidt, 2007). Sample items read, "I feel satisfied with my decision to major in my intended field" and "I enjoy the level of intellectual stimulation in my courses." Duffy, Douglas, and Autin (2015) had 412 undergraduates respond to the *CAAS and the* Academic satisfaction Scale. Duffy and colleagues reported that academic satisfactions correlated .44 to the *CAAS* total score, with correlations between .27 and .33 to the four adapt-abilities.

The second study that used the *Academic Satisfaction Scale* (Lent et al., 2007) with college students was conducted in Northwest China by Ma, Chen, and Zeng (2020). They used the adaptation model to investigate satisfaction among college nursing students, and to compare satisfaction between male and female students. Adaptive readiness was represented by proactive personality and core self-evaluation along with three types of support (i.e., emotional, instrumental, and informational). Adaptability resources were represented by four items from the *CAAS*, one item representing each dimension. And, an adaptation result was represented by academic satisfaction. Measures for the adaptive readiness variables were the *Proactive Personality Scale* ((Bateman & Crant, 1993), the *Core Self-Evaluation Scale* (Judge, Erez, Bono, & Thoreson, 2003), the *Emotional and Instrumental Support Scales* (Carver, 1997), and three items that assessed informational support from the *Career Exploration Scale* (Stumpf, Colarelli, & Hartman 1983). The adaptation result was measured with the *Academic Satisfaction Scale* (Lent et al., 2007). The participants were 1062 students at a vocational college. The sample included 165 males and 897 females with a mean age of 18.74 (SD = 1.64).

Results indicated that the *CAAS* correlated .60 to proactive personality, .59 to core self-evaluations, .44 to emotional support, .46 to instrumental support, .44 to information support, and .37 to academic satisfaction. Results from mediation analyses, shown in Figure 43, indicated that career adaptability mediated the relation of proactive personality, core self-evaluation, and informational support to academic satisfaction.

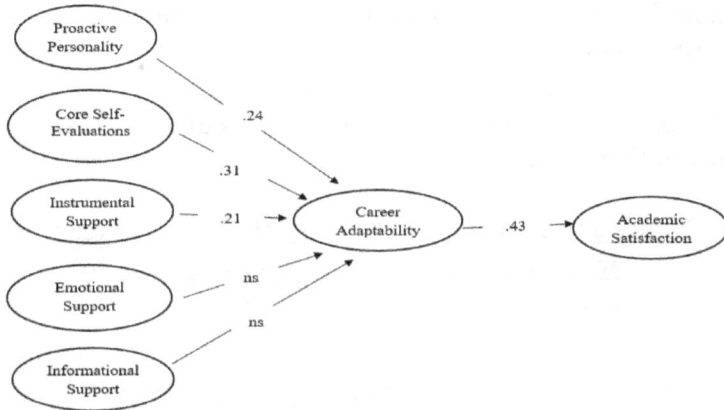

Figure 43. Career Adaptability Mediates between
Adaptivity and Academic Satisfaction

To compare the structural model for males versus females, the researchers used multiple-group analysis to test for a moderating effect. The most important finding of this comparison was that emotional support was important for the male group ($B = 0.31$, $p < .01$) but was not statistically significant for the female group. The researchers concluded that males need emotional support to experience academic satisfaction.

The third study to use the *Academic Satisfaction Scale* (Lent et al., 2007) was conducted in the country of Trinidad and Tobago. Wilkins-Yel, Roach, Tracey, and Yel (2018) They investigated academic satisfaction as a mediator between career adaptability and intended academic persistence. They measured intended academic persistence using two pairs of two items from Lent and his colleagues (2003). Intent to remain in one's major was measured by "I intend to remain enrolled in my current major over the next semester" and "I intend to remain enrolled in my current major over the next year." Intent to succeed in one's major was measured with "I intend to excel in my current major," and "I intend to complete the upper level required courses in my major with an overall G.P.A. of B or better." The two pairs of items correlated .36. As predicted, career adaptability associated positively with academic satisfaction (.33) as well as with intended major persistence (.11) and intended success in that major (.26). Additionally, the relation between career adaptability and intended academic persistence was mediated by academic satisfaction as shown in Figure 44. The findings indicated that students who score higher on career adaptability were more likely to feel content with their academic achievement and exhibit academic satisfaction, and in turn feel more committed to both succeeding and remaining enrolled in their academic major.

Figure 44. Academic Satisfaction Mediates between
Adaptability and Academic Performance

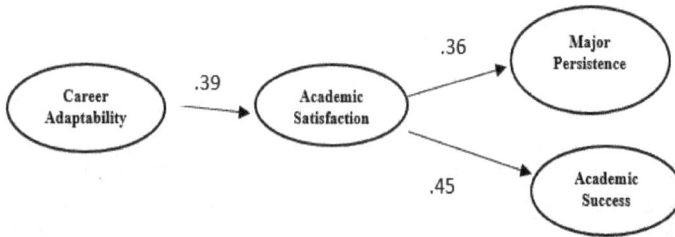

In the three studies with college students that related the *CAAS* to the *Academic Satisfaction Scale* (Lent et al., 2007), the correlations were quite similar: .44 in the USA, .37 in China, and .33 Trinidad and Tobago.

Another study of academic satisfaction among college students reported similar results. Akkermans, Paradnike, Van der Heijden, and DeVos (2019) compared the *CAAS* to the *Academic Major Satisfaction Scale* (Nauta, 2007). The participants were 672 students (68% females with a mean age of 20.62 years) from nine Lithuanian colleges and universities. The *CAAS* correlated .39 to satisfaction with one's academic major.

Job Satisfaction

The relation of job satisfaction to career adaptability was studied by Fiori, Bollmand, and Rossier (2015). They investigated the impact of career adaptability on job satisfaction and work stress, as mediated by affective states. They used a 3-wave cross-lagged longitudinal approach with a representative sample of the Swiss population (N = 1,671). They hypothesized that, over time, career adaptability amplifies job satisfaction and attenuates work stress through higher positive affect and lower negative affect, respectively. They administered the *Minnesota Satisfaction Questionnaire* (Weiss, Dawis, England, & Lofquist, 1967) to assess global job satisfaction; the *General Work Stress Scale* (De Bruin, 2006) to assess work stress; and the *Positive and Negative Affect Scale* (Mroczek & Kolarz, 1998) to assess affect.

The *CAAS* total score at Time 1 correlated at Time 2 to job satisfaction .16, work stress -.15, positive affect .25, and negative affect -.22. The *CAAS* total score at Time 1 correlated at Time 3 to job satisfaction .19, work stress -.17, positive affect .25, and negative affect -.23. Results of model testing showed that employees with higher *CAAS* scores at Time 1 experienced higher job satisfaction and lower work stress at Time 3. However, the effect of career adaptability on job satisfaction was explained only by negative affect (not positive affect), with lower negative affect relating to higher job satisfaction. The researchers concluded that career adaptability makes adaptation to the work environment more effective by reducing generalized negative affect, which helps to buffer work stress and protects against decreases in job satisfaction. Thus, career adaptability is a factor that protects against adversities more than a factor that promotes positive experiences. Overall, the results of their study support the conception of career adaptability as a self-regulatory skill that may model affective reactions in a way that protects from deterioration of job attitudes due to negative affect.

In another study of job satisfaction, Tokar, Savickas, and Kaut (2020) examined the correlations between Judge, Locke, Durham, and Kluger's (1998) 5-item adaptation of the *Job Satisfaction Index* (Brayfield & Rothe, 1951) and the *CAAS* among 243 employed adults. The results indicated that job satisfaction correlated .28 to the *CAAS* total score and .28 to Concern, .12 to Control, .21 to Curiosity, and .27 to Confidence.

The relation of job satisfaction to career adaptability was studied by Maggori, Johnston, Krings, Massoudi, and Rossier (2013). They used a representative sample of employed and unemployed adults living in Switzerland that included 2002 respondents from the French and German-speaking regions. The mean age was 41.99 years (SD = 8.61) and 1033 of the participants were women (51.6%). The researchers measured job satisfaction with the *JobSat Inventory* (Massoudi, 2009). The *CAAS* total score correlated .21 with job satisfaction.

For the three studies of the correlation between the *CAAS* total score and job satisfaction the coefficients were .21, .28, and .21.

Career Satisfaction and Success

Career satisfaction refers to subjective feelings of success. Researchers typically measure individuals' evaluation of their progress toward meeting goals for income, achievement, development, and career-related success as indications of subjective career success. The most widely used operational definition of career satisfaction is the *Career Satisfaction Scale* (Greenhaus, Parasuraman, & Wormley, 1990). The scale has five items, each beginning with the stem "I am satisfied with the ..." Different phrases complete each item: (a) "success I have achieve in my career," (b) " progress I have made towards meeting my overall career goals," (c) "progress I have made towards meeting my goals for income," (d) progress I have made towards meeting my goals for advancement," and (e) progress I have made toward meeting my goals for the development of new skills."

In Serbia, Mirkovic, Suvajdzic, and Dostanic (2020) administered the *Career Satisfaction Scale* (Greenhaus, Parasuraman, & Wormley, 1990) to 374 adult (57.5% female) employees in small and medium-sized enterprises. The participants ranged in age from 21 to 64 years (M = 39; SD = 11.35) years. The *CAAS* total score correlated to career satisfaction .20, with correlations of .18 to Control, .20 to Curiosity, and .22 to Confidence. The correlation of Concern to career satisfaction (.04) was not significant.

The relation of career adaptability to career satisfaction and objective success was examined by Yu, Dai, Guan, and Wang (2020) in China. Career adaptability was measured with the *CAAS-SF* and career satisfaction was measured with *Career Satisfaction Scale* (Greenhaus, Parasuraman, & Wormley, 1990). Career success was indicated by supervisor-rated job performance, which was defined as an individual's behavior that supports the organization's development. It was measured using the 3-item scale developed by Motowidlo and van Scotter (1994). An example item has managers rate an employee's level of "contribution to unit effectiveness." The measures were administered to two samples of workers. The first sample consisted of 905 civil servants (46.6% females). The second sample consisted of 1,250 enterprise employees (57% females) in the manufacturing, information technology, and service industries. For civil servants, career satisfaction correlated .48 to the *CAAS-SF* total score, with correlations of .45 to Concern, .31 to Control, .37 to Curiosity, and .38 to Confidence. Job performance rated by supervisors correlated .25 to the *CAAS-SF* total score, with correlations of .20 to Concern, .19 to Control, .20 to Curiosity, and .22 to Confidence. For enterprise employees, career satisfaction correlated .26 to the *CAAS* total score, with correlations of .25 to Concern, .18 to Control, .17 Curiosity, and .19 to Confidence. Job performance rated by supervisors correlated .16 to the *CAAS-SF* total score, with correlations of .12 to Concern, .15 to Control, .07 to Curiosity, and .15 to Confidence.

The relation of adaptability to career satisfaction and success was studied by Tolentino, Garcia, Lu, Restubog, Bordia, and Tang (2013) in The Phillipines. They obtained data from 495 full-time employees (56% females) who were enrolled in various post-graduate academic programs. Their sample had a mean age of 31.71 years and an average tenure of 5.18 years. The researchers measured career satisfaction using the *Career Satisfaction Scale* (Greenhaus, Parasuraman, & Wormley, 1990). Career success was indicated by promotability as measured by four items drawn from previous research (Shore, Barksdale, & Shore, 1995). A sample item reads, "I am likely to be promoted to a higher position sometime during my career." The *CAAS* total score correlated .43 to career satisfaction and .56 to promotability.

The joint and interactive effects of perceived organizational career management and career adaptability on indicators of career success (i.e., salary and career satisfaction) and turnover intention were examined by Guan, Zhiou, Ye, Jiang, and Zhou (2015). Organizational career management refers to the management practices that facilitate employees' career development in organizations such as individual assessment, training courses, mentoring, and job rotation (Baruch, 1999; Baruch & Peiperl, 2000). Perceived organizational career management denotes employees' subjective perception of organizational support for their career development and the extent to which they have access to these career development opportunities. Chinese employees (361 males and 293 females) reported their perception of organizational career management practices on 11 items that measured the extent to which they perceived that their organizations provided satisfactory career management practices, such as succession planning, career ladders and paths, job posting, and individual counseling. Subjective career satisfaction was measured with the five-item scale developed by Greenhaus, Parasuraman, and Wormley (1990). Participants rated their turnover intention using the 3-item scale developed by Cammann, Fichman, Jenkins, and Klesh (1979) to measure intention to quit the current organization.

The *CAAS* total score correlated .45 to perceived organizational career management, .25 to salary, .54 to career satisfaction, and -.33 to turnover intention. The results showed that career adaptability predicted both salary and career satisfaction, after controlling for the effects of demographics and perceived organizational career management. It was also found that both perceived organizational career management and career adaptability correlated negatively with turnover intention, with these relationships mediated by career satisfaction. The results further showed that career adaptability moderated the relationship between perceived organizational career management and career satisfaction such that the positive relationship was stronger among employees with a higher level of career adaptability. In support of the hypothesized moderated-mediation model, for employees with a higher level of career adaptability the indirect effect of perceived career management on turnover intention through career satisfaction was stronger. Overall, these results demonstrated the unique role of career adaptability in individuals' career success and that employees with a high level of career adaptability are less likely to quit their organizations due to their high level of career satisfaction.

The relation of career satisfaction and entrepreneurship to career adaptability was studied by McKenna, Zacher, Ardabili, and Mohebbi (2016). Career satisfaction was measured by the *Career Satisfaction Scale* (Greenhaus et al., 1990). They operationally defined entrepreneurship with two outcomes that are central constructs in the field of entrepreneurship. Entrepreneurial intentions involve the extent to which people aim or expect to engage in business start-up activities to pursue a career as self-employed in the future. Entrepreneurial intentions were measured with four items: "Do you intend to engage in activities to start a new business in the next six months?" "In the next six months, I will take actions to start a new business," "How likely is it that you will pursue a career as self-employed?" and "Estimate the probability you'll start your own business in the next three years." The second construct, opportunity identification, refers to recognizing and developing opportunities for creating a new business. The researchers operationally defined the construct as the number of opportunities identified by participants within the last six months. The questions were: "How many opportunities for creating a new business have you identified within the last six months?" "Out of all those opportunities, how many were in your opinion promising for creating a new and profitable business?" and "How many opportunities for creating a new business have you pursued, that is committed time and resources to, within the last 6 months?"

Participants were 204 workers (70% males; Mean age 36 years) from various jobs and organizations in Iran. Results indicated that the *CAAS* total score correlated .45 to career satisfaction and .24 to entrepreneurial intentions but not to opportunity identification. All four career adapt-abilities correlated to career satisfaction (ranging from .36 to .42) and entrepreneurial intentions (ranging from .15 to .30). Regression analyses controlling for demographic and employment characteristics showed a R^2 of .24 for adaptability to career satisfaction and .30 to entrepreneurial intentions. Contrary to expectations, overall career adaptability did not correlate significantly to opportunity identification. In regression analyses of the four career adapt-abilities, only Concern positively predicted career satisfaction and entrepreneurial intentions. Despite the lack of a relationship between total adaptability and opportunity identification, Concern (.30) and Control (-.28) did correlate to opportunity identification. While the relation of Concern to opportunity identification makes sense, the negative relation between Control and opportunity identification seems puzzling. The researchers speculated that the Control adapt-ability may lead employees to make a stronger commitment to their current work tasks and careers.

Career Satisfaction and Turnover Intentions

Intentions to leave the organization and the career were studied by Omar and Noordin (2013) among 303 employees in Information and Communication Technology at 15 organizations in Malaysia. The participants were 59 % males with 63% having a Bachelors degree and 9 % having a Masters degrees. The researchers used three items to measure the aspects of searching, thinking about, and intending to leave the job (e.g., "Presently I am actively search for another job"). The items were modified to represent leaving the career (e.g., "Presently, I am actively searching for a career other than ICT"). Intention to leave the job correlated -.44 to Concern, -.48 to Control, -.43 to Curiosity, and -,47 to Confidence. Intention to leave the career correlated -.38 to Concern, -.43 to Control, -.38 to Curiosity, and -,45 to Confidence. This suggests that strong career adaptability resources may reduce the chance of ICT professionals' intending to leave both the organization and the career. Although all four adapt-abilities correlated significantly with intentions to not leave the organization or the career, multiple

290

regression analyses showed that only Control and Confidence significantly explained the intention to leave both organization and career.

A dual-path model linking the negative relationship between career adaptability and turnover intentions was conducted Zhu, Cai, Buchtel, and Guan (2019). They studied two potential mediators, namely, career satisfaction and perceived organizational support. They measured the variables with the *CAAS-SF*; the *Perceived Organizational Support Scale* (Eisenberger, Huntington, Hutchison, & Sowa, 1986); *Career Satisfaction Scale* (Greenhaus, Parasuraman, & Wormley, 1990); and a turnover intentions scale developed by Farh, Tsui, Xin, and Cheng (1998). The participants consisted of 1013 employees (51.4% males) from 200 Chinese organizations, primarily banks (82) and securities firms (68).

As expected, career adaptability related positively to career satisfaction (.33) and perceived organizational support (.36), and negatively to turnover intention (-.28). Structural equation modeling indicated that career adaptability influenced turnover intention through career satisfaction and perceived organizational support. As shown in the Figure 45, after controlling for career adaptability, career satisfaction ($\beta=-.19$) and perceived organizational support ($\beta = -.36$) still related significantly to turnover intention. The analyses showed that mediation through career satisfaction was significant ($\beta = -.08$), as was mediation through perceived organizational support ($\beta = -.16$). The researchers concluded that their findings responded to Johnston's (2018) call to adopt new theoretical perspectives to deepen understanding of career adaptability and extend CCT. Drawing upon social exchange theory, they showed that individuals with high career adaptability intend to stay in their organization not only because they experience more career satisfaction, but also because they receive more support from organizations.

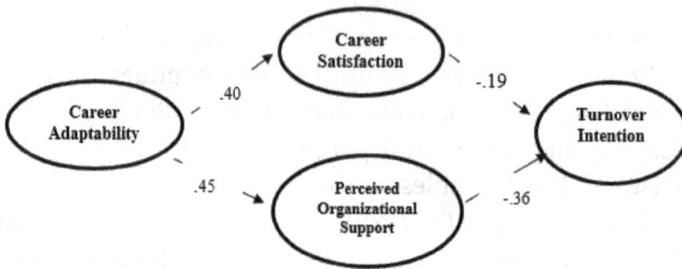

Relations of career adaptability to career satisfaction and turnover intentions were examined in two studies by Chan and his colleagues. Chan and Mai (2015) investigated the linkage between career adaptability, turnover intentions, and career satisfaction for 368 (190 males and 178 females) low-ranking employees working in Macau. They defined career satisfaction as an individual's appraisal of distinct career-associated objectives (e.g., achievement and income) and subjective accomplishments. All these employees were required to work on shifts, and received lower wages in comparison to other ranks. A majority of the respondents originated from Mainland China (76.4%), were non-Macau resident (79.6%), less than 40 years old (77.4%), and had completed at least a college-level education (69.9%). The respondents had worked in the company for less than three years (58.8%), and were earning a monthly salary of less than 1260 US dollars (74.6%) at the time the study was conducted. The researchers measured career satisfaction using the *Career Satisfaction Scale* (Greenhaus, Parasuraman, & Wormley, 1990). They measured turnover intentions with the 3-item scale developed by Tett and Meyer (1993). An example item reads, "It is likely that I will search for a job in another organization."

The results showed that the *CAAS* total score related .34 to career satisfaction and -.14 to turnover intentions. Career satisfaction related -.30 to turnover intentions, and it mediated the association between adaptability and turnover intentions. Career adaptability did not mediate the relation between career satisfaction and turnover intentions. The findings suggest that employees scoring higher in career adaptability are more likely to express career satisfaction and be content with the achievement of their current goals and thus are less likely to leave their positions. In other words, if the employees are adaptable, competent, and have confidence in their work, then they will have less tendency to voluntarily leave the organization.

In a related second study, Chan, Mai, Kuok, and Kong (2016) examined the relation between career adaptability, promotability, and career satisfaction, and their impacts on turnover intentions for 431 service sector employees in Macau. They again used the *Turnover Intentions Scale* (Tett & Meyer, 1993) and the *Career Satisfaction Scale* (Greenhaus, et al., 1990). They measured promotability with a 4-item scale based on earlier studies (Tolentino et al., 2013). An example item reads, "If my boss wants to select someone to succeed him in his position, it will be me." The *CAAS* total score correlated .36 to promotability, .30 to career satisfaction, and -.13 to turnover intentions after controlling for the influences of age, gender, education and tenure. The Concern scale had the highest correlation to promotability at .40. The results showed that promotability and career satisfaction mediated the effect of career adaptability on turnover intentions. This link suggests that when individuals perceive themselves as adaptable to changes at work and able to develop their career, they will be more optimistic about achieving career goals, and therefore less inclined to leave the organization because they are satisfied with their achievements. The findings also suggest that career satisfaction and promotability are stronger predictors of turnover intention than career adaptability.

The relation of career adaptability to career satisfaction and turnover intentions was also studied by Santra and Giri (2019). They measured career adaptability with the *CAAS-SF*, career satisfaction with the *Career Satisfaction Scale* (Greenhaus et al., 1990), and turnover intentions with a 4-item scale developed by O'Reilly, Chatman, and Caldwell (1991). A sample item from the turnover scale reads, "I have seriously thought about leaving this company." The participants were 434 IT professionals in India (28.6% females and 71.4% males) with an average age of 34.41 years (SD = 4.65). Results indicated that career satisfaction correlated .48 to the *CAAS-SF* total score, with correlations to the four adapt-abilities ranging from .33 to .44. Turnover intentions did not correlate significantly to the *CAAS-SF* total score, and only correlated significantly (.19) to the Concern adapt-ability.

Table 16 presents a summary of the correlations between the *CAAS* and the *Career Satisfaction Scale* for eleven studies in seven different countries. The mean correlation between the *CAAS* and *CSS* was .38, with coefficient that ranged from .20 to .54. Thus, career adaptability and career satisfaction share abut 14% variance. The high correlation of .54 came from a sample of full-time employees who also were enrolled in a post-graduate academic program. They may have been particularly satisfied with their career progress in that they were studying in the hopes of advancing even further along the career path. The mean correlation between the *CAAS* and turnover intentions was -.28, with coefficients that ranged from -.13 to -.43. Employees with stronger adaptability resources appear less likely to be thinking abut changing positions, although one must assume that some well-resourced employees might be considering changing positions in terms of a promotion. This possibility makes the relations between the *CAAS* and turnover intentions more ambiguous than that between the *CAAS* and career satisfaction.

Table 16. Relation of Career Adaptability to Career Satisfaction in 11 Studies

	CAAS Correlation to Career Satisfaction Scale	CAAS Correlation to Turnover Intentions
374 employees in Serbia (Mirkovic)	.20	
905 civil servants in China (Yu)	.48	
1,250 enterprise employees in China (Yu)	.26	
495 full-time employees in The Phillipines (Tolentino)	.54	-.33
368 low ranking employees in Macau (Chan)	.34	-.14
431 service sector employees in Macau (Chan)	.30	-.13
1013 employees in China (Zhu)	.33	-.28
434 IT employees in India (Santra)	.48	ns
204 employees in Iran (McKenna)	.45	
234 hospitality employees in China(Rasheed)		-.39
303 IT employees in Malaysia (Omar)		-.43
Mean Correlation	**.38**	**-.28**

Career Entrenchment and Retention Factors

Employee's career entrenchment and employer's retention factors may forestall turnover intentions. Career entrenchment has been defined as employees' feelings of "immobility resulting from substantial economic and psychological investments in a career that make change difficult" (Carson, Carson, Phillips, & Roe, 1996, p. 274). The concept consists of three dimensions: perceived career investments, limited career alternatives, and emotional costs. Career investments involve employees' beliefs that they have invested substantial amounts of time, money, and effort in their current careers, and that they would lose these accrued investments, or substantially reduce their worth, if they changed careers. Limited career alternatives mean that employees' do not perceive new career opportunities. Emotional costs mean the expected socio-emotional risks associated with the pursuit of a new career, such as the disruption of friendships with coworkers and professional contacts.

Working in Brazil, Zacher, Ambiel, and Noronha (2015) hypothesized that highly adaptable employees are less entrenched because they are more open to new career opportunities and they possess more resources to potentially change career fields. Data for their study that examined the relation between career adaptability and job entrenchment came from 404 employees (70% females), whose ages ranged from 18 to 65 years (Mean = 30.6; SD = 9.3. Participants responded to the *CAAS* and the Brazilian version of *Career Entrenchment Scale* (Magalhães, 2008). The results indicated that the *CAAS* total score did not correlate significantly (-.08, ns) to total entrenchment yet did correlate significantly (-21) to limited career alternatives. This finding suggests that career adaptability relates to employees' perceptions of alternative career options

Among the relations between the four adapt-abilities and the three dimensions of entrenchment, the only significant correlations were between limited career alternatives and Control (-.21), Curiosity (-.23), and Confidence (-.14). No adapt-ability correlated significantly to career investments nor emotional costs. Results of structural equation modeling showed that overall career adaptability weakly and negatively predicted overall career entrenchment ($\beta = -.13$), after controlling for age, gender, education, and job tenure. Of the four career adapt-abilities, only Concern ($\beta = .27$, p < .02) and Curiosity ($\beta = -.61$, p < 001) predicted overall career entrenchment, whereas Control and Confidence did not have significant effects. It seems that employees with high levels of Curiosity are interested in pursuing new career opportunities and therefore should perceive themselves as less immobile in their career, and they should be less worried about the loss of career investments, lack of alternatives, and emotional costs. Interestingly, Concern related positively to perceived career investments ($\beta = .25$), suggesting that employees who anticipate new career tasks in the future tend to feel too invested in their current careers to consider changing careers.

Retention factors. Retention is the logical inverse of turnover. Retention factors refers to tactics that an employer may use to retain employees and prevent turnover. The relation of satisfaction with retention factors to career adaptability was studied by Coetzee and Stoltz (2015). They measured satisfaction with the factors of compensation (13 items; e.g., "On my present job this is how I feel about my benefits package"), job characteristics (4 items; e.g., "The job requires me to use a number of complex or high-level skills"), training and development opportunities (six items; e.g., "The company is providing me with job-specific training"), supervisor support (6 items; e.g., "My supervisor looks for opportunities to praise positive employee performance, both privately and in front of others"), career opportunities (six items; e.g., "My chances for being promoted are good"), work–life balance (four items; e.g., "I often feel like there is too much work to do") and commitment to the organization (three items; e.g., "How would you rate your chances of still working at this company a year from now"). The participants were 321 employees in a South African automotive industry. The majority of the respondents were at a managerial level (79%) with the rest being operation staff. The *CAAS* total score correlated significantly to only one retention factor, .20 to career

297

opportunities with the highest adapt-ability correlation being to Concern at .28.

Delegation of authority may also be use as a retention tactic to prevent turnover. Perceived delegation means the extent to which employees believe that their supervisors empower them to take new responsibilities because they recognize the subordinates' job competence and problem-solving skills. The relation of perceived delegation to career adaptability was studied by Yang, Guan, Lai, She, and Lockwood (2015). Scores from the *CAAS* were correlated to six items from the *Perceived Delegation Scale* (Chen & Aryee, 2007). A sample items was "My supervisor does not require that I get his/her input or approval before making decisions." The *CAAS* total score correlated .29 to perceived delegation, with the highest adapt-ability correlation being .41 to Curiosity.

Life Satisfaction

The relation between career adaptability and life satisfaction has been examined in 14 different studies with school-age adolescents, college students, unemployed emerging adults, and employed adults. Each of these studies has operationally defined life satisfaction with the *Satisfaction with Life Scale* (Diener, Emmons, Larsen, & Griffin, 1985). The scale is a 5-item inventory that measures global judgements of satisfaction with one's life. Two example items read, ""I am satisfied with my life" and "So far I have gotten the important things I want in life."

Adolescents. The relation of life satisfaction to career adaptability among middle school students (Mean age = 13.27 years; SD = .67) in Italy was studied by Di Maggio, Ginevra, Nota, Ferrari, and Soresi (2015). They administered the *Satisfaction with Life Scale* (Diener, Emmons, Larsen, & Griffin, 1985) to 838 students. Global life satisfaction correlated .39 to the *CAAS* total score, with correlations ranging from .31 to .33 between the four adapt-abilities and life satisfaction.

In two studies with young adolescents (Mean age = 14.35 years; SD = 2.34), Santilli, Marcionetti, Rochat, Rossier, and Nota (2017) administered the *CAAS* and the *Satisfaction with Life Scale* (Diener et al., 1985) to 726 Italian and 533 Swiss students between the ages of 12 and 16 years. The *CAAS* total score correlated to satisfaction with life .40 among Italian students and .35 among Swiss students.

Studying adolescents in Turkey, Bolukbasi and Kirdok (2019) also investigated the relation of life satisfaction to career adaptability. The participants were 617 high school students (52% females; 48% males) from the city of Adana. The participants ranged in age from 14 to 18 years (Mean age = 16.08; SD=1.09). They were enrolled in the ninth grade (N= 158, 25.6%), tenth grade (N = 160, 25.9%), eleventh grade (N = 153, 24.8%) and twelfth grade (N =146, 23.7%). In terms of high school type, participants studied at two Vocational and Technical High Schools (N = 212, 34.4%), at two state-funded High Schools (N = 290, 47%), and at one private High School (n= 115, 18.6%). The *CAAS* total score correlated .47 with the *Satisfaction with Life Scale* (Diener et al., 1985).

In a study concerning the adaptability-adapting-adaptation path, Ginevra, Magnano, Lodi, Annovazzi, Camussi, Patrizi, and Nota (2018) examined behavioral courage as a mediator between adaptability and adaptation. They used the *CAAS* to represent adaptability resources and the *Satisfaction with Life Scale* (Diener et al., 1985) to represent an adaptation result. As an indicator of adapting responses, they used the construct of courage. Typically, courage has been portrayed as a trait or a stable disposition (i.e., adaptivity). However, recently it has been re-conceptualized as an act or behavior, especially persistent effort despite fear. Ginevra and her colleagues explained that persistence despite fear, as an adapting response, is malleable and may be influenced by other constructs such as career adaptability resources. They used six items from *The Courage Measure* (Norton & Weiss, 2009) that specifically measure persistence despite fear (Howard & Alipour, (2012). An example reads, "Even if I feel terrified, I will stay in that situation until I have done what I need to do." The study participants were 1202 Italian adolescents (602 females and 600 females) who ranged in age from 14 to 20 years (M = 16.87; SD = 1.47).

Zero-order correlations showed that the *CAAS* total score correlated .47 to persistence despite fear and .36 to life satisfaction. Results of the mediation analysis shown in Figure 46 indicated that the direct and indirect relationships between career adaptability and life satisfaction were significant. The 95% confidence intervals for the indirect effect between career adaptability and life satisfaction ranged from 0.23 to 0.59, supporting this indirect effect.

Figure 46. Persistence Mediates between Adaptability and Life Satisfaction

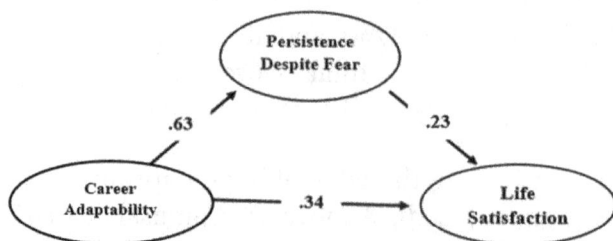

The results suggest that persistence despite fear may be conceptualized as an adapting behavior in coping with career challenges and changes. Ginevra and colleagues concluded that career adaptability may prompt perceptions of possibilities and opportunities that instigate actions to deal with obstacles and to succeed in reaching goals.

Undergraduate students. The relation of life satisfaction to career adaptability was studied by Buyukgoze-Kavas, Duffy, and Douglas (2015) in Turkey. They recruited 1727 undergraduate students from various departments in a public university. Of the participants, 641 (37.1%) were males, 1079 (62.5%) were females, and 7 (.4%) did not report gender. The mean age of the participants was 21.09 years (SD=1.79 years). The class distribution was 32.4% freshmen, 21.1%

sophomores, 25.8% juniors, and 16.9% seniors. The participants respond to the *CAAS* and the *Satisfaction with Life Scale* (Diener et al., 1985). Life satisfaction correlated to .44 to the *CAAS* total score, with correlations to the four adapt-abilities ranging between .32 and .42.

In a study that used university students in Italy as participants, Di Fabio and Kenny (2016) administered the *CAAS* and the *Satisfaction with Life Scale* (Diener et al., 1985) to 184 (44% males and 56% females) who ranged in age from 22 to 27 years (Mean = 24.13; *SD* = 1.79). Satisfaction with life correlated .35 to Concern, .39 to Control, .37 to Curiosity, and .33 to Confidence. They also measured life meaning with the *Meaningful Life Measure* (Morgan & Farsides, 2009). Life meaning correlated .33 to Concern, .37 to Control, .30 to Curiosity, and .32 to Confidence.

A study by Akkermans, Paradnike, Van der Heijden, and DeVos (2019) also compared the *CAAS* to the *Satisfaction with Life Scale* (Diener, Emmons, Larsen, & Griffin, 1985). The participants were 672 students (68% females with a mean age of 20.62 years) from nine Lithuanian colleges and universities. The *CAAS* correlated .42 to life satisfaction.

In yet another study, Cabras and Mondo (2018), reported that for 373 university students (197 in Italy and 176 in Spain), the *Satisfaction with Life Scale* (Diener, Emmons, Larsen, & Griffin, 1985) correlated .35 to the *CAAS* total score, with correlations of .30 to Concern, .22 to Control, .22 to Curiosity, and .33 to Confidence.

Emerging adults. The relation of life satisfaction and affect to career adaptability was examined in an unemployment study by Celen-Demirtas, Konstam, and Tomek (2015). They administered the *Satisfaction with Life Scale* (Diener et al., 1985) and the *Positive and Negative Affect Scales* (Watson, Clark, & Tellegen, 1988) to 184 unemployed emerging adults (84 women, 100 men; Mean age = 25.10, 72% with a bachelor's degree) in the USA. The researchers did not report results for the *CAAS* total score, just for the four adapt-abilities. Life satisfaction correlated .24 to Concern,

.34 to Control, .21 to Curiosity, and .37 to Confidence. Positive affect correlated .48 to Concern, .50 to Control, .42 to Curiosity, and .46 to Confidence. Negative affect correlated -.21 to Control but not to the other three adapt-abilities. In multivariate analyses, career adaptability accounted for 16% (r. = .40) of the total variance in life satisfaction scores. Higher levels of Confidence and Control correlated with higher life satisfaction scores. Additionally, career adaptability accounted for 31% of the total variance in positive affect and 7% of the total variance in negative affect. Concern related to positive affect. Control related to higher levels of positive affect and lower levels of negative affect. Curiosity and Confidence, in the multiple regression analysis, did not related significantly to positive affect nor negative affect.

Adults. The relation of life satisfaction variable to career adaptability was studied by Maggori, Johnston, Krings, Massoudi, and Rossier (2013). They used a representative sample of employed and unemployed adults living in Switzerland that included 2002 respondents from the French and German-speaking regions. The mean age was 41.99 years (SD = 8.61) and 1033 of the participants were women (51.6%). The researchers measured life satisfaction with the *Satisfaction with Life Scale* (Diener et al., 1985), job satisfaction with the *JobSat Inventory* (Massoudi, 2009), and work stress with the *General Work Stress Scale* (DeBruin, 2006). The *CAAS* total score correlated .35 to life satisfaction, .21 with job satisfaction, and -17 to general work stress.

Using the *CAAS-SF*, Kozan, Isik, and Blustein (2019) report a correlation of .51 to the *Satisfaction with Life Scale* (Diener et al., 1985) for 401 low-income employees in Turkey. The participants ranged in age from 18 to 59 years (Mean = 28.9, SD = 8.9) and were 47.1% females.

The relation of life satisfaction to career adaptability among employed adults (N=243) was also studied by Tokar, Savickas, and Kaut (2020). They measured the variables with the *CAAS* and the *Satisfaction with Life Scale* (Diener et al., 1985). Life satisfaction correlated .27 to the *CAAS* total score and .35 to Concern, .18 to Control, .14 to Curiosity, and .17 to Confidence.

The role of career adaptability in employee job and life satisfaction over a two-year period was investigated by Urbanaviciute, Udayar, and Rossier (2019). The participants consisted of a representative sample of 1007 employed adults (51.6% females) with a mean age of 42.77 years (SD = 8.42).from the French- and German-speaking parts of Switzerland. The participants responded twice (two years apart) to the *CAAS-SF*, *Satisfaction with Life Scale* (Diener et al, 1985), *Perceived Stress Scale* (Cohen, Kamarck, & Mermelstein, 1983), and five items from the *JobSat Inventory* (Massoudi, 2009) that measure satisfaction with general working conditions, salary, job security, relationship with supervisor, and relationships with coworkers.

At Time 1, the *CAAS* total score correlated .17 to job satisfaction, .30 to life satisfaction, and -.33 to perceived stress. As shown in the Figure 47 from Urbanaviciute, Udayar, and Rossier (2019, p. 82), cross-lagged structural equation modeling analysis indicated that the *CAAS* correlated to life satisfaction .31 at Time 1. Furthermore, the model demonstrated a positive cross-lagged effect from Time 1 career adaptability to Time 2 job and life satisfaction. Conversely, a negative effect was observed with regard to perceived stress in life. The findings suggest that career adaptability resources may foster both adaptation to an immediate change or challenge as well as sustain longer-term adaptation within and outside of work. Thus, career adaptability may have a two-fold effect on well-being. On the one hand, it serves as a resource for immediate reactions to vocational challenges and changes in the vocational environment. On the other hand, its stable part may also have a foundational role in longer-term adaptation to vocational constraints. The researchers concluded that career adaptability may be beneficial not only for individuals at the beginning of a career who must make choice and secure employment but also for individuals at mid-career who must manage psychological stress as well as maintain a work-life balance.

Figure 47. Career Adaptability Fosters Adaptation

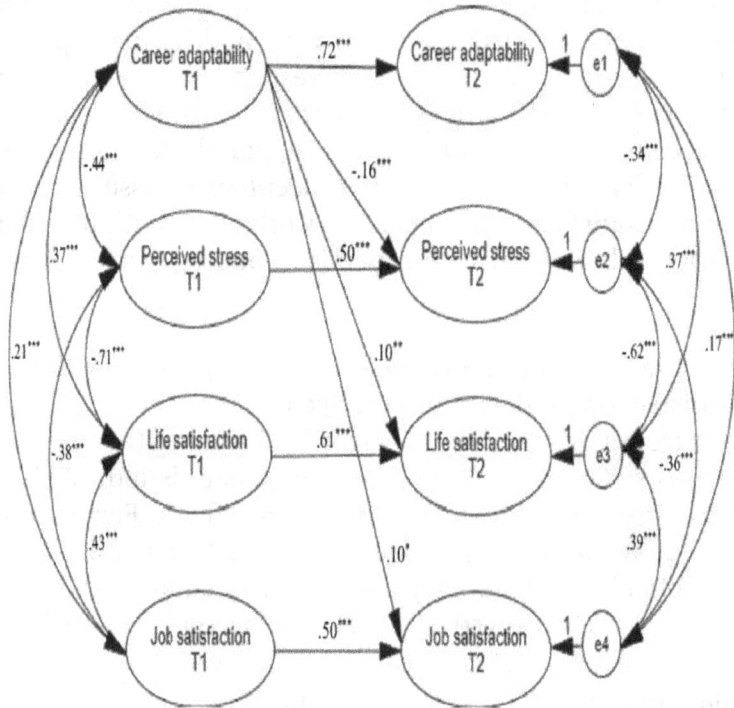

Table 17 reports the correlation coefficients between *CAAS* and the *Satisfaction with Life Scale* for 13 separate studies. The mean correlation was .40, with coefficients that ranged from .27 to .51.

Table 17. Correlation of *CAAS* to *Satisfaction with Life Scale*

838 middle school students in Italy (Dimaggio et al.)	.39
726 adolescents in Italy (Santilli et al.)	.40
533 adolescents in Switzerland (Santilli et al.)	.35
617 high school students in Turkey (Bolukbasi et al.)	.47
1202 adolescents in Italy (Ginevra et al.)	.47
1727 college students in Turkey (Buyukgoze-Kavas et al.)	.44
184 college students in Italy (DiFabio et al.)	.36
672 college students in Lithuania (Akkermans et al.)	.42
373 college students in Italy and Spain (Cabras et al.)	.35
184 unemployed adults in USA (Celen-Demirtas)	.49
2002 adults in Switzerland (Maggori et al.)	.35
243 adults in USA (Tokar et al.)	.27
1007 employed adults in Switzerland (Urbanaviciute et al.)	.31
401 low-income employees in Turkey (Kozan et al.)	.51
Mean Correlation	**.40**

A study conducted by Kirdok and Boluksai (2018) in Turkey used the *Satisfaction with Life Scale* (Diener et al., 1985) but combined it with measures of affect in a subjective well-being indicator. They examined whether career adaptability and the separate adapt-abilities could predict subjective well-being among undergraduate university students in their senior year. A total of 310 students (55.8% females and 44.2% males) enrolled at a public university in the Mediterranean region of Turkey participated in this study. They ranged in age between 20 and 28 years (Mean age = 22.72; SD = 1.59). The researchers assessed subjective well-being by combining scores from the *Satisfaction with Life Scale* (Diener et al., 1985) with scores from the *Positive and Negative Affect Schedule* (Watson, Clark, & Tellegen, 1988). To combine scores they subtracted negative affect from satisfaction with life plus positive affect to represent a participant's global evaluation of affect and life satisfaction. The results showed that subjective well-being correlated .59 to the *CAAS* total score, and .48 to Concern, .59 to Control, .35 to Curiosity, and .51 to Control. A simple regression analysis of career adaptability predicting subjective well-being produced $R = .59$, thus career adaptability accounted for 35% of the variance in subjective well-being. Next, the researchers used scores for the four adapt-abilities to predict subjective well-being. Together the four subscale scores significantly predicted subjective well-being ($R = .64$) and accounted for 41% of the variance in subjective well-being. The Control adapt-ability ($\beta = .41$, $p < .001$) was the strongest predictor of subjective well-being followed by Concern ($\beta = .23$) and Confidence ($\beta = .20$). However, Curiosity ($\beta = -.10$) did not significantly predict subjective well-being among senior university students.

One study used a completely different operational definition of life satisfaction. Rasheed, Okumus, Weng, Hameed, and Nawaz (2020) investigated whether life satisfaction mediates the relation between career adaptability and turnover intentions, and whether perceived opportunities moderate the relation of satisfaction to turnover intentions. The participants were 234 frontline hospitality industry employees. The data were collected in three waves, one month apart. At Time 1, the researchers administered the *CAAS* along with the three-item *Perceived Career Opportunities Scale* (Kraimer, Seibert, Wayne, Linden, & Bravo, 2011). The items read, "There are job opportunities available within this company that are of interest to me," "There are career opportunities within this company that are attractive to me," and "This company offers many job opportunities that match my career goals." At Time 2, they measured contentment and fulfillment with the *Orientations to Happiness and Life Satisfaction Scale* (Peterson, Park, & Seligman, 2005). The scale measures life satisfaction in terms of three different ways to be happy -- through pleasure, engagement, and meaning. Example items read, "For me, the good life is the pleasurable life," "My life serves a higher purpose," and "I am rarely distracted by what is going on around me." The total score indicates degree of fulfillment and contentment, or a summary appraisal of a full or empty life. At Time 3, turnover intentions were measured using a four-item scale from O'Reilly, Chatman, and Caldwell (1991). The items are: "The extent to which you would prefer to work for a different employer," "The extent to which you have thought about changing the organization since beginning to work here," "If you had your own way, you would be working for this employer three years from now," and "How long would you intend to remain with this employer."

Results indicated that the *CAAS* total score correlated .32 to life satisfaction, -.22 to perceived career opportunities, and -.39 to turnover intentions. They tested the mediation model using path analysis and conducted bootstrapping to assess the significance of indirect effects. Time 1 career adaptability associated negatively with Time 3 turnover intentions ($B = -.52$, $p < .001$). Moreover, Time 1 career adaptability associated positively with Time 2 orientation to happiness ($B = .46$, $p < .001$) and Time 2 orientation to happiness associated negatively with Time 3 turnover intentions ($B = -.20$, $p < .01$). There was a significant negative indirect effect of Time 1 career adaptability on Time 3 turnover intentions via Time 2 life satisfaction (-.14). A significant negative effect of career adaptability on turnover intentions after including the mediator ($B = -.51$, $p < .01$) further suggested that life satisfaction played a partial mediating role in the model. The researchers concluded that career adaptability related directly and indirectly to turnover intentions, suggesting that career adaptability is important because it increases life satisfaction, which in turn reduces turnover intentions. They also calculated the conditional indirect effect of career adaptability on turnover intentions through life satisfaction across levels (at -1 SD and $+1$ SD) for the moderator of perceived career opportunities. The conditional indirect effect of career adaptability on turnover intentions through life satisfaction was weaker under low perceived opportunities (effect estimate = -0.04, ns) compared to high perceived opportunities (effect estimate = -0.15), which provides support for moderated mediation, meaning that the relationship between life satisfaction and turnover intentions weakens when perceived career opportunities are low. The researchers recommended that HR professionals and frontline supervisors find ways to develop employees' adaptability resources that enable individuals to better adjust to the demanding working conditions inherent in the hospitality industry while enhancing their careers.

Conclusion

This Chapter reviewed the relation of adaptability resources to adaptation results, independent of adapting behaviors. The first section addressed outcomes that pertain to individuals, namely vocational identity, professional identity, personal growth, quality of life, and career exploration and plans. The second section addressed the adaptation outcomes that pertain to the job, namely work engagement, job performance, job plateauing, and work-family conflict. And, the third section addressed adaptation outcomes that pertain to contentment, namely academic satisfaction, career satisfaction and success, entrenchment, and life satisfaction. The next Chapter examines how adaptability mediates the relation between adaptive readiness and adapting responses.

CHAPTER 12

ADAPTABILITY MEDIATES BETWEEN
ADAPTIVITY AND ADAPTING

The Career Construction Theory adaptation model positions adaptability resources as a mediator between adaptive readiness and actual adaptation responses, as depicted in Figure 48. Several studies have directly tested this proposition about relations among adaptivity, adaptability, and adapting.

Figure 48. Adaptability Mediates between
Adaptivity and Adapting

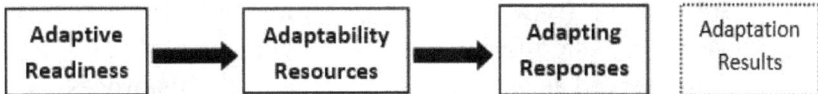

The studies in this section were organized according to how the researchers represented adaptation responses, namely as exploring, deciding, managing, and engaging.

Career Exploring as Adapting Responses

In a study of the adapting response represented by career exploring, Li, Guan, Wang, Zhou, Guo, Jiang, Mo, Li, and Fang (2015) tested whether adaptability mediates between adaptive personality traits and adapting behaviors. Adaptivity was operational defined as the FFM personality traits (Hahn, Gottschling, & Spinath, 2012) along with the Behavioral Inhibition (BIS) and Behavioral Activation (BAS) motivational systems (Carver & White, 1994). BIS represents a disposition that motivates individuals to avoid negative stimuli whereas BAS represents a disposition to approach positive stimuli. Adapting was measured with both subscales from the *Career Exploration Survey* (Stumpf, Colarelli, & Hartman, 1983) -- five items for self- exploration and six items for environmental exploration. The data were collected from 264 undergraduates enrolled in a management course at a university in North China.

309

The participants were 71% females with a mean age of 20.97 years (SD = 1.32). Effects of FFM traits and BIS/BAS on career adaptability were analyzed first. The results showed that openness to experience (β = .12, p < .01), agreeableness (β = .10, p < .05), conscientiousness (β = .16, p < .001) and BAS (β = .39, p < .001) were significant predictors of career adaptability after controlling for the effects of gender, age, faculty, and grade. Adding career adaptability to the model significantly predicted career exploration (β= .62, p < .001), and reduced effects of openness to experience (β = .04, ns), agreeableness (β = .05, ns), BAS (β = .05, ns) and conscientiousness (β = .12, p <.05). The results also showed that the indirect effect of openness to experience on career exploration through career adaptability was significant (95% CI= [.03, .13]). Similarly, the indirect effects of agreeableness (95% CI = [.01, .12]) conscientiousness (95% CI = [.05, .17]) and BAS (95% CI = [.15, .35]) were also significant. These results suggest that career adaptability served as an important mediator in this process.

The researchers further examined the mediating roles of the four adapt-abilities. First, the effects of BIS, BAS, and FFM traits on the four adapt-abilities were tested. Second, when the four adapt-abilities were all added into the model, Concern (β = .25, p < .001) and Curiosity (β = .35, p < .001) significantly predicted career exploration. In addition, the bootstrapping results showed that the indirect effects of BAS through Concern (95% CI= [.04, .16]) and Curiosity (95% CI= [.10, .27]) were both significant. The results of this study suggest that career adaptability plays an important role in guiding and sustaining individuals' career exploration behavior. Moreover, among the four adaptabilities, Concern and Curiosity served as the most important mediators in the personality trait–exploration behavior relationship. These results coincide with previous finding that Concern and Curiosity are more closely related to individuals' exploration of career goals.

Career Exploring, Deciding, and Planning
as Adapting Responses

The career adapt-abilities were studied as mediators in a two-wave design with 1260 university students conducted in Germany by Hirschi, Hermann, and Keller (2015). At Time 1, they measured adaptivity with the *Core Self-Evaluation Scale* (Judge, Erez, Bono, & Thoresen, 2003) and proactivity with the *Personal Initiative Scale* (Frese, Fay, Hilburger, Leng, & Tag,1997). They measured the adapt-abilities with the *CAAS*. They administered four adapting response measures that could be particularly conditioned by each of the four adaptability dimensions. Relative to Concern, they used the *Career Planning Scale* (Gould, 1979). Relative to Control, they measured career decision making with the *Vocational Identity Scale* (Holland, Daiger, & Power, 1980). Relative to Curiosity, they administered the *Career Exploration Scale* (Hirschi, 2009), which has six items to assess environment exploration and four items to assess self-exploration. Relative to Confidence, they administered the *Occupational Self-Efficacy Scale* (Rigotti, Schyns, & Mohr, 2008). In the CCT model of adaptation, self-efficacy is placed between confidence and adapting responses. In retrospect, a more precise indicator of adapting behavior in this study would have been problem-solving behaviors. However, three of the six items in the scale do appear to measure problem-solving efficacy. Results of confirmatory factor analysis showed that the career adaptability and the adapting responses, although related, were empirically distinct from each other.

Six months later, the participants again responded to the four measures of adapting responses. Regarding the relation of adaptivity to adaptability, results indicated that higher levels of adaptivity associated with higher levels of adaptability. Core self-evaluation and proactivity correlated moderately with each other (.42). These indicators of adaptivity both correlated significantly to all four of the adapt-abilities with the exception of the path from core self-evaluation to curiosity. Proactivity correlated somewhat higher than self-evaluation with Concern, Curiosity, and Confidence, but not Control.

Regarding the relation between adaptivity and adapting, core self-evaluation and proactivity both predicted significantly all the adapting responses, showing positive associations with career planning, career exploration, and occupational self-efficacy beliefs and negative associations with career decision-making difficulties. The highest correlations occurred between the adaptivity variables and occupational self-efficacy.

Regarding the relation between adaptability and adapting, Concern related significantly to all four indicators of career adapting. Six months later, higher levels of Concern predicted higher levels of planning, exploring, and self-efficacy as well as fewer decision-making difficulties. Control predicted positively career planning and negatively decision-making difficulties. Curiosity did not relate significantly to career planning and even emerged as a negative predictor six months later. This finding suggests that being curious and inquisitive can be unrelated to, and even inhibit, career planning, especially when considering the part of Curiosity that is unrelated to the other adaptability dimensions of Concern, Control, and Confidence. Of course, individuals who are still curious and exploring are not yet ready to make plans. Future research should examine the role of Curiosity in different circumstances and outcomes. For example, what does Curiosity mean when career planning or vocational identity is high versus low. Of the four adaptability variables, Confidence was the only that did not predict any of the four career adapting variables.

Regarding the relations of adaptivity to adaptability to adapting, the results indicated that individuals who perceive themselves as taking initiative as well as being confident tended to report higher levels of Concern and Control which in turn increased career planning and decreased decision-making difficulties. Furthermore, Concern was a significant mediator of the relationship between proactivity and career exploration and the relationship between proactivity and occupational self-efficacy. Again, individuals who reported higher levels of proactivity tended to be more concerned about their career, which in turn associated with more career exploration and higher occupational self-efficacy beliefs. The researchers also reported a significant indirect negative effect from proactivity through Curiosity on career planning. People who perceived themselves as taking initiative tended to be more inquisitive, which in turn related to less career planning. There were no significant indirect effects for the fourth indicator of adaptability (i.e., Confidence). The data did not support clear matches between adaptability resources and their theoretically corresponding aspects of behavioral career adapting. Overall, these cross-sectional and longitudinal analyses suggest that the four adapt-abilities as measured by the *CAAS* have a broad impact on different manifestations of adapting and not just, or even primarily, on the form of adapting conceptually corresponding to the same resource. The results especially highlighted the important role of the adapt-ability resource of Concern, which showed on average the highest correlation to different adapting measures in both the cross-sectional and the longitudinal analyses. These results support the CCT conceptualization that positions career adaptability resources between more basic aspects of personality that represent adaptivity characteristics and more specific forms of adapting behaviors. The researchers suggested that career adaptability should be treated as a multi-dimensional construct whose components are not mutually interchangeable and thus merit further investigation of the differential effects of the four adapt-abilities regarding outcomes of interest.

Using the CCT model of adaptation, as shown in Figure 49, Neureiter and Traut-Mattausch (2017) positioned the impostor phenomenon between adaptive readiness and adapting responses as a negative mediator, with career adaptability as a positive mediator. Impostor Phenomenon refers to thoughts of intellectual phoniness and fear of being discovered as incompetent. Impostor phenomenon can produce feeling of self-doubt, intellectual inadequacy, and anticipated failure as well as attributions of success to luck or help from others rather than their own abilities (Nelson, 2011).

Figure 49. Adaptability Mediates between
Adaptivity and Adapting

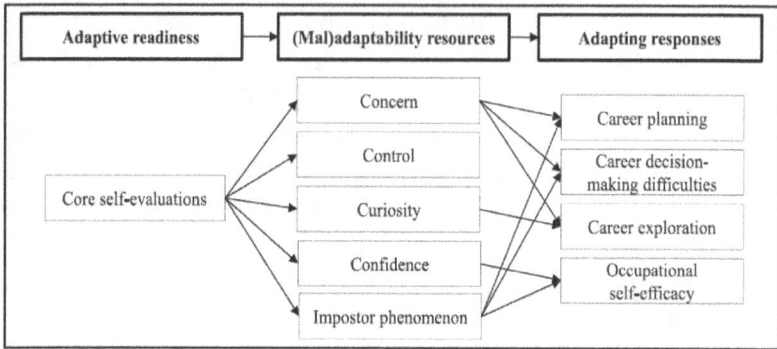

They measured impostor phenomenon with the 20-item German version of the *Clance Impostor Phenomenon Scale* (Clance & Imes, 1978). An example item reads "I can give the impression that I'm more competent than I really am." Considering impostor phenomenon as maladaptability, the measured adaptability with the *CAAS* subscales. The researchers represented adaptive readiness as core self-evaluations, and measured it with the *Core Self-Evaluation Scale* (Judge, Erez, Bono, & Thoreson, 2003). They represented adapting responses as career exploration, career decision-making difficulties, career planning, and occupational self-efficacy. Career exploration was measured with the German 10-item *Career Exploration Scale* (Hirschi, 2009). The scale uses four items for self-evaluation (e.g., "reflecting about vocational interests") and six items for environment exploration (e.g., "collecting information about different vocational options"), which can be combined into a total score for career exploration. Career decision-making difficulties were measured with the 12-item *Attitudes toward Career Choice and Professional Work Questionnaire* (Seifert & Stangl, 1986). Occupational self-efficacy was measured with the 10-item German *Occupational Self-Efficacy Scale* (Schyns & Collani, 2002).

The participants in the study consisted of 289 (75% females, 25% males; Mean age = 24.57 years, SD = 6.49) university students in

314

Austria. Most of the students were German (60%) and Austrian (30%). The bivariate correlations between all of the scales appear in Table 18. Of note, the imposter phenomenon correlated highest to Concern (-.50). Also of note -- as in the study by Fang, Zhang, Mei, Chai, and Fan (2018) -- the Confidence adapt-ability had the strongest correlation to occupational self-efficacy.

Table 18. Correlation of Adapt-Abilities to Adapting Responses

	Self-Evaluation	Career Exploration	Decision Difficulties	Career Planning	Occupational Self-Efficacy	Imposter Phenomenon
Concern	.27	.41	-.26	.52	.37	-.18
Control	.60	.18	-.30	.32	.51	-.50
Curiosity	.20	.28	-.14	.20	.31	-.12
Confidence	.47	.30	-.26	.38	.57	-.35

Mediation analyses indicated that the impostor phenomenon fully and negatively mediated the effects of core self-evaluation on career planning, decision-making difficulties, and occupational self-efficacy, but not on career exploration. This was shown by significant correlations in the expected way and was further supported by regressions between adaptive readiness, (mal)adaptability resources, and adapting responses in mediation analyses, as they indicated consistently significant indirect effects.

To gain more specific information about which adapt-abilities were particularly effective, the researchers conducted parallel multiple mediation analyses to compare the specific indirect effects. These analyses showed that Concern mediated the effects of core self-evaluation on career planning, career decision-making difficulties, and career exploration. Moreover, mediation analyses showed that the adapt-ability of Concern was the most significant mediator in the relation between adaptive readiness and adapting responses. In particular, Concern fostered more career planning. Because Concern is directed to the future and connected with the consideration of upcoming tasks and challenges, it is reasonable that it would have an impact on the extent of career planning and to be the most prominent mediator in this relationship. The Control

315

adapt-ability did not mediate the relationship between core self-evaluation and any of the adapting responses. The Curiosity adapt-ability, as well as the Concern adapt-ability, mediated between core self-evaluation and career exploration. The adapt-ability of Confidence mediated the relation between core self-evaluation and occupational self-efficacy. The researchers concluded that although the career adapt-abilities have commonalities, they play different roles in predicting adaptation outcomes and even suppress each other when considered in parallel.

Career Management Behaviors as Adapting Responses

Two studies used career management behaviors to represent adapting responses. The behaviors are typically grouped as strategies such as seeking a mentor, maintaining flexibility, and building networks. To study these behaviors as adapting responses, Chong and Leong (2017) represented adaptivity with conscientiousness, cognitive flexibility, and environmental exploration. From the perspective of CCT, environmental exploration would have been better positioned as an adapting behavior. They measured conscientiousness with two items: "dependable, self-disciplined," and "disorganized/careless" (reverse scored). They used the 12-item scale developed by Martin and Rubin (1965) to measure cognitive flexibility. An example item reads, "I have many possible ways of behaving in any given situation." The *Career Exploration Scale* (Stumpf & Colarelli, 1980) was used to measure environmental exploration. Career adapting was operationally defined by the *Career Management Strategy Scale* (Guthrie, Coate, & Schwoerer, 1998), which measures five distinct groups of career management behaviors (a) seeking a mentor or guidance, (b) maintaining career flexibility, (c) building a broad network of contacts, (d) extending involvement in work, and (e) self-presentation. The study participants were 307 undergraduate students who had held a past or current job working at least 20 hours per week for at least six months. The participants were 74.3% females and had a mean age of 19.64 years (SD = 1.73).

Bivariate correlations showed the *CAAS* total score correlated .40 to conscientiousness, .53 to cognitive flexibility, .44 to environmental exploration, and .52 to strategic career management. Environmental exploration correlated only .12 to conscientiousness and .19 to cognitive flexibility but .52 to strategic career management. This pattern of correlations supports the idea that exploration is better positioned as an adapting behavior than as an adaptivity trait.

As shown if the Figure 50, the results generally supported the model in which conscientiousness, cognitive flexibility, and environmental exploration positively predicted strategic career management indirectly through career adaptability. The researchers did note that the results only supported partial indirect relation between environmental exploration and career management via career adaptability. This result may be due to not positioning exploration as an adapting response as recommended.

Figure 50. Adaptability Mediates between FFM Traits and Career Management

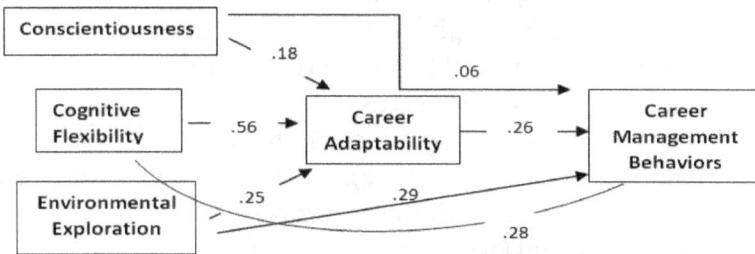

In a second study of career management behaviors as an adapting responses, Gao, Xin, Zhou, and Jepsen (2019) represented adaptivity as proactive personality and adaptation as job performance. They examined how the interactive effects of proactive personality and career adaptability on job performance outcomes may be mediated by career self-management behaviors. Career self-management denotes intentional activities and behaviors used to construct and maintain one's career. These behaviors include self-exploration, environment exploration, learning, goal setting, planning, monitoring actions, job crafting, networking, boundary setting, and feedback processing (Wilhelm, & Hirschi, 2019).

The researchers measured career self-management with an 11-item scale developed for Chinese participants by Weng and McElroy (2010). The scale consists of three subscales: career exploration, development of career goals and career strategy implementation. The three career exploration questions are: "I usually search for detailed information about the vocational areas and jobs in which I am interested;" "I usually consider how to combine my early work experiences with my future career development;" and "I often try to lay new roles at work to explore whether I am suitable for them." The four career development questions are: "My career goal is very definite;" "I have established detailed career development plans;" "I am very clear about how my present position is related to my career objectives;" and "I am very clear about what efforts are needed to realize my career goals." The four career strategy implementation questions are: "I always attempt to learn more new knowledge and skills to realize my career objectives;" I try to let my boos know about what I am doing to pursue my career and career objectives;" "I have established a helpful interpersonal network inside my company which can promote my career development;" and "I usually consult with my boss and experienced colleagues for helpful career guidance." They measured job performance with four items from Chen, Tsui, and Farh (2002). A sample item reads, "I can finish my work on time." They measured proactive personality with the Bateman and Crant (1993) scale and career adaptability with the *CAAS*. They collected data from 232 employees who worked for a Chinese manufacturing company with branches in Beijing, Tianjin, Shanghai and Shenzhen. The participants were 40% females and 60% males, with an average age of 32.7 years (SD = 5.27).

Zero-order correlation coefficients indicated that proactive personality correlated .73 to the *CAAS* total score, with correlations of .60 to Concern, .61 to Control, .66 to Curiosity, and .69 to confidence. Career self-management correlated .41 to the *CAAS* total score, with correlations of .38 to Concern, .32 to Control, .41

to Curiosity, and .31 to Confidence. Performance correlated .32 to the *CAAS* total score, with correlations of .20 to Concern, .28 to Control, .31 to Curiosity, and .34 to Confidence. Regression analyses indicated that career adaptability partially mediated the effect of career self-management on performance. From the CCT perspective, it would be better to examined career management as the mediator. Interestingly, adding the interaction term of "proactivity x adaptability" to the regression model showed that career adaptability (B = .19, p < .05), proactive personality (B = .38, p < .001), and the interaction item (B = .24, p < .001) each had significant positive effects on career self-management. Results also indicated that the interaction term did not have an effect on performance.

The researchers concluded that, in the CCT framework, when examining the effects of proactivity and adaptability on adapting behaviors, researchers may consider the combined effect between proactivity and career adaptability instead of only their separate effects on the adapting behavior. As an indicator of an adapting responses, career self-management serves as an important explanatory link in the relationship between adaptability resources and adaptation results under the CCT framework. These results are in line with the CCT which highlights the mediation role that career self-management plays in the relationship between career adaptability and performance. Individuals who are good at managing their career are more likely to have high degrees of personal initiative and be better at dealing with career construction tasks, compared to those with lower levels of career self-management.

Career Engagement as Adapting Responses

In Iran, Nilforooshan and Salimi (2016) tested whether career adaptability resources mediate the relationship of adaptive readiness to career adapting responses among 101 female and 100 male university students in Iran. The researchers represented adaptivity with the *Zuckerman–Kuhlman–Aluja Personality Questionnaire* (Aluja, Kuhlman & Zuckerman, 2010). The inventory is based on alternative five-factor model (AFFM) with dimensions of aggressiveness, activity, extraversion, neuroticism, and sensation seeking. Adaptability resources were measured with the *CAAS*. They measured adapting behaviors with the *Career Engagement Scale* (Hirschi, Freund, & Herrmann; 2014). Participants indicated to what extent during the last six months they had engaged in specific, overt vocational development behaviors such as career planning, career self-exploration, environmental career exploration, networking, voluntary human capital/skill development, and positioning behavior.

Career adaptability correlated .66 to career engagement, -.22 to aggression, .39 to activity, .37 to extraversion, and -.40 to neuroticism. The relation of adaptability to sensation seeking (.12) was not significant), although sensation seeking did correlate .18 to the adapt-ability of Curiosity. Structural equation modeling indicated that the model fit well to the data (x^2/df = .88, CFI = 1.00, RMSEA = .000) and explained 23% of the career engagement variance. All of the path coefficients of activity and neuroticism to each of the four career adaptability dimensions were significant in such a way that an increase in activity and decrease in neuroticism related to an increase in the career adapt-abilities. For sensation seeking, only the path coefficient to Curiosity was significant. The meditation conditions were not met for the relationships of extraversion and aggressiveness through career adaptability to career engagement. For extraversion, only the path coefficient to Control was significant. Aggression did not have a significant path coefficient to any of the four adapt-abilities.

Neuroticism. In comparison, the four career adapt-abilities each had a full mediation role in the relationship between neuroticism and career engagement. Increases in neuroticism, through the career adapt-abilities related to decreases in career engagement. Neuroticism may hinder development of career adaptabilities as well as thwart engagement in adapting behaviors.

Activity. The results showed that each of the four career adapt-abilities partially mediated the relationship between activity and career engagement in such a way that an increase in activity, directly and indirectly through the career adapt-abilities, related to an increase in career engagement. This finding suggests that individuals who are more active are more likely to have better psychosocial resources for coping with changes. Future research might examine whether the work compulsion and work energy facets of activity may explain more of this relationship than do the facets of general activity and restlessness.

Curiosity. The total effect of sensation seeking upon career engagement was significant ($p < .05$) but very low. Curiosity fully mediated the effect of sensation seeking on career engagement yet its indirect effects through Concern, Control, and Confidence were not significant. Experience seeking may promote the adaptability of Curiosity which in turn may promote career exploration and information-seeking behaviors. In summary, the results suggest that career adapt-abilities mediate between specific personality dimensions (i.e., activity, neuroticism, and sensation seeking) and career engagement.

Conclusion

This Chapter discussed the proposition that adaptability resources mediate between adaptive readiness and actual adaptation responses. The studies in this Chapter were organized according to how the researchers represented adaptation responses, namely as exploring, deciding, managing, and engaging.

CHAPTER 13

ADAPTABILITY MEDIATES BETWEEN
ADAPTIVITY AND ADAPTATION

Several studies have examined the CCT proposition that adaptability resources mediate between adaptive readiness and adaptation results, as depicted in Figure 51.

Figure 51. Adaptability Mediates between
Adaptivity and Adaptation

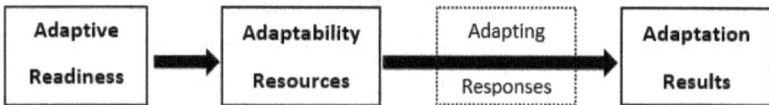

In these studies, researchers have operationally defined adaptation results as academic satisfaction, job performance, career success and satisfaction, work identification, work engagement, and personal growth initiative.

Academic Satisfaction as Adaptation Result

A study by Wilkins, Santilli, Ferrari, Tracey, and Soresi (2014) explored the relationships between adaptivity as represented by positive emotional dispositions (i.e., hope and optimism) to adaptation results (i.e., seven dimensions of satisfaction with school) as mediated by career adaptability. They hypothesized that the underlying pathway from hope and optimism to satisfaction was through career adaptability and its four dimensions of Concern, Control, Curiosity, and Control. Both hope and optimism, two separate yet related constructs, represent relatively stable general expectations about the future; they differ in how they influence behaviors. Dispositional optimism refers to the general belief that good things will happen in the future. Hope refers to a cognitive set of expectations more directed at goal attainment through agentic thinking about pathways to desired goals. Research has demonstrated that a clear relationship exists between positive

322

emotional dispositions (i.e., optimism and hope) and various dimensions of satisfaction (e.g. school, life, academic). However, few studies have examined mediators.

The researchers administered four inventories to a sample of 242 Italian high school students with a mean age of 18.07 years. They measured optimism with the *Life Orientation Test—Revised* (Scheier, Carver, & Bridges, 1994), which assesses a respondent's generalized expectations for positive (three items; e.g., "I'm always optimistic about my future") versus negative outcomes (three items; e.g., "I hardly ever expect things to go my way"). They measured hope with the *Adult Dispositional Hope Scale* (Snyder et al., 1991), which uses 12 items to assess both the agency component (e.g., "I've been pretty successful in life") and pathways component (e.g., "I can think of many ways to get the things in life that are most important to me"). They measured satisfaction with *My Life as a Student* (Soresi & Nota, 2003), which uses 26 items to assess students' quality of life of students. The measure is comprised of seven scales measuring satisfaction with the school experience, opportunities to make decisions autonomously (empowerment), relationships with classmates, current life conditions, relationships with family members; praise received when due; and help availability. The researchers measured adaptability with the *CAAS*.

Zero-order correlations indicated that each of four *CAAS* subscales related statistically significantly to each of the seven student satisfaction variables ranging from a low of .12 between Curiosity and current life conditions to a high of .39 between Confidence and student decision making. The *CAAS* subscale that was the strongest relative to the seven school satisfaction variables was Confidence. Its correlations ranged across the seven scales from a high correlation of .39 to decision making (e.g., "I am a free individual who can actually plan his/her own life in an autonomous way") to a low correlation of .25 to satisfaction with current conditions (e.g., "I think things are working out better for me than for my classmates"). Optimism correlated to the four adapt-abilities ranging from .10 to .24, with highest correlation being to Control .24. Hope correlated to the four adapt-abilities ranging from .42 to

.57, with the highest correlations being .57 to Control and .55 to Confidence.

Mediation analyses indicated that Confidence and Curiosity, but neither Concern nor Control, significantly mediated the relations between hope and satisfaction. Confidence significantly mediated the relationship between hope and six of the satisfaction scales, but not with satisfaction with school experience. Students who possessed both the agency and pathways to achieving their stated goals tended to report feeling more confident about coping with current and anticipated problems which in turn related to: (a) experiencing more satisfaction with the opportunities to make decisions (empowerment); (b) heightened satisfaction with the relationships with classmates and family members; (c) increased satisfaction with current life conditions; (d) greater satisfaction with the praise received in the instances when they were earned; and lastly, and (e) more satisfaction with the support available to them.

Although satisfaction with school experience ("I am really happy with the school I am attending) was not mediated by Confidence, the results demonstrated that Curiosity was a significant mediator of its relation with hope. This implies that those who perceive themselves as possessing both the agency and pathways to attain their goals had a propensity towards exhibiting Curiosity about possible solutions to challenges which in turn enhanced their satisfaction with their school experience. These findings suggest that students with both a greater sense of perceived capacity to derive pathways to desired goals and possess the ability to use such pathways may be likely to display more adaptability resources and better adaptation outcomes in terms of satisfaction.

In mediation-moderation study, Urbanaviciute, Pociute, Kairys, and Liniauskaite (2016) explored the role of career adaptability in the relation of perceived career barriers to academic satisfaction and vocational identity commitment. They hypothesized that career adaptability moderates the link between perceived career barriers and academic major satisfaction, so that respondents who

324

demonstrate high career adaptability report higher satisfaction and, in turn, higher vocational identity commitment compared to respondents who demonstrate low career adaptability (moderated-mediation effect).

Perceived career barriers were measured with a 9-item scale (a = .81), which consisted of two subscales measuring student perceptions of internal (four items; a = .75) and external (five items; a = .71) barriers. Internal barriers referred to, for instance, a lack of ability or interest to pursue the chosen vocational track, whereas external barriers referred to family, financial, labor market, or similar restrictions. Career adaptability was measured with the *CAAS*. Academic major satisfaction was measured by a single item that asked respondents to indicate their overall satisfaction with the chosen academic major on a 10-point scale (1 – not at all satisfied, 10 – absolutely satisfied). Vocational identity commitment was measured with the 5-item Commitment subscale of the *Utrecht Management of Identity Commitments Scale* (Crocetti, Rubini, & Meeus, 2008). Data were obtained at three public universities in Lithuania from 288 first- and second-year undergraduate students enrolled in over 20 academic disciplines.

The results indicated that career adaptability moderated the link between both internal and external perceived career barriers and academic major satisfaction. Regarding the internal career barriers, the moderated indirect effects were more salient at low values of adaptability. Moreover, in the case of external career barriers, they were significant only when the values of career adaptability were low. Notably, the moderated-mediation effects were shown to be stronger when the values of career adaptability were set to low. This suggests that when individuals encounter career barriers, lack of adaptability seems to account for lower academic major satisfaction and vocational identity commitment. Urbanaviciute, Pociute, Kairys, and Liniauskaite interpreted the findings to suggest that career adaptability is a resource and a tool for meeting vocational challenges.

Job Performance as an Adaptation Result

Three studies examined job performance as an adaptation result from adaptivity mediated by adaptability. Safavi and Karatepe (2018) used organizational practices instead of using personality characteristics to represent adaptivity. They investigated the relation of high-performance work practices by an organization to employee job performance via career adaptability. The participants were 313 (58.5% females) front desk agents, food servers, and bell attendants in the twelve 4-star and six 5-star hotels in Iran. The employees' rated their perceptions of the hotel's high-performance work practices on 37 items organized in eight scales: selective staffing, job security, training, empowerment, rewards, teamwork, career opportunities and work–life balance. The scales ranged in internal consistency from .77 to .92. To avoid common method bias, the researchers waited two weeks before having the participants respond to the *CAAS*. Another two weeks later, the participants responded to nine items that assessed how well the organization's practices met their expectations. Also at Time 3, the employees' supervisors rated them for extra-role performance (three items) and creative performance (six items).

The four career adapt-abilities each associated significantly with sense of fulfillment of the psychological contract by employers in that met expectations correlated .23 to Concern, .21 to Control, .19 to Curiosity, and .14 to Confidence. The adapt-abilities also correlated significantly to supervisors' rating of employee performance. Extra-role performance as rated by supervisors correlated .28 to Concern, .15 to Control, .26 to Curiosity, and .27 to Confidence. Creative performance as rated by supervisors correlated .40 to Concern, .05 to Control, .31 to Curiosity, and .23 to Confidence. As shown in Figure 52, high-performance work practices had a positive effect on career adaptability ($\beta = .92$) and career adaptability had a positive effect on met expectations ($\beta = .57$), creative performance ($\beta = .79$) and extra-role performance ($\beta = 0.84$). Furthermore, career adaptability fully mediated the effects of high-performance work practices on met expectations, creative performance, and extra-role performance. The researchers concluded that high-performance work practices enable staff to manage their careers more successfully, which in turn leads to met expectations, creative performance, and extra-role performance.

Figure 52. Adaptability Mediates between Company Practices and Employee Performance

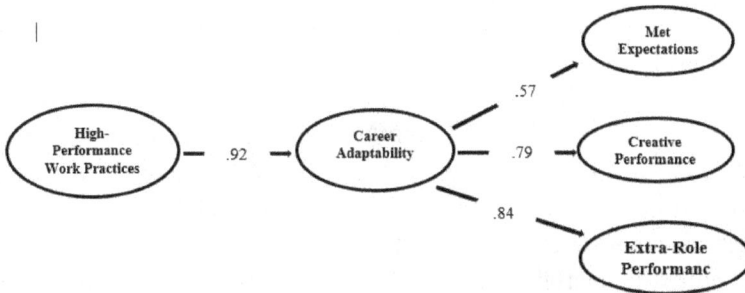

A second study used job performance ratings to represent an adaptation result. Ohme and Zacher (2015) used a policy-capturing approach to study adaptability as a mediator between between adaptivity (i.e., mental ability and conscientiousness) and adaptation results (i.e., job performance ratings). Policy-capturing methodology uses an experimental vignette design for studying implicit decision processes (Aguinis & Bradley, 2014). The participants in the Ohme and Zacher (2015) study responded to 40 scenarios that manipulated the independent variables of adaptability, mental ability, and conscientiousness. Scenario sentences to represent the four career adapt-abilities had high, medium, and low (i.e., frequently, occasionally, or rarely) versions of the following basic statements.

Concern: The employee thinks about the future and prepares for upcoming tasks and challenges.

Control: The employee takes responsibility to change his future development and work environment.

Curiosity: The employee explores various options and is curious about new opportunities.

Confidence: The employee is confident to achieve goals and overcome obstacles.

The researchers also constructed four scenario sentences to represent mental ability (i.e., learning, problem solving, information processing, and reasoning) and four sentences to represent conscientiousness (achievement, order, cautiousness, and dependability).

The sample consisted of 114 men and 21 women who ranged in age from 21 to 66 years (Mean = 42.90; SD = 10.25). Most participants worked in engineering (26.7%) or economics (18.5%), followed by 11 participants (8.1%) in an education profession. Slightly more than half of participants (54.8%) had previous experience in completing performance appraisals for employees. The participants read each of the randomly presented scenarios and then rated the overall job performance of the fictitious employees on a 7-point scale. Next, the participants rated their own mental ability, conscientiousness, and career adaptability using the same statements that were used for the scenarios. The items were changed to state "I" instead of "Employee" and to refer only to high levels of the characteristics, resulting in 12 items in total (i.e., four each for adaptability, mental ability, and conscientiousness). Participants indicated on a 7-point scale (1=not true at all, 7 = very true) the extent to which each statement applied to them.

The researchers examined the predictive and incremental validity of career adaptability by investigating the relative effect of each participant's career adaptability on their job performance ratings compared to the effects of mental ability and conscientiousness, which are two well-established predictors of job performance ratings. The results indicated that a significant positive effect of career adaptability on job performance ratings, yet relatively larger effects for mental ability and conscientiousness than for career adaptability. Raters' judgments about job performance were then used to compute the relative importance of each independent variable in the form of regression weights. As predicted, mental ability and conscientiousness had larger effects on performance ratings than did career adaptability. The results indicated that the order of standardized predictor variables regarding the relative importance for performance ratings were conscientiousness (γ = .66), mental ability (γ = .58), and career adaptability (γ = .41). Contrast analyses revealed that both the difference in the effects of mental ability and career adaptability ($\chi2$ /2 = 2091.74, p<.001) and the difference in the effects of conscientiousness and career adaptability (X^2/2] = 1960.05, p < .001) were significant.

A third study of job performance as an adaptation result concentrated on effective job performance by Human Resource professionals. Job performance was defined as six strategic competencies described by Ulrich, Younger, Brockbank, and Ulrich (2012): strategic positioning, credible activism, capacity building, championing change, innovating and integrating, and levering technology. In a study with Chinese human resource managers, Guan, Yang, Zhou, Tian, and Eves (2016) tested whether identification, support, and variety have a positive effect on strategic competence through the mediation of career adaptability. As indicators of career adaptivity, they selected professional identification (i.e., the extent to which an individual's profession is incorporated in his/her self-concept), career variety (i.e., the diversity of functional areas and institutional context experiences accumulated in an individual's career), and organizational support for the human resource department. They measured professional identification a four-item scale (Hekman, Steensma, Bigley, & Hereford, 2009). They operationally defined career variety with participants' reports of the specific number of different sectors, firms, and functional areas in which they had worked. They measured organizational support with an eight-item measure developed by Law, Song, Wong, and Chen (2009). Strategic competence was measured by the 20-item scale developed by Ulrich, Younger, Brockbank, and Ulrich (2012). The *CAAS* was used as the measure of career adaptability. The five inventories were administered to 220 Chinese human resource managers (85 males and 135 females). The results showed that professional identification, career variety, and organizational support for

329

strategic human resource management predicted strategic competence.

The *CAAS* total score correlated .40 to professional identity, .23 to career variety, .27 to organizational support, and .56 to strategic competence (ranging from .39 for Control to .56 for Curiosity). In addition, career adaptability served as a significant mediator for the above relations, as shown in Figure 53. Moreover, the indirect effect on strategic competence were significant for professional identity (.26), career variety (.20), and organizational support (.16). The results showed that career adaptability partially mediated the effect of professional identification, and fully mediated the effects of career variety and organizational support on strategic competence. It is possible that the effect of professional identification can also be explained by variables more specific to HRM expertise, rather than just career adaptability. The results further showed that the effects of professional identification on career adaptability and strategic competence were stronger among employees who perceived a higher level of organizational support for human resource management.

Figure 53. Adaptability Mediates between Identity/Support and Competence

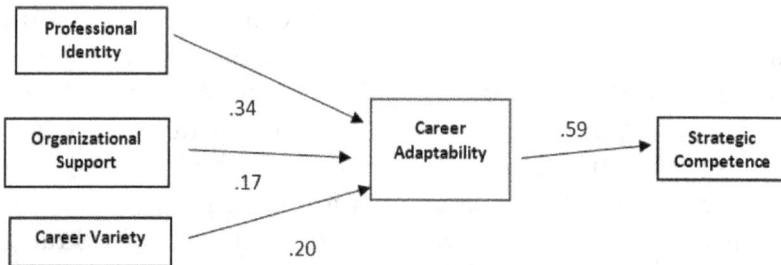

Career Success as an Adaptation Result

Career success was used to represent an adaptation result in a study that represented adaptivity by self-esteem and optimism and positioned career adaptability as a mediator. Haenggli and Hirschi (2020) investigated career adaptability as a mediator from the perspective of Conservation of Resources Theory (COR; Hobfoll, 2002), which proposes that different resources often co-exist and jointly lead to positive outcomes. They investigated how other key resources differentially relate to career adaptability resources as well as their differential relation to the career adaptation results of subjective and objective career success. COR defines career resources as entities that are valuable in their own right (e.g., adaptivity traits) or entities that function as means (e.g., adaptability resources) to acquiring valued career outcomes (e.g., adaptation results). Haenggli and Hirschi studied the adaptivity traits of self-esteem and optimism as entities in themselves representative of career adaptivity.

Participants were recruited through an on-line panel service that invited people on the basis of selection criteria: employed in private industry (not self-employed nor in public service), aged between 18 and 65, and working a minimum of 16 hours per week. The final sample at Time 1 consisted of 574 people (55% women), 30% had secondary school as their highest educational achievement, 13% had obtained a high school degree, 33% had completed vocational training, and 23% had a university degree. The majority of the participants were German (98%) and worked an average of 35 hours per week and had an average organizational tenure of 10 years.

At Time 1, 574 participants responded to the *Rosenberg Self-Esteem Scale* (Rosenberg, 1956) and the *Life-Orientation Test* (Scheier, Carver, & Bridges, 1994), which measures optimism. A month later at Time 2, 395 participants responded to the *CAAS–Short Form* and to the *Career Resources Questionnaire* (Hirschi, Nagy, Baumeler, Johnston, & Spurk, 2018), which measures knowledge and skills, motivation, and environmental career resources. Knowledge and skill resources encompass occupational expertise and soft skills. Motivational career resources encompass involvement, confidence, and clarity. Environmental resources encompass career opportunities, organizational support, job challenge, and social support.

Two months later at Time 3 (360 responders), adaptation outcomes were indicated by objective success measured as gross income for the last month and by the *Subjective Career Success Inventory* (Shockley, Ureksoy, Rodopman, Poteat, & Dullaghan, 2016), which consists of 24 items divided equally into eight subscales, with three items each: satisfaction (e.g., "My career is personally satisfying"), growth and development (e.g., "I have stayed current with changes in my field"), authenticity (e.g., "I have chosen my own career path"), influence ("Decisions that I have made have impacted my organization"), personal life (e.g., "I have been able to have a satisfying life outside of work"), meaningful work (e.g., "I believe my work has made a difference"), quality work (e.g., "I am proud of the quality of the work I have produced"), and recognition (e.g., "I have been recognized for my contributions").

Results showed that the *CAAS* total score did not correlate to salary but did correlate .47 to subjective career success, with correlations to the dimensions ranging from .35 for recognition to .51 for growth and development. Time 2 career adaptability correlated to Time 1 self-esteem .29 and optimism .32. The Time 2 measures of resources indicated that career adaptability correlated .51 to knowledge and skill, .57 to motivation, and .42 to environment. Structural equation modeling indicated that career adaptability related significantly to other types of career resources. Furthermore, career adaptability, knowledge and skills, and motivational and environmental career resources each explain unique variance in different facets of career success. Motivational and environmental resources seem to have incremental utility beyond career adaptability resources in predicting different facets of career success. Specifically, relative weight analyses suggested that especially motivational and environmental career resources may be more important to attaining subjective career success compared to career adaptability. Moreover, knowledge and skill career resources seem to be most important to attain objective career success in terms of salary.

This study was innovative in comparing career adaptability to different career resources. It is not surprising that the motivational and environmental opportunity dimensions fared better in differential analyses than did career adaptability in predicting the adaptation outcome of career success. It would be interesting to replicate the study using outcome criteria more closely related to adaptability such as job search success, career progress, and promotability. It would also be interesting to compare the different career resources to the next dimension in the career construction theory model of adaptation, namely adapting behaviors such as planning, exploring, and deciding.

Career Satisfaction as an Adaptation Result

Four studies have examined adaptability as a mediator between adaptivity and the adaptation result of career satisfaction as indicated by the *Career Satisfaction Scale* (Greenhaus et al., 1990). The first study used the FFM traits to represent adaptive readiness. Zacher (2014b) measured the FFM traits with the four-item scales developed by Donnellan, Oswald, Baird, and Lucas (2006). As a second indicator of adaptivity, he used the *Core Self-Evaluation Scale* (Judge, Erez, Bono, & Thoresen (2003). Career adaptability was measured with the *CAAS*. Zacher represented adaptation results with two indicators of subjective career success, namely career satisfaction and self-rated career performance. Career satisfaction was measured with the *Career Satisfaction Scale* (Greenhaus et al., 1990). Self-rated career performance was measured with four items from Welbourne, Johnson, and Erez' (1998) role-based performance scale. Participants were asked to consider how their supervisor or boss would rate them on items such as "Obtaining personal career goals" and "Making progress in your career." Data for this study came from 1723 employees (961 females and 762 males) who worked in a broad range of jobs in Australia. They ranged in age from 18 to 70 years (Mean = 46.67; SD = 11.31). Only three participants had not finished high school (0.2%), 491 (28.5%) had finished high school, 500 (29.0%) held a technical college degree, 460 (26.7%) held an undergraduate university degree, and 269 (15.6%) held a postgraduate university degree.

333

Results indicated that the *CAAS* total score correlated .44 to core self-evaluation, .25 to openness, .24 to conscientiousness, .24 to extraversion, .25 to agreeableness, -.30 to neuroticism, .40 to career satisfaction, and .39 to self-rated career performance. Furthermore, career adaptability predicted career satisfaction (.25) and self-rated career performance (.30) above and beyond the FFM traits and core self-evaluations. Additional analyses indicated that mediation by the individual adapt-abilities was only partially supported. Concern and Confidence predicted both career satisfaction and self-rated career performance above and beyond the adaptivity variables. In contrast, Curiosity and Control did not have significant effects on career satisfaction. Control had a weak and negative effect on self-rated career performance, and Curiosity did not have a significant effect on self-rated career performance. Zacher reasoned that the extent to which employees are future oriented (Concern) and believe that they can solve problems in reaching their career goals (Confidence) may be important in achieving subjective career success independent of the effects of personality traits and core self-evaluations.

In sum, the mediation effect observed in this study clearly indicated that career adaptability might be considered as a variable contributing to adaptation in terms of career performance and satisfaction. Personality could also be seen as a point of view or perspective for individuals that helps them to interpret the environment and to activate self-regulation processes (in this case career adapt-abilities) in order to better adjust to their environment. Finally, the incremental validity of career adaptability over personality measurements confirmed that it is an important construct to consider for understanding and predicting work-related outcomes, such as success in the workplace, job satisfaction, job tenure, and work engagement.

A second study used the *Career Satisfaction Scale* (Greenhaus et al., 1990) along with a measure of promotability as indicators of adaptation results. Ocampo, Restubog, Liwag, Wang, and Petelczyc (2018) developed and examined a model for mid-career employees that linked support from the organization and the spouse to career success through career adaptability. The participants were 217 married full-time employees (57.5% females) who worked in various business sectors in The Philippines. They ranged in age from 40 to 64 years (Mean = 47.83; SD=6.02) with an average tenure of 14.94 years (SD = 9.72). They responded to the *CAAS* and two scales that measure support. Perceived organizational support was measured using seven items from the scale developed by Eisenberger, Huntington, Hutchison, and Sowa (1986). Example items read, "My organization strongly considers my goals and values" and "My organization takes pride in my accomplishments at work." Perceived spousal support was assessed using 10 items drawn from research by Parasuraman, Greenhaus, and Granrose (1992). Example items read, "My spouse gives advice or suggestions when I have a problem" and "My spouse shows willingness to listen to my problems." Six weeks later at Time 2, 192 supervisors rated their employees' on two measures of success. Subjective career success was indicated by the *Career Satisfaction Scale* (Greenhaus et al., 1990). Objective career success was rated by asking supervisors who indicated the employees' likelihood of promotability using five items from a scale developed by (Colarelli, Dean, and Konstans (1987). Example items read, "How promotable is this employee" and "This person possesses a high potential to assume more challenging work responsibilities." This resulted in 178 independent employee-supervisor dyads. At Time 3 (24 months after Time 2), 160 participants indicated whether they had been promoted to a higher position within the same organization.

Results indicated that the *CAAS* total score correlated .39 to perceived organizational support, .49 to perceived spousal support, .33 to supervisor-rated promotability, .30 to supervisor-rated career satisfaction, and .32 to actual promotion two years later. The overarching purpose of their study was to investigate the role of two forms of social support in career success via career adaptability. To do so, they tested three models. Results for the simple mediation model appears in Figure 54.

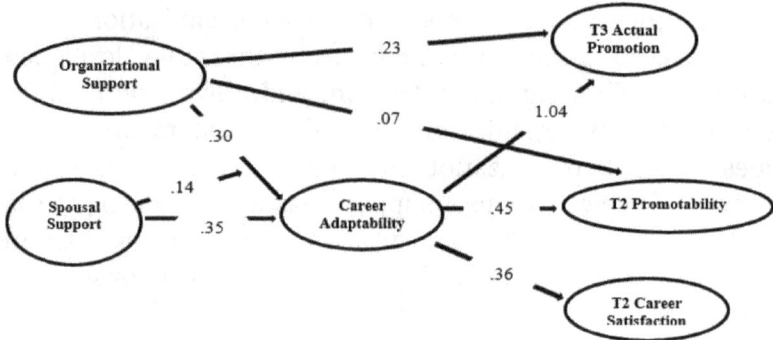

Figure 54. Adaptability Mediates between
Support and Career Outcomes

They also tested the moderating role of perceived spousal support in the relationship between perceived organizational support and career outcomes. Finally, they integrated perceived spousal support into the model to test the overall moderated-mediation model. The results demonstrated that both perceived organizational support, a work-related resource, and perceived spousal support, a non-work, family-related resource, increased career adaptability, which in turn contributed to subjective and objective career success. Furthermore, the benefits of perceived organizational support depended on perceived spousal support. The moderation-mediation model showed that supervisor-rated promotability and actual promotion via career adaptability were significant only for employees who perceived strong support from their spouses. Supplementary analyses indicated that perceived organizational support associated positively with each of the four adapt-abilities, which in turn influenced the association between perceived organizational support and Time 2 supervisor-reported career satisfaction and promotability as well as Time 3 self-reported actual promotion.

A third study also used the *Career Satisfaction Scale* (Greenhaus et al., 1990) along with a measure of work engagement as an indicator of adaptation results. Xie, Xia, Xin, and Zhou (2016) examined the role of career adaptability in the relation of calling to both career satisfaction and work engagement. As an adaptivity variable, they defined calling as transcendent summons, purposeful work, and a prosocial orientation, which they operationally defined with the 12-item Presence of Calling Scale from the *Calling and Vocation Questionnaire* (CVQ; Dik et al., 2012). Career adaptability was operationally defined with the *CAAS*. Work engagement characterized by vigor, dedication, and absorption experienced in work was measured by the 9-item *Utrecht Work Engagement Scale* (UWES-9; Schaufeli, Bakker, & Salanova, 2006). Career satisfaction was measured by the *Career Satisfaction Scale* (Greenhaus et al., 1990). The four inventories were administered to 832 employees (461 females and 371 males) in China who had an average age of 31 years and average organizational tenure of five years.

The analysis tested a mediation model of adaptive readiness (i.e., calling) to adaptability resources to adaptation results (i.e., career satisfaction and work engagement). To reduce common-method variance, the researchers used a time-lagged method in which they first measured calling and adaptability and then three weeks later engagement and satisfaction. Bivariate correlations indicated that calling correlated .59 to career adaptability, .57 to career satisfaction, and .67 to work engagement. In addition, career adaptability correlated .41 to career satisfaction and .47 to work engagement. Engagement and satisfaction correlated .53. The mediation analyses, as shown in Figure 55, indicated that adding career adaptability significantly increased the explanatory power of the regression model, while reducing the magnitude of the coefficient for calling, thus meeting the requirement for mediation. The researchers concluded that calling was an important antecedent of career adaptability. They noted that, while adaptability pertains directly to transitions, their analyses with employed people suggested that adaptability helps maintain a satisfying career yet not as much as calling does.

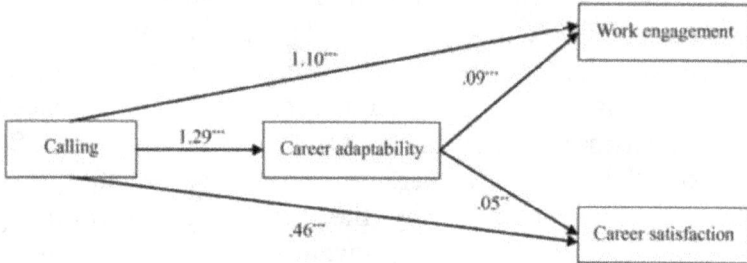

Figure 55. Adaptability Mediates between
Calling and Career Outcomes

Work Identification as an Adaptation Result

A study of the adaptability-adapting-adaption path was conducted by Kirchknopf (2020). The participants in the study consisted of 395 apprentices (59.7% females) who attended commercial schools in Germany. They ranged in age from 16 to 39 years (Mean = 20.27; SD = 3.12). In his structural model, Kirchknoopf represented adaptive readiness as proactivity, operationally defining it with the *Personal Initiative Scale* (Frese, Fay, Hilburger, Leng, & Tag,1997). He represented adaptation results as vocational identity, operationally defining it as occupational and organizational identification. The two forms of identification were each measured with two scales. Cognitive identification was measured with four items. Example items read, "I am aware that I am a member of my occupation group (or training company)." Affective identification was measured with five items. Example items read, "I enjoy working in my occupation (training company)."

A test of the model with a structural equation attained good model fit. As shown in Figure 56, the positive effects of career adaptability on affective occupational identification ($\beta = .36$, p < .001) and on cognitive organizational identification ($\beta = .22$, p <.001) were both significant and also quite similar to the effects on cognitive occupational identification (($\beta = .41$, p< .001) and cognitive organizational identification (β = .28, p< .001). Kirchknopf concluded that apprentices' adaptivity largely predicted their career adaptability, and also career adaptability itself predicted their cognitive and affective identification with both their occupation and their organization.

Figure 56. Adaptability Mediates between Proactivity
and Work Identification

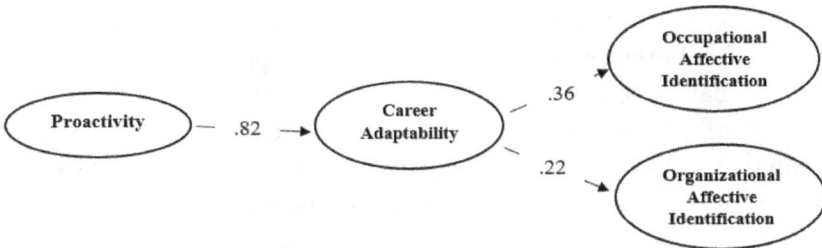

Work Engagement as an Adaptation Result

Two additional studies also used work engagement as an indicator of adaptation results. In a study that used the FFM traits as indicators of adaptivity, Rossier, Zecca, Stauffer, Maggiori, and Dauwalder (2012) investigated whether adaptability mediates between adaptivity traits and the adaptation result of work engagement. They measured the FFM personality traits with both the *NEO-FFI-R* (McCrae & Costa, 2004) and the Alternative FFM (i.e., aggressiveness, activity, extraversion, neuroticism, and sensation seeking) with the *Zuckerman–Kuhlman–Aluja Personality Questionnaire* (Aluja, Kuhlman, & Zuckerman, 2010). They concentrated on the adaptation outcome of work engagement, that is, a persistent, pervasive, and positive state of mind related to work. The researchers measured work engagement with the *Utrecht Work Engagement Scale-9* (Schaufeli, Salanova, González-Romá, & Bakker, 2002) which consists of three items each to asses vigor (e.g., "At my job, I feel strong and vigorous"), dedication (e.g., "I am enthusiastic about my job") and absorption ("I am immersed in my work"). They measured career adaptability with the *CAAS*. They administered the four inventories to 391 French-speaking Swiss participants: 220 females and 171 males with ages ranging from 20 to 79 years (Mean = 39.59; SD = 12.30). The participants consisted of employed people (81.84%), unemployed people seeking employment (2.30%), students (11.25%), and retired people with a private income or those that didn't indicate their professional status (4.61%).

The researchers expected that career adaptability would have some incremental validity over adaptivity traits when predicting work engagement, and that adaptability might fully or partially mediate the relation between personality traits and work engagement. Two hierarchical regressions were performed to assess the incremental validity of the career adapt-abilities over adaptivity traits in predicting work engagement. Age and gender were entered in a first step of the regression as controls. In the second step, the five main personality dimensions were considered in terms of their contribution in predicting work engagement. Finally, the *CAAS* total score was added in a third step in order to evaluate the incremental validity of career adaptability over the revised AFFM or the FFM. Both hierarchical regressions revealed that career adaptability had a significant incremental validity. After controlling for age and gender, the AFFM explained 33%, and the FFM 23% of the work engagement variance. After controlling for age, gender, and personality, adaptability explained at least 5% of the work engagement variance in the two hierarchical regression analyses.

Two further hierarchical regressions were computed for predicting work engagement considering age and gender in step 1, career adaptability in step 2, and personality traits in step 3. Considering that personality related to work engagement and career adaptability, and that career adaptability related to work engagement after controlling for personality, the two further hierarchical regressions suggested that career adaptability partially mediated the relation between personality traits and work engagement. This partial mediation was associated with 14% of work engagement variance for the AFFM and of 6% for the FFM. The difference might be attributed to the fact that the AFFM shares more variance with work engagement (33%) than the FFM (23%). Also, the Activity dimensions of the AFFM measure stable patterns of thoughts and behaviors that relate to work, and which are not as well assessed by the NEO-FFI-R. The effect-size associated with this partial mediation was medium for the AFFM and small for the FFM.

In the second study with work engagement as an adaptation outcome, Bipp, Kleingeld, and van Dam (2018) also investigated the mediating role of career adaptability for the effects of personality structure on engagement. They used the Approach Avoidance Temperament Framework to represent adaptive willingness, measuring it with the 12-item scale developed by Elliot and Thrash (2010). Six items each measured approach temperament ("I'm always on the lookout for positive opportunities and experiences") and avoidance temperament ("It is easy for me to imagine bad things that might happen to me"). Engagement with the study was measured with the 9-item short scale of the *Utrecht Work Engagement Scale for Students* (UWES; Schaufeli, Bakker,& Salanova, 2006). An example item reads, "I get carried away when I'm studying'.' Career adaptability was measured with the *CAAS*. The researchers administered the three inventories to 290 Dutch senior-year students in five academic programs at a University of Applied Science.

The mediation analysis showed no systematic effects for the control variables of age and sex across the three regression steps for career adaptability. Approach temperament related positively (β = .59, p < .01) and avoidance temperament related negatively to career adaptability (β = -.15, p < .01). They also reported a direct effect of approach temperament on engagement (β = .27, p < .01). Although prior studies have reported a negative connection of avoidance motives with job attitudes, avoidance temperament was not directly related to engagement. Nevertheless, the researchers reported a significant indirect effect of both temperament dimensions on engagement through career adaptability. Although avoidance temperament did not have a direct effect on engagement, it did show an indirect, negative effect on engagement through career adaptability, which coincides with findings from Van Vianen et al. (2012) who showed that people pursuing avoidance strategies (i.e., a chronic prevention focus) also reported lower career adaptability.

341

As a group, the studies of career satisfaction and work engagement in this section showed that career adaptability is a transactional, self-regulatory resource that enables employees to achieve the important adaptation outcomes of work engagement and career satisfaction independent of more stable personality dispositions.

Work Stress as Adaptation Result

In another study that investigated career adaptability as a mediator, Johnston, Luciano, Maggori. Ruch, & Rossier (2013) examined its function between orientation to happiness and work stress. Adaptivity was represented by three orientations to happiness (Seligman, 2002). The pleasure orientation concentrates on maximizing pleasure and minimizing pain as the chief route to happiness. The engagement orientation concentrates on the experience of flow enabled by a good match between demands and competences at work. The third orientation entails identifying, cultivating, and living in accordance with one's virtues. Johnston and colleagues measured the orientations with the 9-item version of the *Orientations to Happiness Questionnaire* (Ruch, Martinez-Marti, Heintz, & Brouwers, 2014). Three items are used to measure each orientation: engagement (e.g., "I am always very absorbed in what I do"); pleasure (e.g., "Life is too short to postpone the pleasures it can provide"); and meaning (e.g., "My life serves a higher purpose"). The participants also responded to the *Work Stress Scale* (De Bruin, 2006), which is a unidimensional measure focused on psychological issues generated by stress.

The researchers administered the three inventories to 1204 employed German-speaking adults in Switzerland. Zero-order correlations showed that the *CAAS* total score correlated .29 to the pleasure orientation, .42 to engagement, .31 to meaning, and -.18 to work stress. In a mediation analysis, the *CAAS* total score partially mediated the relations of both the pleasure and engagement orientations to work stress. The researcher then tested mediation models for each of the four career adapt-abilities to test which adapt-abilities carried the mediating effect. They found that only the Control adapt-ability functioned as a significant mediator, even in the presence of Concern, Curiosity, and Confidence. Control represents a self-directed and self-reliant perspective aimed at taking responsibility and making decisions that reflect an individual's self-interest contributing to a positive rather than negative work experience. The researchers concluded that career adaptability seems to serve as one mechanism through which individuals attain their desired life at work.

Commitment to Nursing Career as an Adaptation Result

Another study of the relations among adaptivity, adaptability, and adaptation was conducted by Fang, Zhang, Mei, Chai, and Fan (2018). They operationally defined adaptivity as optimism and educational environment. They measured the personality disposition of optimism with the *Life Orientation Test* (Scheier, Carver, & Bridges, 1994). The 50-item *Dundee Ready Education Environment Measure* (Roff, 2005) was used to assess the students' perceptions of their educational environment. Adaptation was represented by career commitment in terms of occupational self-efficacy and values. The *Nursing Career Motivation Scale* (Tian, Cheng, Cheng, & Fan, 2014) was used to assess motivation in terms of self-efficacy (6 items; e.g., "I think I can do nursing well") and career values (14 items; e.g., "I like to provide nursing services for patients"). The participants were 106 nursing undergraduates (88.3% females) at three universities in China. Their age ranged from 17 to 24 years (Mean = 19.9; SD=1.3). Among these undergraduates, 41.9% were in their first academic year, 36.3% were in their second academic year and 21.8% were in their third academic year.

Results indicated that the *CAAS* total score correlated .43 to an optimistic disposition, .51 to educational environment, .41 to career motivation (.43 to self-efficacy and .35 to values). The correlations of the adapt-abilities ranged from .26 between Control and optimism to .50 between Confidence and educational environment. Of note, the highest correlation between the occupational self-efficacy subscale was .43 to the adapt-ability of Confidence. Further analyses showed that career adaptability partially mediated the relationships of optimism and educational environment to career motivation, as shown in Figure 57. After controlling for independent variables and undergraduates' demographics, career adaptability (β = 0.12, p < .001) associated positively with career motivation, and the effects of optimism (β = 0.06, p < .05) and educational environment (β = 0.51, p < .001) on career motivation were reduced. Optimism (95% CI=[0.13, 0.22]) and educational environment (95% CI=[0.05, 0.14]) had significant indirect effects on career motivation via career adaptability, with zero not included in the confidence interval, indicating the mediating role of career adaptability.

Figure 57. Adaptability Mediates between Optimism and Motivation

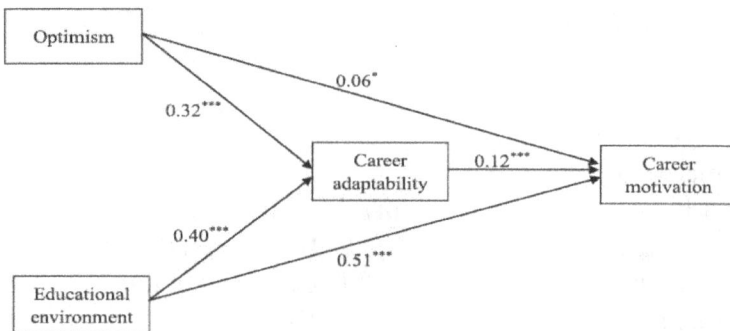

Conclusion

This chapter discussed studies that examined the proposition that adaptability resources mediate between adaptive readiness and adaptation results. In these studies, researchers operationally defined adaptation results as academic satisfaction, job performance, career success and satisfaction, work identification, work engagement, and personal growth initiative.

CHAPTER 14

ADAPTING MEDIATES BETWEEN
ADAPTABILITY AND ADAPTATION

Nine studies have examined the CCT proposition that adapting responses mediate between adaptability resources and adaptation outcomes, as shown in Figure 58.

Figure 58. Adapting Mediates between
Adaptability and Adaptation

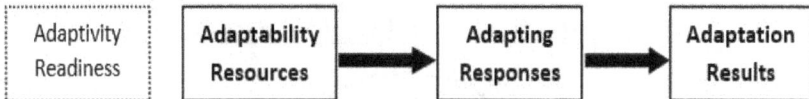

| Adaptivity Readiness | Adaptability Resources | → | Adapting Responses | → | Adaptation Results |

Adaptability-Exploring-Decidedness

A study by Urbanaviciute, Kairys, Pociute, and Liniauskaite (2014) investigated how the adapting responses of career exploration mediate between career adaptability resources and the adaptation result of career decidedness. Career exploration behaviors were measured by seven items asking about the frequency within the last year of career exploration behaviors (e.g., seeking information about educational opportunities and seeking to develop skills). Career decidedness was indicated by one item for which respondents chose one of the three following options: (a) "I have already decided upon one definite career option," (b) "I have several career choice options on my list," and (c) "I haven't decided upon any specific career option yet." The participants consisted of 512 high school students (Mean age = 16.43; SD = 1.18) in Lithuania.

Bivariate correlations showed that the *CAAS* total score correlated .37 to career exploration behaviors with higher correlations to Concern (.36) and Curiosity (.35) than to Control (.22) and Confidence (.24). Career exploration correlated .21 to decidedness and .14 to career adaptability (with the highest correlation being .15

to Concern). A test for mediation produced a significant overall equation, shown in Figure 59, in which the relationship of career exploration behaviors with career decidedness was significant even when controlling for career adaptability, whereas the relationship between career adaptability and career decidedness became non-significant in the model (-.07, ns). Despite the small percentage of variance explained, the results suggest full mediation because the relationship between the predictor variable of career adaptability resources and the dependent variable of career decidedness became non-significant when the mediator of career exploration behaviors was added to the model.

Figure 59. Exploration Mediates between Adaptability and Decidedness

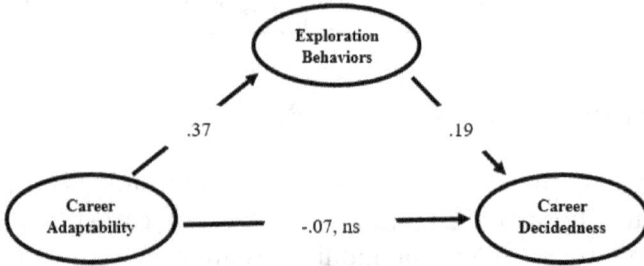

Adaptability-Personal Availability-Work Performance

A second study of the adaptability-adapting-adaption path examined psychological availability/personal engagement as a mediator between adaptability and adaptation outcomes. Personal engagement at work refers to using physical, cognitive, and emotional labor on the job. Kahn (1990) has called this construct "psychological availability," defining it as the physical, emotional, and psychological resources need to perform a role. High psychological availability enables one to fully engage in the work role without being distracted by physical fatigue, depleted emotional energy, feeling insecure about work and work status, or life outside of work. According to Kahn (1990), people's psychological availability is influenced by the resources that they possesses. Jannesair and Sullivan (2019) reasoned that individuals with greater career adaptability should have greater resources to cope with distractions and thus have higher levels of psychological availability. Their study examined whether career adaptability influences work performance and adjustment both directly and indirectly through psychological availability as a mediator.

Data were collected from 273 self-initiated expatriates (SIE) in China. SIEs are individuals who have chosen to relocate to a host country to experience different cultures or further develop their careers in contrast to company-assigned expatriates. The participants in this study were 57% males and 60% were married. Most of the expatriates were between the ages of 31 and 50 (65%). They were highly educated: 1% had a Ph.D. degree, 25% had a Master's, 65% had a Bachelor's, and 9% had a high school diploma. Almost half (49%) of the participants had worked for their current employer for two years or less. They originated from 38 different countries, with most from three major geographic regions: Asia (27.1%), Europe (39.3%), and North America (19.4%). Another 14.2% were from one of nine other countries.

Career adaptability was measured with the *CAAS*. Psychological availability was measured using May, Gilson, and Harter's (2004) 5-item scale. Example items read, "I am confident in my ability to think clearly at work" and "I am confident in my ability to display the appropriate emotions at work". Performance was measured using Lee, Veasna, and Wu's (2013) 7-item scale. Example items read, "My overall performance during my assignment is good" and "I keep good relationships with my local co-workers." Adjustment was measured using the two dimensions of (a) work adjustment (4 items; e.g., "My specific job responsibilities") and (b) interaction adjustment (6 items; e.g., "Collegiality among colleagues") from Chen's (2012) scale.

The *CAAS* total score correlated .50 to psychological availability, .59 to work performance, .37 to work adjustment, and .26 to interaction adjustment. Those participants with higher career adaptability may have demonstrated better performance and adjustment because they had greater resources to draw upon to cope with evolving work demands and cultural uncertainties. Further analyses showed that psychological availability fully mediated the relationship between career adaptability and performance (B = .24). The participants with a higher level of career adaptability may have exhibited higher performance because they felt comfortable about investing their whole self at the workplace. Moreover, participants who had greater career adaptability had more resources to reduce distractions that may have otherwise hindered their psychological availability at work. Contrary to expectations, however, psychological availability did not mediate the relationship between career adaptability and adjustment. Being fully engaged at work may not greatly influence expatriates adjustment because adjustment may be more dependent on other factors (e.g., spouse's adjustment, having a mentor).

Adaptability-Cultural Intelligence-Expatriate Career

The third study of the adaptability-adapting-adaption path examined cultural intelligence as a moderator between adaptability and the adaptation result of intentions for an expatriate career. Increasing knowledge about factors that influence intentions for pursuing an expatriate career prompted a study by Presbitero and Quita (2017). They conceptualized self-initiated expatriation as a form of global employment mobility driven by an individual's self-regulatory capacity to thrive and build one's career in another country. They reasoned that that individuals who want to work overseas probably rely on their adaptability resources to develop their careers. Furthermore, the relation between career adaptability and expatriate intentions may be enhanced by an individual's cultural intelligence, that is, the capability of an individual to function effectively in situations characterized by cultural diversity. Cultural intelligence is distinct from personality and general cognitive ability. To test these assertions among university students, they investigated the relationship between career adaptability and intention for expatriate career as well as an underlying mechanisms that may facilitate an individual's intention to build an expatriate career.

348

A total of 514 students at a private university in The Philippines participated in the study. The participants (70% females and 30% males; Mean age = 19.7 years) were second-year students enrolled in the liberal and communication arts program. Career adaptability was measured with the *CAAS*. Intention for an expatriate career was measured using two items that correlated .86. The items were "I have always wanted to relocate and work overseas" and "If I have the opportunity, I would work and build my career in another country." Cultural intelligence was measured using nine items adapted from a scale developed by Ang and Van Dyne (2008). Sample items read, "I enjoy interacting with people from different cultures," "I am sure I can deal with the stresses of adjusting to a culture that is new to me," and "I am conscious of the cultural knowledge I use when interacting with people from different cultural backgrounds."

The results indicated that the *CAAS* total score correlated .58 to cultural intelligence and .49 to intention for an expatriate career, with cultural intelligence and expatriate intentions correlating .58. Moderation multiple regression analysis showed that *CAAS* had a significant and positive influence on intention for expatriate careers (β = .19, p < .05). In addition, results showed that the interaction term (career adaptability x cultural intelligence) had a significant influence on intention for an expatriate career (β = .27, p < .05), demonstrating that cultural intelligence moderated the relationship such that the relationship was stronger when cultural intelligence was higher, and weaker when cultural intelligence was lower (β = .27, p < .05). The researchers concluded that career adaptability can influence the formation of an intention for an expatriate career and cultural intelligence may enhance the likelihood of forming that intention.

Adaptability-Daily Adapting-Work Performance

In the fourth and fifth studies of the adaptability-adapting-adaptation path, Zacher (2015) examined the inter-relationships among adaptability resources (*CAAS*), intra-individual variations in daily adapting (*CAAS-Behavioral Form*), and daily outcomes on four performance and satisfaction outcomes (i.e., in task performance, career performance, job satisfaction, and career satisfaction). He used two sets of four items to measure daily job performance (e.g., "Quantity of work output") and career outcome (e.g., "Obtaining personal career goals). He used two sets of five items to measure daily job satisfaction (e.g., "Today I felt fairly well-satisfied with my job") and career satisfaction (e.g., "Today I was satisfied with the success I have achieved in my career").

The participants were 234 employees (55% females, mean age = 44.6 years) in the USA. They completed a baseline *CAAS* and then an average of four daily dairies (at least two daily surveys) in which they responded to the *CAAS-Behavioral Form* and rated their daily performance and satisfaction. The *CAAS* total score correlated .60 to daily adapting responses (*CAAS-Behavioral Form*). For the dimensions, Concern as a resource correlated .58 to Concern behaviors, Control as a resource correlated .56 to Control behaviors, Curiosity as a resource correlated .38 to Curiosity behaviors, and Confidence as a resource correlated .52 to Confidence behaviors. Interestingly, Confidence as a resource correlated .54 to Control behaviors. Daily manifestations of Concern and Curiosity behaviors were less frequently enacted by employees than daily manifestations of Control and Confidence behaviors. This may indicate that employees had fewer opportunities in their daily work to show behaviors associated with Concern and Curiosity compared to behaviors associated with Control and Confidence.

The within-person findings indicated that daily career adaptability and its dimensions fluctuated considerably across five work days, and that this variability associated with the outcomes of daily success and daily satisfaction. The career adaptability total score and each of its four subscales measured at baseline correlated positively to the daily job and career outcomes. The *CAAS* total score correlated .52 to daily task performance, .44 to daily career performance, .27 daily job satisfaction, and .40 to daily career satisfaction. With the exception of the correlation between Concern and daily job satisfaction, each of the four adapt-abilities correlated significantly to task and career performance and to job and career satisfaction ranging from .19 (Curiosity to daily job satisfaction) to .54 (Confidence to daily task performance). The average correlations to the four daily outcomes were stronger for the adapt-abilities of Confidence (.40) and Control (.38) than for Concern (.31) and Curiosity (.34). Also, the career adapt-abilities related more to daily career satisfaction than to daily job satisfaction.

Zacher also examined how daily career adapting behaviors related to the four job and career variables. Daily adaptability related to both daily task performance (.49) and daily job satisfaction (.35) yet much higher to daily career performance (.67) and daily career satisfaction (.66). Thus, on days when employees showed more adapting behaviors, they perceived higher performance and satisfaction. Overall, these findings suggest that daily career adapting behaviors fluctuated considerably across five work days, and that there were substantial shares of within-person variability in the daily job and career outcome variables that could potentially be explained by daily manifestations of adapting behaviors.

In a follow-up study to identify daily triggers of daily career adapting rather than daily outcomes, Zacher (2016) examined daily job characteristics (e.g., demands and autonomy) and daily supervisory mentoring. In this study, he again used a diary design to obtain 591 daily entries over a five day period from 156 employees (mean age 45 years) in the USA. He administered the *CAAS-Behavioral Form* to measure the extent to which the employees had engaged in 24 specific adapting behaviors on that day. Also, he had participants rate three items for daily job demands (e.g., "Today there was a great deal to be done."), three items for daily decisional autonomy (e.g., "Today my job allowed me to make a lot of decisions on my own."), and three items for supervisory career mentoring (e.g., "Today my supervisor took a personal interest in my career"). The *CAAS* total score at baseline correlated to .66 to the daily adapting total score. For the dimensions, the correlations between the baseline *CAAS* subscale scores and daily adapting scores were .61 for Concern, .66 for Control, .66 for Curiosity, and .66 for Confidence.

Daily career adapting correlated .33 to daily job demands, .37 to daily job autonomy, and .18 to daily supervisory mentoring. Zacher submitted the data on within-person predictors of daily career adaptability and its four dimensions to multi-level regression analyses. The daily job characteristics were centered at each participant's mean. The results further showed that several daily job characteristics related to daily manifestations of career adapting behaviors at the within-person level. Overall, the findings suggested that daily career adapting and daily job characteristics varied considerably within persons across five work days. In particular, the results indicated substantial proportions of within-person variance in daily overall career adapting (24%) and its four dimensions (between 25% and 36%). In other words, when certain job characteristics were higher or lower on a given day compared to individuals' average scores across days, their daily career adapting behaviors also deviated positively or negatively from their central tendencies across days. In particular, daily job demands related positively to daily Concern .33, daily Confidence .33, and daily overall career adaptability .33, suggesting that employees adapt their behavior to focus on future tasks and plans, and they strive to manage their tasks and work-related changes effectively when they face high job demands. Daily job autonomy correlated .37 to daily career adapting, .31 to daily Control (e.g., making independent decisions, taking responsibility for one's action) and .33 to daily Confidence. Daily supervisory career mentoring correlated .11 to daily adapting, .23 to daily Control, .23 daily to Curiosity, and .17 to daily Confidence but not to daily Concern (.03 ns). Thus, it appears that daily job characteristic and daily supervisory mentoring can trigger manifestation of daily adapt-abilities.

Adaptability-Task Adapting-Job Satisfaction

A sixth study of the adaptability-adapting-adaption path was conducted by Dong, Heng, and Wang (2020. They examined whether task adapting mediated positively the relationship between career adaptability and job satisfaction as well as whether perceived over-qualification mediated negatively between career adaptability and job satisfaction. They recruited 218 participants along with their supervisors from companies that were undergoing business adjustments or introducing new technology. The participants consisted of half males and half females, with a mean age of 29.9 years and an average tenure of 7.5 years. The researchers measured career adaptability with the *CAAS*. They represented adaptation outcomes as job satisfaction and turnover intentions, measuring both with subscales from the *Michigan Organizational Assessment Questionnaire* (Cammann, Fichman, Jenkins, & Klesh, 1979). An example item for job satisfaction reads, "All in all, I am satisfied with my job." An example item for turnover intention reads, "It is likely that I will search for a job in another organization." Adapting beliefs were measured negatively as perceived over-qualification using a scale developed by Johnson, Morrow, and Johnson (2002). Two of the ten items read, "My formal education over-qualifies me for my present job" and "My talents are not fully utilized on my job." They measured adapting behaviors with the *Task Adaptivity Scale* (Griffin, Neal, & Parker, 2007). In CCT terms, the adaptivity performance scale represents adapting responses. The scale measures the degree to which individuals not only complete their core tasks but also adapt to changes or adjustments associated with their work roles. Participants' adapting behaviors were assessed by the supervisors who evaluated employees' behavioral outcomes over the last week using a 7-point scale. Three items read, "Over the past week, this employee (a) adapted well to changes in core tasks"; (b) Over the past week, this employee coped with changes in the way he or she did their core tasks"; and (c) "Over the past week this employee learned new skills to help her or him adapt to changes in core tasks."

Results showed that the *CAAS* total score correlated .14 to task adaptivity, .19 to perceived over-qualification, .34 to job satisfaction, and -.22 to turnover intention. As shown in Figure 60, career adaptability related positively to task adapting ($\beta = .16$, $p < .05$) and perceived over-qualification ($\beta = .26$, $p < .01$). Task adapting related positively to job satisfaction ($\beta = .48$, $p < .01$) while perceived over-qualification related negatively to job satisfaction ($\beta = -.22$, $p < .01$). The results indicated that both task adapting and perceived over-qualification mediated the relationship between career adaptability and job satisfaction. Furthermore, career adaptability related to job satisfaction ($\beta = .38$, $p < .01$), indicating that the mediation was partial. The researchers concluded that employees who possess adequate adaptability resources are able to adapt to changes yet may perceive themselves as over-qualified. These adapting beliefs and behaviors influence employees' levels of job satisfaction, which is an important mediator of turnover intention.

Figure 60. Task Adapting Mediates between Adaptability and Job Satisfaction

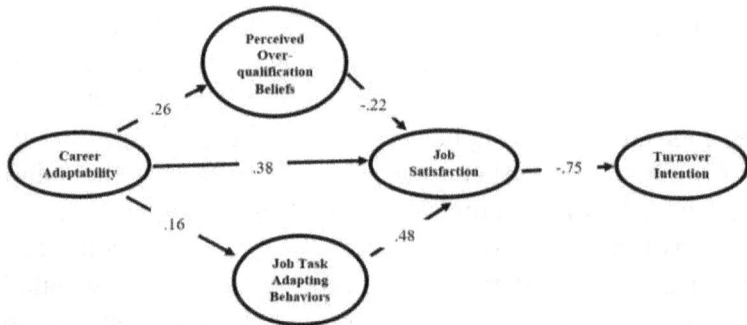

Adaptability-Ingratiation-Adaptation

In a seventh study concerning the adaptability-adapting-adaptation path, Sibunruang, Garcia, and Tolentino (2016) examined adapting responses relevant to sustainable career management. They reasoned that employees with more adaptability resources are more capable of achieving career advancement by using adapting behaviors to actively manage work roles and cope with complex work demands. They focused on ingratiation as an adapting response to barriers in career progression. Described as social influence attempts to positively shape decisions made by their supervisors about performance assessments, salary increases, and promotions. The researchers asserted that individuals rely on their adaptability resources and implement adapting responses, in the form of ingratiation, to increase their promotability at work. The researchers used a mediation model shown in Figure 61 to link adaptability to career advancement through adaptability, and also examined a mediation-moderation function that examined whether the mediation is further strengthened by high career sponsorship.

Figure 61. Ingratiation Mediates between
Adaptability and Promotability

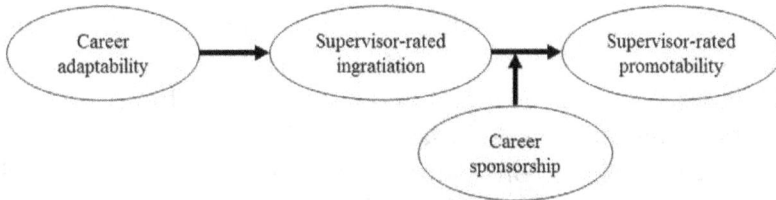

Four measured were used in the study. Sibunruang, Garcia, and Tolentino measured career adaptability with the *CAAS*. They operationally defined ingratiation by asking supervisors to rate their subordinates on a nine-item scale developed by Kumar and Beyerlein (1991), which included three general types of ingratiatory behaviors: opinion conformity, other enhancement, and favor rendering. Example items read, "This subordinate highlights the achievements made under my leadership" and "This subordinate goes out of his/her way to run an errand for me." Supervisors also rated the promotability of their subordinate using a four-item scale developed by Wayne, Liden, Graf, and Ferris (1997). Some of the items were, "I believe that this employee has what it takes to be promoted to a higher-level position" and "If I had to select a successor for my position, it would be this employee." Subordinates rated the degree of career support they received from the immediate supervisor using the seven-item scale developed by Greenhaus, Parasuraman and Wormley (1990). Example items read, "My supervisor takes the time to learn about my career goals and aspirations" and "My supervisor keeps me informed about different career opportunities for me in the organization."

The participants were full-time employees from three different organizations in Thailand (i.e., two from manufacturing and one from the hospitality industry). With the help of each company's human resource department, 284 matched supervisor–subordinate questionnaires were collected. Bivariate correlations indicated that the *CAAS* total score correlated .23 to supervisor-rated ingratiation, .36 to subordinate rated career sponsorship, and .13 to supervisor-rated promotability (with significant correlations only to the adapt-abilities of .13 to Curiosity and .19 to Confidence).

Results from the mediation analysis indicated that career adaptability had an indirect effect on supervisor-rated promotability (indirect effect = .06, *SE* = .03, [95% CI from .02 to .12)] via supervisor-rated ingratiation. Results from the moderated-mediation analysis revealed that the conditional indirect effect of career adaptability on supervisor-rated promotability via supervisor-rated ingratiation was significant under high levels of subordinate-rated career sponsorship (indirect effect = .11, SE =.05, [95% [CI from .03 to .22]) but not under low levels of subordinate-rated career sponsorship (indirect effect= .02, SE= .02, [95% CI from −.01 to .08]). Thus, the results indicate that the effectiveness of ingratiation attempts in positively influencing promotability ratings is enhanced by the resources and support employees receive in the presence of career sponsorship. In sum, the moderated-mediation model was supported and as expected: (a) ingratiation, as an adapting response, mediated the positive relationship between career adaptability and promotability, and (b) the mediated relationship between career adaptability and promotability via ingratiation was stronger for individuals with higher career sponsorship.

Adaptability-LMX-Career Prospects

The eighth and ninth studies of the adaptability-adapting-adaptation path both focused on leader-member theory. Combining career construction theory with leader-member exchange (LMX) theory, Yang, Guan, Zhang, She, Buchtel, Mak, and Hu (2020) examined the effect of career adaptability on LMX, and the indirect effect of career adaptability via LMX on career prospects. LMX theory states that through numerous interactions supervisors develop differential relationships with their employees. According to the theory, high quality LMX produces mutual understanding, trust, and support. Yang and colleagues hypothesized that LMX mediates the relationship between career adaptability and career prospects, and in a second study they hypothesized that this mediation is moderated by agreeableness.

In the first study, Yang and colleagues tested 252 employees (127 males and 125 females) and 69 supervisors, who worked in China. At Time 1, they measured career adaptability with the *CAAS*. At Time 2 one month later, they measured LMX and career prospects as rated by supervisors. An example item from the *LMX Scale* (Chen & Tjosvold, 2006) reads, "He/She and I are inclined to pool our available resources to solve the problems in his/her work." Career prospects were measured with two items developed by Bedeian, Kemery, and Pizzolatto (1991): "He/She will attain his/her career goals in this organization" and "He/She is likely to gain growth and development in this organization." Results indicated that the *CAAS* total score correlated .28 to LMX and .20 to career prospects, with LMX correlating .71 to career prospects. Multi-level mediation analyses showed that career adaptability related to LMX (β = .22), after controlling for employees' age, gender, education, and organizational tenure. In addition, LMX related to career prospects (β = .66), after controlling career adaptability and control variables. The indirect effect was significant (β = .15).

In the second study, Yang and colleagues tested 149 employees (75% males) and 47 supervisors with a time lag of four months. In addition to measuring career adaptability and LMX at Time 1, they assessed agreeableness using three items from the *Big Five Inventory-Short* (Hahn, Gottschling, & Spinath, 2012). At Time 2, the measured career adaptability and LMX, along with career prospects. At Time 1, the *CAAS* total score correlated .25 to LMX and .30 to agreeableness. At Time 2, the *CAAS* total score correlated .39 to LMX .28 to career prospects, with LMX correlating .63 to career prospects. Agreeableness at T1 correlated .30 to *CAAS* at T1 but not at T2 and not to LMX at T1 nor T2 nor career prospects at T2. Mediation results showed that career adaptability at T1 related to LMX at T2 (β = .41) which in turn related to career prospects

357

(β =.42) and the indirect effect (β = .17) was also significant. Interaction effects of career adaptability and agreeableness predicting LMX were significant (β =.36, p < .05)) when agreeableness was high but not significant (β =-.25, ns) when agreeableness was low. The relationship between career adaptability and LMX was moderated by agreeableness (β = .63). The researchers noted that the cross-lagged design of study two provided strong evidence for the unidirectional effect from career adaptability to LMX, but not vice versa. The researchers concluded that LMX is a relational mechanism that links career adaptability to career prospects. The results for both studies appear in Figure 62.

Figure 62. LMX Mediates between Adaptability and Career Prospects

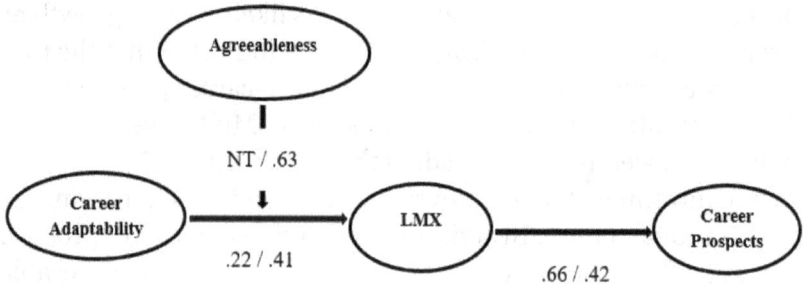

Conclusion

This Chapter reviewed nine studies that examined the CCT proposition that adapting responses mediate between adaptability resources and adaptation outcomes. The next Chapter reviews studies that tested the full career adaptation model.

CHAPTER 15

ADAPTIVITY TO ADAPTABILITY TO ADAPTING TO ADAPTATION

The CCT full model of adaptation, as shown in Figure 63, has been tested by eight studies in seven countries: Australia, Spain, China, Croatia, Iran, Turkey, and the USA.

<u>Figure 63. CCT Adaptation Model</u>

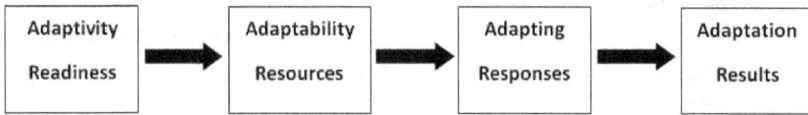

Adaptivity Readiness		Adaptability Resources		Adapting Responses		Adaptation Results
	→		→		→	

Australia

In a study with 1566 students at an Australian university, Perera and McIlveen (2017) used mixture analysis to examine how the FFM personality traits combine to represent adaptivity. They operationally operationally defined the FFM traits with the *NEO-Five Factor Inventory* (Costa & McCrae, 1992); adaptability with the *CAAS*; adapting with the *Organized Study Scale* (Entwistle, 1997); and adaptation with the *Academic Major Satisfaction Scale* (Nauta, 2007) and the *Career Choice Status Inventory* (Savickas, 1993). With regard to the FFM traits, the *CAAS* total score correlated -.43 to neuroticism, .37 to extraversion, .26 to openness, .14 to agreeableness, and .44 to conscientiousness. In turn, the *CAAS* total score correlated .28 to organized study, .29 to academic satisfaction, and .26 to career satisfaction. The authors concluded that, although not a direct test of mediated relations among the variables, the results aligned with the CCT adaptation model in showing that greater adapting behaviors and better adaptation outcomes related to more adaptivity and adaptability.

Spain

A direct test of the mediation model was conducted by Merino-Tejedor, Hontnaga, and Boada-Grau (2016). To test the CCT adaptation model, they operationally defined adaptivity with the *Self-Regulation Scale (SR;* Luszczynska, Diehl, Gutiérrez-Doña, Kuusinen, & Schwarzer, 2004); adaptability with the *CAAS*; adapting with the *Student Career Construction Inventory (SCCI;* M. Savickas, Porfeli, Hilton, & S. Savickas, 2018); and adaptation with the *Academic Burnout Scale - University Form* (Boada-Grau, Merino-Tejedor, Sánchez-García, Prizmic-Kuzmica, & Vigil-Colet, 2015) plus the *Utrecht Work Engagement Scale (UWES)* adapted for university students (Schaufeli, Salanova, González-Romá, & Bakker, 2002). They administered these five inventories to 577 students at a university in Spain.

As shown in Figure 64, they tested first a three-step sequence of adaptivity to adaptability to adapting (Model 1). Goodness of fit was acceptable, both when direct effects were not included (NNFI = .909, CFI = .929, SRMS = .053, RMSEA = .081), and when these were introduced (similar values), with no statistically significant differences between them ($\Delta\chi$ =1.02, Δdf = 1, p = .313). The indirect effect of adaptivity (*SR*) upon the adapting behaviors (*SCCI*) was statistically significant (γ = .371, p < .001), but not the direct effect (γ = .054, p = .308). Therefore, these results confirmed the mediation model presented in Figure 64 that shows self-regulation (SR) influences career constructing behaviors (SCCI) through the effect it has on the *CAAS*.

Figure 64. Adaptability Mediates between Self-Regulation and Adapting Responses

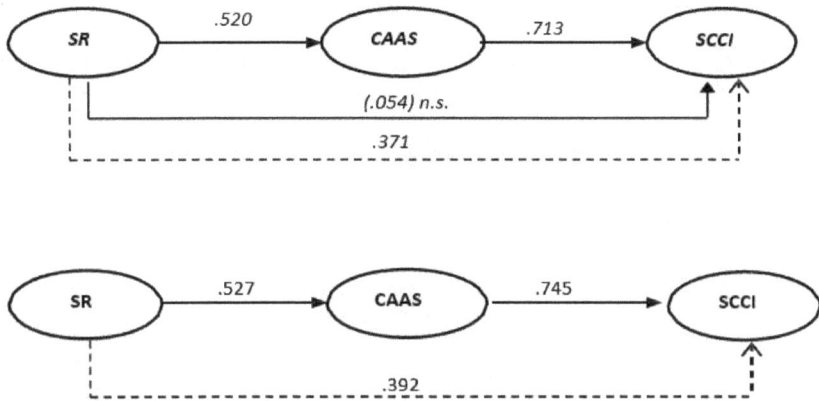

Model 1 with 3 steps. Indirect effects above and direct effects below.

They next tested the four-step sequence (Model 2) that added adaptation at the end. Adaptation was represented as academic engagement (*EN*) and indicated by *Academic Burnout Scale* and the *Utrecht Work Engagement Scale*. The results showed acceptable goodness of fit indices when the direct effects were not included (NNFI = .886, CFI = .905, SRMS = .075, RMSEA = .086), improving significantly when these were introduced (NNFI = .910, CFI = .928, SRMS = .052, RMSEA = .076; $\Delta\chi^2$ = 91.88, Δdf = 3, p < .001). The direct effect of self-regulation on the adapting behaviors was not statistically significant (γ = .06, p = .28), although the indirect effect was (γ = .36, p < .001), confirming the mediation role of the *CAAS* (see Figure 65). However, the mediation by the *SCCI* between the *CAAS* and engagement was not supported as neither the direct influence of the *SCCI* upon engagement was significant (γ = −.06, p = .40), nor the indirect effect of the *CAAS* (γ = −.04, p = .40). However, the results did indicate that the *CAAS* had a strong direct effect upon engagement (γ = .61, p < .001), and exercised a partial mediation between self-regulation and engagement, given that both the direct effect (γ = .123, p = .024), and the indirect effect (γ = .294, p < .001) of self-regulation were statistically significant.

Figure 65. Relations among Adaptivity, Adaptability, Adapting, and Adaptation

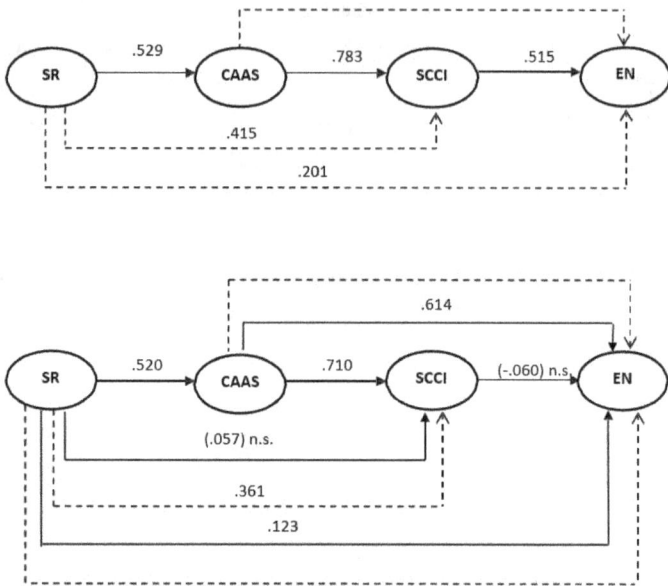

Model 2 with 4 steps. Indirect effects above and direct effects below.

The mediation analysis confirmed the three-sequence model with the variables of self-regulation (adaptivity), career adaptability (adaptability resources), and adapting responses (*SCCI*). However, the results did not support the four-sequence model as the relationship between the *SCCI* and engagement was not supported. Therefore, the four-sequence model presents a limitation in the final phase with the incorporation of engagement and burnout (adaptation results). The researchers recommended that future studies replicate these results using a better representations of adaptation results (e.g., career satisfaction, job success, occupational stability) in a longitudinal study which would reduce common-method variance and test the sequence of casual relationships in the model.

China

Two other studies that tested the CCT adaptation model reduced common-method bias by using time-lag designs. Guan and colleagues (2014) used a three-wave design with 270 new graduates who had just received their bachelors or masters degree from a Chinese university and who intended to seek employment immediately after graduation. In the first wave, adaptivity was operationally defined with the *Future Work Self Scale* (Strauss, Griffin, & Parke, 2012) and career adaptability was measured with the *CAAS*. A month later the students responded to a measure of adapting (*Jobs Search Self-Efficacy Scale*, Wanberg, Zhang, & Diehn, 2010). Two months later, the graduates reported yes or no as to whether they had signed an employment contract.

The results indicated that adaptivity predicted adaptability and adapting responses. As shown in the Figure 66, after controlling for the effects of gender, age, education level and faculty, future work self (measured at Time 1) significantly predicted career adaptability measured at Time 1 (β = .27, p <. 01). Furthermore, when simultaneously added in the equation, both future work self (β = .18, p < .01) and career adaptability (β = .47, p < .01) manifested strong predictive effects on job search self-efficacy measured at Time 2, a result indicating that career adaptability partially mediated the relationship between future work self and job search self-efficacy. Moreover, in the equation predicting employment status measured at Time 3, future work self (β = .52, p < .01) and job search self-efficacy (β = .48, p < .05) but not career adaptability (β = −.17, ns) were significantly related to employment status. These results suggested that job search self-efficacy fully mediated the effect of career adaptability on employment status.

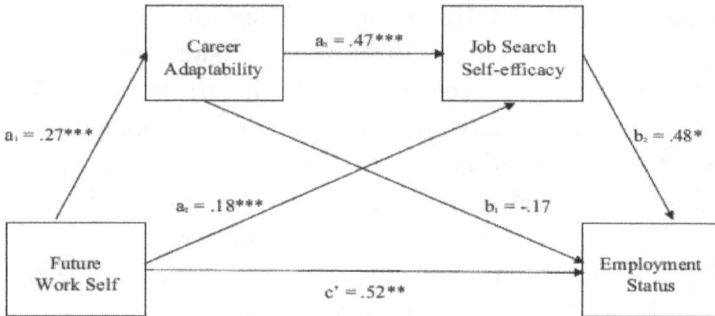

Figure 66. Self-Efficacy Mediates between
Adaptability and Employment Status

As portrayed by the mediation model in Figure 66, job self-efficacy fully mediated the effect of adaptability on the adaptation outcome of employment status. Job search self-efficacy measures the extent to which individuals report that they believe they could perform well in job search tasks. Thus, self-efficacy is neither an adaptability resource nor adapting behavior itself. It is an adapting belief, a belief that one can perform the adapting behaviors. As such, the CCT model places it between adaptability and adapting. The finding that self-efficacy fully mediated the effect of adaptability on adaptation calls for more research to understand self-efficacy beliefs. In addition to the results from the mediation model, the results of a moderated-mediation model further revealed that the positive effect of future work self on job search self-efficacy was stronger among the graduates who had a higher level of career adaptability. For individuals with a higher level of career adaptability, the indirect effect of future work self on employment status through job search self-efficacy was stronger.

In a second study that controlled for common-method variance, Zhuang, She, Cai, Huang, Xiang, Wang, and Zhu (2018) conducted a two-wave study with 165 Chinese university students. In the first wave 1,194 students responded to two measures of adaptivity: *Chinese Big-Five Personality Scale- Short Form* (Li et al., 2015) and *Approach-Avoidant Temperament* (Elliot & Thrash, 2010). A month later, 165 of the original participants completed the *CAAS,* two measures of adapting in terms of search for and presence of life meaning (*Meaning in Life Questionnaire*, Steger, Frazier, Oishi, & Kaler, 2006), and a measure of adaptation in terms of psychological well-being (*The Flourishing Scale*, Diener, Wirtz, Tov, Kim-Prieto, Choi, Oishi, & Biswas-Diener, 2009).

As shown in figure 67, after controlling for the effects of age and gender, career adaptability was significantly predicted by openness to experience (β = .12, p < .05), conscientiousness (β = .21, p < .001), the approach trait (β = .38, p < .001), and the avoidance trait (β = -.24, p < .001). And, career adaptability positively predicted presence of meaning in life (β = .57, p < .001) and search for meaning in life (β = .35, p < .01). The effects of extraversion, neuroticism, and agreeableness on career adaptability were not significant in this model. Furthermore, after controlling the effects of age, gender, basic traits, and career adaptability, presence of life meaning showed significant correlation with psychological flourishing (β = .18, p < .01), while no significant effect was found for search for life meaning.

Figure 67. Relations among FFM, Motivation, Adaptability, Meaning, and Flourishing

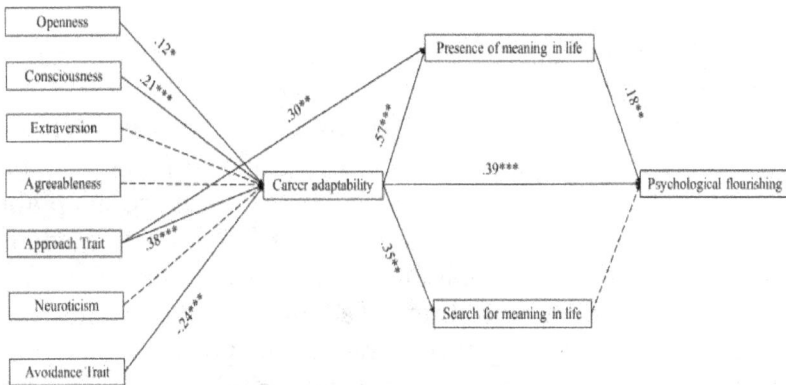

In sum, career adaptivity predicted career adaptability, which in turn predicted adapting responses and adaptation results. While the study supported the model, there are better measures of

adapting response than life meaning, which seems to be closer to an adaptation outcome and similar in some ways to psychological flourishing.

Croatia

In two studies, Sverko and Babarovic (2019) tested the full CCT adaptation model by examining readiness, resources, responses, and results of after-school career transition. Their first study used a cross-sectional design that concentrated on the first three dimensions in the adaptation model. The researchers operationally defined adaptive readiness as high school grade point average (GPA), viewing it as a proxy for cognitive abilities. They measured career adaptability resources with the *CAAS*. Adapting responses were measured in terms of engagement and difficulties. The *Student Career Construction Inventory* (*SCCI*; Savickas, Porfeli, Hilton, Savickas, 2018) measured enactment of adapting responses. The *Career Decision-Making Difficulties-Revised* (*CDMD-R*; Gati, Krausz, & Osipow, 1996) measured difficulties that people may face when making career decisions. The participants consisted of 622 students (62.2% females) attending the first (N= 223; age 15) and the fourth grade (N = 399; age 18)) of different high schools in Croatia.

Results indicated that the *SCC* total scored correlated to the four adapt-abilities from .39 to .56 and -.30 to difficulties. The *CDMD-R* total score correlated to the four adapt-abilities from -.14 to -.31. The path diagram in Figure 68 shows significant paths that follow the CCT model of adaptation. GPA weakly predicted adaptability resources, and adaptability resources further predicted adapting responses. Among adaptability resources, Concern had the strongest effect on the enactment of adapting behaviors and Control on difficulties. Higher Concern related to greater enactment of adapting behaviors, and higher Control related to less career decision-making difficulties. No direct effects of adaptivity to adapting responses were suggested by modification indices, thus this model confirms the mediating role of career adaptability in the CCT model of adaptation. The researchers also tested the reverse model in which adaptability resources and adapting responses switched places (all other relations remained the same). The reverse model showed worse fit, indicating that the original model more accurately represents the process of adaptation.

Figure 68. Relations among GPA, Adaptability, Adapting, and Difficulties

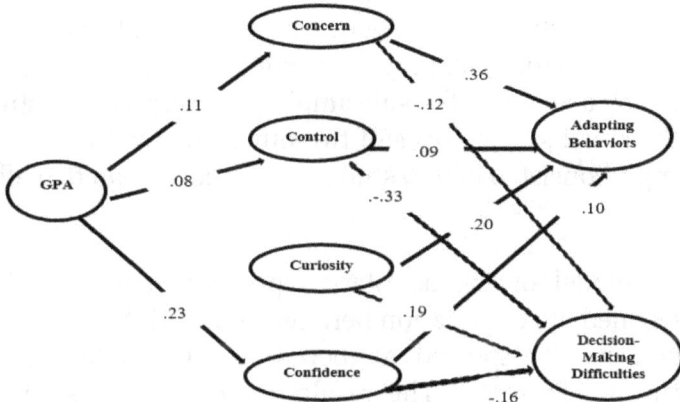

The second study conducted by Sverko and Babarovic (2019) tested the four dimensions in the full model of career adaptation using a longitudinal design that followed high school student for 18 months to explore the transition process after high school. At the beginning of the last year of high school (Time 1) the researchers measured adaptive readiness three ways: (a) the personality traits of conscientiousness, openness, and Extraversion with the HEXACO-60 (Ashton & Lee, 2009), (b) self-appraisal with the *Core Self-Evaluations Scale* (Judge, Erez, Bono, & Thoresen, 2003), and (c) academic achievement with the GPA in the last year of schooling. At the end of the last year of high school (Time 2), they measured adaptability resources with the *CAAS* and adapting responses with the *SCCI* and the *CDMDQ-R*. Finally, one year later after the participants transitioned to employment or college (Time 3), the researchers measured adaptation results with three scales. Study satisfaction was measured using a 4-item scale that reflects general satisfaction with one's studies. Self-reported study performance was measured with five items depicting subjective parameters of achievement in university studies. Example items read, "How satisfied are you with your grades at the university?" and "Compared to other students in your study program, how would you rate your success as a student?" Work engagement was measured with the *Utrecht Work Engagement Scale for Students* (Schaufeli, Martinez, Marques Pinto, Salanova, & Bakker, 2002). Gender and socio-economic status were measured as covariates. Of the 405 participants remaining at Time 3, 321 were enrolled in undergraduate studies, 50 were employed, and 34 were not involved in education, employment, nor training. The researchers continued by using only the subsample of undergraduate students, due to the small sample sizes of two other groups. In the end, the total sample consisted of 299 students who participated in all three waves.

The CCT model of the adaptation process in which adapting responses mediate the relation between adaptability resources and adaptation results showed a good fit to the data, as shown previously in Figure 63. The results indicate that the strongest correlations occurred between constructs within the same dimension. Among adaptivity indicators, core self-evaluations related .62 to extraversion and .43 to conscientiousness, while GPA related .37 to conscientiousness. Correlations between the four adapt-abilities ranged from .35 to .53. The correlations between the *SCCI* behaviors and *CDMDQ-R* difficulties was .49. Correlations between the three adaptation results ranged from .46 to .71. Correlations between the different dimensions were strongest between the *CAAS* adaptability resources and the *SCCI* adapting behaviors (ranging from .31 to .46) and between *CAAS* and *CDMDQ-R* difficulties (ranging from −.07 to −.41). Figure 69 shows the significant paths in the career adaptation model. In addition, support for the model was found in the significance of several indirect effects. First, the indirect effects of adaptive readiness on adapting responses via adaptability resources were significant. There were medium-size indirect effects of (a) core self-evaluations on *SCCI* behaviors (.10) and *CDMDQ-R* difficulties (−.14, respectively), (b) extraversion on *SCCI* behaviors (.12) and *CDMDQ-R* difficulties (−.07), and (c) conscientiousness on *SCCI* behaviors (.18). In addition, small indirect effects of core self-evaluations and conscientiousness were observed on all three adaptation results, as well as indirect effects of extraversion on self-reported study performance and study engagement. Finally, significant small to medium indirect effects of adaptability resources on the adaptation results via adapting responses were also observed. Concern and Control indirectly effected all three outcomes (effects ranged from .05 to .09). The researchers tested a reverse model in which adapting responses precede adaptability resources and found significantly worse fit.

Figure 69. Relations among Adaptivity, Adaptability, Adapting, and Adaptation in Croatia

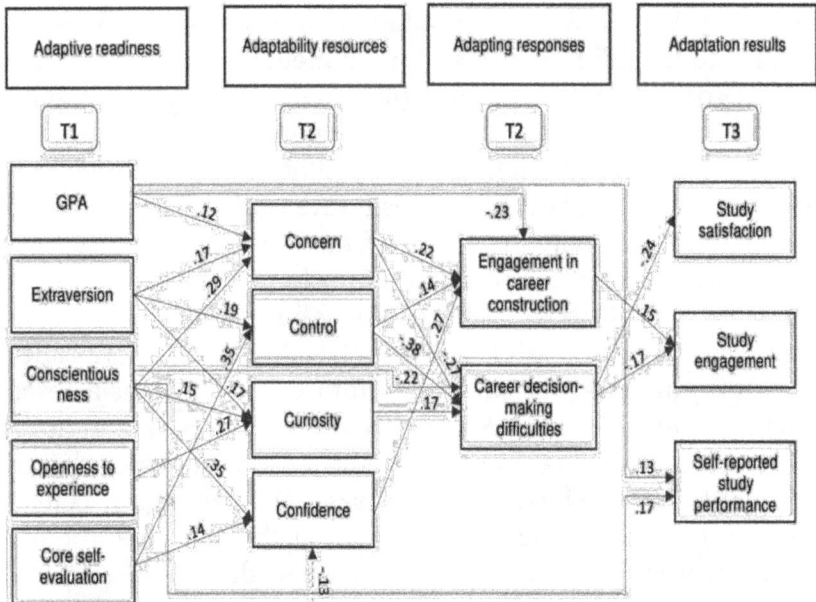

My inspection of the path model prompted two comments. First, the relatively weaker paths between *SCCI* behaviors and adaptation results may have occurred because the adaptation indicators were for academic not career outcomes, such as decidedness or vocational identity. Furthermore, the adaptation results were measured when the participants were in college, one year after taking the *SCCI* while in the final year of high school. Second, the positive path between Curiosity and decisional difficulties is the same as reported by Karacan-Ozdemir (2019) who used the same two measures. However, he reported subscale scores for the *CDMDQ* and indicated that Curiosity positively predicted (β = .61) increase in difficulties due to a lack of readiness, which involves difficulties prior to beginning the decisional process, namely, lack of motivation, general indecisiveness, and dysfunctional beliefs. He interpreted this finding as suggesting that exploring oneself is harder than exploring occupations.

Iran

A study by Nilforooshan (2020) also examined the complete theoretical model of career adaptation (Savickas, 2013). He attended to the full multiple mediation model by concentrating on two types of adaptivity (i.e., willingness and readiness), adaptability resources, two types of adapting responses (i.e., beliefs and behaviors), and an adaptation result. Nilforooshan conceptualized adaptivity in terms of willingness as future work self and readiness in terms of proactivity. The term *future work* self refers to an individual's representation of himself or herself in the future that reflects his or her hopes and aspirations in relation to work. The clearer and more accessible this representation, the more salient the future work self. The salience of future work self was assessed with the *Future Work Self Scale* (Strauss, Griffin, & Parker, 2012), which consists of five items. Proactivity was assessed by the *Personal Initiative Questionnaire* (Frese, Fay, Hilburger, Leng, & Tag, 1997), which includes seven items such as "I take initiative immediately even when others don't." Career adaptability resources were measured with the *CAAS*. Adapting responses were conceptualized as self-efficacy beliefs and engagement behaviors. Participants' self-efficacy in career decision-making was measured with the *Career Decision-Making Self-Efficacy Scale–Short Form* (Betz, Klein, & Taylor, 1996 2005). The *Career Engagement Scale* (Hirschi, Hermann, & Keller, 2014) contains nine items (e.g., "Caring for the development of your career") about general and specific career engagement behaviors. Adaptation results were conceptualized as academic satisfaction and assessed by the *Academic Satisfaction Scale* (Lent, Singley, Sheu, Gainor, Brenner, Treistman, & Ades, 2005). The participants were 282 students at a university in Iran. They had a mean age of 27.72 years (*SD* = 4.57). the participants were 150 females and 132 males. In terms of academic status 17.7% were Ph.D. students, 28.7% were master's degree students, and 52.8% were bachelor's degree students.

Results indicated that career adaptability correlated .54 to future work self, .43 to proactivity, .68 to decision-making self-efficacy beliefs, .58 to career engagement behaviors, and .32 to academic satisfaction. The indirect and direct relationships in the hypothesized multiple-mediation model were examined with structural equation modeling. As presented in Figure 70, the indirect relations of both future work self and proactivity with academic satisfaction through the mediator variables was significant whereas their direct relation were not. Therefore, the mediators fully mediated the relation of both future work self and proactivity to academic satisfaction. Analyses also indicated that that career adaptability had a partial mediation role in the relationships of both future work self and proactivity with career decision-making self-efficacy. The relation between career adaptability and academic satisfaction was fully mediated by career decision-making self-efficacy and career engagement. And finally, additional analyses indicated that career adaptability did not moderate the relations between adaptivity indices (i.e., future work self and proactivity) and adapting indices (i.e., self-efficacy beliefs and career engagement). These findings support the series of influences delineated in the CCT adaptation model. It seems that adapting responses employ the individual's adaptability resources in order to reach adaptation results. Willingness to change and readiness to change indirectly promoted adapting behaviors by facilitating adaptability resources.

371

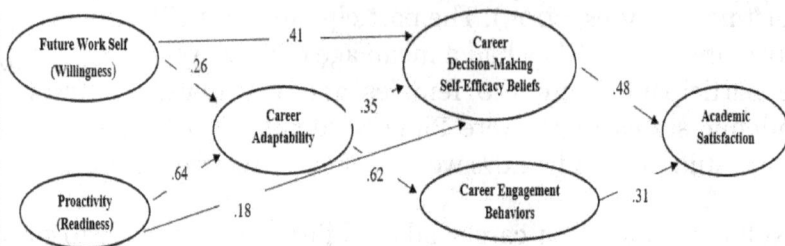

TURKEY

The role of the components in the CCT adaptation model was investigated sequentially as a whole by Oztemel and Akyo (2021). The participants were 694 students at five high schools in Turkey. The 299 females and 395 males had a mean age of 15.2 years (SD = 1.11). The researchers represented adaptivity with the *Rosenberg Self-Esteem Scale* (Rosenberg, 1965), adaptability with the *CAAS*, adapting behaviors with the *Student Career Construction Inventory* (*SCCI*; Savickas et al., 2018), and adaptation with the *Oxford Happiness Questionnaire-Short Form* (Hills & Argyle, 2002). The happiness measure consists of seven items such as "I feel that life is very rewarding" and "I am well satisfied with everything in my life."

The researchers used serial mediation analysis to test the CCT model of sequential components such that adaptive readiness (self-esteem) facilitates adaptability resources (career adaptability), which further improves adapting responses (career construction behaviors), and ends in adaptation results (happiness). In serial mediation analysis, all path parameters are estimated simultaneously. A three-way mediator effect was tested in the structural model. The advantage of this approach was that it distinguished the indirect effects of both the *CAAS* and *SCCI* from both mediator variables in the CCT model. This approach also allows discovery of an indirect effect that passes through both mediators in a series.

Results of the model test, portrayed in Figure 71, showed that self-esteem sequentially associated with career adaptability (β = .14, p < .001), adapting responses (β = .60, p < .001), and eventually happiness (β = .10, p < .001). Self-esteem related .23 directly to happiness. The sequential pathway from "self-esteem to career adaptability to adapting responses to happiness" was significant (indirect effect = .008, SE = .004, 95% CI = [0.001, 0.015]). Therefore, career adaptability and adapting responses mediated the relation between self-esteem and happiness. The results support the view that individuals with high self-esteem mediate their happiness in being ready to fulfill their career development tasks and deal with career transitions in a way that leads to happiness.

Figure 71. Serial Mediation Results for the CCT Adaptation Model

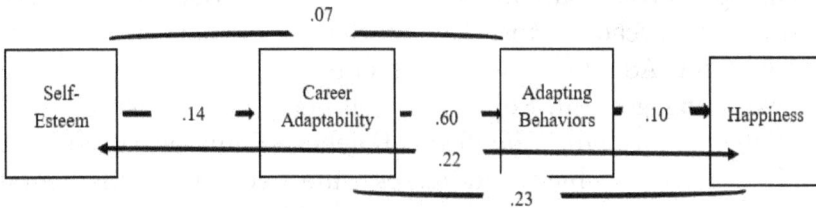

USA

A study by Tokar, Savickas, and Kaut (2020) tested the full CCT adaptation model with a sample of employed adults to examine its validity beyond adolescents and emerging adults. Moreover, the researchers purposefully sought to test the model in an adult sample who routinely face serious adaptive challenges as part of their employment. Participants were 289 employed adults (261 women, 26 men, 2 not stated) diagnosed with Chiari malformation, which is a chronic health condition with varying degrees of cognitive (e.g., attention, memory), sensory (e.g., pain, numbness/tingling), motor (e.g., weakness), and psychosocial (e.g., depression, anxiety) complications. More than half of the participants (55%) had been diagnosed with at least one additional illness (e.g., Ehlers-Danlos Syndrome, hypothyroidism, syringomelia). The participants' ages ranged from 18 to 61 years (Mean = 37.12; SD = 9.43). The majority (68.2%) of participants were employed full-time outside the home, with 22.1% employed part-time outside home, 6.6% self-employed part-time at home, and 3.1% self-employed full-time at home. The mean number of hours worked per week was 33.90 (SD = 12.14).

Tokar, Savickas, and Kaut represented adaptivity as proactivity with the *Proactive Personality Scale* (Seibert, Crant, & Kraimer, 1999) and the FFM personality traits of conscientiousness and openness with the *Mini-International Personality Item Pool* (Donnellan, Oswald, Baird, & Lucas, 2006). Career adaptability was measured with the *CAAS-SF* (Maggiori, Rossier, & Savickas, 2017). Adapting was represented as competence need satisfaction, that is, one's level of competence at activities that maintain effective performance and facilitate goal attainment, measured by the *Basic Psychological Need Satisfaction at Work Scale* (Deci et al., 2001). A sample item reads, "Most days I feel a sense of accomplishment from working. Adaptation was represented by subjective well-being and work engagement. Subjective well-being was measured with the *Satisfaction with Life Scale* (Diener, Emmons, Larsen, & Griffin, 1985), which addresses the cognitive-judgmental component of subjective well-being (e.g., "I am satisfied with my life"). Work engagement was a latent variable inferred by scores on the directly measured variables of work engagement, job satisfaction, and meaningful work. Work engagement as an observed variable was assessed with the 9-item *Utrecht Work Engagement Scale* (Schaufeli, Bakker, & Salanova, 2006). Overall job satisfaction was measured with Judge, Locke, Durham, and Kluger's (1998) 5-item adaptation of Brayfield and Rothe's *Job Satisfaction Index* (1951). The experience of meaningful work was measured with the 10-item *Work as Meaning Scale* (Steger, Dik, & Duffy, 2012), which addresses positive meaning (e.g., "I have found a meaningful career"), meaning making through work (e.g., "My work helps me better understand myself"), and greater good motivation (e.g., "I know my work makes a positive difference in the world").

Observed relationships among adaptivity readiness, adaptability resources, adapting responses, and adaptation results in Figure 72 provided strong support for the CCT adaptation model in workers with Chiari malformation. As hypothesized, higher levels of adaptivity --operationally defined as the dispositions of proactivity, conscientiousness, and openness --were associated with higher levels of career adaptability, adapting responses, and adaptation results. Positive associations of adaptivity with adapting responses (i.e., competence need satisfaction at work) were fully mediated via adaptability resources, as posited by the CCT model of adaptation. Significant effects of adaptivity on adaptation results (i.e., work engagement and subjective well-being) occurred via adaptability and adapting responses, which coincides with the sequence of mediated relations proposed by the CCT model. Career adaptability associated positively with adapting responses (i.e., competence need satisfaction at work) and the two adaptation results. The positive association of adaptability resources with adapting responses suggested that workers with Chiari malformation who possess the psychosocial capacities to respond to career tasks and challenges are more likely to experience competence at work activities that facilitate development and effective performance. Associations of adaptability with adaptation results were fully mediated via adapting (i.e., competence need satisfaction), as posited by the CCT model.

Figure 72. Relations among Adaptivity, Adaptability, Adapting, and Adaptation in USA

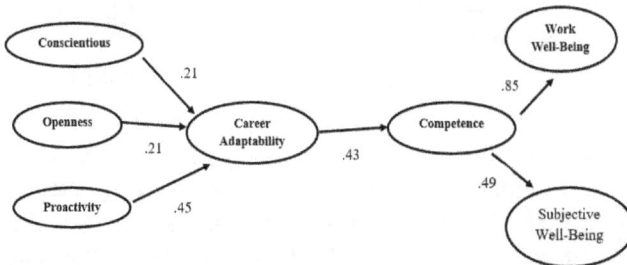

375

A different perspective on the career adaptation model and a different approach to testing the full model was taken by Xu (2020c). He aimed to examine the incremental predictive power of the *CAAS* over and above a measure of general self-efficacy. Rather than place general self-efficacy between adaptability resources and adapting responses as prescribed by the CCT model, he positioned general self-efficacy as an indicator of adaptive readiness and sequenced it before career adaptability resources. Then he tested whether the *CAAS* total score could predict unique variance in career criteria over and beyond generalized self-efficacy. The CCT model considers generalized self-efficacy as beliefs about enacting adapting behaviors, and expects that generalized self-efficacy beliefs have a stronger relationship than adaptability resources to adapting behaviors and adaptation results. Selecting generalized self-efficacy beliefs to represent adaptive readiness, and sequencing it before adaptability resources, may be justifiable from a certain perspective but it is not used and sequenced that way in the CCT model of career adaptation. CCT positions self-efficacy beliefs, both general and specific, as a moderator not a predictor.

For CCT self-efficacy influences adapting behaviors because it refers to "beliefs in one's capabilities to mobilize the motivation, cognitive resources, and courses of action needed to meet given situational demands" (Wood & Bandura, 1989, p. 408). Adapting behaviors -- such as initiation, effort, and persistence -- are consequences of self-efficacy adapting beliefs. Self-efficacy energizes the resource-responding link. The CCT adaptation model also views general self-efficacy as malleable, rather than as a stable adaptive trait, because it emerges over the life span as one accumulates successes and failures across different task domains. CCT also views general self-efficacy as pertaining to a broad array of task and contexts and thus subsuming specific self-efficacy beliefs about particular tasks such as career decision making. Both general self-efficacy and career decision-making self-efficacy denote beliefs about performing behaviors, with one being general and the other being specific. In his studies, Xu (2020c) reported that general self-efficacy correlated .63 to career decision-making self-efficacy for students and .64 to occupational self-efficacy for employed adults. In contrast to self-efficacy beliefs, career adapt-abilities are psychosocial resources or capacities for self-regulation with which individuals can support and shape adapting behaviors.

In a second difference from the previous studies that tested the full CCT adaptation model, Xu (2020c) represented the *CAAS* as a multi-dimensional bi-factor model with all the items loading on one general factor and corresponding subscale factors instead of the previously researched multi-dimensional hierarchical model with items loading on corresponding subscale factors and then the subscale factors loading on one general factor. The bi-factor model directly generates a *CAAS* total score from items, whereas the hierarchical model indirectly generates a *CAAS* total score based on the four first-order factors. The second-order confirmatory factor models used in previous studies of the *CAAS* are typically used in non-cognitive domains, where bi-factor models have seldom been used. In the last ten years, a few personality assessment researchers have begun to use bi-factor models. In 2010, Reise, Moore and Haviland suggested that the bi-factor model is poorly understood by personality assessment researchers, who still view it with skepticism and seldom apply it. Today, even those who use bi-factor models seem to agree that inferences on dimensionality should not be based solely on statistical fit any more than they should be purely based on expert judgment of item content (Dunn, & McCray, 2020).

Given his use of a bi-factor model, Xu (2020c) expected that the *CAAS* total score would likely overlap with general self-efficacy, and that general self-efficacy would associate more strongly with the *CAAS* total score than with the four specific subscale factors. He conducted two sophisticated studies to investigate his conceptualization of a career adaptation model and bi-factor measurement of career adaptability resources.

The participants in the first study, recruited from MTurk, consisted of 284 employees (63% females) from the United States with a mean age of 38.99 years (SD = 11.89). The *CAAS* was used to measure career adaptability resources and the 8-item *New General Self-Efficacy Scale* (Chen, Gully, & Eden, 2001) was used to measure beliefs in ones' confidence about performing adapting behaviors effectively across different tasks and situations. Example items read, "I believe I can succeed at most any endeavor to which I set my mind"; "I will be able to successfully overcome many challenges"; "I am confident that I can perform effectively on many different tasks"; and "Even when things are tough, I can perform quite well."

Xu (2020c) appropriately chose occupational self-efficacy and career decision ambiguity aversion to represent adapting responses in terms of beliefs -- not behaviors -- and career satisfaction and career indecision to represent adaptation results. Adapting responses were represented by two indicators of the beliefs component and no indicators of the behaviors component (i.e., actions such as exploring and planning). The two sets of adapting beliefs were occupational self-efficacy and career decision ambiguity aversion. The 6-item *Occupational Self-Efficacy Scale* (Rigotti, Schyns, & Mohr, 2008) was used to measure one's confidence in coping with difficult vocational tasks (e.g., "I can remain calm when facing difficulties in my job because I can rely on my abilities") or problems (e.g., "When I am confronted with a problem in my job, I can usually find several solutions"). Xu used the *Career Decision Aversion Scale-R* (*CDAR-R*; Xu & Tracey, 2015) to measure career decision ambiguity aversion, which is defined as the tendency to find ambiguity anxiety-provoking and avoid it in career decision making (e.g., "I want to avoid processing conflictual information about a career"). Adaptation results were represented by career satisfaction and career indecision. The *Career Satisfaction Scale* (Greenhaus et al., 1990) was used to measure career satisfaction in terms of one's estimated progress toward meeting various career-related goals. Xu used the choice/commitment anxiety subscale of the *Career Indecision Profile-Short* (*CIP-Short*; Xu & Tracey, 2017) to measure career indecision, operationally defined as resistance/hesitance in committing to one choice (e.g., "Often feel discouraged about deciding").

Results indicated that general self-efficacy correlated .64 to the *CAAS* total score, with correlations of .48 to Concern, .58 to Control, .44 to Curiosity, and .66 to Confidence. Occupational self-efficacy correlated .50 to career adaptability and .65 to general self-efficacy. Career satisfaction correlated .46 to adaptability and .56 to self-efficacy while career indecision correlated -.25 to adaptability and-.36 to self-efficacy. This pattern of zero-order correlations fit expectations from the CCT model of career adaptation.

Based on his model of adaptation, Xu hypothesized that the *CAAS* total score adds no or little incremental prediction for career criteria over and beyond general self-efficacy. He used hierarchical multiple regression to examine the incremental predictions of the *CAAS* total score for occupational self-efficacy, career decision ambiguity aversion, career satisfaction, and career indecision over and beyond general self-efficacy. Results showed that the *CAAS* total score added no or little incremental predictions for career criteria over and beyond general self-efficacy. The CCT adaptation model would anticipate this finding because it sequences self-efficacy after adaptability resources and before the adapting response and adaptation outcomes. Regarding the *CAAS* itself, the bi-factor model supported the existence of a general adaptability factor derived from the items, and that score associated strongly with general self-efficacy ($r = .70$). In addition to the main analysis, Xu examined the incremental predictions of the *CAAS* four subscales beyond general self-efficacy. He reported significant ΔF test results for occupational self-efficacy (ΔF [4278] = 3.76, p < .05, $\Delta R2$ = 0.03), career satisfaction (ΔF [4278] = 3.22, p < .05, $\Delta R2$ = 0.03), and career indecision (ΔF [4278] = 5.34, p < .05, $\Delta R2$=0.06) and a non-significant ΔF test for ambiguity aversion. He concluded that the *CAAS* subscales showed a stronger incremental predictive pattern than the *CAAS* total score among employees.

The participants in the second study, also recruited from MTurk, consisted of 279 students (58.8% females) from the United States with a mean age of 23.63 years (SD = 3.24). Given the mean ages of 23.6 years, it would be interesting to know the level of education at which they were enrolled. The *CAAS* and *New General Self-Efficacy*

Scale were also used in this study. Xu appropriately chose career decision-making self-efficacy and career decision ambiguity aversion to represent adaptation responses and academic satisfaction and career indecision to represent adaptation results. Adapting responses were represented as by two indicators of the beliefs component and no indicators of the behaviors component (i.e., actions such as exploring and planning). The two sets of adapting beliefs were career decision-making self-efficacy and career decision ambiguity aversion. Xu used the 25-item *Career Decision-Making Self-Efficacy Scale* (Betz, Klein, & Taylor, 1996) to measure specific self-efficacy (as opposed to general self-efficacy) and the *CDAR-R* (Xu & Tracey, 2015) to measure career decision ambiguity aversion. To measure adaptation outcomes, Xu used the 6-item *Academic Major Satisfaction Scale* (Nauta, 2007) to assess students' satisfaction with their academic majors (e.g., "I feel good about the major I've selected") and the choice/commitment anxiety subscale of the *CIP-Short* (Xu & Tracey, 2017) to assess career indecision.

Results indicated that general self-efficacy correlated .64 to the *CAAS* total score, with correlations of .60 to Concern, .55 to Control, .48 to Curiosity, and .63 to Confidence. Career decision-making self-efficacy correlated .70 to adaptability and .63 to generalized self-efficacy. Aversion correlated -.04 to adaptability and -.05 to general self-efficacy. Major satisfaction correlated .20 to adaptability and .39 to general self-efficacy. Career indecision correlated -.22 to adaptability and -.26 to self-efficacy.

Again using hierarchical multiple regression, Xu reported a significant ΔF test result for career decision-making self-efficacy (ΔF [1276] = 95.29, p < .05) with an incremental effect size ($\Delta R2$) of 0.16. He reported non-significant results and for career decision ambiguity aversion, and career indecision. In addition to the main analysis, he further examined the incremental predictions of the *CAAS* four subscales over and beyond general self-efficacy among students. He reported significant ΔF test results for both career decision self-efficacy (ΔF [4273] = 24.20, p < .05, $\Delta R2$ = 0.16) and career indecision (ΔF [4278] = 2.63, p < .05, $\Delta R2$ = 0.04) but not for ambiguity aversion nor major satisfaction. He concluded that the *CAAS* subscales showed a slightly stronger incremental predictive pattern than the *CAAS* total score among students. The results of Study 2 again supported the bi-factor model of a general factor derived from the *CAAS* items. Correlations to general self-efficacy were strong for the *CAAS* total score and weak for Concern (.16), Curiosity (-.19), and Confidence (.20).

Based on the two studies, Xu concluded that the *CAAS* total score may not provide incremental predictive power for career criteria over and beyond dispositional constructs. This conclusion hinges on conceptualizing self-efficacy as a stable dispositional trait similar to proactivity and the FFM traits, rather than malleable beliefs about performing behaviors effectively in diverse contexts. Xu's conceptualization of an alternative career construction model that begins with self-efficacy beliefs merits further research, especially using the familiar hierarchical second-order confirmatory factor analysis model for *CAAS*, rather than the bi-factor model. At his point, it seems premature to replace the *CAAS* with the 8-item *General Self-Efficacy Scale* in research and practice regarding the CCT model of career adaptation. Career adaptability self-regulation resources just seem to differ substantially from self-efficacy beliefs about adapting behaviors, which will continue for now to be sequenced in the CCT model between adapt-ability resources and adapting behaviors.

Conclusion

This Chapter reviewed nine studies that tested the full CCT model of adaptation in seven countries: Australia, Spain, China, Croatia, Iran, Turkey, and the USA. The next chapter reports research reviews of the *CAAS* literature.

CHAPTER 16

CAREER ADAPTABILITY RESEARCH REVIEWS

The research findings on career adaptability have been reviewed and described using three different approaches. Narrative reviews of the literature have focused on particular research questions posed by the reviewer. Meta-analysis has been used to statistically synthesize and summarize the quantitative research literature. And, scientometrics has been used to identify the frequent authors and central topics and their evolution.

Narrative Reviews

A narrative literature review analyzes existing research and reflection on a particular topic, and in some ways resembles a book chapter. The reviewer systematically collates available empirical evidence that fits pre-specified eligibility criteria to answer a particular research question. A literature review conducted by Sulistiani and Handoyo (2017) addressed the following research question, "What factors influence the readiness and success of career adaptability in the educational context?" They evaluated 45 articles, and concluded that only 16 article met their pre-specified criteria. Based on these studies, they concluded that the influential factors consisted of (a) demographic characteristics such as gender; (b) personality traits including conscientiousness and future orientation; and (c) social support from families and teachers.

In another systematic review of research and reflection on career adaptability, Johnston (2018) addressed the following question: "What is career adaptability and where did it come from? Her goals were to synthesize the research on career adaptability and to suggest directions for future development. The 116 published entries covered in the review consisted of book chapters and journal articles, including cross-sectional, longitudinal, and qualitative papers, along with intervention studies and theoretical contributions. The review began by describing and discussing the different instruments available to measure career adaptability.

Next, Johnston integrated the research on both adaptability resources and adapting responses. She concluded that both resources and responses contribute to positive transitions and personal functioning in teenagers and adults. She ended the review by offering several suggestions for future research, highlighting theoretical, practical, empirical, and methodological contributions that could be made by additional research on the CCT adaptation model.

In a review of literature on career adaptability published in the Portuguese language, Fiorini, Bardagi, and Silva (2016) analyzed the epistemological, theoretical, and methodological perspectives within an evolutionary framework in the field of organizational and work psychology, and more specifically in the area of career counseling. The reviewers also discussed the importance of career adaptability in the contemporary world of work, as well as the multifaceted and dynamic aspects that various studies and career counseling practice have adopted regarding the concept, from both paradigmatic and methodological approaches.

Meta-Analytic Review

A different type of review called a meta-analysis combines the findings from disparate quantitative studies using statistical methods to objectively evaluate, synthesize, and summarize results. In a meta-analysis of 90 published studies, Rudolph, Lavigne, and Zacher (2017) synthesized research findings on the relation of career adaptability resources to adaptive readiness, adapting responses, and adaptation results. They concluded that career adaptability associated significantly with measures of adaptivity (i.e., cognitive ability, FFM traits, self-esteem, core self-evaluations, proactive personality, future orientation, hope, and optimism), adapting (i.e., career planning, career exploration, occupational self-efficacy, and career decision-making self-efficacy), and adaptation (i.e., career identity, calling, career/job/school satisfaction, affective organizational commitment, job stress, employability, promotability, turnover intentions, income, engagement, self-reported work performance, entrepreneurial outcomes, life satisfaction, and negative affect). They computed multiple regression analyses based on meta-analytic correlations. The results documented the incremental predictive validity of career adaptability, above and beyond other individual difference characteristics, for a variety of career, work, and subjective well-being outcomes. Overall, the findings from their meta-analysis supported the CCT model of adaptation. Based on their analyses, they offered excellent suggestions for future research on adaptability and the career adaptation model.

Scientometric Review

To analyze the research literature on career adaptability, Chen, Fang, Liu, Pang, Wen, Chen, and Gu (2020) used scientometrics. This methodology is a sub-field of bibliometrics, one that produces quantitative descriptions of scientific topics by measuring and analyzing scholarly texts. Chen and colleagues searched the Web of Science database for the period 2010 to March 2020. They identified 20,871 documents as empirical units of data. They then analyzed this data to describe the themes, performance, and location of sub-domains of the constructs connected to career adaptability. A co-cited network map of career adaptability authors had 346 network nodes and 739 connections. The important node positions indicated that central figures in the field of career adaptability research were Savickas, Hirschi, Guan, Koen, Zacher, and Rudolph. A ranking of keywords indicated that the research hotspots in this field were mainly focused on the issues of career adaptability and scale development, the relationship with personality, structure establishment, and psychometric attributes. And finally, Chen and colleagues used keyword processing to produce a career adaptability research frontier map to show the evolution of research on career adaptability. Five clusters automatically appeared: boundaryless mindset, career adaptability scale, career construction, proactive personality, and life design. Additional topics were job success, life satisfaction, job performance, and self-efficacy. When reviewing the literature for 2010 to 2015, they found that the research mainly concentrated on two groups of topics. The first group of topics consisted of relationships to individuals, such as gender, grade, age, and personality traits. The second group of topics focused on learning. From 2016 to 2020, research attention moved to diversity of research subjects, including different types of students, refugees, corporate employees, and immigrants. Additional topics included parenting style, social support, and socioeconomic status. Chen and colleagues suggested that future research might attend to the research groups that have not received much attention, such as the adaptation of female workers to the workplace and the adjustment of diverse populations to the pandemic. Moreover they suggested that because the development of the career adaptability scale had matured, future research might use qualitative methods and field research to examine in-depth various factors that influence subjects' career adaptability.

Conclusion

Overall, the research reviews supported the CCT model of career adaptation. They also described the current state of *CAAS* research and offered excellent suggestions for future research on adaptability and the career adaptation model. The next Chapter reviews research on career-related experiences that foster the development of career adaptability resources.

CHAPTER 17

CAREER-RELATED EXPERIENCES
DEVELOP ADAPTABILITY

Career-related experiences have been shown to develop career adaptability resources. In particular, academic advising, internships, and supervisor feedback can each increase individuals' adaptability resources.

Affective Academic Advising

Academic advising assists individuals of any age by providing educational and vocational information to manage their careers. Tuna, Kanten, Yesiltas, Kanten, and Alparslan (2014) investigated the relation of career adaptability to students' description of their experience with their academic advisors. The participants consisted of 397 students who were in their final year of studying tourism and hotel management at five different universities in Turkey. Students' perceptions of academic advising were measured with 21 items (Noy & Ray, 2012) organized into three separate scales: affective, intellectual, and instrumental. Affective advising is sensitive to student needs, provides emotional support, and shows concern for both professional and personal life. Intellectual advising provides feedback, assesses progress, directs research training, and focuses on research matters. Instrumental advising focuses on professional demands of training such as funding, publishing, networking, conducting research, and teaching. In a structural model, career adaptability correlated .28 to affective advising, .13 to intellectual advising, and -.25 to instrumental advising. The focus on feelings and plans related more strongly to adaptability than did instrumental advising. It may be that instrumental advising, by concentrating on training and evaluating students, places the authority on the advisor and does not encourage students to develop adaptability resources.

Internship Experiences

During their last two years at Chinese universities, many undergraduate students participate in internships that involve structured and career-relevant work experiences. Viewing an internship as a career intervention, Pan, Guan, Wu, Han, Zhu, Fu, and Yu (2018) investigated whether internships increased career adaptability. In addition, they examined whether career adaptability mediates the relationship between proactive personality and job-search success in terms of number of job offers and starting salary. They also examined whether internship quality served as a moderator between proactive personality and career adaptability.

The researchers measured career adaptability with the *CAAS* before and after students' internships (Time 1 and Time 3). At Time 2, which was during the middle of an internship, they assessed proactive personality with the *Proactive Personality Scale* (Bateman & Crant, 1993). They also assessed internship quality with an adaptation of the *Job Diagnostic Survey* (Hackman &.Oldham, 1975). The 13-item survey measured skill variety (3 items; e.g., "How much variety in work does your internship offer?"), task identity (2 items; e.g., "How often do you complete work that has been started by another employee?"), task significance (3 items; e.g., "To what extent do the results of your work influence your co-workers?"), autonomy (3 items; e.g., "To what extent are you able to do your internship independently of others?"), and feedback (2 items; e.g., "To what extent do you receive information from your superior on your job performance?"). Job search success was measured at Time 4, which was one month before graduation, because most of the students had accepted job offers by that time. Success was indicated by when the first job offer was received and the starting salary. A total of 207 students from different Chinese universities completed the measures at all four time points.

The *CAAS* total score at Time 1 correlated .54 to the *CAAS* total score at Time 2. The *CAAS* total score at Time 2 correlated .36 to internship quality and .65 to proactive personality. The *CAAS* total score correlated to number of job offers .27 at Time 1 and .29 at Time 2. The *CAAS* total score correlated .25 to salary at Time 1 and .29 at Time 2. The path model shown in Figure 73 indicates that career adaptability related significantly to the number of offers (β = .19) and salary (β = .26). There was an indirect effect of proactive personality on the number of offers (indirect effect = .12) and salary (indirect effect = .14) via career adaptability. Furthermore, internship quality moderated the relationship between proactive personality and career adaptability. The results suggested that the interactive effects of internship quality on the link between proactive personality and career adaptability were significant (β = −.28). Career adaptability was stronger when internship quality was lower.

Figure 73. Internship Quality Influences Adaptability

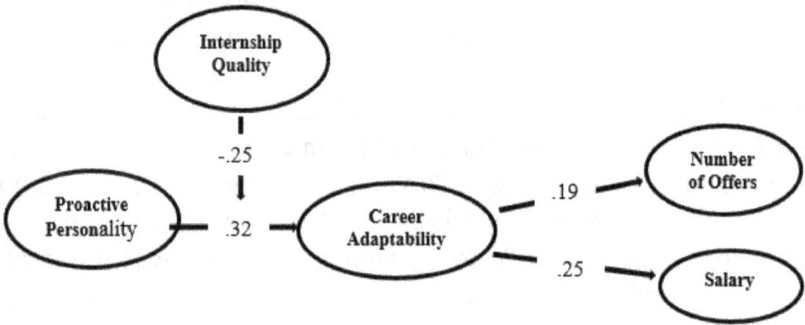

To test the mediated-moderation relationship, they examined the indirect effects at the contingent level of internship quality. Results indicated that when internship quality was low, the indirect effect was significantly positive (number of offers had indirect effect of .33; salary had an indirect effect of .40). However, when internship quality was high, the indirect effect was not significant. This suggests that contextual factors in general and internship quality in particular are more essential in determining career adaptability for those who are not very proactive. The results provide empirical

388

support for the interactive effects of adaptive readiness (i.e., proactive personality) and context (i.e., internship) on career adaptability. In sum, the researchers concluded that a high quality internship can greatly ease the process of searching for a job by fostering career adaptability.

A second study that examined internship experiences as an intervention that increases career adaptability was conducted by Ocampo, Reyes, Chen, Restubog, Chih, Chua-Garcia, and Guan (2020). They reasoned that internship experience can foster reflection, exploration, and the development of career adaptability. They suggested that not all students who participate in internships are likely to develop high levels of career adaptability because certain individual traits are likely to set crucial boundary conditions for the career-enhancing benefits of internship. They thought that the FFM trait of conscientiousness -- which involves responsibility, dutifulness, and achievement -- may be an adaptive characteristic that supports development of career adaptability during an internship. They hypothesized that, over time, highly conscientious interns exhibit greater increases in Concern, Control, Curiosity, and Confidence. To test their reasoning, they studied student interns at a five-star hotel in Guangzhou, China. The eight-week internship program was designed in accordance with the students' academic program requirements. The participants were 173 fourth-year undergraduate tourism management students. These participants were divided into internship and control groups. The internship group consisted of 48 participants (84% females) with a mean age of 21.5 years (SD = 0.8). The control group included 124 non-internship participants (70% females) with a mean age of 21.7 years (SD = 0.8). The participants were surveyed at five time points prior and after the internship program. Two months (Time 1) and two weeks (Time 2) before commencement of the internship program, participants from both the internship and control groups responded to measures of conscientiousness and career adaptability (pre-test). The internship group then completed a post-test which assessed their career adaptability immediately after the internship (Time 3), and again at two months (Time 4) and five months after the internship (Time 5). The control group also

389

completed the post-tests assessing career adaptability at the same time points as those in the internship group. Conscientiousness was measured using the 9-item scale developed by John and Srivastava (1999). The *CAAS* was used to measure career adaptability.

Results indicated that two months before the internship, the intern and control groups did not differ significantly in GPA, conscientiousness, nor all four adapt-abilities. Two weeks before the internship, students who participated in the internship had a higher level of Curiosity. The internship group generally demonstrated a continuous growth in all four career adapt-abilities. In contrast, the control group showed no growth in career adaptability except for the dimension of Concern than the control group. The estimated means of the time slope were statistically significant in the internship group, whereas the slope was only significant for the Concern dimension in the control group.

Having established an effect of internship on the growth trajectories of career adapt-abilities, the researchers examined whether conscientiousness influenced the growth trajectories for both the intern and control groups. Students who were high on conscientiousness did not experience steeper growth trajectories than students who are low on conscientiousness. Although not hypothesized, it was noteworthy that the effect of conscientiousness on the intercept term of the dimension of Curiosity (.60, $p < .05$) was significant for the internship group. Also, the effect of conscientiousness on the intercept term of the dimension of Confidence (.34, $p < .01$) was significant for the control group. For the internship group, with every one unit increase in conscientiousness, the initial level of Curiosity increased by .60. For the control group, with every one unit increase in conscientiousness, the initial level of Confidence increased by .34. A related finding was the negative covariance between the intercept and slope in all models. In the internship group, the higher the pre-internship level of a career adaptability, the more slowly it developed. The interns who scored higher on a career adaptability dimension to start with were the ones who would develop that dimension more slowly. High-conscientious interns had higher initial levels of Curiosity, but high conscientious non-interns had higher initial levels of Confidence. Conscientious and Curious students elected to enroll in the internship, while conscientious and Confident students did not do so. It seems that students who decided to pursue internship did so, in part, because they were curious about their impending careers. The researchers surmised that students make career-related decisions that they deem appropriate given their current levels of career adaptability, albeit only when the conscientiousness trait is high. This finding suggests that students with different career adaptability profiles diverge in the career paths they select. Overall, these results show that, at the outset of a career-related task, individuals' current levels of career adaptability are either constraints or facilitators of the further development of career adaptability.

Supervisor Feedback

The career management strategy of seeking feedback was studied by Gong and Tiantian (2019) who investigated relations of career adaptability to feedback environment, feedback seeking, and political skill. The participants were nurses from China who had experience in clinical practice. Their mentors were more experienced nurses or the head nurse. A total of 303 nurses (81.2% females, 18.8% males) under the age of 40 years completed the survey. In addition to measuring career adaptability with the *CAAS*, the researchers measured the feedback environment by editing Steelman and Wolfeld's (2004) scale to use "a mentor" instead of "a supervisor." The items assess seven dimensions: source credibility, feedback quality, feedback delivery, accuracy of favorable feedback, accuracy of unfavorable feedback, source availability and promoting feedback seeking. An example item reads, "My mentor gives me useful feedback about my job performance." Feedback seeking, was assessed with a 4-item measure (Callister & Turban, 1999). An example item reads, 'From my mentors' reactions, I can tell how well I am doing in my work." They also used 18 items from the *Political Skills Inventory* (Ferris, Treadway, Kolodinsky, Hochwarter, Kacmar, Douglas, & Finket, 2016) to measure social acuity (five items), interpersonal influence (four items), social ability (six items), and explicit sincerity (three items). An example item reads, "I am good at building relationships with influential people at work."

The *CAAS* total score correlated .19 to the feedback environment established by a mentor, .35 to feedback seeking, and .62 to political skill. Feedback seeking correlated .44 to political skill. The results of hierarchical regression about mediation and moderation effects indicted that the feedback environment established by a mentor associated with both nurses' feedback-seeking behavior and career adaptability. The indirect association of feedback environment with career adaptability via feedback seeking was stronger for employees with high political skill than those with low political skill. The researchers concluded that when mentors create a suitable context for feedback, nurses' career adaptability can be enhanced through feedback seeking. This was especially true for nurses with high political skill, which moderated the relationship between feedback environment and career adaptability.

A second study conducted by Gong and colleagues also investigated the relation of career adaptability to supervisor feedback environment, this time examining their relation to autonomous motivation and psychological safety. A psychologically-safe workplace is populated by supervisors and coworkers who support and respect each others' competence and can engage in constructive conflict. Research on antecedents of psychological safety among employees has focused on coworker relationships and supportive feedback, viewing an individual's beliefs about psychological safety as a result of passively accepting the influences of external factors without looking at their initiative in actively adapting to the environment. Gong, Yang, Gilal, Van Swol, and Yin (2020) addressed this oversight by viewing employees' psychological safety beliefs through the lens of career adaptability.

They conducted the study with a sample of 295 police officers from four provinces in China. Among the participants, 80.3% were males and 19.7% were females, with an average age of 31.2 years (SD = .79) and average organizational tenure of 8.62 years. The researchers operationally defined psychological safety with seven items, including the following: "On my team, it is safe to take risks and take chances on new ideas" and "When working with members of my team, my competences and talents are valued and used." They measured supervisor feedback environment using the scale constructed by Steelman, Levy, and Snell. (2004) and autonomous motivation with the goal-self concordance index devised by Deci and Ryan (2003). The researchers assessed officers' career adaptability by having supervisors rate subordinates on the 24 items of the CAAS.

The results indicated that the *CAAS* total score correlated .40 to psychological safety, .22 to autonomous motivation, and .13 to feedback environment. Psychological safety correlated .11 to autonomous motivation and .35 to feedback environment. The feedback environment played a mediating role in the relationship between career adaptability and police officers' beliefs about their psychological safety, and the relationship between career adaptability and feedback environment was more positive for individuals with lower autonomous motivation. Individuals with stronger autonomous motivation benefited less from career adaptability in terms of the feedback environment or psychological safety. The findings suggest that career adaptability resources may be more important for individuals having trouble balancing internal and external motivations. The researchers concluded that individuals with lower autonomous motivation need to give more consideration to their future work roles, control their personal professional activities, make education and career choices based on curiosity, and be confident in performing their own careers. In sum, when propelled by heteronomous motivation, individuals may rely more on supervisor feedback and need to draw more on career adaptability resources.

Conclusion

This Chapter reviewed studies that showed career-related experiences can develop career adaptability resources. In particular, academic advising, internships, and supervisor feedback can each increase individuals' adaptability resources. The next Chapter concentrates on career construction interventions that foster the development of career adaptability resources.

CHAPTER 18

CAREER ADAPTABILITY INTERVENTIONS

The discussion of interventions in this chapter is divided into four sections: psycho-education, existing interventions effect on career adaptability, interventions designed to foster career adaptability, and interventions designed to prompt adapting responses.

Psycho-Education Interventions

Psycho-education is a form of education that offers individuals generic knowledge about how to cope with specific concerns and challenges. When psycho-education concentrates on vocational behavior, CCT considers it to be a form of career education for students and career coaching for adults. Only two studies have dealt with psycho-education related to career adaptability, one involving a written text and the other a digital video.

Psycho-Education Text

To study the relation between career adaptability and intentions to seek vocational guidance, Ambiel, Moreira, Oliveira, Pereira, and Hernandez (2018) prepared a written text about the process of vocational guidance. They administered the *CAAS* to high school students (52% females) in Brazil and inquired about their intentions to seek vocational guidance. The participants consisted of 272 adolescents who ranged in age from 14 to 19 years (Mean = 16.34, SD = 0.99). The students were in the first year (36.6%), second year (32.1%), or third year (31.3%). They were asked about their interest in participating in vocational guidance after reading a text that informed them about the process. The students then selected one of three options: (1) "I would not seek vocational guidance, because I am already sure of what I want to do in the future," (2) "Although I already know what I want to do in the future, I would do a vocational guidance, because it could help me to be sure I'm on the right track," and (3) "I would seek vocational guidance, as I have no idea what I'm going to do next year." Based on the students' responses, the researchers formed three groups: Group 1 (N = 480) had no interest in seeking vocational guidance; Group 2 (N = 170) had already made a choice for the next year; and Group 3 (N = 44) had not decided about the future. To evaluate differences among the three groups, the researchers performed ANOVA tests with Tukey post hoc along with Cohen's d to determine the effect sizes for any differences. Lower levels of adaptability associated with an interest in vocational guidance. In particular, significant differences occurred on the Concern subscale between Groups 1 and 3 ($d = .53$); between Groups 2 and 3 ($d = .69$); and on the Control subscale between Groups 1 and 3 ($d = .63$). An effect size of .2 is considered small, .4 is considered medium, and .6 is considered large.

Psycho-Education Video

A unique intervention was constructed by Burrows and McArdle (2020) who developed a digital video to increase a viewer's knowledge about career adaptability as a means to prepare athletes, coaches, and athlete support providers for career transitions following upcoming Olympic and Paralympic games. The video aimed to educate viewers about upcoming career transitions including strategies they could use to adapt to the experience. In designing the 150-second video, they used entertainment-education theory to present learning points and their associated career adaptability resources pertaining to the Games experience and to strategies that could be applied to ease the transition through this experience. Each learning point addressed at least one of the adaptability resources. Entertainment-education theory proposes that outcomes can be measured by examining viewer subjective and objective recall of the intended learning points in the video because recall predicts both attitudes and intentions to change behaviors. Typically, viewers can accurately recall about 30% of the communicated information.

To be eligible to participate in this study, participants had to be older than 18 years as well as a current competitor or involved in the preparation (e.g. coach, physiotherapist, sport psychologist, performance director and physiologist) of an athlete for the Games. Participants included 116 athletes with a mean age of 26.46 years, 10 coaches with a mean age of 40.20 years and 42 athlete support providers with a mean age of 39.77.

Subjective recall was assessed by asking participants to indicate yes or no to the question, "Did you learn anything from watching this video?" To measure objective recall, participants were asked to describe what they believed they had learned from watching the video in an open text-box style question immediately following viewing and again 72 hours after viewing. Appreciation was measured by seven question such as "This video was relevant to me." Social validity was measured by two open-text box questions relating to what they liked about the video and what suggestions they had to improve the video.

Relative to subjective recall, 141 participants indicated that "yes" they learned something from the video and 14 indicated "no" they did not learn something from the video. Overall, participants accurately recalled between 1 and 3 learning points (Mean = 1.13; SD = 0.65) immediately following viewing. Sixty-six participants answered the follow-up questions at 72 hours post-viewing. At this point, participants accurately recalled between 1 and 2 learning points (Mean = 0.58; SD = 0.70). Learning point 5 ("An athlete can plan in advance for the post-Games meta-transition") was the most frequently recalled immediately post-viewing (N = 83) and 72 hours later (N = 23). Overall, participants agreed (score > 4) that they found the video enjoyable (Mean = 4.08; SD = 0.70), relevant (Mean = 4.06; SD = 0.86), and informative (Mean = 4.11; SD = 0.60). The participants said they would recommend the video to a friend (Mean = 4.14; SD = 0.74) and would watch it again (Mean = 3.96; SD = 0.87). Social validity comments centered on the length, volume of information, and suggestions for improvement. The researchers concluded that the results support the development of career adaptability videos using education-entertainment theory as a psycho-education intervention for Olympic and Paralympic athletes and their supporters.

Existing Interventions Effect on Adaptability

Four studies have examined the effects of existing workshops or courses on the career adaptability resources of the participants.

Manual-Based Workshop

Because psychosocial resources are malleable rather than fixed, Koen, Klehe, and Van Vianen (2012) investigated whether a pre-existing training workshop enhances career adaptability resources. Structured by a step-by-step manual, the workshop aimed to assist university graduates search for suitable employment during the transition from school to work. It was not designed to concentrate specifically on the four adapt-ability dimensions in particular. However, the researchers were able to match elements of the pre-existing intervention to fit the adapt-ability dimensions. They conducted a field quasi-experiment among recent university graduates, examining whether there were changes in career adaptability related to the training, as well as whether these changes remained stable over six months. A three-wave longitudinal design allowed them to compare the accomplishments of university graduates who received the career adaptability training (i.e., training group) to graduates who did not receive the training (i.e., control group). The sample consisted of students with a Bachelor's degree who were about to graduate or who had just graduated with a Master's degree from one of the largest universities in the Netherlands. A total of 93 participants took part in the study, from which 49.5% (N = 46) formed the training group and 50.5% (N = 47) formed the control group. The sample of participants that had completed all the measures at all three time periods consisted of 28 men (50%) and 28 women (50%) with an average age of 26.47 years (SD = 2.12).

Participants' career adaptability was assessed with the *CAAS* one week before the training (Time 1), three days after the training (Time 2), and six months later with the addition of measures to determine their employment status and quality (Time 3). The one-day training, offered to up to 15 participants at a time with a total duration of 8.5 hours was given by two experienced trainers from the recruitment agency who knew about the training's purpose (enhance participants' career adaptability) but who were left blind to the research questions regarding the malleability of career adaptability and its impact on employment quality.

At pre-training, the control group scored slightly higher on all four *CAAS* subscales. At post-training, the control group scored lower on three subscales but still the same degree higher on the Confidence subscale. At follow-up, the training group scored higher on all four *CAAS* subscales, with an even stronger gap on Control and Curiosity. Results of the multivariate analyses of variance (MANOVAs) indicated that the two groups showed no significant difference directly after the training (Time 2), except for a marginally significant higher mean of career Concern for the training group. However, the two groups did differ significantly at the follow-up measurement (Time 3) in Control ($p < .01$) and Curiosity ($p < .01$), with the training group showing higher scores on both dimensions.

Although the mean differences between training group and control group were not yet apparent immediately after training, the training group did show higher Control and Curiosity at the follow-up measurement than the control group, implying that the training succeeded in enhancing participants' Control and Curiosity in a more sustainable way. The effect sizes showed that training effects were detectable post-training, but were larger at the follow-up measurement, with the exception of career Concern. Arguably, the training increased participants' career adaptability resources and helped to buffer against a decrease of career adaptability. Lastly, employed participants who had taken part in the training reported higher employment quality than those who had not. Last but certainly not least, six months later among the university graduates who had found employment, the training participants reported higher employment quality than non-participants -- as reflected in higher job satisfaction, lower turnover intentions, better person-organization fit, and greater career success. However, note that the proportion of graduates who had found employment did not differ between the two groups.

Career Education versus Career Development Courses

Two different types of career courses were compared by Kim and Shin (2020) to determine their differential effectiveness in fostering career adaptability resources among first-year nursing students in Korea. They described one course as a career education intervention that provided information about careers in nursing. They described the other course as a career development intervention that prompted exploring, choosing, and planning a nursing career. The courses met for one hour each week for 15 weeks. The participants were first-year nursing students, 44 in the career education course and 46 in the career development course. Students in both courses showed significant increases in *CAAS* scores after eight weeks and after 15 weeks. The improvement in *CAAS* scores was significantly ($p < .001$) but not meaningfully higher for students in the career development course.

Career Exploration Course

A college course designed specifically to promote career exploration indirectly produced small yet significant gains in career adaptability according to a study by Cheung and Jin (2016). The theoretically-driven course was designed to enhance exploration behavior concerning the self and occupations. The course content had two foci. The first focus was on understanding career and career management issues in the 21st-century working world through lectures and seminars that presented the perspectives of sociology, psychology, and organizational behavior. The second focus was on students' understanding of their own vocational selves through group projects and workshop sessions on aptitudes, personality, vocational interests, and life-long career development. The course was delivered over 13 sessions, once a week for three hours.

A non-equivalent comparison group design was used to assess the effects of the course on students' career exploration and career adaptability by comparing results for students in the course to those

400

for students in a General Education course unrelated to career development. The data were collected during the first week of class for the pre-test and again during the last week of class for the post-test. This resulted in 172 valid responses at pre-test and 125 valid responses at post-test for the intervention group, and 218 valid responses at pre-test and 86 valid responses at post-test for the comparison group. The *CAAS* was used to measure career adaptability. Career exploration was assessed by the self-exploration and environment exploration scales of the *Career Exploration Survey* (Stumpf, Colarelli, & Hartman, 1983). Environment exploration was defined as exploration activities related to occupations, jobs, and organizations during the past three months and self-exploration as activities of self-assessment and introspection during the past three months.

The researchers anticipated that participation in the career exploration course should produce in and of itself substantial post-test gains in exploratory behaviors during the previous three months given the course content and requirements. Despite being addressed indirectly, career adaptability should increase somewhat at post-test, especially the Curiosity adapt-ability because it relates more closely to career exploration.

There were no significant differences in pre-test scores between the two groups. At post-test, the results suggested that the intervention group increased overall scores for career adaptability from 3.17 to 3.29 and three of the adapt-abilities but not Confidence. On post-test, the comparison group remained unchanged on all the dimensions of career adaptability. Repeated measures analysis of variance (ANOVA) was performed to test the Group x Time interaction effect. A significant Group x Time interaction effect suggested that the effect of time on the measure depends on the group, implying that the size of change found in the measure is significantly different between the intervention group and comparison group. In such a case, it can be argued that changes in the intervention group's measures are exclusively due to the intervention. The Group x Time ANOVA was significant for career exploration scores but not for *CAAS* scores. Although there was a

401

post-test increase in career adaptability in the intervention group, it was not significant enough when analyzed together with the comparison group, probably because the course was designed to foster career exploration and elements needed to boost career adaptability were missing.

The researchers then performed analyses of covariance (ANCOVAs) for all post-test scores. Examining the subscales of *CAAS*, they did find a significant difference for the Curiosity adapt-ability. The course effect on Curiosity became significant ($p = .027$) after controlling for pre-test group differences in gender, decidedness, and decision-making confidence. This result was not surprising considering the fact that the ANOVA Group x Time interaction effect ($p = .07$) was already close to the cut-off value of .05. Of the four adapt-abilities, it was Curiosity that was most likely to be enhanced indirectly by a course dealing with exploratory behavior.

My Career Story Workbook

An intervention centered on the *My Career Story* workbook (*MCS*; Savickas & Hartung, 2012) was developed for middle schools students by Santilli, Nota, and Hartung (2019). Using the *MCS*, the instructors prompted participants to reflect on and narrate their emerging career stories. The *MCS* includes goal-setting activities identified as critical to the efficacy of career interventions. The course did not explicitly concentrate on the career adaptation model of the motivated agent but rather the career story of the autobiographical actor. This means that the career adaptability resources were not explicitly addressed during the intervention. The researchers designed the study to evaluate the *MCS* intervention using both an experimental and a control group.

The experimental group intervention activities were conducted across three two-hour sessions spaced one week apart. This spacing allowed students to reflect on the issues addressed in the activity. During the first session, participants were also encouraged to explore their interests by completing a card sort of work activities. During the same time period, a control group engaged in activities traditionally carried out in Italian middle schools and required by the Italian school programs (MIUR, 2014). During the first two-hour session, students in both groups completed the same measures of career adaptability, hope, optimism, resilience, and orientation toward the future along with other measure related to interests, values, and study motivation. During a two to three-hour session one week later, the students in the control group received a personalized report that included suggestions about future school programs and job activities associated with their interests, values, and study motivation. This report was similar in content to the *MCS* summary life portrait written by the students in the experimental group. These reports were discussed with students in groups and a range of information about local high schools and job opportunities was also provided. The control group intervention lasted a total of about four to five hours over two sessions.

The participants were 108 middle-school students (54 girls, 54 boys) with a mean age of 13.1 years (SD = .47). The participants attended seven different classes of two public middle schools in Northeastern Italy. A total of 54 students from three separate classes within one public school participated in the career construction intervention. A control group consisted of 54 students who were recruited from four classes at another public school. Each group consisted of 27 females and 27 males.

To evaluate the effectiveness of the experimental and traditional interventions, the researchers tested the statistical significance of post-intervention change in career development variables and evaluated indicators of the social validity of the intervention. To measure hope and optimism about the future, they used the *Visions about Future* scale (Santilli, Ginevra, Sgaramella, Nota, Ferrari, & Soresi, 2015), which consists of two subscales that measures hope (e.g., "Certainly, in the future I'll be able to realize something interesting for me") and optimism (e.g., "I think I am an optimist"). To measure resilience and future orientation, they used the *Design My Future* scale (Santilli et al., 2015), which has two subscales that measure resilience (e.g., "I think I'm able to meet the difficult situations that may arise in the future for me") and future orientation (e.g., "Looking ahead and thinking about what will happen in the future makes me feel full of energy"). The *CAAS* was used to measure career adaptability. Social validity was assessed by five items that inquired about the experimental-intervention participants' satisfaction with the intervention and its utility for career planning, self- reflection, and decision making. Three items related to perceived utility of a career construction workbook (e.g., "Has it been useful for you to have completed the *MCS* workbook?"). The last two questions assessed participants' level of satisfaction with the overall program ("On the whole, how satisfied are you with the MCS project you did at school?").

Results indicated that there were no significant differences between the experimental and control groups at pre-test. The post-test analysis for treatment effects indicated that students in the experimental group experienced increases in career adaptability and future orientation compared to students in the control group in which these changes were not observed. In particular, students in the experimental group experienced increases in Concern (β = .30, p < .01) and Control (β =. 27, p < .02) compared to students in a control group. The *CAAS* total scores for males in the experimental group were 84.43 at pre-test and 91.30 at post-test. For females, the *CAAS* total scores were 88.79 at pre-test and 96.42 at post-test. The effect size was about .5. In terms of social validity, 16% were extremely satisfied with the overall program, 43% were satisfied, 30% were neutral about it, 9% reported being a little satisfied, and 2% indicated that they were not at all satisfied with the program. Specific to the *MCS* workbook, 10% of participants were extremely satisfied to have completed it, 43% were satisfied with it, 27% responded that they were neutral about it, 8% were a little satisfied, and 2% responded that they were not at all satisfied with the *MCS*. The researchers concluded that narrative interventions incorporating the *MCS* either alone or in tandem with ancillary materials may prove to be an effective and efficient means of fostering career adaptability and associated life-design goals for early adolescent youth.

Courses Designed to Increase Career Adaptability

Researchers have evaluated the effects of three different courses that were designed specifically to increase college students' career adaptability resources.

Group Guidance Career Course

Zorver (2018) designed an eight-week Career Group Guidance Program to increase students' career adaptability resources. He evaluated the course with college students in Turkey using a pre- and post-test design with a follow-up. The experimental group consisted of 11 students and the control group consisted of 28 students. The *CAAS-SF* was used to measure career adaptability. Mann Whitney U test and Wilcoxon Signed Rank Test were used to compare the significance of differences between the measurements. Results indicated a meaningful difference in favor of the experimental group. A follow-up two months later indicated the gains made by the experimental group were maintained across all four *CAAS-SF* subscales.

Career Navigation Course

A course based explicitly on CCT, called the Career Navigation Course, was designed by Lara (2009, 2016) for undecided, first-year college students in the USA. After working with Lara, Kepir Savoly adapted the course to fit the needs and characteristics of university students in Turkey. The modified course consisted of 12 weekly sessions, each lasting 90 minutes Then Kepir Savoly and Dost (2020) field tested the course at a university in Turkey. The participants were 32 college seniors who responded to an e-mail from the Registrar announcing the course. Half were assigned to the intervention group and half to the control group. The evaluation measures were the *CAAS* and the *Career Optimism Scale* (Kepir Saoly, 2017), which consists of 23 items such as "I can make the right career decisions for myself" and "I can develop necessary skills to reach my career goals." Participants responded to the measures at pre-test, post-test, and three-month follow-up. A Mann–Whitney U test indicated that at pre-test, there were no significant differences between the two groups groups on career adaptability. After the intervention, there were significant differences between the post-test scores on adaptability and optimism for the two groups, in favor of the intervention group. Also, there were significant differences between the intervention group's pre-test and post-test scores for career adaptability and career optimism in favor of the post-tests. At the three-month follow-up of the intervention group, there were no significant differences in test scores between the post-test and follow-up.

Career Adaptability Modules in a Business Course

Career adaptability interventions were embedded in an an undergraduate course in organizational behavior by Salvador and Teckchandani (2020). The four modules consisted of activities that provide opportunities for career exploration, each with the goal of developing a higher level of career adaptability. Salvador and Teckchandani outlined the four modules in Figure 74. They include detailed lesson plans for each module in appendices to their article.

Figure 74. Career Exploration and Adaptability Modules

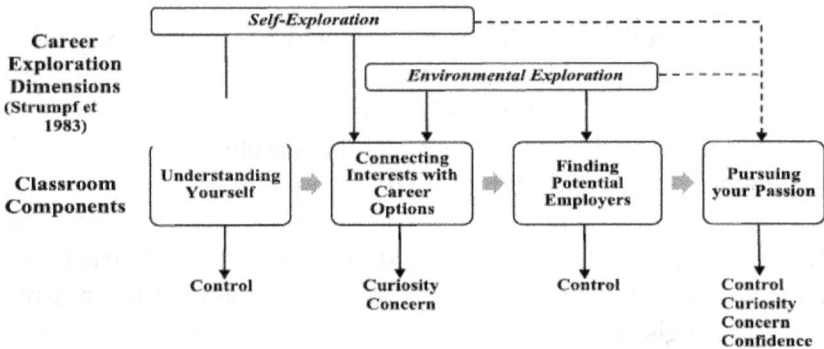

Courses Designed to Increase Adapting Responses

The previous three courses concentrated directly on increasing students' career adaptability resources. The three studies in this section report results for courses that concentrated directly on increasing students' career adapting responses and indirectly on increasing students' career adaptability resources. The researchers anticipated that developing adapting responses would also enhance students' adaptability resources.

Career Planning Course

The effectiveness of an intervention that concentrated on adapting behaviors was investigated by Fouad, Ghosh, Chang, Figueiredo, and Bachhuber (2016). The career planning course was a two-credit hour course offered by the university to help first- and second-year college students choose their majors and plan their future careers. Of the students, 56 (37 females and 19 males) completed both the pre-test and post-test measures. The majority of students (48) were in their first year. They responded to three inventories. The first inventory measured adapting behaviors with the *Occupational Engagement Scale for Students* (Krieshok, Black, & McKay, 2009), which consists of 14 items that assess activities students engage in to explore their vocational identities and the world of work. The second inventory of adapting behaviors was the *Student Career Construction Inventory* (Savickas, M., Porfeli, Hilton, & Savickas, S., 2018). The third inventory, the *CAAS*, assessed adaptability resources rather than adapting behaviors. The post-test results showed increases in adapting behaviors but not adaptability resources. The findings indicated significant (p < . 05) increases on the *Occupational Engagement Scale* and three scales from the *Student Career Construction Inventory*, namely occupational exploration, career decision making, and instrumentation. The results indicated that the course's concentration on behaviors did indeed increase career adapting responses. However, the intervention did not meaningfully effect the career adaptability resources of the students. The *CAAS* post-test scores increased slightly for three subscales but not the Concern subscale.

On-Line Module

Based on the career adaptation model, Teychenne, Sahlqvist, Teychenne, Macfarlane, Dawson, and Costigan (2017) developed an on-line module specifically for university students who were enrolled in a public health curriculum. The two-hour module aims to help students develop adapting beliefs and behaviors relative to effective job planning and seeking. The authors asserted that developing these responses would also enhance students' adaptability and employability. The materials targeted adapting behaviors directly related to the four adapt-abilities. Relative to Concern, the materials deal with career planning strategies; Control materials deal with decision-making self-efficacy. Curiosity materials deal with exploring career paths relevant to their course of study; and Confidence materials deal with skills awareness and problem solving. Teychenne and colleagues (2017) evaluated the module with a pilot test in which 22 students reported their perceptions of the module. Most students reported that the module motivated them to reflect on additional qualifications as well as skills and work experience needed to increase competitiveness when applying for relevant jobs. Furthermore, most students reported that the module activities inspired them to conduct their own research into potential jobs and guided them make choices about their career direction.

In a second study, Teychenne and colleagues (2019) tested the effectiveness of the on-line module using a pre-test/post-test design. The study included 80 participants who completed both the pre- and post-test. Findings indicated that taking the on-line module resulted in small yet significant improvements in career adapting responses including preparing for the future, learning planning strategies, identifying new career choice alternatives, increasing decision-making skill, and enhancing problem-solving confidence,

Career Adaptation Course

An innovative course based on the adaptation model of career construction theory was designed by Green, Noor, and Hashemi (2020). Rather than just focus on career adaptability as most courses have, they implemented training components for the first three dimensions of the career adaptation model, omitting the

408

fourth dimension of adaptation results. They represented the components in the model using (a) proactive personality to represent adaptive readiness, (b) the four career adapt-ability resources to represent adaptability resources, and (c) planning, exploring, and occupational self-efficacy behaviors to represent adapting responses. The theory-driven training course included a facilitator's manual to guide the training leaders. The training components were delivered over seven sessions as well as an introductory and a closing session. Session 1 concentrated on proactive personality and Session 2 focused on career adaptability and its dimensions. Session three dealt with "predict," including such topics as developing foresight and visualizing future scenarios of success. Session 4 dealt with "prevent" in terms of identifying and addressing barriers to a successful transition into the workplace as well as the importance of problem-solving skills. Session 5 dealt with "plan" in terms of decision making and planning competencies as well as a personal Strengths, Weaknesses, Opportunities, and Threats (SWOT) analysis. Session 6 focused on career "explore." Session 7 deal with how to "perform" the school-to-work transition and building resilience. The trainer delivered this content using lectures and a variety of experiential learning activities

The participants were 98 students in the final year of a Bachelor of Business Administration degree at Islamabad University. The 57 men and 41 women, with a mean age of 24.21 years (SD = 1.32) were randomly assigned to a training and a control group. Adaptivity was measured with the 17-item version of the *Proactive Personality Scale* (*PPS*; Bateman & Crant, 1993). Adaptability was measured with the *CAAS*. The *CAAS* and *PPS* were administered at one month pre-training (Time 1), post-training (Time 2), and follow-up six months later (Time 3). Adapting responses were measured only at Time 3. The adapting responses were measured with the (a) Thinking and Planning subscale of the *Career Salience Inventory* (Greenhaus, 1971); (b) *Environmental Exploration Scale* (Stumpf, Colarelli, & Hartmann, 1983); (c) *Occupational Self-Efficacy Scale* (Schyns & von Collani, 2002); and the *Career Decision-Making Self-Efficacy Scale* (Betz, Klein, & Taylor, 1996).

There were no statistically significant differences at pre-test between the two groups on gender, age, proactivity, nor career adaptability. Results at both Time 2 and Time 3 indicated that the training enhanced students' proactivity and career adaptability resources in a more sustainable manner. The effect sizes showed that the intervention effects were visible at Time 2 (post-test) yet were larger at Time 3 (follow-up). The effect sizes were for Concern .75 at Time 2 and 1.34 at Time 3; Control .69 at Time 2 and 1.42 at Time 3; Curiosity .80 at Time 2 and 1.17 at Time 3; and Confidence .75 at Time 2 and .91 at Time 3. Thus, the pattern of effect sizes indicated that the training increased students' proactivity and career adaptability resources both immediately and in the long run. Furthermore, proactive personality and career adaptability resources related more strongly to each of the career adapting responses in the training group than in the control group at Time 3. For example, at Time 3, proactivity and Concern correlated .51 for the training group and .32 for the control group. This suggests that the intervention may have been responsible for strengthening associations between the aforementioned variables at Time 3.

Even more impressive was the finding of a significant difference between the training and the control group with regard to the development of overall adapting responses six months later, ($F = 19.85$, $p < .001$). Recall that the four adapting responses were measured only at Time 3 so there was no practice effect. The effect sizes were 1.39 for planning, 1.21 for exploring, 1.03 for career decision-making self-efficacy, and .71 for occupational self-efficacy.

Conclusion

This Chapter discussed interventions that have been shown to increase participants' career adaptability resources. Four groups of interventions were considered: psycho-education, existing interventions effect on career adaptability, intervention designed to foster career adaptability, and interventions designed to prompt adapting responses.

CHAPTER 19

AFTERWORD

The preceding Chapters reviewed and synthesized empirical findings that have accumulated during the first decade of research on career adaptability. The findings have come from many different sources and diverse disciplines. In the present book, I formally integrated them into a body of scientific knowledge that can serve as a basis for further conceptualization and investigation. The integration was organized by a conceptual framework for programmatic research suggested by Edwards and Cronbach (1952) and Crites (1969).

The programmatic research on career adaptability has followed a sequential strategy that progressed across five distinct stages with different research methods: survey, technique, critical, theoretical, and applied. The program of research on career adaptability began with a *survey study* of existing literature related to the construct of career adaptability, followed by reflection on the findings to identify dimensions of the construct and variables to which it may relate. The survey led to understanding how career adaptability differs from career maturity, its possible dimensions, proposed definitions, and place in a model of career adaptation. The second stage in the programmatic strategy involved *technique research* that developed an operational definition with which to make the construct of career adaptability observable, quantifiable, and measurable. This strategy produced the *Career Adapt-Abilities Scale* and the *Student Career Construction Inventory*. The third stage consisted of *critical research* that used the inventories to establish a coherent nomological network of empirical relationships between career adaptability and related constructs. The fourth stage involved *theoretical research* that tested hypotheses concerning relations among adaptivity, adaptability, adapting, and adaptation. The final stage, which has begun just recently, is *applied research* to determine how educational, counseling, and coaching interventions might develop the career adaptability of students and employees.

411

Increased understanding of career adaptability and the Career Construction Theory model of adaptation continues to progress through a series of successive approximations advanced by reflection and research. Reflecting on the studies reported in the present book led me to identify several research suggestions. The research ideas follow, in no particular order.

An immediate research need is the creation and validation of educational, counseling, and coaching intervention methods and materials to develop career adaptability resources among students and employees.

Future research could investigate adding an interaction term of "work volition beliefs x self-efficacy beliefs" in a regression model to explore whether the interaction term shows a combined effect instead of only their separate effects on adapting behavior.

It would be illuminating to study simultaneously the relations of career adaptability to beliefs about both work volition and self-efficacy, and their consequent relations to adaptation results.

The research that has examined adaptivity in terms of personality traits indicates that further research might concentrate on crafting a specific measure of career adaptivity that is a compound of proactivity, conscientiousness, and openness ... possibly imitating how the *Core Self-Evaluation Scale* was designed and developed by Judge, Erez, Bono, and Thoresen (2003).

It may be useful to further examine the potential of emotional intelligence as an indicator of adaptivity, particularly in comparison to proactivity, openness, and conscientiousness.

Preliminary research suggests further examination of how intrapersonal career adaptation variables relate to interpersonal cooperation during times of career transition. This research could test that proposition that the *CAAS* measures internal resources activated within the self, whereas the *Cooperation Scale* measures external resources activated within the community.

Longitudinal studies may test whether career adaptability continues to develop during adulthood. Based on the current research findings, one might conclude that career adaptability increases with age through childhood and adolescence yet does not keep developing during adulthood. In adulthood, the resources may be activated and strengthened during times of occupational transitions.

Developmental research could investigate the assertion by Shin and Lee (2017) that secure attachment may foster career adaptability resources and promote adapting responses. In contrast, insecure attachment may cause individuals to under-develop adaptability resources and adopt dysfunctional strategies to deal with vocational tasks, occupational transitions, and work troubles.

Current research findings suggest that career adaptability should be treated as a multi-dimensional construct whose dimensions are not mutually interchangeable and thus merit further investigation of the four adapt-abilities' differential effects regarding outcomes of interest.

Future research should examine the role of the four adapt-abilities in different circumstances and outcomes. For example, what does Curiosity mean when career planning or vocational identity is high versus low.

It would be useful to study variability of profile shapes among individuals with the same level of adaptability and consider nuances of interpretation for commonly occurring distinct profiles.

Although the career adapt-abilities have commonalities, they play different roles in predicting adaptation outcomes and even suppress each other when considered in parallel. For example, the pairing of Control and Confidence seems to be more strongly related to social outcomes than does the pairing of Control and Curiosity. Another example involves time perspective, with Concern relating to future focus while Control relates to present focus.

In sum, while the research reported herein has done much to explain the construct of career adaptability, full understanding of its meaning, measurement, and malleability is far from complete. The construct of career adaptability will become even more comprehensible with the continued study of a number and variety of empirical and hypothetical relationships.

REFERENCES

Aguinis, H., & Bradley, K. J. (2014). Best practice recommendations for designing and implementing experimental vignette methodology studies. *Organizational Research Methods, 17*, 351–371.

Ahari, Z. H. M., Azman, N., Rasul, M. S. (2019). Factors predicting career choice among Malaysian students in skills-based training institutions. *International Journal for Educational and Vocational Guidance, 19*, 19-39.

Akca, Y., Ozer, G., & Kalaycioglu, E. (2018). Impact of career adaptability on employee performance. *International Journal of Business and Management Invention, 7*, 24-28.

Akkermans, J., Brenninkmeijer, V., Huibers, M., and Blonk, R. W. B. (2013). Competencies for the contemporary career: Development and preliminary validation of the career competencies questionnaire. *Journal of Career Development, 40*, 245–267.

Akkermans, J., Paradnike, K., Van der Heijden, M., DeVos, A. (2019). The best of both worlds: The role of career adaptability and career competencies in students' well-being and performance. *Frontiers in Psychology, 12*, https://doi.org/10.3389/fpsyg.2018.01678

Albien, A. J., Kidd, M., Naidoo, A. V., & Maree, J. G. (2020). Mixed-methods analysis of the applicability of the *Career Adapt-Abilities Scale* for isiXhosa-speaking South African township adolescents. *International Journal of Educational and Vocational Guidance, 20*, 1–29.

Allport, G. W. (1961). *Pattern and growth in personality*. (1961). New York: Holt, Rinehart, & Winston.

Aluja, A., Kuhlman, M., & Zuckerman, M. (2010). Development of the Zuckerman–Kuhlman–Aluja Personality Questionnaire (ZKA-PQ): A factor/facet version of the Zuckerman–Kuhlman Personality Questionnaire (ZKPQ). *Journal of Personality Assessment, 92*, 416–431.

Amarnani, R., Garcia, P. R. J. M., Restubog, S. L. D., Bordia, P., & Bordia, S. (2018). Do you think I'm worth it? The self-verifying role of parental engagement in career adaptability and career persistence among STEM students. *Journal of Career Assessment, 26*, 77-94.

Ambiel, R. A. M., Carvalho, L. F., Martins, G. H., Tofoli, L. (2016). Comparing the adaptabilities of Brazilian adolescent students and adult workers. *Journal of Vocational Behavior, 94*, 20-27.

Ambiel, R. A. M., Moreira, T. C., Oliveira, D. A., Pereira, E. C., & Hernandez, D. N. (2018). Self-efficacy, adaptability, and intention of searching for vocational guidance in adolescents. *Paideia, 28*, 1-18.

Ambiel, R. A. M., &, Noronha, A. P. P. (2012). *Escala de Autoeficácia para Escolha Profissional: manual técnico*. São Paulo, Brazil: Casa do Psicológo.

Ang, S., & Van Dyne, L. (2008). *Handbook of cultural intelligence: Theory, measurement and applications*. Armonk, NY: ME Sharpe.

Antonovsky, A. (1987). *Unraveling the mystery of health: How people manage stress and stay well*. San Francisco, CA: Jossey-Bass.

Arthur, M. B., Claman, P. H., & DeFillippi, R. J. (1995). Intelligent enterprise, intelligent careers. *Academy of Management Executive, 9*, 7–20.

Arthur, S &. Sheffrin , S. M. (2003). *Economics: Principles in action*. Upper Saddle River, New Jersey: Pearson Prentice Hall.

Ashton, M. C., & Lee, K. (2009). The HEXACO-60: A short measure of the major dimensions of personality. *Journal of Personality Assessment, 91*, 340–345.

Atac, L. O., Dirik, D., & Tetik, H. T. (2018). Predicting career adaptability through self-esteem and social support: A research on young adults. *International Journal of Educational and Vocational Guidance, 18*, 45-61.

Autin, K. L., Douglass, R. P., Duffy, R. D., England, J. W., & Allan, B. A. (2017). Subjective social status, work volition, and career adaptability: A longitudinal study. *Journal of Vocational Behavior, 99*, 1-10.

Avram, E., Burtaverde, V., Zanfirescu, A-S. (2019). The incremental validity of career adaptability in predicting academic performance. *Social Psychology of Education, 22*, 867-882.

Bacanli, H., İlhan, T., & Aslan, S. (2009). The development of a personality scale based on the five factor theory: the personality test based on adjustments (SDKT). *Turkish Journal of Educational Sciences, 7*, 261-279.

Bass, B. M. (1985). *Leadership and performance beyond expectations*. New York: Free Press.

416

Bateman, T. S., & Crant, J. M. (1993). The proactive component of organizational behavior: A measure and correlates. *Journal of Organizational Behavior, 14*, 103–118.

Baumeister, R. F., & Vohs, K. D. (2007). Self-regulation, ego depletion, and motivation. *Social and Personality Psychology Compass, 1*, 1-14.

Bedeian, A. G., Kemery, E. R., & Pizzolatto, A. B. (1991). Career commitment and expected utility of present job as predictors of turnover intentions and turnover behavior. *Journal of Vocational Behavior, 39*, 331–343.

Berzonsky, M. (1989). Identity style. *Journal of Adolescent Research 4*, 268-282.

Betz, N. E., Klein, K. L., & Taylor, K. M. (1996). Evaluation of a short form of the Career Decision-Making Self-Efficacy Scale. *Journal of Career Assessment, 4*, 47-57.

Bimrose, J., & Hearne, L. (2012). Resilience and career adaptability: Qualitative studies of adult career counseling. *Journal of Vocational Behavior, 81*, 338-344.

Bipp, T., Kleingeld, A., & van Dam, K. (2018). Approach and avoidance temperament: An examination of its construct and predictive validity at work. *European Journal of Psychological Assessment. 34*, 284.

Bloch, A. (2002). *Refugees' opportunities and barriers in employment and training*. Leeds, UK: Corporate Document Services.

Blustein, D. L. (2006). *The psychology of working: A new perspective for career development, counseling, and public policy*. New York, NY: Routledge.

Bolukbasi, A., & Kirdok, O. (2019). The mediating role of future orientation in the relationship between career adaptability and life satisfaction in high school students. *Education and Science, 44*, 77-91.

Brandtstadter, J., & Renner, G. (1990). Tenacious goal pursuit and flexible goal adjustment: Explication and age-related analysis of assimilative and accommodative strategies of coping. *Psychology of Aging, 5*, 58-67.

Brandstadter, J. & Rothermund, K. (2002). The life-course dynamics of goal pursuit and goal adjustment: A two-process framework. *Developmental Review, 22*, 117-150.

Brasseur, S., Gregoire, J., Bourdu, R., & Mikolajczak, M. (2013). The profile of emotional competence (PEC): Development and validation of a self-reported measure that fits dimensions of emotional competence theory. *PLoS One, 8,* 1–8.

Brayfield, A. H., & Rothe, H. F. (1951). An index of job satisfaction. *Journal of Applied Psychology, 35,* 307-311.

Brisbin, L. A., & Savickas, M. L. (1994). Career indecision scales do not measure foreclosure. *Journal of Career Assessment, 2,* 352–363.

Briscoe, J. P., Hall, D. T., & DeMuth, R. I. (2006). Protean and boundaryless careers: An empirical exploration. *Journal of Vocational Behavior, 69,* 30-47.

Brown, A., Bimrose, J., Barnes, S. A., & Hughes, D. (2012). The role of career adaptabilities for mid-career changers. *Journal of Vocational Behavior, 80,* 754-761.

Brown, S. D., Hacker, J., Abrams, M., Carr, A., Rector, C., Lamp, K., Telander, K. J., & Siena, A. (2012). Validation of a four-factor model of career indecision. *Journal of Career Assessment, 20,* 3–21.

Bruchon-Schweizer, M., & Paulhand, I. (1993). *The French adaptation of the Spielberger STAI-Y manual.* Paris, France, ECPA.

Buyukgoze-Kavas, A., (2014). Validation of the Career Adapt-Abilities Scale-Turkish Form and its relation to hope and optimism. *Australian Journal of Career Development, 23,* 125-132.

Buyukgoze-Kavas, A., Duffy, R. D., & Douglas, R. P. (2015). Exploring links between career adaptability, work volition, and well-being among Turkish students. *Journal of Vocational Behavior 90,* 122–131.

Cable, D. M., & DeRue, D. S. (2002). The convergent and discriminant validity of subjective fit perceptions. *Journal of Applied Psychology, 87,* 875–884.

Cable, D. M., & Judge, T. A. (1996). Person–organization fit, job choice decisions, and organizational entry. *Organizational Behavior and Human Decision Processes, 67,* 294–311.

Cabras, C. & Mondo, M. (2018). Future orientation as a mediator between career adaptability and life satisfaction in university students. *Journal of Career Development, 45,* 597-609.

Cai Z, Guan Y, Li H, Shi W, Guo K, Liu Y, Li Q, Han X, Jiang P, Fang Z, Hua H. (2015) Self-esteem and proactive personality as predictors of future work self and career adaptability: An examination of mediating and moderating processes. *Journal of Vocational Behavior*, 86, 86-94.

Callister, R. R., & Turban, D. B. (1999). Feedback seeking following career transitions. *Academy of Management Journal*, *42*, 429–438.

Cammann, C., Fichman, M., Jenkins, D., & Klesh, J. (1979). *Michigan Organizational Assessment Questionnaire*. Ann Arbor: University of Michigan.

Campion. E. D. (2018). The career adaptive refugee: Exploring the structural and personal barriers to refugee resettlement. *Journal of Vocational Behavior, 105*, 6-16.

Carson, K. D., Carson, P. P., Phillips, J. S., & Roe, C. W. (1996). A career entrenchment model: Theoretical development and empirical outcomes. *Journal of Career Development, 22*, 273–286.

Carver, C. S. (1997. You want to measure coping but your protocol's too long: Consider the Brief Cope. *International Journal of Behavioral Medicine 4*, 92.

Carver, C. S., & White, T. L. (1994). Behavioral inhibition, behavioral activation, and affective responses to impending reward and punishment: The BIS/BAS Scales. *Journal of Personality and Social Psychology, 67*, 319–333.

Celen-Demirtas, S., Konstam, V., & Tomek, S. (2015). Leisure activities in unemployed emerging adults: Links to career adaptability and subjective well-being. *Career Development Quarterly, 63*, 209-222.

Celik, P., & Storme, M. (2018). Trait emotional intelligence predicts academic satisfaction through career adaptability. *Journal of Career Assessment, 26*, 666-677.

Chan, K.Y., Ho, M.H.R., Chernyshenko, O. S., Bedford, O., Uy, M. A., Gomulya, D. et.al. (2012). Entrepreneurship, professionalism, leadership: A framework and measure for understanding boundaryless careers. *Journal of Vocational Behavior, 81*, 73-88.

Chan, K. Y., Uy, M. A., Ho, M. R., San, Y. L., Chernyshenko, O. S., Yu, K. T. (2015). Comparing two career adaptability measures for career construction theory: Relations with boundaryless mindset and protean career attitudes. *Journal of Vocational Behavior, 87*, 22-33.

419

Chen, H., Fang, T., Liu, F., Pang, L., Wen, Y. Chen, S., & Gu, X. (2020). Career adaptability research: A literature review with scientific knowledge mapping in Web of Science. *International Journal of Environmental Research and Public Health, 17*, 5986.

Chen, G., Gully, S. M., & Eden, D. (2001). Validation of a new General Self-Efficacy Scale. *Organizational Research Methods, 4*, 62–83.

Chen, Y. F., & Tjosvold, D. (2006). Participative leadership by American and Chinese managers in China: The role of relationships. *Journal of Management Studies, 43*, 1727–1752.

Chen, Y. P. (2012). *A three-stage process model of self-initiated expatriate career transitions: A self-determination theory perspective.* Unpublished doctoral dissertation, University of Wisconsin-Milwaukee.

Chen, Y., Friedman, R., Yu, E., Fang, W., and Lu, X. (2009). Supervisor–subordinate guanxi: Developing a three-dimensional model and scale. *Management and Organizational Review, 5*, 375–399.

Chen, Z. X., & Aryee, S. (2007). Delegation and employee work outcomes: An examination of the cultural context of mediating processes in China. *Academy of Management Journal, 50*, 226–238.

Chen, Z. X., Tsui, A. S., & Farh, J. L. (2002). Loyalty to supervisor vs. organizational commitment: Relationships to employee performance in China. *Journal of Occupational and Organizational Psychology, 75*, 339–356.

Cheung, G. W., & Rensvold, R. B. (2002). Evaluating goodness-of-fit indexes for testing measurement invariance. *Structural Equation Modeling: A Multidisciplinary Journal, 9*, 233–255.

Cheung, R., & Jin, Q., (2916). Impact of a career exploration course on career decision making, adaptability, and relational support in Hong Kong. *Journal of Career Assessment, 24*, 481-496.

Chong, S., & Leong, F. T. L. (2017). Antecedents of career adaptability in strategic career management. *Journal of Career Assessment, 25*, 268-280.

Clance, P. R., & Imes, S. A. (1978). The imposter phenomenon in high achieving women: Dynamics and therapeutic intervention. *Psychotherapy: Theory, Research & Practice, 15*, 241–247.

Cohen, J. (1988). *Statistical power analysis for the behavioral sciences.* Hillsdale, NJ: Erlbaum.

Cohen, S., Kamarck, T., & Mermelstein, R. (1983). A global measure of perceived stress. *Journal of Health and Social Behavior, 24*, 385–396.

Coetzee, M. (2008). Psychological career resources and subjective work experiences of working adults: A South African survey. *South African Journal of Industrial Psychology, 34*, 32–41.

Coetzee, M. (2012). A framework for developing student graduateness and employability in the economic and management sciences at the University of South Africa. In M. Coetzee, J. Botha, N. Eccles, N. Holtzhausen, & H. Nienabe (Eds). *Developing student graduateness and employability: Issues, provocations, theory and practical guidelines* (pp. 119-152). Randburg: Knowres.

Coetzee, M., Ferreira, N., & Potgieter, I. L. (2015). Assessing employability capacities and career adaptability in a sample of human resource professionals. *SA Journal of Human Resource Management/SA Tydskrif vir Menslikehulpbronbestuur, 13*, Art. #682, 9 pages.

Coetzee, M., & Harry, N. (2014). Emotional intelligence as a predictor of employees' career adaptability. *Journal of Vocational Behavior, 84*, 90-97.

Coetzee, M., & Harry, N. (2015). Gender and hardiness as predictors of career adaptability: An exploratory study among Black call centre agents. *South Africa Journal of Psychology, 45*, 81–92.

Coetzee, M., & Schreuder, D. (2018). Proactive career self-management: Exploring links among psychosocial career attributes and adaptability resources. *South African Journal of Psychology, 48*, 206-218.

Coetzee, M., & Stoltz, E. (2015). Employees' satisfaction with retention factors: Exploring the role of career adaptability. *Journal of Vocational Behavior, 89*, 83-91.

Colarelli, S. M., Dean, R. A., & Konstans, C. (1987). Comparative effects of personal and situational influences on job outcomes of new professionals. *Journal of Applied Psychology, 72*, 558–566.

Costa, P. T., & MacCrae, R. R. (1992). *Revised NEO personality inventory (NEO PI-R) and NEO five-factor inventory (NEO FFI): Professional manual*. Odessa, FL: Psychological Assessment Resources.

Crant, J. M. (2000). Proactive behavior in organizations. *Journal of Management, 26,* 435–462.

Crocetti, E., Rubini, M., & Meeus, W. (2008). Capturing the dynamics of identity formation in various ethnic groups: Development and validation of a three-dimensional model. *Journal of Adolescence, 31,* 207–222.

Crites, J. O. (1965). Measurement of vocational maturity in adolescence: 1. Attitude Scale of the Vocational Development Inventory. *Psychological Monographs, 79* (2, Whole no. 595).

Crites, J. O., (1969). *Vocational psychology: The study of vocational behavior and development.* New York: McGraw-Hill.

Crites, J. O. (1981). *Career Mastery Inventory.* Rootstown, OH: Vocopher.com

D'Alessio, M., Guarino, A., Pascalis, V. D., & Zimbardo, P. G. (2003). Testing Zimbardo's Stanford Time Perspective Inventory (STPI) — Short Form. *Time & Society, 2,* 333–347.

De Bruin, G. P. (2006). The dimensionality of the General Work Stress Scale: A hierarchical exploratory factor analysis. *SA Journal of Industrial Psychology, 32,* 68–75.

de Guzman, A. B., & Choi, K. O. (2013)). The relations of employability skills to career adaptability among technical skill students. *Journal of Vocational Behavior, 82,* 199-207.

Deci, E. L., & Ryan, R. M. (2003). *Intrinsic motivation inventory. Self-determination theory.* http://selfdeterminationtheory.org

Deci, E. L., Ryan, R. M., Gagné, M., Leone, D. R., Usunov, J., & Kornazheva, B. P. (2001). Need satisfaction, motivation, and well-being in the work organizations of a former Eastern bloc country: A cross-cultural study of self-determination. *Personality and Social Psychology Bulletin, 27,* 930–942.

Department of Skills Development (2012). *Level of acceptance on skills training in Malaysia* (Internal Report). Putrajaya, Malaysia.

Diener, E. D., Emmons, R. A., Larsen, R. J., & Griffin, S. (1985). The Satisfaction with Life Scale. *Journal of Personality Assessment, 49*, 71–75.

Diener, E., Wirtz, D., Tov, W., Kim-Prieto, C., Choi, D., Oishi, S., & Biswas-Diener, R. (2009). New measures of well-being: Flourishing and positive and negative feelings. *Social Indicators Research, 39*, 247-266

Dietrich, J., & Kracke, B. (2009). Career-specific parental behaviors in adolescents' development. *Journal of Vocational Behavior, 75*, 109,-119.

Di Fabio, A., & Kenny, M. E. (2016). From decent work to decent lives: Positive self and relational management in the twenty-first century. *Frontiers in Psychology, 7*, 361.

Dik, B. J., Eldridge, B. M., Steger, M. F., & Duffy, R. D. (2012). Development and validation of the Calling and Vocation Questionnaire (CVQ) and Brief Calling Scale (BCS). *Journal of Career Assessment, 20*, 242–263.

Di Maggio, I., Ginevra, M. C., Nota, L., Ferrari, L., & Soresi, S. (2015). Career Adapt-Abilities Scale-Italian Form: Psychometric proprieties with Italian pre-adolescents. *Journal of Vocational Behavior, 91*, 46-53.

Di Maggio, I., Ginevra, M. C., Nota, L., & Soresi, S. (2016). Development and validation of an instrument to assess future orientation and resilience in adolescence. *Journal of Adolescence, 51*, 114-122.

Donnellan, M. B., Oswald, F. L., Baird, B. M., & Lucas, R. E. (2006). The Mini-IPIP: Tiny-yet-effective measures of the Big Five factors of personality. *Psychological Assessment, 18*, 192-203.

Douglass, R. P., Duffy, R. D. (2015). Calling and career adaptability among undergraduate students. *Journal of Vocational Behavior, 86*, 58-65.

Dries, N., Van Esbroeck, R., van Vianen, A. E. M., De Cooman, R., & Pepermans, R. (2012). Career Adapt-Abilities Scale - Belgium Form: Psychometric characteristics and construct validity. *Journal of Vocational Behavior, 80*, 674-679.

Duarte, M. E., Soares, M. C., Fraga, S., Rafael, M., Lima, M. R., Paredes, I., Agostinho, R., & Djaló, A. (2012). Career Adapt-Abilities Scale– Portugal Form: Psychometric properties and relationships to employment status. *Journal of Vocational Behavior 80*, 725-729.

Duffy, R. D., Allan, B. A., England, J. W., Blustein, D. L., Autin, K. L., Douglass, R. P., Santos, E. J. R. (2017). The development and initial validation of the Decent Work Scale. *Journal of Counseling Psychology, 64*, 206–221.

Duffy, R. D., Deimer, M. A., & Jadidian, A. (2011). The development and initial validation of the Work Volition Scale - Student Version. *The Counseling Psychologist, 40*, 291-319.

Duffy, R. D., Diemer, M. A., Perry, J. C., Laurenzi, C., & Torrey, C .L. (2012). The construction and initial validation of the Work Volition Scale. *Journal of Vocational Behavior, 80*, 400–411.

Duffy, R. D., Douglas, R. P., & Autin, K. L. (2015). Career adaptability and academic satisfaction: Examining work volition and self-efficacy of as mediators. *Journal of Vocational Behavior, 90*, 46-54.

Dumulescu, D., Balazsi, R., & Opre, A. (2015). Calling and career competencies among Romanian students: The mediating role of career adaptability. *Procedia: Social and Behavioral Sciences, 209*, 25-32.

Dunn, K. J., & McCray, G. (2020). The place of the bi-factor model in confirmatory factor analysis investigations into construct dimensionality in language testing. *Frontiers in Psychology*, doi.org/10.3389/fpsyg.2020.01357.

Ebenehi, A. S., Rashid, A. M., & Bakar, A. R. (2016). Predictors of career adaptability skill among higher education students in Nigeria. *International Journal for Research in Vocational Education and Training, 3*, 212-229.

Edwards, A. L., & Cronbach, L. J. (1952). Experimental design for research in psychotherapy. *Journal of Clinical Psychology, 8*, 51-59.

Einarsdóttir, S., Vilhjálmsdóttir, G., Smáradóttir, S. B., & Kjartansdóttir, G. B. (2015). A culture-sensitive approach in the development of the

Career Adapt-Abilities Scale in Iceland: Theoretical and operational considerations. *Journal of Vocational Behavior, 89*, 172-181.

Eisenberger, R., Huntington, R., Hutchison, S. & Sowa, D. (1986). Perceived organizational support, *Journal of Applied Psychology, 71*, 500-507.

Elliot, A. J., & Thrash, T. M. (2002). Approach-avoidance motivation in personality: Approach and avoidance temperaments and goals. *Journal of Personality and Social Psychology, 82*, 804-818.

Elliot, A. J., & Thrash, T. M. (2010). Approach and avoidance temperament as basic dimensions of personality. *Journal of Personality, 78*, 865–906.

Ellis, R. A., & Taylor, M. S. (1983). Role of self-esteem within the job search process. *Journal of Applied Psychology, 68*, 632–640.

Elshout, J. J., & Akkerman, A. E. (1975). *Vijf Persoonlijkheids-faktoren test 5PFT*. Nijmegen: Berkhout BV.

Entwistle, N. J. (1997). The *approaches and study skills inventory for students (ASSIST)*. Edinburgh, Scotland: Centre for Research on Learning and Instruction, University of Edinburgh.

Eryilmaz, A., & Kara, Ahmet (2017). Development of the Career Adaptability Scale for Psychological Counsellors. *The Online Journal of Counseling and Education, 6*, 18-29.

Fan, W., Hao, D., & Yuen, M. (2013). Psychometric properties of the career and talent development self-efficacy scale when used with Chinese university students. *Asian Journal of Counselling, 20*, 59–84.

Fang, W., Zhang, Y., Mei, J., Chai, X., & Fan, X. (2018). Relationships between optimism, educational environment, career adaptability and career motivation in nursing undergraduates: A cross-sectional study. *Nurse Education Today, 68*, 33-39.

Farh, J.-L., Tsui, A. S., Xin, K., & Cheng, B.-S. (1998). The influence of relational demography and Guanxi: The Chinese case. *Organization Science, 9*, 471–488.

Fasbender, U., Wohrmann, A. M., Wang, M., & Klehe, U-C (2019). Is the future still open? The mediating role of occupational future time perspective in the effects of career adaptability and aging experience on late career planning. *Journal of Vocational Behavior, 111*, 24-38.

Fawehinmi, O. O., & Yahya, K. K. (2018). Investigating the linkage between proactive personality and social support on career adaptability amidst undergraduate students. *Journal of Business and Social Review in Emerging Economies, 4*, 81-92.

Ferris, G. R., Treadway, D. C., Kolodinsky, R. W., Hochwarter, W. A., Kacmar, C. J., Douglas, C., & Frink, D. D. (2016). Development and validation of the political skill inventory. *Journal of Management, 31*, 126–152.

Fiori, M. Bollmand, G., & Rossier, J. (2015). Exploring the path through which career adaptability increases job satisfaction and lowers job stress: The role of affect. *Journal of Vocational Behavior, 91*, 113-121.

Forner, Y. (2005). À propos de la motivation à la réussite scolaire. *Carriérologie, 10, 183-194.*

Fouad, N. A., Ghosh, A, Chang, W-h., Figueiredo, C., & Bachhuber, T. (2016). Career exploration among college students. *Journal of College Student Development, 57*, 460-464.

Fraley, R. C., Waller, N. G., & Brennan, K. A. (2000). An item response theory analysis of self-report measures of adult attachment. *Journal of Personality and Social Psychology, 78*, 350–365.

Frese, M., Fay, D., Hilburger, T., Leng, K., & Tag, A. (1997). The concept of personal initiative: Operationalization, reliability and validity in two German samples. *Journal of Occupational and Organizational Psychology, 70*, 139–161

Fugate, M., Kinicki, A. J.., Ashforth, B. E. (2004). Employability: A psycho-social construct, its dimensions, and applications. *Journal of Vocational Behavior, 65*, 14-38.

Funder, D. C. (1991). Global traits: A neo-Allportian approach to personality. *Psychological Science, 2*, 31-39.

Furness, M. P. (2020). What predicts career adaptability? An application of achievement goal theory and adult attachment theory. *Journal of Career Development, 47*, 671-685.

Gao X., Xin, X., Zhou, W., & Jepsen, D. M. (2019) Combine your "Will" and "Able": Career
adaptability's influence on performance. *Frontiers in Psychology, 9*, 2695.

Gati, I., Krausz, M., & Osipow, S. H. (1996). A taxonomy of difficulties in career decision making. *Journal of Counseling Psychology, 43*, 510–526.

Ghosh, A., & Fouad, N. A. (2016). Career transitions of student veterans. *Journal of Career Assessment, 24*, 99-111.

Ghosh, A., & Fouad, N. A. (2017). Career adaptability and social support among graduating college seniors. *Career Development Quarterly, 65*, 278-283.

Ghosh, A., Kessler, M., Heyrman, K., Opelt, B., Carbonelli, M., & Fouad, N. A. (2019). Student veteran career transition readiness, career adaptability, and academic and life satisfaction. *Career Development Quarterly, 67*, 365-371.

Ginevra, M. C. (2013, December). Vision about Future: Uno strumento per misurare la speranza e l'ottimismo nel counseling [Visions About Future: An instrument to assess hope and optimism in counseling]. Paper presented at the Italian Conference "Counselling e Career Counselling: valutazioni e certificazioni," Padova, Italy.

Ginevra, M. C., Magnano, P., Lodi, E., Annovazzi, C., Camussi, E., Patrizi, P., & Nota, L. (2018). The role of career adaptability and courage on life satisfaction in adolescence. *Journal of Adolescence, 62*, 1-8.

Ginevra, M. C., Sgaramella, T. M., Ferrari, L., Nota, L., Santilli, S., & Soresi, S. (2016). Visions About Future: A new scale assessing optimism, pessimism, and hope in adolescents. *International Journal for Educational and Vocational Guidance, 17*, 187-210.

427

Goldberg, L. (1992). The development of markers for the Big-Five factor structure. *Psychological Assessment, 4*, 26–42.

Gong, Z. & Tiantian, L. (2019). Relationship between feedback environment established by mentor and nurses' career adaptability: A cross-sectional study. *Journal of Nursing Management, 27*, 1568-1575.

Gong, Z., Yang, J., Gilal, F. G., Van Swol, L. M., & Yin, K. (2020). Repairing police psychological safety: The role of career adaptability, feedback environment, and goal-self concordance based on the conservation of resources theory. *SAGE Open.* doi.org/10.1177/21582440209195

Goodman, J. (1994). Career adaptability in adults: A construct whose time has come. *Career Development Quarterly, 43*, 74-84.

Gosling, S. D., Rentfrow, P. J., Swann Jr., W. B. (2003). A very brief measure of the Big Five personality domains. *Journal Research in Personality 37*, 504–528.

Gould, S., (1979).Characteristics of career planners in upwardly mobile occupations. *Academy of Management Journal, 15*, 135-156.

Gray, J. A. (1970). The psychophysiological basis of introversion–extraversion. *Behaviour Research & Therapy, 8*, 249–266.

Gray, J. A., McNaughton, N. (2008). *The neuropsychology of anxiety: An enquiry into the function of the sept-hippocampal system.* New York: Oxford University Press.

Gray, M. P., & O'Brien, K. M. (2007). Advancing the assessment of women's career choices: The Career Aspiration Scale. *Journal of Career Assessment, 15*, 317–337.

Green, Z. A., Noor, U., Hashemi, M. N. (2020). Furthering proactivity and career adaptability among university students: Test of an intervention. *Journal of Career Assessment, 28*, 402-424.

Greenhaus, J. H. (1971). An investigation of the role of career salience in vocational behavior. *Journal of Vocational Behavior, 1*, 209–216.

Greenhaus, J. H., Parasuraman, S., & Wormley, W. M. (1990). Effects of race on organizational experiences, job performance evaluations, and career outcomes. *Academy of Management Journal, 33*, 64–86.

Gregor, M.A., Weigold, I. K. Wolfe, G., Campbell-Halfaker, D. Martin-Fernandez, Javier, & Gangis Del Pino, H. V. (2021). Positive predictors of career adaptability among diverse community college students. *Journal of Career Assessment, 29*, 115-128.

Guan, M., Capezio, A., Restubog, S. L. D., Read, S., Lajom, J. A. L., & Li, M. (2016). The Role of traditionality in the relationship among parental support, career decision-making self-efficacy and career adaptability. *Journal of Vocational Behavior, 94*, 114-123.

Guan, Y., Deng, H., Sun, J., Wang, Y., Cai, Z., Ye, L., ... Li, Y. (2013). Career adaptability, job search self-efficacy and outcomes: A three-wave investigation among Chinese university graduates. *Journal of Vocational Behavior, 83*, 561–570.

Guan, Y., Guo, Y., Bond, M. H., Cai, Z., Zhou, X., Xu, J., Zhu, F., Wang, Z., Fu, R., Wang, Y., Hu, T., & Ye, L. (2014). New job entrants' future work self, career adaptability and job search outcomes: Examining mediating and moderating models. *Journal of Vocational Behavior, 85*, 136-145.

Guan, Y., Liu, S., Guo, M. J., Li, M., Wu, M., Chen, S. X, Xu, S. L., & Tian, L. (2018). Acculturation orientations and Chinese student sojourners' career adaptability: The roles of career exploration and cultural distance. *Journal of Vocational Behavior, 104*, 228-239.

Guan, Y., Wang, Z., Dong, Z., Liu, Y., Yue, Y., Liu, H., & Liu, H. (2013). Career locus of control and career success among Chinese employees: A multi-dimensional approach. *Journal of Career Assessment, 21,* 295-310.

Guan Y, Wang F, Liu H, Ji Y, Jia X, Fang Z, Li Y, Hua H, Li C. (2015). Career-specific parental behaviors, career exploration and career adaptability: A three-wave investigation among Chinese undergraduates. *Journal of Vocational Behavior, 86*, 95-103.

Guan, Y., Wang, Z., Gong, Q., Cai, Z., Xu, S. L., Xiang, Q., Wang, Y., Chen, S. X., Hu, H., & Tian, L. (2018). Parents' career values, adaptability, career-specific parenting behaviors, and undergraduates' career adaptability. *The Counseling Psychologist, 46*, 922-946.

Guan, Y., Yang, W., Zhou, X., Tian, Z., & Eves, A. (2016). Predicting Chinese human resource managers' strategic competence: Roles of identity, career variety, organizational support and career adaptability. *Journal of Vocational Behavior*, 92, 116-124

Guay, F. (2005). Motivations underlying career decision-making activities: The career decision-making autonomy scale (CDMAS). *Journal of Career Assessment, 13*, 77–97.

Guo, Y., Guan, Y., Yang, X., Xu, J., Zhou, X., She, Z., et al. (2014). Career adaptability, calling and the professional competence of social work students in China: A career construction perspective. *Journal of Vocational Behavior, 85*, 394–402.

Guthrie, J. P., Coate, C. J., & Schwoerer, C. E. (1998). Career management strategies: The role of personality. *Journal of Managerial Psychology, 13*, 371–386.

Haan, N. (1977). *Coping and defending: Processes of self-environment organization*. San Diego, CA: Academic Press.

Hackman, J. R., & Oldham, G. R. (1974). The Job Diagnostic Survey: An instrument for the diagnosis of jobs and the evaluation of job redesign projects. *Affective Behavior, 4*, 159-170.

Haenggli, M., & Hirschi, A. (2020). Career adaptability and career success in the context of broader career resources framework. *Journal of Vocational Behavior, 119*, 103414.

Hahn, E., Gottschling, J., & Spinath, F. M. (2012). Short measurements of personality—Validity and reliability of the GSOEP Big Five Inventory (BFI-S). *Journal of Research in Personality, 46*, 355–359.

Hall, D. T. (1986). *Career development in organizations*. San Francisco, CA: Jossey-Bass.

Hall, D. T. (2004). The protean career: A quarter-century journey. *Journal of Vocational Behavior, 65*, 1-13.

Hall, D. T., & Mirvis, P. H. (1995). The new career contract: Developing the whole person at midlife and beyond. *Journal of Vocational Behavior, 47*, 269-289.

Hagmaier, T., & Abele, A. E. (2012). The multidimensionality of calling: Conceptualization, measurement and a bicultural perspective. *Journal of Vocational Behavior, 81*, 39-51.

Haibo, Y., Xiaoyu, G., Xiaoming, Z., & Zhihin, H. (2018). Career adaptability with or without career identity: How career adaptability leads to organizational success and individual career success. *Journal of Career Assessment, 26*, 717-731.

Hamtiaux, A., Houssemand, C., & Vrignaud, P. (2013). Individual and career adaptability: Comparing models and measures. *Journal of Vocational Behavior, 83*, 130-141.

Hardin, E. E., Leong, F. T., & Osipow, S. H. (2001). Cultural relativity in the conceptualization of career maturity. *Journal of Vocational Behavior, 58*, 36–52.

Harry, N., & Coetzee, M. (2013). Sense of coherence, career adaptability and burnout of early-career Black staff in the call centre environment. *SA Journal of Industrial Psychology, 39*, Art. #1138, 10 pages.

Hartung, P. J., Porfeli, E. J., & Vondracek, F. W. (2008). Career adaptability in childhood. *Career Development Quarterly, 57*, 63–74.

Hekman, D. R., Steensma, H. K., Bigley, G. A., & Hereford, J. F. (2009). Effects of organizational and professional identification on the relationship between administrators' social influence and professional employees' adoption of new work behavior. *Journal of Applied Psychology, 94*, 1325–1335.

Heppner, M. J. (1998). The Career Transitions Inventory: Measuring internal resources in adulthood. *Journal of Career Assessment, 6*, 329–346.

Higgins, E. (1997). Beyond pleasure and pain. *American Psychologist, 52*, 1280–1300.

Hirschi, A. (2009). Career adaptability development in adolescence: Multiple predictors and effect on sense of power and life satisfaction. *Journal of Vocational Behavior, 74*, 145–155.

Hirschi, A., Freund, P. A., & Herrmann, A. (2014). The career engagement scale: Development and validation of a measure of proactive career behaviors. *Journal of Career Assessment*, 22, 575-594.

Hirschi, A., Hermann, A., & Keller, A. C. (2015). Career adaptivity, adaptability, and adapting: A conceptual and empirical investigation. *Journal of Vocational Behavior, 87*, 1-10.

Hirschi, A., Nagy, N., Baumeler, F., Johnston, C., & Spurk, D. (2018). Assessing key predictors of career success: Development and validation of the career resources questionnaire. *Journal of Career Assessment, 26*, 338-358.

Hirschi, A., & Valero, D. (2015). Career adaptability profiles and their relationship to adaptivity and adapting. *Journal of Vocational Behavior, 88*, 220-229.

Hlad¢o, P., & Je˘zek, S. (2018). Measurement of career-specific parental behaviors perceived by Czech adolescents. *Studia Paedagogica, 23*, 101–135.

Ho, E. S. C., & Sum, K. W. (2018). Construction and validation of the Career and Educational Decision Self-Efficacy Inventory for secondary students (CEDSIS). *Journal of Psycho-educational Assessment, 36*, 162–174.

Hobfoll, S. E. (2002). Social and psychological resources and adaptation. *Review of General Psychology, 6*, 307.

Holland, J. L., Daiger, D. C., & Power, P. G. (1980). *My Vocational Situation*. Palo Alto, CA: Consulting Psychologists Press.

Hou, C., Wu, L., & Liu, Z. (2014). Effect of proactive personality and decision-making self-efficacy on career adaptability among Chinese graduates. *Social Behavior and Personality, 42*, 903-912.

Hou, Z- J., Leung, S. A., Li, X., Li, Xu., & Xu, H. (2012). Career Adapt-Abilities Scale—China Form: Construction and initial validation. *Journal of Vocational Behavior, 89,* 686-691.

Howard, M. C., & Alipour, K. K. (2014). Does the courage measure really measure courage? A theoretical and empirical evaluation. *Journal of Positive Psychology, 9,* 449–459.

Hu, Y., & Gan, Y. (2008). Development and psychometric validity of the resilience scale for Chinese adolescents. *Acta Psychologica Sinica, 40,* 902–912.

Hui, T., Yuen, M., & Chen, G. (2018a). Career adaptability, self-esteem, and social support among Hong Kong university students. *Career Development Quarterly, 66,* 94-106.

Hui, T., Yuen, M., & Chen, G. (2018b). Career-related filial piety and career adaptability in Hong Kong university students. *Career Development Quarterly, 66,* 358-370.

Hutz, C. S., Nunes, C. H., Silveira, A. D., Serra, J., Anton, M., & Wieczorek, L. S. (1998). O desenvolvimento demarcadores para a avaliação da personalidade nomodelo dos cinco grandes fatores [The development of markers for personality assessment according to the Big Five Factor Model]. *Psicologia: Reflexão e Crítica, 11,* 395–415.

Inkson, K. H. (2006). *Understanding careers: The metaphors of working lives.* Thousand Oaks, CA: Sage.

Isik, E., Yegin, F., Koyuncu, S., Eser, A., Comlekeiler, F. & Yildirum, K. (2018). Validation of the Career Adapt-Abilities Scale-Short Form across different age groups in the Turkish context. *International Journal of Educational and Vocational Guidance, 18,* 297-314.

Ispir, O., Elibol. E., & Sonmez, B. (2019). The relationship of personality traits and entrepreneurship tendencies with career adaptability of nursing students. *Nurse Education Today, 79,* 41-47.

Jahoda, M. (1981). Work, employment, and unemployment: Values, theories, and approaches in social research. *American Psychologist, 36,* 184-191.

Jannesari, M. & Sullivan, S. (2019). Career adaptability and the success of self-initiated expatriates in China. *Career Development International, 24,* 331-349.

Jiang, Z. (2016). The relationship between career adaptability and job content plateau: The mediating roles of fit perceptions. *Journal of Vocational Behavior, 95-96,*1-10.

Jiang, Z. (2017). Proactive personality and career adaptability: The role of thriving at work. *Journal of Vocational Behavior, 98,* 85-97.

Jiang, Z., Hu, X., & Wang, Z. (2018). Career adaptability and plateaus: The moderating effects of tenure and job self-efficacy. *Journal of Vocational Behavior, 104,* 59-71.

Jin, L. L. (2009). *The role of personality and filial piety in the career commitment process among Chinese university students* (Unpublished doctoral thesis). University of Hong Kong, China.

John, O. P., & Srivastava, S. (1999). The big five trait taxonomy: History, measurement, and theoretical perspectives. In L. A. Pervin, & O. P. John (Eds.). *Handbook of personality: Theory and research* (102-138). New York: Guilford.

Johnston, C. S., Broonen, J. P., Stauffer, S. D., Hamtiaux, A., Pouyard, J., Zecca, G., Houssemand, C., & Rossier, J. (2013). Validation of an adapted French form of the Career Adapt-Abilities Scale in four Francophone countries. *Journal of Vocational Behavior, 83,* 1-10.

Johnston, C. S., Maggiori, C., & Rossier, J. (2016). Personal trajectories, individual characteristics, and staying satisfied and healthy. *Journal of Career Development, 43,* 81-98.

Judge, T. A., Erez, A., Bono, J. E., & Thoresen, C. J. (2003). The Core Self-Evaluations Scale (CSES): Development of a measure. *Personnel Psychology, 56,* 303–331.

Judge, T. A.; Locke, E. A.; Durham, C. C. (1997). The dispositional causes of job satisfaction: A core evaluations approach. *Research in Organizational Behavior, 1,* 151–188.

Judge, T. A., Locke E. A., Durham, C. C., & Kluger, A. N. (1998). Dispositional effects on job and life satisfaction: The role of core evaluations. *Journal of Applied Psychology, 83,* 17-34.

Kahn, W. A. (1990). Psychological conditions of personal engagement and disengagement at work. *Academy of Management Journal, 33,* 692-724.

Kanten, S. (2012). Kaeiyer uyum yetenekleri olcegi: Gecerlilik ve guvenilirlik carlismasi [Career Adaptability Scale: A study of validity and reliability]. *Journal of Süleyman Demirel University Institute of Social Sciences, 16,* 191-205.

Karacan-Ozdemir, N. (2019). Associations between career adaptability and career decision-making difficulties among Turkish high school students. *International Journal for Educational and Vocational Guidance, 19,* 475-495.

Karcher, M. J., & Lee, Y. (2002). Connectedness among Taiwanese middle school students: A validation study of the Hemingway Measure of Adolescent Connectedness. *Asia Pacific Education Review, 3,* 92–114.

Karoly, P. (1993). Mechanisms of self-regulation: A systems view. *Annual Review of Psychology, 44,* 23-52.

Kasperzack, D., Ernst, A. L., & Pinquart, M. (2014). Ambivalence during and after career decision making of high school graduates. *Journal of Career Assessment, 22,* 248–260.

Kaur, H., & Kaur, R. (2020). The relationship between career adaptability and job outcomes via fit perceptions: A three-wave longitudinal study. *Australian Journal of Career Development, 29,* 196-204.

Keller, B. K., & Whiston, S. C. (2008). The role of parental influences on young adolescents' career development. *Journal of Career Assessment, 16,* 198–217.

Kenny, M. E., Blustein, D. L., Ling, B., Kelein, T., & Etchie, Q. (2019). Applying the psychology of working theory for transformative career education. *Journal of Career Development, 46,* 623-636.

Kim, J. H., & Shin, H. S. (2020). Effects of self-reflection-focused career course on career search efficacy, career maturity, and career adaptability in nursing students: A mixed-methods study. *Journal of Professional Nursing, 36,* 395-403.

Kirchknopf, S. (2020). Career adaptability and vocational identity of commercial apprentices in the German dual system. *Vocations and Learning, 13,* 503-526.

Kirdok, O., & Boluksai, A. (2018). The role of senior university students' career adaptability in predicting their subjective well-being. *Journal of Education and Training Studies, 6,* 47-54.

Koen, J., Klehe, U. C., Van Vianen, A. E., Zikic, J., & Nauta, A. (2010). Job-search strategies and reemployment quality: The impact of career adaptability. *Journal of Vocational Behavior, 77,* 126–139.

Konovsky, M. A., & Cropanzano, R. (1991). Perceived fairness of employee drug testing as a predictor of employee attitudes and job performance. *Journal of Applied Psychology, 76,* 698–707.

Kozan, S., Isik, E., & Blustein, D. L. (2019). Decent work and well-being among low-income Turkish employees: Testing the psychology of working theory. *Journal of Counseling Psychology, 66,* 317-327.

Kraimer, M. L., Seibert, S. E., Wayne, S. J., Liden, R. C., & Bravo, J. (2011). Antecedents and outcomes of organizational support for development: The critical role of career opportunities. *Journal of Applied Psychology, 96,* 485.

Kristof, A. L. (1996). Person-organization fit: An integrative review of its conceptualizations, measurement, and implications. *Personnel Psychology, 49,* 1–49.

Kumar, K., & Beyerlein, M. (1991). Construction and validation of an instrument for measuring ingratiatory behaviors in organizational settings. *Journal of Applied Psychology, 76,* 619–627.

Kwon, J. E. (2019). Work volition and career adaptability as predictors of employability: Examining a moderated mediating model. *Sustainability, 11,* 7089.

Lang, J. W., Lievens, F., De Fruyt, F., Zettler, I., & Tackett, J. L. (2019). Assessing meaningful within-person variability in Likert-Scale rated personality descriptions: An IRT tree approach. *Psychological Assessment, 31*, 474-487.

Law, K. S., Song, L. J., Wong, C. S., & Chen, D. H. (2009). The antecedents and consequences of successful localization. *Journal of International Business Studies, 40*, 1359–1373.

Lee, J.-Y., & Kwon, S.-M. (2005). Development of Scale for Dispositional Self-Focused Attention in Social Situations. *The Korean Journal of Clinical Psychology, 24,* 451–464.

Lee, K., & Ashton, M. C. (2004). Psychometric properties of the HEXACO personality inventory. *Multivariate Behavioral Research, 39*, 329-358.

Lee, L-Y., Veasna, S., & Wu, W-Y. (2013). The effects of social support and transformational leadership on expatriate adjustment and performance: The moderating roles of socialization experience and cultural intelligence. *Career Development International, 18*, 377-415.

Leiter, M. P., Day, A., & Price, L. (2015). Attachment styles at work: Measurement, collegial relationships, and burnout. *Burnout Research, 2*, 25–35.

Lent, R. W. (2013). Career-life preparedness: Revisiting career planning and adjustment in the new workplace. *Career Development Quarterly, 61*, 2-14.

Lent, R. W., & Brown, S. D. (2013). Social cognitive model of career self-management: Toward a unifying view of adaptive career behavior across the life span. *Journal of Counseling Psychology, 60*, 557-568

Lent, R. W., Brown, S. D., Schmidt, J., Brenner, B., Lyons, H., & Treistman, D. (2003). Relation of contextual supports and barriers to choice behavior in engineering majors: Test of alternative social cognitive models. *Journal of Counseling Psychology, 50*, 458–465.

Lent, R. W., Singley, D., Sheu, H., Gainor, K., Brenner, B. R., Treistman, D., & Ades, L. (2005). Social cognitive predictors of domain and life satisfaction: Exploring the theoretical precursors of subjective well-being. *Journal of Counseling Psychology, 52,* 429–442.

Lent, R. W., Singley, D., Sheu, H. B., Schmidt, J. A., & Schmidt, L. C. (2007). Relation of social-cognitive factors to academic satisfaction in engineering students. *Journal of Career Assessment, 15,* 87–97.

Leong, F. T. L., & Walsh, W. B. (Eds.) (2012). Career adaptability [Special issue]. *Journal of Vocational Behavior, 80*(3).

LePine, J. A., Colquitt, J. A., & Erez, A. (2000). Adaptability to changing tasks context: Effects of general cognitive ability, conscientiousness, and openness to experience. *Personnel Psychology, 53,* 563-593.

Levenson, H. (1981). Differentiating between internality, powerful others, and chance. In H. M. Lefcourt (Ed.), *Research with the locus of control construct, Vol. 1.* (pp. 15–63). New York: Academic Press.

Li, H., Ngo, H-y., & Cheung, F. (2019). Linking protean career orientation and career decidedness: The mediating role of career decision self-efficacy. *Journal of Vocational Behavior, 115,* 103322.

Li, Y., Guan, Y., Wang, F., Zhou, X., Guo, K., Jiang, P., Mo, Z., Li, Y., & Fang, Z. (2015). Big-five personality and BIS/BAS traits as predictors of career exploration: The mediation role of career adaptability. *Journal of Vocational Behavior, 89,* 39-45.

Liang, Y., Dou, K., Li, J-B., Liang, Y, Zhou, N., Cao, H., Wu, Q., & Lin, Z. (2020). Career-related parental behaviors, adolescents' consideration of future consequences, and career adaptability: A three-wave longitudinal study. *Journal of Counseling Psychology, 67,* 208-221.

Life Design International Research Group (2008, December). *Summary Report for Modeling Career Adaptability*, Fourth International Seminar on Career Psychology, Humboldt University, Berlin, Germany.

Liñán, F., & Chen, Y. W. (2009). Development and cross-cultural application of a specific instrument to measure entrepreneurial intentions. *Entrepreneurship Theory and Practice, 33,* 593–617.

Lockwood, P., Jordon, C. H., & Kunda, Z. (2002). Motivation by positive or negative role models: Regulatory focus determines who will best inspire us. *Journal of Personality and Social Psychology, 83*, 854–864.

Lorenz, T., Beer, C., Pütz, J., & Heinitz, K. (2016). Measuring psychological capital: Construction and validation of the Compound PsyCap Scale (CPC-12). *PLoS ONE, 11*, e0152892.

Lounsbury, J. W., Hutchens, T., & Loveland, J. M. (2005). An investigation of big five personality traits and career decidedness among early and middle adolescents. *Journal of Career Assessment, 13*, 25–39.

Luke, J., McIlveen, P., & Perera, H. N. (2016). A thematic analysis of career adaptability in retirees who return to work. *Frontiers in Psychology, 7*:193.

Luszczynska, A., Diehl, M., Gutiérrez-Doña, B., Kuusinen, P., & Schwarzer, R. (2004). Measuring one component of dispositional self-regulation: Attention control in goal pursuit. *Personality and Individual Differences, 37*, 555-566.

Luthans, F., Avolio, B. J., Avey, J. B., & Norman, S. M. (2007). Positive psychological capital: Measurement and relationship with performance and satisfaction. *Personnel Psychology, 60*, 541–572.

Ma, Y., Chen, S-C., & Zeng, H. (2020). Male student nurses need more support: Understanding the determinants and consequences of career adaptability in nursing college students. *Nursing Education Today, 91*, 104435.

Maddi, S. (1987). Hardiness training at Illinois Bell Telephone. In J. P. Opatz (Ed.), *Health promotion evaluation: Measuring the organizational impact* (pp. 101–115). Stevens Point, WI: National Wellness Institute.

Magalhães, M. D. O. (2008). Propriedades psicométricas da versão brasileira da Escala de Entrincheiramento na Carreira [Psychometric properties of the Brazilian version of the Career Entrenchment Scale]. *PsicoUSF, 13*, 13–19.

Maggori, C., Johnston, C. S., Krings, F., Massoudi, K., & Rossier, J. (2013). The role of career adaptability and work conditions on general and professional well-being. *Journal of Vocational Behavior, 83*, 437-449.

Maggiori, C., Rossier, J., & Savickas, M. L. (2015). Career Adapt-Abilities Scale–Short Form (CAAS-SF): Construction and validation. *Journal of Career Assessment, 25*, 312-325.

Maslach, C., & Jackson, S. E. (1981) The measurement of experienced burnout. *Journal of Organizational Behavior, 2*, 99–113.

Martin, M. M., & Rubin, R. B. (1995). A new measure of cognitive flexibility. *Psychological Reports, 76*, 623–626.

Meade, A. W., Johnson, E. C., & Braddy, P. W. (2008). Power and sensitivity of alternative fit indices in tests of measurement invariance. *Journal of Applied Psychology, 93*, 568–592.

Morrison, R. F. (1977). Career adaptivity: The effective adaptation of managers to changing role demands. *Journal of Applied Psychology, 62*, 549-558.

Manczak, E. M., Zapata-Gietl, C., & McAdams, D. P. (2014). Regulatory focus in the life story: Prevention as expressed in three layers of personality. *Journal of Personality and Social Psychology, 106*, 169-181.

Marcia, J. E. (1966). Development and validation of ego-identity status. *Journal of Personality and Social Psychology, 3*, 551–558.

Massoudi, K. (2009). *Le stress professionnel: Une analyse des vulnérabilités individuelles et des facteurs de risque environnementaux* [Professional stress: Analysis of individuals vulnerabilities and environmental risk factors]. Bern, Switzerland: Peter Lang.

Matheny, K. B., Curlette, W. L., Aycock, D. W., Pugh, J. L. & Taylor, H. F. (1987). *The Coping Resources Inventory for Stress*. Fayetteville, GA: Health Prisms.

May, D. R., Gilson, R. L., & Harter, L. M. (2004). The psychological conditions of meaningfulness, safety and availability and the engagement of the human spirit at work. *Journal of Occupational and Organizational Psychology, 77*, 11–37.

Maynard, D. C., Joseph, T. A., & Maynard, A. M. (2006). Underemployment, job attitudes, and turnover intentions. *Journal of Organizational Behavior, 27*, 509–536.

McCrae, R. R., & Costa, P. T., Jr. (2004). A contemplated revision of the NEO Five-Factor Inventory. *Personality and Individual Differences, 36*, 587–596.

McIlveen, P., Burton, L. J., & Beccaria, G. (2013). A short form of the Career Futures Inventory, *Journal of Career Assessment, 21*, 127–138.

McIlveen, P. & Midgley, W. (2015). A semantic and pragmatic analysis of career adaptability. In K. Maree & A. DiFabio (Eds.), *Exploring new horizons in career counseling: Turning challenges into opportunities* (pp. 235-247). Rotterdam, The Netherlands: Sense Publishers.

McIlveen, P., Perera, H. N., Hoare, P. N., & McLennan, B. (2018). The validity of CAAS scores in divergent social occupations. *Journal of Career Assessment, 26*, 31-51.

McKenna, B., Zacher, H., Ardabili, F. S., & Mohebbi, H. (2016). Career Adapt-Abilities Scale-Iran Form: Psychometric properties and relationships with career satisfaction and entrepreneurial intentions. *Journal of Vocational Behavior, 92*, 81-91.

McLenna, B., McIlveen, P., & Perera, H. N. (2017). Pre-service teachers' self-efficacy mediates the relationship between career adaptability and career optimism. *Teaching and Teacher Education, 63*, 176-185.

McMahon, M., Watson, M., & Bimrose, J. (2012). Career adaptability: A qualitative understanding from the stories of older women. *Journal of Vocational Behavior, 80*, 762-768.

Merino-Tejedor, E. Hontangas-Beltran, P. M, & Boada-Grau, J. (2016). Career adaptability and its relation to self-regulation, career construction, and academic engagement among Spanish university students. *Journal of Vocational Behavior, 93*, 92-102.

Merino-Tejedor, E., Hontangas, P. M., & Petrides, K. V. (2018). Career adaptability mediates the effect of trait emotional intelligence on academic engagement. *Revista de Psicodidactica, 23*, 77-85.

Metheny, J., McWhirter, E. H., & O'Neil, M. E. (2008). Measuring perceived teacher support and its influence on adolescent career development. *Journal of Career Assessment, 16*, 218–237.

Meyer, J., & Allen, N. (1997). *Commitment in the workplace: Theory, research and application.* Thousand Oaks, CA: Sage.

Milliman, J. F. (1992). *Causes, consequences, and moderating factors of career plateauing.* (Unpublished doctoral dissertation), University of Southern California, Los Angeles, CA.

Mirkovic, B., Suvajdzic, K., & Dostanic, J. (2020). Career adaptability in Syria: Examining the CAAS model. *Psihologija, 53*, 1-21.

Mitchell, T., Holtom, B., & Lee, T. (2001). How to keep your best employees: The development of an effective retention policy. *Academy of Management Executive, 15*, 96–108.

MIUR (2014). Linee guida nazionali per l'orientamento permanente [National guidelines for lifelong guidance]. Retrieved from http://www.istruzione.it/allegati/2014/prot4232_14.pdf.

Monteiro, D., & Almeida, L. S. (2015). The relation of career adaptability to work experience, extracurricular activities, and work transition in Portuguese graduate students. *Journal of Vocational Behavior, 91*, 106-112.

Morgan, J., & Farsides, T. (2009). Measuring meaning in life. *Journal of Happiness Studies, 10*, 197-214.

Morrison, R. F., & Hall, D. T. (2002). Career adaptability. In D. T. Hall (Ed.), *Careers in and out of organizations* (pp. 205-234). Thousand Oaks, C. A.: Sage.

Morsunbul, U. (2016). The relations between personal growth initiative and identity styles among youth. *Online Journal of Counseling and Education, 5*, 31-38.

Motowidlo, D. J., & Scotter, J. R. V. (1994). Evidence that task performance should be distinguished from contextual performance. *Journal of Applied Psychology, 79*, 475–480.

Mroczek, D. K., & Kolarz, C. M. (1998). The effect of age on positive and negative affect: A developmental perspective on happiness. *Journal of Personality and Social Psychology, 75*, 1333–1349.

Nastam K. A. (2007). *Influence of career self-efficacy beliefs on career exploration behaviors*. Thesis submitted to the Psychology Department at the State University of New York at New Palz.

Nauta, M. M. (2007). Assessing college students' satisfaction with their academic majors. *Journal of Career Assessment, 15*, 446–462.

Ndlovu, V., & Ferreira, N. (2019). Students' psychological hardiness in relation to career adaptability. *Journal of Psychology in Africa, 29*, 598-604.

Negru-Subtirica, O., & Pop, E. I. (2016). Longitudinal links between career adaptability and academic achievement in adolescence. *Journal of Vocational Behavior, 93*, 163-170

Nelson, J. (2011). What's behind the impostor syndrome. *Canadian Business, 84*, 129-129.

Netemeyer, R., Boles, J., & McMurrian, R. (1996) Development and validation of work–family conflict and family–work conflict scales. *Journal of Applied Psychology, 81*, 400–410.

Neureiter, M., & Traut-Mattausch, E. (2017). Two sides of the career resources coin: Career adaptability resources and the imposter phenomenon. *Journal of Vocational Behavior, 98*, 56-69.

Nilforooshan, P. (2020). From adaptivity to adaptation: Examining the career construction model of adaptation. *Career Development Quarterly, 68*, 98-111.

Nilforooshan, P., & Salimi, S. (2016). Career adaptability as a mediator between personality and career engagement. *Journal of Vocational Behavior, 94*, 1-10.

Norton, P. J., & Weiss, B. J. (2009). The role of courage on behavioral approach in a fear-eliciting situation: A proof-of-concept pilot study. *Journal of Anxiety Disorders, 23*, 212–217.

Nota, L., & Soresi, S. (2013). *ProSpera: Programma di orientamento all'universit*a *e al lavoro.* [ProSpera: Vocational guidance program for college and work]. Florence, Italy: Hogrefe.

Noy, S., & Ray, R., 2012. Graduate students' perceptions of their advisors: İs there systematic disadvantage in mentorship? *The Journal of Higher Education.* 83, 876-914.

Nuttin, J. (1987). Affective consequences of mere ownership: The name letter effect in twelve European languages. *European Journal of Social Psychology, 17*, 381–402.

Ocampo. A. C. G., Restubog, S. L. D., Liwag, M. E., Wang, L., & Petelczyc, C. (2018). My spouse is my strength: Interactive effects of perceived organizational and spousal support in predicting career adaptability and career outcomes. *Journal of Vocational Behavior, 108*, 165-177.

Ohme, M., & Zacher, H. (2015). Job performance ratings: The relative importance of mental ability, conscientiousness, and career adaptability. *Journal of Vocational Behavior, 87*, 161-170.

Olugbade, O. A. (2016). The Career Adapt-Abilities Scale – Nigeria Form: Psychometric properties and construct validity. *Journal of Vocational Behavior, 95-96*, 111-113.

Omar, S., & Noordin, F. (2013). Career adaptability and intention to leave among ICT professionals: An exploratory study. *Turkish Journal of Educational Technology, 12*, 11-18.

Omar, S., & Noordin, F. (2016). Moderator influences on individualism-collectivism and career adaptability among ICT professionals in Malaysia. *Procedia Economics and Finance*, 37, 529-537.

Oncel, L. (2014). Career Adapt-Abilities Scale: Convergent validity of subscale scores. *Journal of Vocational Behavior, 85*, 13-17.

O'Reilly, C. A., Chatman, J., & Caldwell, D. F. (1991). People and organizational culture: A profile comparison approach to assessing person-organization fit. *Academy of Management Journal, 34*, 487–516.

Ozdemir, N. K. (2019). Qualitative exploration of career adaptability of Turkish adolescents. *Australian Journal of Career Development, 28*, 83-91.

Pajic, S., Ulcelsue, M., Kismihok, G., Mol, S. T., & den Hartong, D. N (2018). Antecedents of job search self-efficacy of Syrian refugees in Greece and the Netherlands, *Journal of Vocational Behavior, 105*, 159-172.

Pan, J., Guan, Y., Wu, J., Han, L., Zhu, F., Fu, X., & Yu, J. (2018). The interplay of proactive personality and internship quality in Chinese university graduates' job search success: The role of career adaptability. *Journal of Vocational Behavior, 109*, 14-26.

Parasuraman, S., Greenhaus, J. H., & Granrose, C. S. (1992). Role stressors, social support, and well-being among two-career couples. *Journal of Organizational Behavior, 13*, 339–356.

Parmentier, M., Pirsoul, T., & Nils, F. (2019). Examining the impact of emotional intelligence on career adaptability: A two-wave cross-lagged study. *Personality and Individual Differences, 151*, 109446.

Pavot, W., & Diener, E. (1993). Review of the Satisfaction with Life Scale. *Psychological Assessment, 5,* 164–172.

Peltier, M., Hay, A., & Drago, W. (2006). Reflecting on reflection: Scale extension and a comparison of undergraduate business students in the United States and the United Kingdom. *Journal of Marketing Education, 28*, 250–263.

Perera, H. N., & McIlveen, P. (2017). Profiles of career adaptivity and their relations with adaptability, adapting, and adaptation. *Journal of Vocational Behavior*, 98, 70-84.

Peterson, C., Park, N., & Seligman, M. E. (2005). Orientations to happiness and life satisfaction: The full life versus the empty life. *Journal of Happiness Studies, 6*, 25–41.

Petrides, K. V. (2009). Psychometric properties of the trait emotional intelligence questionnaire (TEIQue). In A. J. D. Parker, H. D. Saklofske, & C. Stough (Eds.), *Assessing emotional intelligence: Theory, research, and applications* (pp. 85–101). Boston, MA: Springer USA.

Petrides, K. V., & Furnham, A. (2006). The role of trait emotional intelligence in a gender-specific model of organizational variables. *Journal of Applied Social Psychology, 36*, 552–569.

Pociūtė, B. Kairys, A., Urbanavičiūtė, L., & Liniauskaitė, A. (2014). High school students' vocational identity and adaptability. *Acta Paedegogia Vilnensia, 33*, 46-59.

Polyhart, R. E., & Bliese, P. D. (2006). Individual adaptability (I-ADAPT) theory: Conceptualizing the antecedents, consequences, and measurement of individual differences in adaptability. In C. S. Burke, L. G. Pierce, & E. Salas (Eds.) *Understanding adaptability: A prerequisite for effective performance within complex environments* (pp. 3-40). Amsterdam, The Netherlands: Elsevier B.V.

Porath, C., Spreitzer, G., Gibson, C., & Garnett, F. G. (2012). Thriving at work: Toward its measurement, construct validation, and theoretical refinement. *Journal of Organizational Behavior, 33*, 250-275.

Porfeli, E. J., Lee, B., Vondracek, F. W., & Weigold, I. K. (2011). A multi-dimensional measure of vocational identity status. *Journal of Adolescence, 34*, 853–887.

Pouyaud, J., Vignoli, E., Dosnon, O., Lallemand, N. (2012). Career Adapt-Abilities Scale-France Form: Psychometric properties and relationships to anxiety and motivation. *Journal of Vocational Behavior, 80*, 692-697.

Preacher, K. J., & Hayes, A. F. (2008). Asymptotic and resampling strategies for assessing and comparing indirect effects in multiple mediator models. *Behavior Research Methods, 40*, 879–891.
.

Presbitero, A., & Quita, C. (2017). Expatriate career intentions: Links to career adaptability and culture intelligence. *Journal of Vocational Behavior, 98*, 118-126.

Prescod, D. J., & Zeligman, M. (2018**).** Career adaptability of trauma survivors: The moderating role of posttraumatic growth. *Career Development Quarterly, 66*, 107-120.

Puffer, K. A. (2011). Emotional intelligence as a salient predictor for collegians' career decision making. *Journal of Career Assessment, 19*, 130–150.

Pulakos, E. D., Arad, S., Donovan, M. A., & Plamondon, K. E. 2000. Adaptability in the workplace: Development of a taxonomy of adaptive performance. *Journal of Applied Psychology, 85*, 612-624.

Quigley, N. R., & Tymon, J. W. G. (2006). Toward an integrated model of intrinsic motivation and career self-management. *Career Development International, 11*, 522-543.

Ragins, B. R., & McFarlin, D. B. (1990). Perceptions of mentor roles in cross-gender mentoring relationships. *Journal of Vocational Behavior, 37*, 321–339.

Ramos, K., & Lopez, F. G. (2018). Attachment security and career adaptability as predictors of subjective well-being among career transitioners. *Journal of Vocational Behavior, 104*, 72-85.

Rasheed, I., Okumus, F., Weng, Q., Hameed, Z., & Nawaz, M. S., (2020). Career adaptability and employee turnover intentions: The role of perceived career opportunities and orientation to happiness in the hospitality industry. *Journal of Hospitality Management, 44*, 98-107.

Raven, J., Raven, J. C., & Court, J. H. (2000). *Standard Progressive Matrices: Raven manua*l (Section 3). Oxford, UK: Oxford Psychologists Press.

447

Reise, S. P., Moore, T. M., & Haviland, M. G. (2010). Bifactor models and rotations: Exploring the extent to which multidimensional data yield univocal scale scores. *Journal of Personality Assessment, 92*, 544-559.

Rigotti, T., Schyns, B., & Mohr, G. (2008). A short version of the Occupational Self-Efficacy Scale: Structural and construct validity across five countries. *Journal of Career Assessment, 16*, 238–255.

Ringle, P. M., & Savickas, M. L. (1983). Administrative leadership: Planning and time perspective. *Journal of Higher Education, 54*, 649-661.

Robitschek, C. (1997). Life/career renewal: An intervention for vocational and other life transitions. *Journal of Career Development, 24*, 133–146

Robitschek, S. (1998). Personal growth initiative: The construct and its measure. *Measurement and Evaluation in Counseling and Development, 30*, 183–198.

Robitschek, S. (2003). Validity of Personal Growth Initiative Scale scores with a Mexican-American college student population. *Journal of Counseling Psychology, 50*, 496-502.

Robitschek, C., Ashton, M. W., Spering, C. C., Geiger, N., Byers, D., Schotts, G. C., & Thoen, M. A. (2012). Development and psychometric evaluation of the Personal Growth Initiative Scale-II. *Journal of Counseling Psychology, 59*, 274-287.

Roff, S., 2005. The Dundee Ready Educational Environment Measure (DREEM): A generic instrument for measuring students' perceptions of undergraduate health professions curricula. *Medical Teacher, 27*, 322–325.

Rosenberg, M. (1965). *Society and adolescent self-image*. Princeton, NJ: Princeton University.

Rossier, J., Hansenne, M., Baudin, N., & Merizot, J. (2012). Zuckerman's revised alternative five-factor model: Validation of the Zuckerman-Kuhlman-Aluja Personality Questionnaire in four French-speaking countries. *Journal of Personality Assessment, 94*, 358-365.

Rossier, J., Zecca, G., Stauffer, S. D., Maggiori, C., & Dauwalder, J. P. (2012). Career Adapt-Abilities Scale in a French-speaking Swiss sample: Psychometric properties and relationships to personality and work engagement. *Journal of Vocational Behavior, 80*, 734-743.

Rothwell, A., & Arnold, J. (2007). Self-perceived employability: Development and validation of a scale. *Personnel Review, 36*, 23–41.

Rottinghaus, P. J., Buelow, K., Matyja, A., & Schneider, M. (2012). The Career Futures Inventory - Revised: Assessing multiple dimensions of career adaptability. *Journal of Career Assessment, 20*, 123-139.

Rottinghaus, P. J., Day, S. X., & Borgen, F. H. (2005). The Career Futures Inventory: A measure of career-related adaptability and optimism. Journal *of Career Assessment, 13*, 3-24.

Ruch, W., Brouwers, S. A., & Luciano, E. C. (2013). Nine items to assess orientations to happiness: Development and validation of a short version of the OTH questionnaire. *Swiss Journal of Psychology 73,*225-234.

Rudolph, C. W., Lavigne, K. N., & Zacher, H. (2017). Career adaptability: A meta-analysis of relationships with measures of adaptivity, adapting responses, and adaptation. *Journal of Vocational Behavior, 98*, 17-34.

Rusu, A., Măirean, C., Hojbotă, A. M., Gherasim, L. R., & Gavriloaiei, S. I. (2015). Relationships of career adaptabilities with explicit and implicit self-concepts. *Journal of Vocational Behavior, 89*, 92-101.

Rusu, S., Maricuțoiu, L., Macsinga, I., Vîrgă, D., & Sava, F. (2012). Evaluarea personalității din perspectiva modelului Big Five. Date privind adaptarea chestionarului IPIP-50 pe un eșantion de studenți români [Personality assessment in terms of the Big Five model. Data concerning the adaptation of the IPIP-50 questionnaire on a sample of Romanian students]. *Psihologia Resurselor Umane, 10*, 39–56.

Safavi, H. P., & Bouzari, M. (2019). The association of psychological capital, career adaptability and career competency among hotel frontline employees. *Tourism Management Perspectives, 30*, 65-74.

Safavi, H. P., & Karatepe, O. K. (2018). High-performance work practices and hotel employee outcomes: The mediating role of career adaptability. *International Journal of Contemporary Hospitality Management, 30,* 1112-1133.

Saka, N., & Gati, I. (2007). Emotional and personality-related aspects of persistent career decision-making difficulties. *Journal of Vocational Behavior, 71,* 340–358.

Saka, N., Gati, I., & Kelly, K. R. (2008). Emotional and personality-related aspects of career-decision-making difficulties. *Journal of Career Assessment, 16,* 403–424.

Saks, A. M., Zikic, J., & Koen, J. (2015). Job search self-efficacy: Reconceptualizing the construct and its measurement. *Journal of Vocational Behavior, 86,* 104–114.

Salovey, P., & Mayer, J. D. (1990). Emotional intelligence. *Imagination, Cognition and Personality, 9,* 185–211.

Santilli, S., Ginevra, M. C., Sgaramella, T. M., Nota, L., Ferrari, L., & Soresi, S. (2015). Design My Future: An instrument to assess future orientation and resilience. *Journal of Career Assessment, 25,* 281–295.

Santilli, S., Grossen, S., & Nota, L. (2020). Career adaptability, resilience, and life satisfaction among Italian and Belgian middle school students. *Career Development Quarterly, 68,* 194-207.

Santilli, S., Marcionetti, J., Rochat, S., Rossier, J., & Nota, L. (2917). Career adaptability, hope, optimism, and life staifaction in Italian and Swiss adolescents. *Journal of Career Development, 44,* 62-76.

Santilli, S., Nota, L., Ginvera, M. C., & Soresi, S. (2014). Career adaptability, hope, and life satisfaction in workers with intellectual disability. *Journal of Vocational Behavior, 85,* 67-74.

Santilli, S., Nota, L., & Hartung, P. J. (2019). Efficacy of a group career construction intervention with early adolescent youth. *Journal of Vocational Behavior, 111,* 49-58.

Santra, S., & Giri, V. N. (2019). Role of career adaptability and its resources in predicting vocational attitudes of Indian IT professional. *Management and Labour Studies, 44*, 168-192.

Sassenberg, K. & Scholl, A. If I can do it my way...The influence of regulatory focus on job related values and job selection. *Journal of Economic Psychology, 38,* 58-70.

Sattar, M., A., Rasheed, M. I., Khan, I., U., Tariq, H., & Iqbal, J. (2017). Why adaptable individuals perform better: The role of orientation to happiness. *Australian Journal of Career Development, 26*, 134-141.

Savickas, M. L. (1984). *Interpreting the Career Maturity Attitude Scale's relationship to measures of mental ability*. Paper presented at the Annual Meeting of the American Psychological Association. Toronto, Canada. http://files.eric.ed.gov/fulltext/ED248442.pdf

Savickas, M. L. (1992). New directions in career assessment. In D. H. Montross, & C. J. Shinkman (Eds.), *Career development: Theory and practice* (pp. 336-355). Springfield, IL: Charles C. Thomas.

Savickas, M. L. (1993). *Career Choice Status Inventory*. Rootstown, OH: Northeastern Ohio Universities College of Medicine.

Savickas, M. L. (1997). Adaptability: An integrative construct for life-span, life-space theory. *Career Development Quarterly*, 45, 247–259.

Savickas, M. L. (2005). The theory and practice of career construction. In S. D. Brown, & R. W. Lent (Eds.), *Career development and counseling: Putting theory and research to work* (pp. 42–70). Hoboken, NJ: Wiley.

Savickas, M. L. (2013). Career construction theory and practice. In S. D. Brown, & R. W. Lent (Eds.), *Career development and counseling: Putting theory and research to work* (pp. 147–183). Hoboken, NJ: Wiley.

Savickas, M. L. (2016). Reflection and reflexivity during life-design intervention: Comments on Career Construction Counseling. *Journal of Vocational Behavior, 97,* 84-89.

Savickas, M. L. (2019a). *Career construction theory: Life portraits of attachment, adaptability, and identity*. Rootstown, OH: Vocopher.com

Savickas, M. L. (2019b). *Career counseling* (2nd ed.). Washington, DC: American Psychological Association.

Savickas, M. L. (2020). Career Construction Theory and Counseling Model. In S. D. Brown & R. W. Lent (Eds) *Career Development and Counseling: Putting Theory to Work* (3rd. ed.; pp. 165-199). Hoboken, NJ: John Wiley Sons.

Savickas, M. L., Nota, L., Rossier, J., Dauwalder, J. P., Duarte, M. E., Guichard, J., et al. (2009). Life designing: A paradigm for career construction in the 21st century. *Journal of Vocational Behavior*, 75, 239–250.

Savickas, M. L., & Porfeli, E. J. (2011). Revision of the Career Maturity Inventory: The adaptability form. *Journal of Career Assessment, 19*, 335–374.

Savickas, M. L., & Porfeli, E. J. (2012). Career Adapt-Abilities Scale: Construction, reliability, and measurement equivalence across 13 countries. *Journal of Vocational Behavior*, 80, 661–673.

Savickas, M. L., Porfeli, E. J., Hilton, T. L., & Savickas, S. (2018). The Student Career Construction Inventory. *Journal of Vocational Behavior, 106*, 138-152.

Sawitri, D. R., Creed, P. A., & Zimmer-Gembeck, M. J. (2012). The Adolescent–Parent Career Congruence Scale: Development and initial validation. *Journal of Career Assessment, 21*, 210–226.

Schaufeli, W. B., Bakker, A. B., & Salanova, M. (2006). The measurement of work engagement with a short questionnaire: A cross-national study. *Educational and Psychological Measurement, 66*, 701–716.

Schaufeli, W. B., Salanova, M., González-Romá, V., & Bakker, A. B. (2002). The measurement of engagement and burnout: A two sample confirmatory factor analytic approach. *Journal of Happiness Studies, 3*, 71–92.

Schein, E. H., (1978) *Career dynamics: Matching individual and organizational needs*. Reading, MA: Addison-Wesley.

Schein, E. H. (1990). *Career anchors: Discovering your real values*. San Diego, CA: Pfeiffer & Company, University Associates

452

Scheier, M. F., Carver, C. S., & Bridges, M. W. (1994). Distinguishing optimism from neuroticism (and trait anxiety, self mastery, and self-esteem): A reevaluation of the Life Orientation Test. *Journal of Personality and Social Psychology, 67*, 1063–1078.

Schutte, N. S., Malouff, J. M., & Bhullar, N. (2009). The Assessing Emotions Scale. In C. Stough, D. Saklofske, & J. Parker (Eds.), *The assessment of emotional intelligence* (pp. 119–135). New York: Springer.
Schaufeli, W., Martinez, I. M., Marques Pinto, A., Salanova, M., & Bakker, A. B. (2002). Burnout and engagement in university students: A cross-national study. *Journal of Cross-Cultural Psychology, 33*, 464–481.

Schaufeli, W. B., Salanova, M., González-Romá, V., & Bakker, A. B. (2002). The measurement of engagement and burnout: A two sample confirmatory factor analytic approach. *Journal of Happiness Studies, 3*, 71–92.

Schuesslbauer, A. F., Volmer, J., & Goritz, (2018). The goal paves the way: Inspirational motivation as a predictor of career adaptability. *Journal of Career Development, 45*, 489-503.

Schwarzer, R., & Jerusalem, M. (1995). Self-efficacy Scale. In J. S. Weinman, & M. Johnston (Eds.), *Health psychology: A user's portfolio. Causal and control beliefs.* (pp. 35–37). UK: NFER-NELSON

Seibert, S. E., Crant, J. M., & Kraimer, M. L. (1999). Proactive personality and career success. *Journal of Applied Psychology, 84,* 416-427.

Seibert, K. H., & Stangl, W. (1986). Der fragebogen einstellung zur berufswahl und beruflichen arbeit [The questionnaire of attitudes toward career choice and professional work]. *Diagnostica, 32*, 153–164.

Seligman, M. E. P. (2002). *Authentic happiness: Using the new positive psychology to realize your potential for lasting fulfillment.* New York: Free Press.

Shabeer, S., Mohammed, S. J., Jawahar, I. M., & Bilal, A. R. (2019). The mediating influence of fit perceptions on the relationship between career adaptability and job content and hierarchical plateaus. *Journal of Career Development, 19*, 332-345.

Shafer, L. F. (1936). *The psychology of adjustment: An objective approach to mental hygiene*. Boston: Houghton-Mifflin.

Sharma, S., Sunny, N., & Parmar, J. S. (2017). Role of work values in predicting career adaptability: A study of university students of the State of Himachal Pradesh. *Global Journal of Commerce & Management Perspective, 6*, 14-18.

Shin, Y-J., & Lee, J-Y. (2017). Attachment, career-choice pessimism, and intrinsic motivation as predictors of college students' career adaptability. *Journal of Career Development, 44*, 311-326.

Shin, Y-J., & Lee, J-Y. (2019). Self-focused attention and anxiety: The mediating role of career adaptability. *Career Development Quarterly, 67*, 110-125.

Shin, Y-J., Lee, E. S., & Seo, Y. (2019). Does traditional stereotyping of career as male affect college women's, but not college men's, career decision self-efficacy and ultimately their career adaptability? *Sex Roles, 81*, 74-86.

Shipp, A. J., Edwards, J. R., & Lambert, L. S. (2009). Conceptualization and measurement of temporal focus: The subjective experience of the past, present, and future. *Organizational Behavior and Human Decision Processes, 110*, 1–22

Shockley, K. M., Ureksoy, H., Rodopman, O. B., Poteat, L. F., & Dullaghan, T. R. (2016). Development of a new scale to measure subjective career success: A mixed-methods study. *Journal of Organizational Behavior, 37*(1), 128–153.

Shore, L. M., Barksdale, K., & Shore, T. H. (1995). Managerial perceptions of employee commitment to the organization. *Academy of Management Journal, 38*, 1593–1615.

Sibunruang, H. Garcia, P. R. J. M., & Tolentino, L. R. (2016). Ingratiation as an adapting strategy: Its relationship with career adaptability, career sponsorship, and promotability. *Journal of Vocational Behavior, 92*, 135-144.

Sidiropoulou-Dimakakou1, D., Mikedaki, K., Argyropoulou, K., & Kaliris, A., (2018). A psychometric analysis of the Greek Career Adapt-

Abilities Scale in university students. *International Journal of Psychological Studies, 10*, 95-108.

Singelis, T. M., Triandis, H., Bhawuk, D. P. S., & Gelfand, M. J. (1995). Horizontal and vertical dimensions of individualism and collectivism: A theoretical and measurement refinement. *Cross-Cultural Research, 29*, 240-275.
Slack, N. (1994). The importance-performance matrix as a determinant of improvement priority. *International Journal of Operations and Production Management, 14*, 59-75.

Slaney, R. B., Rice, K. G., Mobley, M., Trippi, J., & Ashby, J. S. (2001). The revised Almost Perfect Scale. *Measurement and Evaluation in Counseling and Development, 34*, 130–145.

Slemp, G. R., & Vella-Brodrick, D. A. (2013). The job crafting questionnaire: A new scale to measure the extent to which employees engage in job crafting. *International Journal of Wellbeing, 3, 126–146.*

Snyder, C. R., Harris, C., Anderson, J. R., Holleran, S. A., Irving, L. M., Sigmon, S. T., et al. (1991). The will and the ways: Development and validation of an individual differences measure of hope. *Journal of Personality and Social Psychology, 60*, 570–585.

Soares, J., do Céu Taveira, M., de Oliveira, M. C. et al. (2021). Factors influencing adaptation from university to employment in Portugal and Brazil. *International Journal of Educational and Vocational Guidance.* https://doi.org/10.1007/s10775-020-09450-3

Son, S. (2018). The more reflective, the more career adaptable: A two-wave mediation and moderation analysis. *Journal of Vocational Behavior, 109*, 44-53.

Soresi, S., & Nota, L. (2003). *Portfolio Clipper per l'orientamento dagli 15 ai 19 anni - Volume II°: Autoefficacia e decision making.* Firenze: ITER-Organizzazioni Speciali.

Soresi, S., Nota, L., & Ferrari, L. (2012). Career Adapt-Abilities Scale-Italian Form: Psychometric properties and relationships to breadth of interests, quality of life, and perceived barriers. *Journal of Vocational Behavior, 80*, 705-711.

455

Spurk, D., Volmer, J., Orth, M., Goritz, A. S. (2020). How do career adaptability and proactive career behaviors interrelate over time? An inter- and intra-individual investigation. *Journal of Occupational and Organizational Psychology, 93*, 158-186.

Steelman, L. A., Levy, P. E., & Snell, A. F. (2004). The Feedback Environment Scale: Construct definition, measurement, and validation. *Educational and Psychological Measurement, 6*, 165–184.

Steger, M. F., Frazier, P., Oishi, S., & Kaler, M. (2006). The Meaning in Life Questionnaire: Assessing the presence of and search for meaning in life. *Journal of Counseling Psychology, 53*, 80–93.

Steger, M. F., Dik, B. J., & Duffy, R. D. (2012). Measuring meaningful work: The Work as Meaning Inventory (WAMI). *Journal of Career Assessment, 20,* 322-337.

Stern, P. C., Dietz, T., & Guagnano, G. A. (1998). A brief inventory of values. *Educational and Psychological Measurement, 58*, 984–1001.

Storme, M., Celik, P., & Myszkowski, N. (2019). Career decision ambiguity tolerance and career decision-making difficulties in a French sample: The mediating role of career decision self-efficacy. *Journal of Career Assessment, 27*, 273-288.

Strome, M., Celik, P., & Myszkowski, N. (2020). A forgotten antecedent of career adaptability: A study on the predictive role of with-in person variability in personality. *Personality and Individual Differences, 160,* 109936.

Strauss, K., Griffin, M. A., & Parker, S. K. (2012). Future work selves: How salient hoped-for identities motivate proactive career behaviors. *Journal of Applied Psychology, 87*, 580–598.

Stumpf, S.A., Colarelli, S.M., & Hartman, K. (1983). Development of the Career Exploration Survey (CES). *Journal of Vocational Behavior, 22*, 191–226.

Schyns, B., & Collani, G. (2002). A new occupational self-efficacy scale and its relation to personality constructs and organizational variables. *European Journal of Work and Organizational Psychology, 11*, 219–241.

Strathman, A., Gleicher, F., Boninger, D. S., & Edwards, C. S. (1994). The consideration of future consequences: Weighing immediate and distant outcomes of behavior. *Journal of Personality and Social Psychology, 66,*742–752.

Super, D. E. (1955). Dimensions and measurement of vocational maturity. *Teachers College Record, 57,* 151–165.

Super, D. E. (1970). *Work Values Inventory Manual.* Boston: Houghton-Mifflin.

Super, D. E. (1980). A Life-span, life-space approach to career development. *Journal of Vocational Behavior 16,* 282-298.

Super, D. E., & Knasel, E. G. (1981). Career development in adulthood: Some theoretical problems and a possible solution. *British Journal of Guidance & Counselling,, 9,* 194-201.

Super, D. E., Thompson, A. S., & Lindeman, R. H. (1988). *Adult Career Concerns Inventory: Manual for research and exploratory use in counseling.* Palo Alto, CA: Consulting Psychologist Press.

Super, D. E., Thompson, A. S., Lindeman, R. H., Jordaan, J. P., & Myers, R. A. (1981). *Career Development Inventory.* Palo Alto, CA: Consulting Psychologists Press.

Super, D. E., Zelkowitz, R. S., & Thompson, A. S. (1988). *Career Development Inventory – Adult Form 1,* New York: Teachers College.

Sverko, I., & Babarovic, T. (2016). Integrating personality and career adaptability into vocational interest space. *Journal of Vocational Behavior, 94,* 89-103.

Šverko, I., Babarović, I., & Babarović, T. (2019). Applying career construction model of adaption to career transition in adolescence: A two study paper. *Journal of Vocational Behavior, 111,* 59-73.

Šverko, I., Babarović, T., &Matić, I. P. (2015, May*). Career adaptability in Croatia: Validation of career adapt-abilities scale and its relation to career maturity.* Oslo, Norway: EAWOP Congress.

Taber, B. J., & Blankemeyer, M. (2015) Future work self and career adaptability in the prediction of career behaviors. *Journal of Vocational Behavior, 86*, 20-27.

Tang, J., Kacmar, K. M., & Busenitz, L. (2012). Entrepreneurial alertness in the pursuit of new opportunities. *Journal of Business Venturing, 27*, 77–94.

Tedeschi, R. G., & Calhoun, L. G. (1996). The Posttraumatic Growth Inventory: Measuring the positive legacy of trauma. *Journal of Traumatic Stress, 9*, 455–471

Teixeira, M. A. P., Bardagi, M. P., Lassance, M. C. P., Magalhaes, M. D. O., & Duarte, M. E. (2012). Career Adapt-Abilities Scale—Brazilian Form: Psychometric properties and relationships to personality. *Journal of Vocational Behavior, 80*, 680-685.

Tett, R. P., & Meyer, J. P. (1993). Job satisfaction, organizational commitment, turnover intention, and turnover: Path analyses based on meta-analytic findings. *Personnel Psychology, 46*, 259–293.

Tian, Y., Cheng, M., Cheng, C., Fan, X. (2014). The impact of clinical learning environment and career motivation on career adaptability of student nurses. *Journal of Nursing Science, 29*, 63–65.

Tian, Y., & Fan, X. (2014). Adversity quotients, environmental variables and career adaptability in student nurses. *Journal of Vocational Behavior, 85*, 251–257

Tien, H-S., Wang, Y. C., Chu, H-C., & Huang, T. L. (2012). Career Adapt-Abilities Scale — Taiwan Form: Psychometric properties and construct validity. *Journal of Vocational Behavior, 80*, 744-747.

Tien, H-L. S., Lin, S-H., Hsieh, P-J., & Jin, S-R. ((2014). The Career Adapt-Abilities Scale in Macau: Psychometric characteristics and construct validity. *Journal of Vocational Behavior, 84*, 259-265.

Tokar, D. M., Savickas, M. L., & Kaut, K. P. (2019). A test of the career construction theory model of adaptation in adult workers with Chiari malformation. *Journal of Career Assessment, 28*, 381-401.

Tolentino, L. R., Garcia, P. R. J. M., Lu, V. N., Restubog, S. L. D., Bordia, P., & Plewa, C. (2014). Career adaptation: The relation of adaptability to goal orientation, proactive personality, and career optimism. *Journal of Vocational Behavior, 84*, 39-48.

Tolentino, L. R., Garcia, P. R. J. M., Lu, V. N., Restubog, S. L. D., Bordia, P., & Tang, R. L. (2013). Validation of the Career Adapt-Abilities Scale and an examination of a model of career adaptation in The Philippine context. *Journal of Vocational Behavior, 83*, 410-418.

Tolentino, L. R., Sedoglavich, V., Lu, V. N., Raymund, J., P., Garcia, J. M., Restubog, S. L. D. (2014). The role of career adaptability in predicting entrepreneurial intentions. A moderated-mediation model. *Journal of Vocational Behavior, 85*, 403-412.

Tolentino, L. R., Sibunruang, H., Garcia, P. R. J. M. (2019) the role of self-monitoring and academic effort in students' career adaptability and job search self-efficacy. *Journal of Career Assessment, 27*, 726-740.

Tracey, T. J. G. (2002). Personal Globe Inventory: Measurement of the spherical model of interest and competence beliefs [Monograph]. *Journal of Vocational Behavior*, 60, 113-172.

Tracey, T. J. G. (2010). Development of an abbreviated Personal Globe Inventory using item response theory: The PGI-Short. *Journal of Vocational Behavior, 76*, 1-15.

Tracey, T. J. G., & Ward, C. C. (1998). The structure of children's interests and competence perceptions. *Journal of Counseling Psychology, 45*, 290-303.

Tschannen-Moran, M., & Woolfolk Hoy, A. (2001). Teacher efficacy: Capturing an elusive construct. *Teaching and Teacher Education, 17*, 783–805.

Tuna, M., Kanten, P., Yesiltas, M., Kanten, S., & Alparslan, A. M. (2014). The effect of academic advising on career adaptabilities: A study on tourism and hotel management students. The *Macrotheme Review: A Multidisciplinary Journal of Global Macro Trends, 3*, 139-155.

Tumer, S. L., Alliman-Brissett, A., Lapan, R. T., Udipi, S., & Ergun, D. (2003). The career-related parent support scale. *Measurement and Evaluation in Counseling and Development, 36*, 83-94.

Udayar, S., Fiori, M., Thalmayer, A. G., & Rossier, J. (2018). Investigating the link between trait emotional intelligence, career indecision, and self-perceived employability: The role of career adaptability. *Personality and Individual Differences, 135*, 7-12.

Ulrich, D., Younger, J., Brockbank, W., & Ulrich, M. D. (2012). HR talent and the new HR competencies. *Strategic HR Review, 11*, 217-222.

Urbanaviciute, L., Kairys, A., Pociute, B., & Liniauskaite, A. (2014) Career adaptability in Lithuania: A test of psychometric properties and a theoretical model. *Journal of Vocational Behavior, 85*, 433-442.

Urbanaviciute, L., Pociute, B., Kairys, A. & Liniauskaite, A. (2016) Perceived career barriers and vocational outcomes among university undergraduates: Exploring mediation and moderation effects. *Journal of Vocational Behavior 92*, 12-21.

Urbanaviciute, I., Udayar, S., Maggori, C., & Rossier, J. (2020). Precariousness profile and career adaptability as determinants of job insecurity: A three-wave study. *Journal of Career Development, 47*, 146-161.

Urbanaviciute, I., Udayar, S., & Rossier, J. (2019). Career adaptability and employee well-being over a two-year period: Investigating cross-lagged effects and their boundary conditions. *Journal of Vocational Behavior, 111*, 74-90.

Vallerand, R. J., Blanchard, C., Mageau, G., Koestner, R., Ratelle, C., Leonard, M., Gagne, M., & Marsolais, J.. (2003) Les passions de l'âme: On obsessive and harmonious passion. *Journal of Personality and Social Psychology, 85*, 756–767

Vandenberg, R. J., & Lance, C. E. (2000). A review and synthesis of the measurement invariance literature: Suggestions, practices, and recommendations for organizational research. *Organizational Research Methods, 3*, 4–70.

Vandenbos, G. R. (Ed.) (2015). *American Psychological Association dictionary of psychology* (2nd ed.). Washington, DC: American Psychological Association.

VandeWalle, D. (1997). Development and validation of a work domain goal orientation instrument. *Educational and Psychological Measurement, 57*, 995–1015.

VandeWalle, D., Cron, W. L., & Slocum Jr., J. W. (2001) The role of goal orientation following performance feedback. *Journal of Applied Psychology, 86*, 629-640.

van Vianen, A. E. M., Klehe, U. C., Koen, J., & Dries, N. (2012). Career Adapt-Abilities Scale — Netherlands Form: Psychometric properties and relationships to ability, personality, and regulatory focus. *Journal of Vocational Behavior, 80*, 716-724.

von Collani, G., & Herzberg, P. Y. (2003). Eine revidierte Fassung der deutschsprachigen Skala zum Selbstwertgefuhl von Rosenberg. *Zeitschrift für Differentielle und Diagnostische Psychologie, 24*, 3–7.

Vilhjálmsdóttir G., Kjartansdóttir, G. B., Smáradóttir, S. B., & Einarsdóttir, S. (2012). Career Adapt-Abilities Scale — Icelandic Form: Psychometric properties and construct validity. *Journal of Vocational Behavior, 80*, 698-704.

Vignoli, E., Croity-Belz, S., Chapeland, V., DeFillipis, A., & Garcia, M. (2005). Career exploration in adolescents: The role of anxiety, attachment and parenting style. *Journal of Vocational Behavior, 67*, 153-168.

Wanberg, C. R., Zhang, Z., & Diehn, E. W. (2010). Development of the "Getting Ready for Your Next Job" inventory for unemployed individuals. *Personnel Psychology, 63*, 439–478.

Wang, D., Hou, Z-J., Ni, J., Tian, L., Zhang, X., Chi, H-Y., & Zhao, A. (2020). The effect of perfectionism on career adaptability and career decision-making difficulties. *Journal of Career Development, 47*, 469-483.

Wang, L. F., & Heppner, P. P. (2002). Assessing the impact of parental expectations and psychological distress on Taiwanese college students. *The Counseling Psychologist, 30*, 582–608.

Wang, Y. C. (2011). *Strength-centered career counseling: Counseling framework, counseling ability, and training program* (Report No. NSC100-2410-H-152-003). Taipei, Taiwan: National Science Council.

Wang, Y-C., & Tien, H-L. S. (2018). The relation of career adaptability to work–family experience and personal growth initiative among Taiwanese working parents. *Journal of Employment Counseling, 55*, 27-40.

Wang, Y. C., Wu, Q. L., & Li, Y. M. (2014). Development of the Work–Family Strength Scale for working parents in Taiwan. *Chinese Journal of Guidance and Counseling, 41,* 57–91.

Wang, Z., & Fu, Y. (2015). Social support, social comparison, and career adaptability: A moderated mediation model. *Social Behavior and Personality: An International Journal, 43*, 649-660.

Warech, M., Smither, J. W., Reilly, R. R., Millsap, R. E., & Reilly, S. P. (1998). Self-monitoring and 360-degree ratings. *Leadership Quarterly, 9*, 449–473.

Watson, D., Clark, L. A., & Tellegen, A. (1988). Development and validation of the brief measures of positive and negative affect: The PANA Scales. *Journal of Personality and Social Psychology, 54*, 1063-1070.

Wayne, S. J., Liden, R. C., Graf, I. K., & Ferris, G. R. (1997). The role of upward influence tactics in human resource decisions. *Personnel Psychology, 50*, 979–1006.

Weiss, D. J., Dawis, R. V., England, G. W., & Lofquist, L. H. (1967). Manual for the Minnesota Satisfaction Questionnaire. *Minnesota Studies in Vocational Rehabilitation. Vol. 22*. Minneapolis, MN: University of Minnesota, Industrial Relations Center.

Wehrle, K., Kira, M. & Klehe, U-C. (2019). Putting career construction in context: Career adaptability among refugees. *Journal of Vocational Behavior, 111*, 107-124.

Wei, M., Russell, D. W., Mallinckrodt, B., & Vogel, D. L. (2007). The Experiences in Close Relationship Scale (ECR)-Short Form: Reliability, validity, and factor structure. *Journal of Personality Assessment, 88*, 187–204.

Weigold, I. K., & Robitschek, C. (2011). Agentic personality characteristics and coping: Their relation to trait anxiety in college students. *American Journal of Orthopsychiatry, 81*, 255–264.

Weiss, D. S., & Marmar, C. R. (1996). The Impact of Event Scale–Revised. In J. Wilson & T. M. Keane (Eds.), *Assessing psychological trauma and PTSD* (pp. 399–411). New York: Guilford Press.

Welbourne, T. M., Johnson, D. E., & Erez, A. (1998). The role-based performance scale: Validity analysis of a theory-based measure. *Academy of Management Journal, 41*, 540-555.

Weng, Q., & McElroy, J. C. (2010). Vocational self-concept crystallization as a mediator of the relationship between career self-management and job decision effectiveness. *Journal of Vocational Behavior, 76*, 234–243.

Werbel, J. D. (2000). Relationships among career exploration, job search intensity, and job search effectiveness in graduating college students. *Journal of Vocational Behavior, 57*, 79–394.

Wheeler, M. S., Kern, R. M., & Curlette, W. L. (1993*). BASIS-A Inventory.* Highlands, NC: TRT Associates.

Whiston, S. C., Feldwisch, R. P., Evans, K. M., Blackman, C. S., & Gilman, L. (2015). Older professional women's views on work: A qualitative analysis. *Career Development Quarterly, 63*, 98- 112.

Wiernik, B. M., & Kostal, J. W. (2019). Protean and boundaryless career orientations: A critical review and meta-analysis. *Journal of Counseling Psychology, 66*, 280–307.

Wilhelm, F., & Hirschi, A. (2019). Career self-management as a key factor for career wellbeing. In I. L. Potgieter, N. Ferreira & M. Coetzee (Eds.). *Theory, Research and Dynamics of Career Wellbeing* (117-137). Switzerland: Springer.

Wilkins-Yel, K. G., Roach, C. M. L., Tracey, T. J. G., & Yel, N. (2018). The effects of career adaptability on intended academic persistence: The mediating role of academic satisfaction. *Journal of Vocational Behavior, 108*, 67–77.

Wilkins, K. G., Santilli, S., Ferrari, L., Nota, L., Tracey, T. J. G., & Soresi, S. (2014). The relationship among positive emotional dispositions, career adaptability, and satisfaction in Italian high school students. *Journal of Vocational Behavior, 85*, 329-338.

Williams, L., & Anderson, S. (1991). Job satisfaction and organizational commitment as predictors of organizational citizenship and in-role behaviors. *Journal of Management* 17, 601–617.

Wohrmann, A. M., Deller, J., & Wang, M. (2013). Outcome expectations and work design characteristics in post-retirement work planning. *Journal of Vocational Behavior, 83*, 219–228.

Woo, H. R. (2020). Perceived over-qualification and job crafting: The curvilinear moderation of career adaptability. *Sustainability. 12(24)*, 10458.

Wood, R., & Bandura, A. (1989). Impact of conceptions of ability on self-regulatory mechanisms and complex decision making. *Journal of Personality and Social Psychology, 56*, 407–415.

Wood, V. R., Chonko, L. B., & Hunt, S. D. (1986). Social responsibility and personal success: Are they incompatible? *Journal of Business Research, 14*, 193–212.

Wrzesniewski, A., & Dutton, J. E. (2001). Crafting a job: Revisioning employees as active crafters of their work. *Academy Management Review, 26*, 179–201.

Xiao, S. Y. (1994). Theoretical foundation and research application of the Social Support Rating Scale [in Chinese]. *Journal of Clinical Psychological Medicine, 4*, 98-100.

Xie, B., Xi, M., Xin, X., & Zhou, W. (2016). Linking calling to work engagement and subjective career success: The perspective of Career Construction Theory. *Journal of Vocational Behavior, 94*, 70-78.

Xu, C., Gong, X., Fu, W., Xu, Y., Xu, H., Chen, W., & Li, M. (2020). The role of career adaptability and resilience in mental health problems in Chinese adolescents. *Children and Youth Services Review, 112*, 104893.

Xu, H. (2020a). Development and initial validation of the Constructivist Beliefs in the Career Decision-Making Scale. *Journal of Career Assessment, 28*, 303-319.

Xu, H. (2020b). Career Indecision Profile-Short: Reliability and validity among employees and measurement invariance across students and employees. *Journal of Career Assessment, 28*, 91-108.

Xu, H. (2020c). Incremental validity of the career adapt-abilities scale total score over general self-efficacy. *Journal of Vocational Behavior, 119*, 103425.

Xu, H., & Tracey, T. J. G. (2015). Career Decision Ambiguity Tolerance Scale: Construction and initial validations. *Journal of Vocational Behavior, 88*, 1–9.

Xu, H., & Tracey, T. J. G. (2017). Development of an abbreviated Career Indecision Profile-65 using item response theory: The CIP-Short. *Journal of Counseling Psychology, 64*, 222–232.

Yang, W., Guan, Y., Lai, X., She, Z., & Lockwood, A. J. (2015). Career adaptability and perceived over-qualification: Testing a dual-path model among Chinese human resource management professionals. *Journal of Vocational Behavior*, 90, 154-162.

Yang, X., Feng, Y., Yuchen, M., & Yong, Q. (2019). Career adaptability, work engagement, and employee well-being among Chinese employees: The role of guanxi. *Frontiers of Psychology, 10*, 1029

Yang, X., Guan, Y., Zhang, Y., She, Z., Buchtel, E. E., Mak, M. C. K., & Hu, H. (2020). A relational model of career adaptability and career prospects: The roles of leader-member exchange and agreeableness. *Journal of Occupational and Organizational Psychology, 93*, 405-430.

Yen, H., Cheng, J., Hsu, C., & Yen, K. (2019). How career adaptability can enhance career satisfaction: Exploring the mediating role of person-job fit. *Journal of Management & Organization*, 1-18.

Yılmaz, E., Sünbül, A. M. (2009). Developing the Scale of University Students' Entrepreneurship. *Selcuk University Journal of the Institute of Social Sciences, 21*, 195–203.

Yu, H., Dai, Y., Guan, X., & Wang, W. (2020). Career Adapt-Abilities Scale – Short Form: Validation across three different samples in the Chinese context. *Journal of Career Assessment, 28*, 219-240.

Yucel, I., & Polat, M. (2015). Career Adapt-Abilities Scale – Turkey Form: Psychometric properties and construct validity. *International Journal of Economics, Commerce and Management, 3*, 67-74.

Yuen, M., & Yau, J. (2015). Relation of career adaptability to meaning in life and connectedness among adolescents in Hong Kong. *Journal of Vocational Behavior, 91*, 147-156.

Zacher, H. (2014a). Career adaptability predicts subjective career success above and beyond personality traits and core self-evaluations. *Journal of Vocational Behavior, 84*, 21-30.

Zacher (2014b). Individual difference predictors of change in career adaptability over time. *Journal of Vocational Behavior, 84*, 188-198.

Zacher, H. (2015). Daily manifestations of career adaptability: Relationships with job and career outcomes. *Journal of Vocational Behavior, 91*, 76-86.

Zacher, H. (2016). Within-person relationships between daily individual and job characteristics and daily manifestations of career adaptability. *Journal of Vocational Behavior, 92,* 105-115.

Zacher, H., Ambiel, R. A. M., & Noronha, A. P. P. (215). Career adaptability and job entrenchment. *Journal of Vocational Behavior, 88*, 164-173.

Zacher, H., & Frese, M. (2009). Remaining time and opportunities at work: Relationships between age, work characteristics, and occupational future time perspective. *Psychology and Aging, 24*, 487–493.

Zacher, H., & Griffin, B. (2015). Older workers' age as moderator of the relationship between career adaptability and job satisfaction. *Working, Aging, and Retirement, 1*, 227-236.

Zhang, J., Chen, G., Yuen, M. (2019). Validation of the Vocational Identity Status Assessment (VISA) using Chinese technical college students. *Journal of Career Assessment, 27*, 675-692.

Zheng, X., Zhu, W., Zhao, H., and Zhang, C. (2015). Employee well-being in organizations: Theoretical model, scale development, and cross-cultural validation. *Journal of Organizational Behavior, 36*, 621–644.

Zhou, B. (1991). *Mental Health Test*. Shanghai: East China Normal University Press

Zhou, N., Nie, Y., Yu, S., Deng, L., Zang, N., Sun, R., Fang, X. Cao, H., Li, X., Liang, Y., & Buehler, C. (2019). Career-related parental processed and career adaptability and ambivalence among Chinese adolescents: A person-centered approach. *Journal of Research on Adolescence, 30*, 234-248.

Zhou, W., Guan, Y., Xin, L., Kuan, M. C. K., & Deng, Y., Mak, M. C. K., & Deng, Y. (2016). Career success criteria and locus of control as indicators of adaptive readiness in the career adaptation model. *Journal of Vocational Behavior, 94*, 124-130.

Zhou, W. X., Sun, J., Guan, Y., Li, Y., & Pan, J. (2013). Criteria of career success among Chinese employees: Developing a multi-dimensional scale with qualitative and quantitative approaches. *Journal of Career Assessment, 21*, 265–277.

Zhuang, M., She, Z., Cai, Z., Huang, Z., Xiang, Q., Wang, P. & Zhu, F. (2018). Examining a sequential mediation model of Chinese university students' well-being: A career construction perspective. *Frontiers in Psychology, 9*:593.

Zimet, G. D., Dahlem, N. W., Zimet, S. G., & Farley, G. K. (1988). The Multidimensional Scale of Perceived Social Support. *Journal of Personality Assessment, 52*, 30-41.

Zuckerman, M. (1999). *Vulnerability to psychopathology: A biosocial model*. Washington, DC: American Psychological Association.

APPENDIX A

Career Adapt-Abilities Scale

Career Adapt-Abilities Scale

Name _____

Age _____   Circle one: Male or Female

DIRECTIONS

Different people use different strengths to build their careers. No one is good at everything, each of us emphasizes some strengths more than others. Please rate how strongly you have developed each of the following abilities using the scale below.

STRENGTHS	Strongest	Very Strong	Strong	Somewhat Strong	Not Strong
1. Thinking about what my future will be like	____	____	____	____	____
2. Realizing that today's choices shape my future	____	____	____	____	____
3. Preparing for the future	____	____	____	____	____
4. Becoming aware of the educational and vocational choices that I must make	____	____	____	____	____
5. Planning how to achieve my goals	____	____	____	____	____
6. Concerned about my career	____	____	____	____	____
7. Keeping upbeat	____	____	____	____	____
8. Making decisions by myself	____	____	____	____	____
9. Taking responsibility for my actions	____	____	____	____	____
10. Sticking up for my beliefs	____	____	____	____	____
11. Counting on myself	____	____	____	____	____
12. Doing what's right for me	____	____	____	____	____

Please rate how strongly you have developed each
of the following abilities using the scale below.

STRENGTHS	Strongest	Very Strong	Strong	Somewhat Strong	Not Strong
13. Exploring my surroundings					
14. Looking for opportunities to grow					
15. Investigating options before making a choice					
16. Observing different ways of doing things					
17. Probing deeply into questions that I have					
18. Becoming curious about new opportunities					
19. Performing tasks efficiently					
20. Taking care to do things well					
21. Learning new skills					
22. Working up to my ability					
23. Overcoming obstacles					
24. Solving problems					

Scoring Key

Concern= 1-6
Control = 7-12
Curiosity = 13-18
Confidence 19-24

APPENDIX B

Student Career Construction Inventory

Student Career Construction Inventory

Name _____

Age _____   Circle one: Male or Female

Please indicate how much thinking or planning you have
done about each one using the following scale.

5 = I have already done this.
4 = I am now doing what needs to be done.
3 = I know what to do about it.
2 = I have thought about it but do not know what to do about it.
1 = I have not yet thought much about it.

Activities	5	4	3	2	1
1. Forming a clear picture of my personality					
2. Recognizing my talents and abilities					
3. Determining what values are important to me					
4. Knowing how other people view me					
5. Identifying people that I want to be like					
6. Finding out what my interests are					
7. Setting goals for myself					
8. Interviewing people in a job that I like					
9. Discussing my career with teachers and advisors					
10. Learning about different types of jobs					
11. Reading about occupations					
12. Investigating occupations that might suit me					
13. Working a part-time job related to my interests					

Activities	5	4	3	2	1
14. Determining the training needed for jobs that interest me					
15. Deciding what I really want to do for a living					
16. Finding a line of work that suits me					
17. Selecting an occupation that will satisfy me					
18. Planning how to get into the occupation I choose					
19. Reassuring myself that I made a good occupational choice					
20. Developing special knowledge or skill that will help me get the job I want					
21. Finding opportunities to get the training and experience I need					
22. Beginning the training I need for my preferred job					
23. Qualifying for the job that I like best					
24. Making plans for my job search					
25. Getting a job once I complete my education or training					

SCCI Scoring Key

Self-concept crystallization   1, 2, 3, 4, 5, 6 reliability =.84

Occupational Exploration 10, 11, 12 reliability = .87

Career decision making 15, 16, 17, 18, 19 reliability = .94

Preparing   21, 22, 23, 24,   reliability = .89

471

APPENDIX C

Career Mastery Inventory

John Orr Crites

Rate the following items from
1 meaning disagree to 7 meaning agree.

1. The job I am doing is the only one I really know anything about.
2. I try to do the best I can.
3. I'd rather my supervisor told me what to do than plan my work myself.
4. Besides my immediate suprvisor, I have little idea who runs the organization
5. I think I'm in the best work for me.
6. I often think about chaning my job.
7. I feel confident most of the time about how well I can do my job.
8. I don't know if I am in the right job for me.
9. Getting ahead on the job is mostly a matter of chance.
10. Even if my job changes, I feel I can go along with it.
11. I feel close to the people and organization where I work.
12. I know who to go to for womething I want at work.
13. I don't think of my self as part of the organization
14. I like to set up and schedule my own work.
15. I always seem to be doing something that's against organizational policy and procedure.
16. I have a plan for where I want to be in my job in five years.
17. I want my job to stay the same.
18. I only work because I have to.
19. I seldom talk with others at work.
20. It is important for me to continually seek opportunity.
21. Doing a good job is very important to me.
22. I seldom think about what I will be doing in the future.
23. I eat lunch with friends at work.
24. I pretty much go along with what the organization expects of me.
25. I only do what is expected of me – nothing more.
26. I have a pretty good idea of how much my organizationmakes in a year.
27. I have friends where I work.
28. I have little or no idea what I have to do to get promoted.
29. I do as well as I have to on my job to keep it.
30. I don't know my way around where I work.
31. I look for opportunities within theorganization
32. I don't know what is expected of me socially on the job.
33. I plan to take additional training so I'll have a better chance of developing myself for future opportunities.
34. Some of my best friends are at work.

35. Work is important to me as a way of life.
36. I often question whether I have the ability to get ahead in my work.
37. I only wiork to get the things I want.
38. I like to be left alone at work.
39. I've discusses with my supervisor/superior what I have to do to get promoted.
40. I go out with my firiends from work.
41. I try to figure out what my organization's policies and procedures are.
42. I may get promoted but there is not much I can do about it.
43. As far as I am concerned, it's either the organization or me.
44. I get in arguments withothers at work.
45. I feel good when I do my work well.
46. I look forward to seeing my friends at work.
47. I feel that others think I do a good job.
48. I wish I had more friends at work.
49. I feel that I have what it takes to get aheadd in my job.
50. It's difficult for me to change what I am doing even when I am told.
51. I really want to know everything I can in my job.
52. I feel like I don't know how my job fits into the "big picture."
53. I think I am as good as others who have been promoted at my level in the organization,
54. I usually have to ask somebody where things are and how use them in my job.
55. If I have a problem on the job, I know who to see about it.
56. I use what I learned in school on my job.
57. I'll probably be doing the same job twenty years from now.
58. The training I'm getting doesn't seem to have anything to do with my job.
59. I feel others like me where I work.
60. I admit mistakes I make in my work.
61. I feel that others at work don't like me.
62. I know what to do, and how to do it, to be promoted.
63. I can see how my work fits into what the organization is doing.
64. I feel "left out" of what's going on where I work.
65. It's important to me to be as good as I possibly can in my job.
66. I feel I chose the wrong line of work.
67. I often feel others have it in for me where I work.
68. Sometimes it's seniority rather than performance that results in promotion.
69. It upsets me when they change the work I'm supposed to do.
70. I feel the organization has the right to expect me to behave in certain ways on the job.
71. I have difficulty doing the best I can in my job.
72. I feel pretty good about the career I chose for myself.
73. I enjoy having friends at work.
74. I'm confused about what I have to do to advance in the organizaiton.
75. If I didn't work, I don't know what I'd do with myself.
76. I don't think my organization cares about me, or how I get along.
77. What I learned in school has helped me do well on my job.
78. I wish I knew where I was headed in my career.
79. I try to avoid others where I work.

80. You have to do the right things to get ahead.
81. I feel like I'm part of the organization where I work.
82. If something goes wrong on the job, it's usually somebody else's fault.
83. I have a good idea of how I can advance in this organizaiton and and what the opportunities are.
84. I don't understand what my on-the-job training has to do with my work.
85. It's not what you know but who you know that's important in getting ahead in this organizaiton.
86. I get along with others where I work.
87. My career plans for the future are uncertain.
88. I try hard as I can to learn my job.
89. I like toplan my own work.
90. I feel lost where I work.

Scoring Key

Organizational Adaptability: 4(R), 12, 15(R), 24, 26, 30(R), 32 (R), 41, 43(R), 55, 65(R), 70, 76(R), 81, 90(R)

Position Performance: 2, 7, 10, 17*, 25*, 47, 52*, 54*, 56, 58*, 63, 71*, 77, 84*, 88

Coworker Relationships: 19, 23, 27, 34, 38*,40, 44*,46, 48*, 59, 61*, 67*, 73, 79*, 87

Work Habits and Attitudes: 3*, 14, 18*,21, 29*,35, 37*,45, 50*, 60, 65, 69*, 75, 82*, 89,

Advancement: 6*, 9*, 16, 28*, 33, 36*, 39, 42*, 49, 62, 63, 68, 74*, 80, 85*

Career Choice and Plans: 1*, 5, 8*, 11, 13*, 20, 22*, 31, 51, 57*, 66*, 72, 78*, 83, 87*

APPENDIX D

Career Maturity Inventory – Form C

John Orr Crites & Mark L. Savickas

Career Maturity Inventory — Form C

Name _____

Age _____   Circle one: Male or Female

DIRECTIONS

There are 24 statements about choosing the kind of job or work that you will probably do when you finish school. Read each statement. If you agree or mostly agree with it, then circle agree next to it. If you disagree or mostly disagree with it, then circle disagree next to it.

1. There is no point in deciding on a job when the future is so uncertain.   Agree   Disagree

2. I know very little about the requirements of jobs.   Agree   Disagree

3. I have so many interests that it is hard to choose just one occupation.   Agree   Disagree

4. Choosing a job is something that you do on your own.   Agree   Disagree

5. I can't seem to become very concerned about my future occupation.   Agree   Disagree

6. I don't know how to go about getting into the kind of work I want to do.   Agree   Disagree

7. Everyone seems to tell me something different; as a result I don't know what kind of work to choose.   Agree   Disagree

8. If you have doubts about what you want to do, ask your parents or friends for advice.   Agree   Disagree

9. I seldom think about the job that I want to enter.   Agree   Disagree

10. I am having difficulty in preparing my self for the work that I want to do.   Agree   Disagree

If you agree or mostly agree with a statement, then mark agree next to it.
If you disagree or mostly disagree with it, then mark disagree next to it.

11. I keep changing my occupational choice.   Agree   Disagree

12. When it comes to choosing a career, I will ask other people to help me.   Agree   Disagree

13. I'm not going to worry about choosing an occupation until I am out of school.   Agree   Disagree

14. I don't know what courses I should take in school.   Agree   Disagree

15. I often daydream about what I want to be, but I really have not chosen an occupation yet.   Agree   Disagree

16. I will choose my career without paying attention to the feelings of other people.   Agree   Disagree

17. As far as choosing an occupation is concerned, something will come along sooner or later.   Agree   Disagree

18. I don't know whether my occupational plans are realistic.   Agree   Disagree

19. There are so many things to consider in choosing an occupation, it is hard to make a decision.   Agree   Disagree

20. It is important to consult close friends and get their ideas before making an occupational choice.   Agree   Disagree

21. I really can't find any work that has much appeal to me.   Agree   Disagree

22. I keep wondering how I can reconcile the kind of person I am with the kind of person I want to be in my occupation.   Agree   Disagree

23. I can't understand how some people can be so certain about what they want to do.   Agree   Disagree

24. In making career choices, one should pay attention to the thoughts and feelings of family members.   Agree   Disagree

Scoring Key

Concern = 1 (D), 5 (D), 9(D), 13(D), 17(D), 21(D)
Curiosity = 2(D), 6(D), 10(D), 14(D), 18(D), 22(D)
Confidence = 3(D), 7(D), 11(D), 15(D), 19(D), 23(D)
Consultation = 4(D), 8(A), 12(A), 16(D), 20(A), 24(A)

Major Topics Index